MW01674444

Comparative Psychology: Evolution and Development of Behavior

Comparative Psychology: Evolution and Development of Behavior

Edited by Talia Gomez

MURPHY & MOORE
www.murphy-moorepublishing.com

Murphy & Moore Publishing,
1 Rockefeller Plaza,
New York City, NY 10020, USA

Copyright © 2021 Murphy & Moore Publishing

This book contains information obtained from authentic and highly regarded sources. Copyright for all individual chapters remain with the respective authors as indicated. All chapters are published with permission under the Creative Commons Attribution License or equivalent. A wide variety of references are listed. Permission and sources are indicated; for detailed attributions, please refer to the permissions page and list of contributors. Reasonable efforts have been made to publish reliable data and information, but the authors, editors and publisher cannot assume any responsibility for the validity of all materials or the consequences of their use.

Trademark Notice: Registered trademark of products or corporate names are used only for explanation and identification without intent to infringe.

ISBN: 978-1-63987-119-3

Cataloging-in-Publication Data

Comparative psychology : evolution and development of behavior / edited by Talia Gomez.
p. cm.
Includes bibliographical references and index.
ISBN 978-1-63987-119-3
1. Psychology, Comparative. 2. Human behavior. 3. Psychology. I. Gomez, Talia.
BF671 .C66 2021
156--dc23

For information on all Murphy & Moore Publications
visit our website at www.murphy-moorepublishing.com

MURPHY & MOORE

Contents

Preface

The world is advancing at a fast pace like never before. Therefore, the need is to keep up with the latest developments. This book was an idea that came to fruition when the specialists in the area realized the need to coordinate together and document essential themes in the subject. That's when I was requested to be the editor. Editing this book has been an honour as it brings together diverse authors researching on different streams of the field. The book collates essential materials contributed by veterans in the area which can be utilized by students and researchers alike.

The sub-field of psychology which focuses on the behavior and mental processes of non-human animals is known as comparative psychology. The two most prominent areas of study under this field are the commonness of behavior across animal species and the relationship of behavior with reproduction. This includes the quantitative and qualitative similarities and differences observed across a wide range of species. The physiological and environmental components which trigger a particular behavior are also studied under this field. It also aims to understand the psychological state of a domesticated or caged species and their corresponding behavior. It also explores typical behavior such as tonic immobility, imitation, hoarding, nest building, etc. This discipline has significant applications in the fields of medicine, ecology and animal training. This book traces the progress of this field and highlights some of its key concepts and applications. While understanding the long-term perspectives of the topics, the book makes an effort in highlighting their impact as a modern tool for the growth of the discipline. It includes contributions of experts and scientists which will provide innovative insights into the field of comparative psychology.

Each chapter is a sole-standing publication that reflects each author´s interpretation. Thus, the book displays a multi-facetted picture of our current understanding of application, resources and aspects of the field. I would like to thank the contributors of this book and my family for their endless support.

Editor

1

Age Influences Male's Mating Preferences for Multiparous and Nulliparous Females in the Laboratory-bred *Macaca Fascicularis*

Maiko Yoshida- Kobayashi[1,2], Takamasa Koyama[1], Yasuhiro Yasutomi[2] and Tadashi Sankai[2]
Japan Women's University, Japan [1], National Institutes of Biomedical Innovation, Health and Nutrition, Japan[2]

Most studies of partner choice and preferences in nonhuman primates have been concerned with male social rank. Females select high-ranking males, and high-ranking females can more readily gain access to males. Although researchers have mentioned males' choices and their preferences in females, papers that focus on male preferences have been few. Past studies suggest that male primates prefer older females. This study was aimed at analyzing the male preference under minimized social factors. We analyzed data collected though the every-other-day mating system, in which a male alternately lived with each of two females. Multiparous and/or older females were more frequently pregnant. In the nulliparous group, females that became pregnant for the first time tended to be younger than the other non-pregnant females paired in the mating set. The results suggest that while males generally prefer females with higher gravidity, males prefer to mate with younger females among females that have never been pregnant. There is the possibility that females of high reproductive ability are chosen for mating. This strategy may be biologically advantageous for both males and females.

Male reproductive success is measured by successful competition with other males to have more offspring. On the other hand, female reproductive success in primates, including humans, is measured by the ability to acquire high-quality genes from a male and to fulfill her purpose to bear a child and bring it up safely (Penn, 2002). Although most studies conform to the notion that females take the initiative in mating partner choice, some studies have examined male mating preferences in nonhuman primates (Anderson, 1986; Muller, Thompson, and Wrangham, 2006; Parga, 2006).

Most studies of mating partner choice in nonhuman primates have been concerned with social rank and female choice. They have revealed that females prefer high-ranking males (Bercovitch & Strum, 1993; Bercovitch & Berard, 1993; Drickamer, 1974; Ellis, 1995; Gowaty, 1997; Huffman, 1991; Manson, 1992; Paul &Thommen, 1984; Small, 1989). Holding a higher rank in a dominance hierarchy seems to guarantee a

Please send correspondence to Dr. Maiko Yoshida-Kobayashi, Japan's Women University, Japan.
(Email:maikoyoshida417@gmail.com)

male's genetic quality (Folstad & Karter, 1992; Havlicek, Roberts, & Flegr, 2005) and to show that he is in good health (Waynforth, Hurtado, & Hill, 1998). On the other hand, Nikitopoulos, Heistermann, de Vries, van Hooff, & Sterck (2005) suggested that female preference is independent of a partner's dominance rank. Their work was congruous with Bercovitch's (1995) finding regarding the mating of female savannah baboons with multiple males apart from their social rank. Thus, since there remain several controversies about female preference and male's social rank in partner choice, this research was excluded social rank factors.

Male preference studies are few. Bercovitch (1997) stated that offspring survivorship is a more important component of female reproductive strategy than choice of mating partner. Some other researchers also suggested that males choose fertile, old females with higher offspring survivorship (Muller et al., 2006). A high gravidity rate suggests that a female is fertile and also guarantees higher offspring survivorship.

This study was aimed at analyzing male preference in females. We focused on the female attributes that determined male preference and led to pregnancy. Which attributes of the female affect male preference? At first, we compared physical and/or biological factors, such as age and past gravidity between the subject females who became pregnant and those that did not within this mating system. Weight also is a good index of physical condition (Bercovitch, 1997); it shows the momentum of the individual and congenital individual differences. In this study, we compared the weight of pregnant and non-pregnant females. These female attributes may induce male preference and will be reflected in the difference in conception rate.

Furthermore, some studies have reported on the peak pregnancy rate (Gardin, Jerome, Jayo, & Weaver, 1989) and mating activity of primates (Kaufman, 1965). Because the number of viable oocytes in the ovaries decreases with age, age should be considered as much as weight or gravidity to be a factor that directly affects reproductive success.

In this study, we used individually housed cynomolgus monkeys (*Macaca fascicularis*) that were free from male–male competition and social rank factors, as much as possible. In order to compare a pair of females under the same condition, we adopted the every-other-day mating system, in which one male was set to copulate alternately with one of two females housed separately in adjacent cages. Although a male lived together with a distinct female for the same period, one female nevertheless became pregnant and the other did not after living together. The advantage of this system is that the condition of the male was controlled as much as possible for both of the females. This system enabled us to investigate male preferences in mating partners by analyzing the attributional or behavioral differences between pregnant and non-pregnant females after mating.

Method

Subjects

The subjects comprised 47 adult male and 94 adult female cynomolgus monkeys (*Macaca fascicularis*) that were born in the Tsukuba Primate Research Center (TPRC) breeding colony. Almost all of the males were confirmed their reproductive capability. Females were random-sampled from the individuals with regular menstruation. NIH safety standards were adhered to in the TPRC breeding and rearing environments.

All adult monkeys were housed in single cages (0.5 m wide × 0.8 m high × 0.9 m deep; stainless steel mesh). The air of the breeding room was replaced 12 times hourly while maintaining a temperature of about 25 °C and a humidity of 50% to 60%. The room was lighted for 12 hours a day, from 0700 to 1900, and the monkeys were provided with fruit (100 g) and monkey chow (70 g) in the morning. All subjects were supplied the same amount of bait every day. Water was available ad libitum. Experienced animal technicians inspected the monkeys daily for any abnormalities and menstruation.

Mating Method

The TPRC uses several mating systems for effective breeding. In this study, we adopted the every-other-day mating system, in which one male is set to house a full day alternately with one of two females, each of which lives in an adjacent cage on either side of the male's cage. In this mating system, a male and a female stayed together without special consideration of the female's ovulation and menstrual cycle. It was randomly decided which female started living with a male at first. Combinations of female subjects' ages, weights and gravidity were not controlled to prevent unexpected deviation. In this experiment, females were housed with a male for up to 99 days. The menstrual cycle of cynomolgus monkey is 29 ±4.3 days on average. The typical gestational period of a cynomolgus monkey in the TPRC was 165 days.

A male's cohabitation with one of the females was started by removing the partition board on one or the other of the three consecutive cages, so there was no chance for the females to come in contact with each other. The female also did not come in contact with other males during the experiment period. Pregnancy was confirmed by ultrasonography, which was conducted on the 35th, 70th and 98th days after the start of cohabitation. This experimental condition assumed that the first ultrasonography included the female's one ovulation. Pregnancy testing and weight measurement were performed under anesthesia.

When pregnancy was confirmed in either of the females, that set of three monkeys was disbanded. If pregnancy was not confirmed in either female by the fourteenth week, we disbanded the mating combination and checked the females for pregnancy five weeks later. Mating ceased if one of the monkeys suffered a serious injury or became anorexic. We excluded several cases in which the females became pregnant simultaneously because the male's preference would not be discernible.

This study was approved by the Ethics Committee of the National Institute of Biomedical Innovation (NIBI), and the experiments were conducted according to NIBI guidelines.

Data Collection and Analysis

Data from 47 male-female-female mating sets were obtained from the records of every-other-day mating systems implemented between 2008 and 2011. The independent variable was a female's pregnancy in this experiment. The independent variable included two groups (pregnant females or non-pregnant females). We used three dependent variables; a female's past gravidity was defined as her number of pregnancies up to the experiment, and her age and weight were those at the start of mating. The females' ages ranged from 3 to 19 years, past gravidity from 0 to 11, and weight from 2410 g to 7770 g.

Since pregnant females and non-pregnant females were individually matched, logistic regression was applied for data analysis. With regard to the nulliparous females, we used one-way ANOVA between pregnant females and non-pregnant females, because of lack of past gravidity and small number of subjects. The statistical package IBM SPSS Statistics 21 was used for these analyses. The nulliparous females had no experience with pregnancy and became pregnant for the first time when mating during this experiment, while the multiparous females had experienced pregnancy before this study.

Results

First, we clarified the relationship between the variables using correlation. The pair-wise correlations between age, weight, and number of previous pregnancies (past gravidity) for the 94 females in the 47 mating sets are shown in Table 1. All three correlations were positive and significant, with the highest correlation seen between age and past gravidity. The lowest correlation was between age and weight; the heavier a female was, the older she was. The correlation between past gravidity and weight indicates that females with more previous pregnancies tend to be heavier.

Table 1. *Correlation between age, past gravidity and weight*

	Age	Past Gravidity	Weight
Age	—	0.85 **	0.60 **
Past Gravidity		—	0.66 **
Weight			—

Note. df = 1 & 92, *n* = 94.
** $p < 0.01$.

Table 2 illustrates the number of factors among pregnant females and non-pregnant females. In Table 2, it can be seen that the pregnant females were significantly older and had more past gravidity than the non-pregnant females.

We then distributed multiparous and nulliparous. First, we compared the multiparous pregnant females with the non-pregnant females that were in the same mating sets ($n = 30$) on three variables (age, past gravidity, and weight). Table 3 shows that the pregnant females were older and had more past gravidity than non-pregnant females.

Second, we compared the age and weight of the pregnant females with no previous gravidity versus the non-pregnant females in the same mating sets ($n = 17$). Table 4 shows that the pregnant females were younger than the non-pregnant females.

Table 2. *Factors of pregnancy: age, past gravidity and weight (logistic regression analysis)*

	Pregnant Females ($n = 47$)	Non-pregnant Females ($n = 47$)	
	Mean ± SD	Mean ± SD	Odds ratio (95% CI)
Age	8.3 ± 3.8	8.0 ± 2.9	0.61 (0.45-0.83) *
Past Gravidity	2.3 ± 2.6	1.0 ± 1.5	2.48 (1.50-4.10) **
Weight (g)	3491.6 ± 901.8	3196.8 ± 557.3	1.00 (1.00-1.00) *n.s*

Note. n = 94. *n.s.* = not significant, SD = Standard Deviation.
* $p < 0.05$. ** $p < 0.001$

Discussion

This study examined the relationship between the feasibility of becoming pregnant and the three variables of age, weight and gravidity in female cynomolgus monkeys. The weight of the females increased with age at the TPRC (even after maturation), and the number of previous pregnancies also rose with age. This means that the age of the female seemed to be most important for this study. As for the relationship between age and gravidity, previous studies reported that increasing age increases the chance of gravidity, and older females with greater gravidity have an increased chance of successful pregnancy (Anderson, 1986; Gardin, 1989; Muller et al., 2006).

Of the positive correlations between the chance to become pregnant and each of the three variables, past gravidity and age significantly affected the feasibility of becoming pregnant. Weight did not statistically influence pregnancy. Although the animals were kept indoors and were supplied with the same amount of food in the TPRC, weight did not influence the feasibility of becoming pregnant in this experiment.

To analyze the features of the females' gravidity in this study, we divided the pregnant females into groups of multiparous females with past gravidity and females with no history of pregnancy (instead of directly analyzing the influence of age). We found that the number of previous pregnancies was an important factor in the former group. The influence of age on pregnancy, however, should be considered in the group of females that became pregnant for the first time. That is to say, older females in the multiparous group became pregnant more readily, whereas the younger females in the group that became pregnant for the first time did so more readily. This means that the age factor appears to affect pregnancy differently, between the multiparous and nulliparous females.

In general, copulation is complete when a female accepts a male; it does not occur if a female refuses a male. In the every-other-day mating system used in this study, every female lived with a male through more than one ovulation cycle, and thus all should have had the opportunity to become pregnant. Nevertheless, we observed two groups of females: those that became pregnant and those that did not became pregnant. This suggests the possibility that males rather than females choose mating partners.

The every-other-day mating system allowed males to choose one of the females living in the adjacent cages. Even though we might suppose the females chose the males based on their reproductive ability, this seems less likely for the following reason: in a given mating set, the female with more previous pregnancies was more likely to become pregnant, whereas the younger female of a pair without a history of previous pregnancies was more apt to become pregnant. Our results suggest that the idea that a male chooses a mating partner is more reasonable than the converse. This is congruous with the male's preference for females (Muller et al., 2006).

It is worthwhile to notice that the male chose a younger female in mating with nulliparous females. If the young female became pregnant in the early stages of maturation, she would give more births to offspring than a female that became pregnant for the first time at an older age. The male who chose a younger, nulliparous female would thus have the possibility of producing more offspring. A male's choice of a younger female would raise the reproductive success for both the male and female.

It is important for males to choose females that more easily and regularly become pregnant and give birth to offspring with higher survival rates, because the male's choice is biologically significant with respect to leaving more offspring (Trivers, 1972). Apart from social rank, there is the possibility that females of high reproductive ability are chosen for mating. This strategy may be biologically advantageous for both males and females.

This study suggests that males may select females as part of their reproductive strategy. There is no evidence yet regarding the characteristics that males use to distinguish females of greater reproductive ability from other females. Who took the initiative in mating, the female or the male? That question will probably be considered in the future. We need further basic data on macaques' mating behaviors to determine whether males choose their mating partners. We could observe such behaviors as which individual initiates mating, the male or female, and whether his ejaculation was successful by checking for sperm in the female's vagina.

Acknowledgments

This work was supported by a Health Labour Sciences Research Grant for the Development of New Drugs from the Ministry of Health, Labour and Welfare of Japan.

References

Anderson, C. M. (1986). Female age: Male preference and reproductive success in primates. *International Journal of Primatology, 7*, 305-326.

Bercovitch, F. B. (1995). Female cooperation, consortship maintenance, and male mating success in savanna baboons. *Animal Behaviour, 50*, 137-149.

Bercovitch, F. B. (1997). Reproductive strategies of rhesus macaques. *Primates, 38*, 247-263.

Bercovitch, F. B., & Berard, J. D. (1993). Life history costs and consequences of rapid reproductive maturation in female rhesus macaques. *Behavioral Ecology and Sociobiology, 32*(2), 103-109.

Bercovitch, F. B., & Strum, S. C. (1993). Dominance rank, resource availability, and reproductive maturation in female savanna baboons. *Behavioral Ecology and Sociobiology, 33*(5), 313-318.

Drickamer, L. C. (1974). A ten-year summary of reproductive data for free-ranging *Macaca mulatta. Folia Primatologica, 21*(1), 61-80.

Ellis, L. (1995). Dominance and reproductive success among nonhuman animals: A cross-species comparison. *Ethology and Sociobiology, 16*, 257-333.

Folstad, I., & Karter, A. J. (1992). Parasites, bright males, and the immunocompetence handicap. *American Naturalist, 139*, 603-622.

Gardin, J. F., Jerome, C. P., Jayo, M. J., & Weaver, D. S. (1989). Maternal factors affecting reproduction in a breeding colony of cynomolgus macaques (*Macaca fascicularis*). *Laboratory Animal Science, 39*, 205-212.

Gowaty, P. A. (1997). Sexual dialectics, sexual selection, and variation in reproductive behavior. In P. A. Gowaty (Ed.), *Feminism and Evolutionary Biology* (pp. 351-384). New York, NY: Chapman & Hall.

Havlicek, J., Roberts, S. C., & Flegr, J. (2005). Women's preference for dominant male odour: Effects of menstrual cycle and relationship status. *Biology Letters, 1*, 256-259.

Huffman, M. A. (1991). Mate selection and partner preferences in female Japanese macaques. In L. M. Fedigan & P. J. Asquith (Eds), *The Monkeys of Arashiyama: Thirty-Five Years of Research in Japan and the West* (pp. 101-122). Albany, NY: SUNY.

Kaufman, J. H. (1965). A three-year study of mating behavior in a free ranging band of rhesus monkeys. *Ecology, 46*, 500-512.

Manson, J. H. (1992). Measuring female mate choice in Cayo Santiago rhesus macaques. *Animal Behaviour, 44*, 405-416.

Muller, M. N., Thompson, M. E., & Wrangham, R. W. (2006). Male chimpanzees prefer mating with old females. *Current Biology, 16*, 2234-2238.

Nikitopoulos, E., Heistermann, M., de Vries, H., van Hooff, J. A. R. A. M, & Sterck, E. H. M. (2005). A pair choice test to identify female mating pattern relative to ovulation in longtailed macaques, *Macaca fascicularis. Animal Behaviour, 70*, 1283-1296.

Parga, J. A. (2006). Male mate choice in *Lemur catta. International Journal of Primatology, 27*, 107-131.

Paul, A., & Thommen, D. (1984). Timing of birth, female reproductive success and infant sex ratio in semifree-ranging Barbary macaques (*Macaca sylvanus*). *Folia Primatologica, 42*(1), 2-16.

Penn, D. J. (2002). The scent of genetic compatibility: Sexual selection and the major histocompatibility complex. *Ethology, 108*, 1-21.

Small, M. F. (1989). Female choice in nonhuman primates. *American Journal of Physical Anthropology, 32*(S10), 103-127.

Trivers, R. (1972). Parental investment and sexual selection. In R. Campbell (Ed.), *Sexual Selection and the Descent of Man* 1871-1971 (pp. 136-179), Chicago, IL: Aldine.

Waynforth, D., Hurtado, A. M., & Hill, K. (1998). Environmentally contingent reproductive strategies in Mayan and Ache males. *Evolution and Human Behavior, 19*(6), 369-385.

2

Early Experience and Incentive Relativity in Adulthood

Lucas Cuenya
Laboratorio de Psicología Experimental y Aplicada, Instituto de Investigaciones Médicas, CONICET – Universidad de Buenos Aires.

Giselle Kamenetzky & Alba E. Mustaca
Laboratorio de Psicología Experimental y Aplicada, Instituto de Investigaciones Médicas, CONICET – Universidad de Buenos Aires.
Centro de Altos Estudios en Ciencias Humanas y de la Salud, Universidad Abierta Interamericana (UAI)

Human and animal studies have shown the long-lasting impact of early life experience on the development of individual differences in stress responsiveness in later life. Despite the numerous works that evaluate the effect of early experience on different behavioral paradigms, which for the most part are related to aversive situations, there are few studies that assess the effects on the unexpected downshift or omission of rewards. The purpose of this article is to review several independent lines of research into how frustration responses during adulthood may be influenced by early experience. Few articles have been found on the subject and in most cases the results were negative or controversial. However, recent research suggests that the response to frustration or euphoria in adults may be modulated by early experience.

Human and animal studies have shown the long-lasting impact of early life experience on the development of individual differences in stress responsiveness in later life. This phenomenon underlies the interplay between genes and the environment. These studies address (1) the effects of early environment on later stress phenotypes, (2) the role of genetic factors in modulating the outcome of environmental influences, and (3) the role of nonshared environmental experience in the outcome of gene × environment interactions (Claessens et al., 2011). Early studies contributed to the notion that the consequences of early life stress exposure are invariantly deleterious. These consequences are achieved through the action of specific environmental cues acting at a specific time during development, that result in permanent alterations in the functioning of the hypothalamic-pituitary-adrenal (HPA) axis (e.g., Andrews & Matthews 2004; De Kloet, Sibug, Helmerhorst & Schmidt, 2005; Matthews, 2002; Meaney, Szyf, & Seckl, 2007; Seckl, 2008). This research shows that the stress of early parental loss, neglect, or abuse produces enhanced fear and anxiety, increased anhedonia, impaired cognition, abnormal brain neurochemistry and neurobiology, and alterations in baseline activity as well as stress reactivity of the HPA axis (e.g., Maestripieri, Lindell, Ayala, Gold, & Higley, 2005; Pryce et al., 2005; Rosenblum, Forger, Noland, Trost, & Coplan, 2001; Stevens, Leckman, Coplan, & Suomi, 2009; Suomi, 1997). However, other research has shown that environmental influences in early life do not always lead to disease or increased vulnerability. There is evidence that early life stress exposure produces a diverse range of developmental outcomes, including resilience to subsequent stressors encountered in adulthood. For example, childhood stress has been linked to attenuated increases in salivary cortisol responses to the Trier Social Stress Test, a protocol in which the subjects have to deliver a free speech and perform mental arithmetic in front of an audience (Gunnar & Donzella, 2002) and lower cerebrospinal fluid levels of corticotropin releasing factor in healthy adults (e.g., Carpenter et al., 2004). Moreover, stress during childhood diminished cardiovascular responses during stressful laboratory tests, such as mental arithmetic task, videogame performance and hand submersion in ice water (e.g., Boyce & Chesterman, 1990). Prior stressful experience also diminishes emotional distress in day-care settings and hospital admissions (e.g., Holmes, 1935; Stacey, Dearden, Pill, & Robinson, 1970), and men and women are found to cope better with stressful events such as spousal loss, major accidents, illness, and work stress if they previously experienced and successfully coped with stressors in childhood (e.g., Forest, 1991; Khoshaba & Maddi, 1999). When early life exposure to stress is examined across a continuum, adults exposed to moderate levels of early life stress exhibit lower levels of state anxiety (Edge et al., 2009) and more resilient cardiovascular responses to a stressful motivated performance task, compared to individuals exposed to either low or high levels of early life stress (Parker & Maestripieri, 2011). These empirical studies suggest that exposure to early life stress may be best conceptualized as a quadratic, rather than linear, function. The outcome of early experience is not necessarily deterministic nor can it be evaluated as positive or negative. Several environmental, cognitive, and genetic inputs are involved in an intricate manner in the modulation of the outcome of early experience on adulthood (Claessens et al., 2011).

Animal models used to study the effects of early experience on stress expression during adult life in rodents include such experimental manipulations as handling, electric shock, exposure to hot or cold temperatures, maternal separation, mild chronic stress and acute stress, and litter size. Typically, behavioral and psychobiological responses are evaluated in adulthood in different tests consisting of the administration of moderate or intense aversive stimuli, such as the exposure to a novel context (e.g., Levine, Haltmeyer, Karas, & Denenberg, 1967) or to avoidance tasks (e.g., Denenberg, 1967), among others.

The majority of studies evaluate the effect of early experience on behavioral paradigms related to aversive situations; only a few studies assess the effects of early experience on the unexpected downshift or omission of rewards. These effects are known as paradoxical reward effects (Amsel, 1992), surprising reward omissions (Papini & Dudley, 1997), or incentive relativity (Flaherty, 1996). A frustration response occurs when an expected appetitive reinforcer is not presented or is reduced in magnitude or quality, even though there are signals for its impending presentation. Different procedures are employed to produce frustration responses, including the total elimination of a reward (extinction), a change of a preferred reward for a less preferred one (contrast effects), a reduction of the reinforcement rate, or an introduction of an impediment or barrier to reach the reward (e.g., Hull, 1943). Although these methods do not apply aversive stimuli, numerous investigations show that these protocols instigate behavioral and neurophysiological responses similar to reactions prompted by the presentation or anticipation of aversive events. Gray (1987) and Gray and McNaughton (2000) stated that both types of experience activate the same brain structures, and different authors have proposed that surprising reward omission is a source of anxiety, stress and psychological pain (e.g., Mustaca, 2013; Papini & Dudley, 1997; Papini, Wood, Daniel, & Norris, 2006).

Based on the above theories and evidence, it could be inferred that situations involving a decrease or loss of positive reinforcers during early childhood might alter adult behavior. However, if early experience affects the stress response, then it should also affect the adjustment to frustrating situations. The purpose of this article is to present several independent lines of research on the influence of early experience on frustration responses. A series of studies related to pharmacological and environmental treatments during infancy and adolescence and their influence on incentive relativity are included, together with designs that evaluate the effect of total or partial reward devaluation (i.e., extinction and negative contrast), random presentation of rewards and extinction (i.e., partial reinforcement), and surprising reward upshift (i.e., positive contrast), either in instrumental or consummatory procedures.

Research on the effects of early experiences on incentive relativity in adulthood has both theoretical and applied implications. From a theoretical level, the evaluation of theories that propose a motivational equivalence between psychological and physiological stress responses caused by aversive stimuli, devaluation or omission of appetitive stimuli can be performed. Moreover, compared to those using aversive conditioning, frustration models have a higher ecological validity. Most stressful events in human lives are related to incentive devaluation or incentive loss (e.g., death of relatives, unemployment; Scully, Tosi, & Banning, 2000). From an applied level, psychological treatments aimed at reducing wasteful consumption of appetitive reinforcers such as food or drugs of abuse usually fail because of frustration responses that subjects experience during the abrupt reduction or elimination of an expected reinforcement. Understanding the mechanisms by which early experiences modulate frustration reactions could contribute to the development of more effective treatments to prevent relapse.

Neonatal Clomipramine and Consummatory Successive Negative Contrast

Neonatal administration of clomipramine (CLI) produces physiological, neuroendocrine, and behavioral abnormalities in rats when they reach adulthood, which are similar to those observed in animal models of depression (Justel, Bentosela, Mustaca, & Ruetti, 2011). This pharmacological manipulation consists in the subcutaneous administration of CLI (15 mg/kg, dissolved in 0.9% saline solution), twice a day, at 08:00 and 20:00 h in rats from postnatal day (PND) 8 to 21. Newborn rats treated with CLI show a decrease in weight (Hansen & Mikkelsen, 1988; Maciag et al., 2006); a decrease in their pleasure-seeking behavior (Vogel, Neill, Kors, & Hagler, 1990); are less aggressive (Martínez-González, Prospero-García, Mihailescu, & Drucker-Colın, 2002); show a lower increase of plasma corticosterone levels during exposure to the stressor, faster return to basal levels, and a reduction in serotoninergic activity (Hansel & Mikkelsen, 1988); and display increased immobility in a forced-swim test, a widely used procedure to assess depressive behaviors (e.g., Bhagya, Srikumar, Taju, & Shankaranarayana Rao, 2008). This background suggests that CLI rats might show an attenuated frustration response. Only one experiment has tested this hypothesis. Ruetti, Burgueño, Justel, Pirola, and Mustaca (2013) evaluated CLI rats in a consummatory successive negative contrast (cSNC) situation. These rats receive daily access to 32% sucrose (preshift phase) and then they are shifted to 4% sucrose (postshift). Compared to unshifted animals that always received access to 4% sucrose, downshifted rats exhibited a sharp suppression of consummatory behavior, followed by a recovery during the next 2-4 trials (Flaherty, 1996). Results were in accordance with the hypothesis: CLI rats showed a cSNC effect only during the first downshift trial, whereas vehicle rats (VEH, subcutaneously administration of saline solution) showed this effect on two post-shift trials, which indicates a faster recovery of CLI animals. Amsel´s theory (1992) suggests that the initial rejection of the 4% solution is triggered by a state of primary frustration induced by the discrepancy between the expectation of a 32% reward acquired during the pre-shift trials and the actual 4% reward encountered on the first post-shift trial. This emotional reaction is hedonically aversive and it induces rejection with minimal or no conflict, serving as an unconditioned stimulus for the acquisition of secondary frustration through Pavlovian conditioning (i.e., pairings of stimuli present at the time of reward downshift with the internal state of primary frustration). Once acquired, secondary frustration plays its role as the avoidance component of the conflict induced at full strength during the second postshift trial. On the basis of Amsel´s theory (1992), the results suggest that both CLI and VEH rats showed a similar response pattern when they face to the downshift solution (unconditioned response). By contrast, the secondary frustration could be attenuated because of a diminished expectative in the CLI rats. Moreover, most of studies have found a significant increase in blood plasma corticosterone in the second post-shift test but not the first one, which coincides with the fact that CLI animals showed a lower increase in plasma corticosterone levels during the exposure to the stressor, and a faster return to basal levels (e.g., Bonilla-Jaime, Retana-Márquez, Vázquez-Palacios, & Velázquez-Moctezuma, 2003). For these reasons the authors concluded that the result may be accounted for by an alteration of the HPA axis, a serotonergic system deficit, a low expectation formation during the pre-shift phase, or by a combination of some of all these factors.

Litter Size and the Frustration Effect

Litter size (i.e., the number of litter siblings) has previously been shown to strongly affect early growth in many small and social mammal species including laboratory rats. Some studies indicate that the effects of litter size also involve stress reactions, although the results were more modest compared to other treatments. For example, Rödel, Meyer, Prager, Stefanski, and Hudson (2010) found, in young Long–Evans rats, a negative correlation between serum corticosterone concentrations and litter size during PND 17 and on PND 33 after a10-min test in an elevated plus maze. The authors suggested two main explanations, not necessarily mutually exclusive: delayed maturation of the HPA axis in the typically lower body-mass pups of large litters. However, pups encountering greater competition for maternal resources adjust to this presumably more stressful developmental environment by down-regulating responsiveness of the HPA axis. Spencer and Tilbrook (2009) found that these differences were higher in females than in males. Wistar rats raised in small litters (4 vs. 16) have greater access to their mothers' milk and weigh more in adulthood than those raised in large litters. Compared to males, females from small litters show enhanced exploratory behavior and reduced anxiety in the elevated plus maze, (i.e., they enter open arms more often), and enhanced central response to restraint stress, including greater activation of the paraventricular nucleus of the hypothalamus and paraventricular nucleus of the thalamus.

We found only one experiment on the effect of litter size on frustration. Amsel and Penick (1962) evaluated the influence of early experience and training on the frustration effect to test the associative theory proposed by Lawson and Marx (1958) and Marx (1956) regarding the frustration effect. The authors reported that the frustration effect in a double-runway situation did not vary as a function of the litter size during rearing. Nevertheless, this result should be taken with caution because Amsel and Penick did not report the sex of the animals. Considering that later experiments have shown that the influence of the litter size on stress is sex-dependent, the lack of a positive result in Amsel and Penick's study could be due to the used of males.

Early Handling and Frustration

Levine (1957) challenged the dominant theory that early life stress invariably contributes to the development of emotional instability. He exposed neonatal rat pups to daily handling sessions, which consisted of brief maternal separation periods (less than 15 min) between PND 1 and 21 (early handling, EH). This manipulation differs from transient isolation from the mother and siblings or maternal separation (MS), which consists of prolonged periods of daily maternal absence ranging from 1 to 24 h. The outcome of these manipulations was unexpected at the time. Levine, and then others, found that early handling (EH) induced long-lasting changes in the adult phenotype, such as HPA axis hypo-responsiveness (e.g., Levine, 2005; Meaney & Aitken, 1985; Meerlo, Horvath, Nag, Bohus, & Koolhaas, 1999), reduced emotionality (Meerlo et al. 1999), and increased cognitive performance (Kosten, Lee, & Kim, 2007), as compared to nonhandled (NH) rats raised in undisturbed laboratory conditions. Compared to normally reared controls, stimulated rats have higher activity levels and lower defecation scores in an open field (Denenberg & Morton, 1962), shorter latencies in an emergence from home-cage test (Williams & Wells, 1970), a lower adrenal response to stress (Levine et al., 1967), and learn a shock avoidance response faster (Levine, 1957). These findings have demonstrated that, in some instances, exposure to moderate stress in early life appeared to be beneficial for the infant by promoting a greater ability to adapt to psychological and physiological stressors in adulthood (Levine, 1957). This same principle also serves as the basis for the stress inoculation-induced resilience theory developed later (Levine & Mody 2003; Lyons, Kim, Schatzberg, & Levine, 1998; Lyons, Martel, Levine, Risch, & Schatzberg, 1999). One interpretation of these results has been that stimulation in infancy reduces emotional reactivity in adulthood (Denenberg, 1967). Using other experimental designs, it was shown that maternal care changed when pups were returned after handling, which leads to the maternal mediation hypothesis on the handling effects observed in adulthood. Nevertheless, a review on experimental results has suggested that variation in active maternal care could be understood as an epiphenomenon rather than as a causal factor in developmental plasticity of HPA axis and low fear responses in EH rats (Macrí & Würbel, 2006).

This evidence suggests that handling might attenuate responses to surprising reward changes. If contrast effects resulted from emotional processes, then animals known to differ in emotional reactivity should behave differently when exposed to frustration. Four studies assessing the EH effect on contrast procedures have been reported. Daly and Rosenberg (1973) evaluated infant male Wistar rats that were either removed from the nest each day (EH) or left undisturbed (NH) in instrumental extinction with or without shock (Experiment1), and in instrumental successive negative contrast (iSNC) employing a runway (Experiment 2). Handling consisted of removing the pups from the nest on a daily basis during the first 20 days after birth and isolating each one for 3 min in individual cages. At the end of the 3-min interval, pups were returned to the nest. The control rats were left completely undisturbed until weaning. In Experiment 1, one handled and one nonhandled groups were given extinction training with no shock (NS), whereas the other two groups were given extinction training plus shock (S) in the goalbox. Two control groups, one handled and one nonhandled, were given runway training with no food reinforcement (0) to determine if baseline running speeds were affected by the handling variable. In instrumental acquisition and extinction, reinforced rats ran faster than nonreinforced rats. Handled rats ran faster than nonhandled rats during the initial trials of runway acquisition, irrespective of the reinforcement condition. During extinction all groups showed decreases in speed of running, but the shocked group's speed decreased faster than the nonshocked group's, and differences between handled and nonhandled groups were larger for shocked than for nonshocked groups. Handled subjects ran faster in all segments of the alley despite the fact that they received more shocks. Nonhandled rats stopped running sooner than handled rats when shock was introduced in the goalbox, but there were small differences between handled and nonhandled rats when given extinction training without shock. Instead, responses on iCSN showed no differences between handled and nonhandled rats in the magnitude of the depression effect after an incentive shift. These results suggest that the handling procedure diminished the suppressive effect of punishment on extinction, but not incentive devaluation. Taken together, these results do not support theories of analogy between incentive devaluation and application of aversive stimuli.

Fagen and Rycek (1980) examined the effects of EH using male and female Long-Evans hooded rats on the response to positive and negative contrast effects in the sucrose-licking paradigm and in open field testing. For handled litters, the mother was removed from the cage and the pups were individually placed into wooden compartments for 3 min daily between PND 2 and 22. Approximately on PND 101, they were given alternating 1-min access periods to two bottles containing either 32 % or 4% sucrose solutions. Measures of lick rate and latency to switch bottles revealed that both EH and NH rats exhibited contrast effects of equal magnitudes. The open-field test showed that, although both infantile treatment groups were equally active, NH rats defecated and urinated more on each of the four open-field days than EH rats. The experimental design employed in this work was simultaneous contrast, which involves sensory adaptation mechanisms (Flaherty, 1996). Therefore, early handling will most likely not have an effect on this type of response as it is not modulated by emotional processes.

Meinrath and Flaherty (1987) handled preweanling male Sprague-Dawley rat pups during 3 min daily from PND 2 to15. The subjects were subsequently evaluated during adulthood in open field, cSNC, and neophobia tests. They observed that EH rats reared and ambulated more, and defecated less than NH subjects (i.e., EH rats exhibited lower emotionality than NH rats). However, the handling manipulation had no effect on the size of the cSNC effect after a shift from 32% to 4% sucrose and did not influence sucrose neophobia in two different test situations.

Finally, de la Torre et al. (2008, unpublished work) tested handled and nonhandled rats in the elevated plus maze, cSNC, and iSNC. They reported that nonhandled rats were more fearful than their handled counterparts in the elevated plus maze. In iSNC, no significant differences were found between handled and nonhandled rats. In cSNC, no contrast effect was exhibited in either group during the first block of two postshift trials. Instead, in the second block (i.e., postshift Trials 3 and 4) only NH rats showed a negative contrast effect. It should be noted that (1) usually, the cSNC effect is observed with greater intensity in the first two postshift trials (Flaherty, 1996), but in this work there was no evidence of the effect on such trials (first block of 2 trials); and (2) as the difference between the EH and NH groups emerged in the second block (postshift Trials 3 and 4), EH might affect the recovery from the negative contrast. In any case, there are misgivings regarding this interpretation because, given the lack of negative contrast in the first two trials, how can it be argued that early handling accelerates recovery from cSNC? In sum, this is a positive result that could indicate some influence of early handling on cSNC, but it should be replicated with more animals and better measurements.

In conclusion, the EH manipulation does not seem to produce an alteration on the adult animal's response in situations involving surprising reward changes. The only study reporting positive results using cSNC should be replicated because there was no contrast effect in the first two devaluation trials, which thus contradicts the results obtained in earlier investigations into cSNC.

Chronic Random Neonatal Stress and Frustration

Sharing the basic thinking behind the early handling approach, some authors found that infant rats isolated during short periods of time from their litters and exposed to moderate and random aversive stimuli exhibited less emotionality in adulthood when subject to moderate or intense stressors (Toth, Avital, Leshem, Richter-Levin, & Braun, 2008). One of the procedures of chronic random neonatal stress (CRNS) consists of unpredictable and repeated stimulation from PND 2 to 15. Pups are daily separated from their mothers (between 6 and 10 h) and different stimuli are presented, including white noise, cold–heat exposure, handling, moderate electric shocks, and tail pinch (Ruetti, González, Justel,Torrecilla, & Mustaca, 2010). González, Rodríguez, Cabrera, and Fóscolo (1991) evaluated adult rats subjected to CRNS, handling, or controls in tests that involved exposure to aversive stimuli. Animals exposed to CRNS showed an attenuated increase in prolactin and corticosterone, and an improvement in a forced-swimming test, compared to EH and control conditions. However, EH was a less effective treatment than CRNS to reduce the behavioral deficit observed in the forced swimming test due to unpredictable electric shocks during the estrous cycle of female rats (González Jatuff, Rodríguez Echandía, Cabrera & Fóscolo, 1991). Considering that frustration triggers emotional states similar to those generated by aversive stimuli, it was hypothesized that CRNS might also modulate the emotional reaction produced by devaluation or omission of an expected reward. Ruetti et al. (2010) evaluated rats exposed to CRNS in cSNC and consummatory extinction (cE) situations. The latter consists of measuring the approach response to an empty tube after acquisition of the consummatory response to an appetitive solution (32% sucrose). Rats exposed to CRNS showed an attenuated cSNC effect and a faster cE (significant decrease in the time of contact with the feeder compared to the no CRNS group). These results suggest that previous research on the handling treatment was probably not strong enough to affect the animals′ frustration responses.

Maternal Separation and Negative and Positive Contrast Effects

Maternal separation (MS) consists of prolonged periods of maternal absence each ranging from 1 to 24 h during the early period of life. The reported effects of MS on adulthood appear to be less consistent compared to the effects of early handling, probably because of the substantial variety of different experimental procedures across different laboratories in terms of duration, frequency, age of onset of the separation, and the choice of control group (e.g., Lehmann, Russig, Feldon, & Pryce, 2002; Rosenfeld, Wetmore, & Levine, 1992). Nevertheless, MS appears to "program" the functioning of the HPA axis. This manipulation was reported to yield a more severe outcome, opposing the effects of early handling and chronic random neonatal stress, including HPA hyper-responsiveness following stress (Plotsky & Meaney, 1993), increased emotionality (Kalinichev, Easterling, Plotsky, & Holtzman, 2002a), altered sensitivity to opioids (Kalinichev, Easterling, & Holtzman, 2002b), and impaired cognitive performance (Levine, 2005). However, two opposite behavioral phenotypes may result from similar neonatal MS protocols. One is characterized by hyperactive/impulsive behaviors in the open-field and defensive withdrawal tests (e.g., Arnold & Siviy, 2002; Braun, Kremz, Wetzel, Wagner, & Peoggel, 2003; Colorado, Shumake, Conejo, Gonzalez-Pardo, & Gonzalez-Lima, 2006; Kaneko, Riley, & Ehlers 1994). The other phenotype expresses hypoactive/anxiety-like behaviors in open-field, defensive withdrawal, and elevated plus-maze tests (e.g., Huot, Thrivikraman, Meaney, & Plotsky, 2001; Janus, 1987; Matthews & Robbins, 2003). The reason of these conflicting results are still unknown, nevertheless it was proposed that it is presumable related to genetic variations in the outcome of environmental influences (see Claessens et al., 2011).

Only one article on the effects of MS on frustration responses was found. Matthews, Wilkinson, and Robbins (1996) studied the effects of repeated MS of preweanling rats on responses to both primary and conditioned incentives in mature rats. The procedure consisted of separating pups on ten occasions spaced randomly between PND 5 and 20. On PND 21 the animals were housed in pairs by gender. When assessed during adulthood, it was observed that MS animals showed enhanced weight gain, a reduction in the immediate exploratory locomotor response to novelty in both sexes, and a decrease of locomotor responsivity to compound cues predictive of food reward in females (Experiment 1). When responding to different sucrose solutions, MS rats did not exhibit changes in either consummatory behavior or sucrose preference. In Experiment 2, the animals were evaluated in positive and negative contrasts. In each session of negative contrast, the animals had access to a 15% sugar solution for 2 min, and then to a 2% sugar solution for 2 min. In sessions of positive contrast, the animals had access to a 2% sugar solution for 2 min, and then to a 15% sugar solution for 2 min. The licking rate was measured every minute. The sessions were conducted 24-h apart. Before evaluating contrast effects, rats were given 3-min access to a 15% sugar solution (when measuring negative contrast) or 3-min access to a 2% sugar solution (when assessing positive contrast). The authors found that MS rats displayed increased negative contrast and attenuated positive contrast as compared to animals with no MS. The method used does not rule out that these differences may be due to carryover or sensory contrast. Therefore, even though the findings are interesting, they should be replicated to eliminate such confounding variable.

Social Isolation in Adolescence and Incentive Relativity

Many behavioral and neurophysiological changes occur during adolescence. These include an increased focus on peer-directed social interactions, novelty seeking and the pursuit of new sensations (see Spear, 2000), changes in the use of appetitive reinforces like food (e.g., Neumark-Sztainer et al., 2006) or drugs of abuse (e.g., Chen & Jacobson, 2012; Cuenya, 2006) and close proximity to incentive situations (see Ernst, Romeo, & Andersen, 2009). In rats, as in other species, adolescence is characterized by behavioral and neurochemical changes from PND 20 to 55 (Spear, 2000). During this period, there is an increase in social interaction and play behaviors with peers (Vanderschuren, Niesink, & Van Ree, 1996), in novelty-seeking and exploratory behaviors (Douglas, Varlinskaya, & Spear, 2003), in the release of gonadal hormones (Sisk & Foster, 2004), and in changes in mesolimbic dopamine function (Wahlstrom, Collins, White, & Luciana, 2010).

The social isolation procedure during adolescence in rats consists usually in socially isolating animals for a specific period of time with as little manipulation as possible. However, subjects keep visual, auditory, and olfactory contact with their littermates in the room (Weiss, Domeney, Heidbreder, Moreau, & Feldon, 2001). The behavioral and neuroendocrinological changes produced as a result of adolescent isolation are mainly observed when the treatment is applied from the first day of weaning until PND 30. Within the wide range of alterations noted during adulthood figure a decrease in social interactions; an impairment of inhibitory mechanisms and sensorimotor gating, shown in low latent inhibition and prepulse inhibition; hyperresponsivity to novel environments; cognitive inflexibility; dopaminergic hyperactivity in the nucleus accumbens (NAc); and glutamatergic and dopaminergic hypoactivity in the prefrontal cortex (Fone & Porkess, 2008). Other studies have shown that adolescent isolation produced alterations in the consumption of appetitive reinforcers during adulthood, like hyperphagia (Jahng, Yoo, Ryu, & Lee, 2012), increased preference for sucrose solutions (Hong et al., 2012), and changes in responsivity to food novelty (Hall, Humby, Wilkinson, & Robbins, 1997).

The impact of social isolation during adolescence on contrast effects has hardly been investigated. Shanab and Ralph (1979) compared adult male rats that were group-housed or isolated from weaning to adulthood in an iSNC situation and in an instrumental partial reinforcement extinction effect (iPREE) situation, using a runway. They found that housing conditions had no effect on the iSNC, but that only isolated animals showed the iPREE, which the authors interpreted as the expression of a higher level of emotionality or anxiety under such conditions. However, the study does not make a distinction between the specific effect of adolescent isolation and the possible effect of adult isolation. Adult isolation is also considered a stressor generating alterations in mammals, although its effects cannot be matched to social isolation since each one produces different patterns of deleterious consequences (Morgan & Tromborg, 2007). Cuenya, Fosacheca, Mustaca, and Kamenetzky (2011, 2012) showed that isolation in adulthood, from PND 60 to testing, did not affect the expression of cSNC, partial reinforcement effect on cSNC, or consummatory successive positive contrast (cSPC). These results suggest that the findings reported by Shanab and Ralph (1979) could be explained by the specific isolation during adolescence. In any case, the kind of design employed by Shanab et al. does not allow testing of this hypothesis.

Hall et al. (1997) showed a study with the same methodological problem. The authors compared adult male *Lister* hooded rats reared in isolation after weaning for eight weeks with rats housed always in groups, in connection with the consumption of sucrose solutions of different concentrations (0.7%, 2.1%, 7%, 21%, and 34%) presented in an ascending and descending order during 5-min trials. The authors concluded that the consummatory positive contrast was increased in isolated animals, while no differences were noted in the negative contrast. The study has yet another problem. Consumption trials were run every 25 min instead of every 24 h, as in standard incentive contrast procedures (e.g., Cuenya et al., 2011; Cuenya et al., 2012), so that differences might be due to a sensory after effect and not to a violation of expectation recovered through a memory process. Finally, the design used did not feature groups receiving the same incentive value throughout the training so as to determine the contrast effect. Therefore, these results do not allow for conclusive interpretations on how social isolation in adolescence affects the animals' response to shifts in reinforcements.

Finally, Cuenya, Kamenetzky, Tassone, and Mustaca (2010) assessed the effect of adolescent isolation in male Wistar rats on elevated plus maze responses, cSNC, cSPC, and cE. The animals were submitted to a period of social isolation from PND 21 to 36. From PND 37 until the end of the experiment, they remained grouped in their home cages, even when evaluated during adulthood. Adolescent isolation generated higher levels of locomotor activity, without affecting anxiety on the elevated plus maze. It also enhanced response to a surprising increase in reinforcement during adulthood, both when going from 0% to a 32% sucrose solution (Experiment 1), and from 4% to 32% (Experiment 2), showing a greater positive contrast, as in the work by Hall et al. (1997). At the same time, it was noted that the treatment did not alter either anxiety levels in adulthood or responses to incentive omission or devaluation in cSNC and cE, just as was reported for the iSNC by Shanab and Ralph (1979). The study, however, was devoid of methodological limitations that characterized previous studies, allowing us to identify adolescence as a period in which, if certain chronic stressors such as isolation occur, long-lasting effects on responses to surprising reward change can be generated.

Conclusions

There is evidence that exposure to stress in early life produces a diverse range of developmental outcomes, including resilience to subsequent stressors encountered in adulthood. There are numerous investigations that analyze the neurobiological and behavioral effects of early experience on adulthood by means of procedures that apply aversive stimuli of varying intensity. However, the effects of early experience on adult behavior when exposed to surprising upshifts or omissions of appetitive reinforcers have hardly been investigated. Table 1 summarizes the research work that evaluated the impact of early experience on incentive relativity.

Table 1. *Early experience and frustration in rats.*

Early treatment	Procedure	Result	Reference
Neonatal clomipramine	cSNC	faster recovery	Ruetti et al. (2013)
Perinatal asphyxia	ID	minor devaluation	Galeano et al. (2011)
Litter size	Double runway	no effect	Amsel & Pennick (1962)
Early handling	iSNC (runway)	no effect	Daly & Rosenberg (1973)
Early handling	Simultaneous positive and negative contrast	no effect	Fagen & Rycek (1980)
Early handling	cSNC	no effect	Meinrath & Flaherty (1987)
Early handling	iSNC (runway)	no effect	De la Torre et al. (2008, unpublished)
Early handling	cSNC	small contrast effect (?)	De la Torre et al. (2008, unpublished)
Chronic random neonatal stress	cSNC	small contrast effect	Ruetti et al. (2010)
Chronic random neonatal stress	cE	facilitated extinction	Ruetti et al. (2010)
Maternal separation	cSPC	small positive contrast (?)	Mattews et al. (1996)
Maternal separation	cSNC	enhanced negative contrast (?)	Mattews et al. (1996)
Adolescent isolation	iPREE	no iPREE in grouped rats (?)	Shanab & Ralph (1979)
Adolescent isolation	iSNC	no effect (?)	Shanab & Ralph (1979)
Adolescent isolation	cSPC	enhanced positive contrast (?)	Hall et al. (1997)
Adolescent isolation	cSNC	no effect (?)	Hall et al. (1997)
Adolescent isolation	cSPC	enhanced positive contrast	Cuenya et al. (2010)
Adolescent isolation	cSNC	no effect	Cuenya et al. (2010)
Adolescent isolation	cE	no effect	Cuenya et al. (2010)

Note. Early experiences and frustration in rats. "?": controversial methods or results; cSNC: Consummatory Successive Negative Contrast; cSPC: consummatory Successive Positive Contrast; iSNC: instrumental Successive Negative Contrast; ID: Incentive devaluation; iPREE: instrumental Partial Reinforcement Extinction Effect; cE: consummatory Extinction.

There are only 12 papers with 19 studies on incentive relativity, of which seven had some methodological problems or lack of information that hinders proper interpretation, six obtained a negative result, and only five had positive results. It should be noted that negative results obtained in early work during the 1960s could be the reason for abandoning this line of research. Flaherty (1996), an author who contributed significantly to the study of incentive relativity, suggested based on negative results on the effects of early handling on cSNC that "the lack of usefulness of emotionality as a general concept does not exclude the possibility that a particular emotion might be involved in contrast." (p. 90).

The hypotheses guiding these experiments were based on theories of emotional frustration that confirm the existence of a neurobiological and functional equivalence between the presentation of aversive stimuli and the devaluation of appetitive reinforcers (e.g., Amsel, 1992; Gray, 1987; Konorsky, 1964). Evidence accumulated over the years has supported these theories. The effect of the devaluation of appetitive reinforcers is modulated by genetic factors (Cuenya et al., 2012), by anxiolytic and analgesic drugs (Justel, Ruetti, Bentosela, Mustaca, & Papini, 2012; Pellegrini, Wood, Daniel, & Papini, 2005), by the application of aversive stimuli prior to reward devaluation (Ortega, Daniel, Davis, Fuchs, & Papini, 2011), by exposure to anxiolytic behaviors before devaluation (Freidin, Kamenetzky, & Mustaca, 2005), by pharmacological manipulations of emotional memory (Bentosela, Ruetti, Muzio, Mustaca, & Papini, 2006), by partial reinforcement (Cuenya et al., 2011; Pellegrini, Muzio, Mustaca, & Papini, 2004), and by exposure to open-field testing prior to reinforcement devaluation (Justel, Pautassi, & Mustaca, 2014), among other manipulations. It is possible that the parameters needed to obtain positive results have yet to be identified. This has been suggested in recent work by Ruetti et al. (2010) and Galeano et al. (2011), who found an attenuation of cSNC and a facilitation of cE in rats exposed to chronic random neonatal stress, an attenuation of cSNC in rats subjected to neonatal clomipramine treatment, and higher consumption in perinatal asphyxia rats. Moreover, the effects of early experience also seem to affect positive contrast, which is difficult to observe. There is at least one paper that reported a stronger positive contrast effect in animals exposed to adolescent isolation (Cuenya et al., 2010). The latter finding may encourage further research into the relationship between early experience and the response of adult animals to the surprising upshift or omission of appetitive reinforcers.

Acknowledgments

We thank the anonymous reviewers who helped improve the manuscript.

References

Amsel, A. (1992). *Frustration theory: An analysis of dispositional learning and memory.* New York, NY: Cambridge University Press.

Amsel, A., & Penick, E. (1962). The influence of early experience on the frustration effect. *Journal of Experimental Psychology, 63,*167-176.

Andrews, M. H., & Matthews, S. G. (2004). Programming of the hypothalamo-pituitary-adrenal axis: serotonergic involvement. *Stress, 7*, 5-27.

Arnold, J. L., & Siviy, S. (2002). Effects of neonatal handling and maternal separation on rough-and-tumble play in the rat. *Developmental Psychobiology, 41*, 205-215.

Bentosela, M., Ruetti, E., Muzio, R., Mustaca, A., & Papini, M. (2006). Administration of corticosterone after the first downshift trial enhances consummatory successive negative contrast. *Behavioral Neuroscience, 120*, 371-380.

Bhagya, V., Srikumar, B., Taju, T., & Shankaranarayana Rao, B. (2008). Neonatal clomipramine induced endogenous depression in rats is associated with learning impairment in adulthood. *Behavioral Brain Research, 187*, 1890-194.

Bonilla-Jaime, H., Retana-Márquez, S., Vázquez-Palacios, G. & Velázquez-Moctezuma, J. (2003). Plasma levels of corticosterone and testosterone after sexual activity in male rats treated neonatally with clomipramine. *Behavioral Pharmacology, 14*, 357-362.

Boyce, W. T., & Chesterman, E., (1990). Life events, social support, and cardiovascular reactivity in adolescence. *Journal of Developmental & Behavioral Pediatrics, 11*, 105-111.

Braun, K., Kremz, P., Wetzel, W., Wagner, T., & Peoggel, G. (2003). Influence of parental deprivation on the behavioral development in *Octodon degus*: Modulation by maternal vocalizations. *Developmental Psychobiology, 42,* 237-245.

Carpenter, L. L., Tyrka, A. R., McDougle, C. J., Malison, R. T., Owens, M. J., Memeroff, C. B., & Price, L. H.(2004). Cerebrospinal fluid corticotropin-releasing factor and perceived early-life stress in depressed patients and healthy control subjects. *Neuropsychopharmacology, 29*, 777-784.

Claessens, S. E., Daskalakis, N. P., van der Veen, R., Oitzl, M. S., Kloet, R., & Champagne, D. L. (2011). Development of individual differences in stress responsiveness: an overview of factors mediating the outcome of early life experience. *Psychopharmacology*, *214*, 141-154.

Chen, P., & Jacobson, K. C. (2012). Developmental trajectories of 622 substance use from early adolescence to young adulthood: Gender and racial/ethnic difference. *Journal of Adolescent Health*, *50,* 154-63.

Colorado, R. A., Shumake, J., Conejo, N. M., Gonzalez-Pardo, H., & Gonzalez-Lima, F.(2006). Effects of maternal separation, early handling, and standard facility rearing on orienting and impulsive behavior of adolescent rats. *Behavioural Processes, 71,* 51-58.

Cuenya, L. (2006). Estresores ocupacionales, soporte social y consumo de alcohol en jóvenes. *Anuario de Investigaciones*, *14*, 211-20.

Cuenya, L., Fosacheca, S., Mustaca, A., & Kamenetzky, G. (2011). Efectos del aislamiento en la adultez sobre el dolor y la frustración. *Psicológica*, *32*, 49-63.

Cuenya, L., Fosacheca, S., Mustaca, A., & Kamenetzky, G. (2012). Effects of isolation in adulthood on frustration and anxiety. *Behavioural Processes, 90*, 155-60.

Cuenya, L., Kamenetzky, G., Tassone, R., & Mustaca, A. (2010). Efecto del aislamiento adolescente sobre las respuestas ante el cambio sorpresivo del refuerzo en ratas. Memorias del II Congreso Internacional de Investigación y Práctica Profesional en Psicología, *XVI Jornadas de Investigación y Sexto Encuentro de Investigadores en Psicología del MERCOSUR, 2*, 523-524.

Cuenya, L., Sabariego, M., Donaire, R., Fernández-Teruel, A., Tobeña, A., Gómez, M. J.,& Torres, M. C. (2012). The effect of partial reinforcement on instrumental successive negative contrast in inbred Roman High- (RHA-I) and Low- (RLA-I) Avoidance rats. *Physiology & Behavior, 105*, 1112-1116.

Daly, H. B., & Rosenberg, K. M (1973). Infantile stimulation and its effects on frustration and fear-motivated behavior in rats. *Learning & Motivation, 4*, 381-396.

De Kloet, E. R, Sibug, R. M, Helmerhorst, F. M, & Schmidt M. V. (2005). Stress, genes and the mechanism of programming the brain for later life. *Neuroscience & Biobehavioral Review, 29*, 271-281.

De la Torre, M. L., Sabariego, M., Espadas, I., Gómez, M. J., Torres, C., Aguilar, R., & Espinet, A. (2008, unpublished work). Does neonatal handling influence aversive emotions triggered by surprising reward loss? *Primer congreso IBRO/LARC de neurociencias da América Latina*. Buziios, Brasil.

Denenberg, V. H. (1967). Stimulation in infancy, emotional reactivity, and exploratory behavior. In D. C. Glass (Ed.), *Neurophysiology & emotion*. New York, NY: Rockefeller University Press and Russell Sage Foundation.

Denenberg, V. H., & Morton, J. R. C. (1962). Effects of environmental complexity and social grouping upon modification of emotional behavior. *Journal of Comparative & Physiological Psychology, 55*, 242-246.

Douglas, L. A., Varlinskaya, E. I., & Spear, L. P. (2003). Novel-object place conditioning in adolescent and adult male and female rats: effects of social isolation. *Physiology & Behavior*, *80*, 317-325.

Edge, M. D., Ramel, W., Drabant, E. M., Kuo, J. R., Parker, K. J., & Gross, J. J. (2009). For better or worse? Stress inoculation effects for implicit but not explicit anxiety. *Depression & Anxiety*, *26*, 831-837.

Ernst, M., Romeo, R. D., & Andersen, S. L. (2009). Neurobiology of the development of motivated behaviors in adolescence: A window into a neural systems model. *Pharmacology, Biochemistry & Behavior, 93*, 199-211.

Fagen, J. W., & Rycek, R. F. (1980). Effect of handling on positive and negative contrast effects. *Developmental Psychobiology, 13,* 37-45.

Flaherty, C. F. (1996). *Incentive Relativity*. Cambridge, UK: Cambridge University Press.

Fone, K. C. F., & Porkess, M. P. (2008). Behavioural and neurochemical effects of post weaning social isolation in rodents-Relevance to developmental neuropsychiatric disorders. *Neuroscience & Biobehavioral Reviews, 32,* 1087-1102.

Forest, K. B. (1991). The interplay of childhood stress and adult life events on women's symptoms of depression. *Dissertation Abstracts International, 51*, 3237.

Freidin, E., Kamenetzky, G., & Mustaca, A. (2005). Anxiolytic-like effect of ejaculation upon frustration. *Learning & Behavior, 33*, 277-286.

Galeano, P., Blanco Calvo, E., Madureira de Olivieira, D., Cuenya, L., Kamenetzky, G., Mustaca, A.,& Capani, F. (2011). Long-lasting effects of perinatal asphyxia on exploration memory and incentive downshift. *International Journal of Developmental Neuroscience, 29*, 609-619.

González Jatuff, A. S., Rodríguez Echandía, R., Cabrera, R., & Fóscolo, R. (1991). Neonatal chronic stress induces subsensitivity to chronic stress in adult rats: II. Effects on estrous cycle in females. *Physiology & Behavior*, *56*, 591-595.

Gray, J. A. (1987). *The psychology of fear and stress.* Cambridge, UK: Cambridge University Press.

Gray, J. A., & McNaughton, N. (2000). *The Neuropsychology of Anxiety.* (2nd ed.). Oxford, UK: Oxford University Press.

Gunnar, M. R., & Donzella, B. (2002). Social regulation of the cortisol levels in early human development. *Psychoneuroendocrinology, 27*,199-220.

Hall, F. S., Humby, T., Wilkinson, L. S., & Robbins, T. W. (1997). The effects of isolation-rearing on sucrose consumption in rats. *Physiology & Behavior, 62*, 291-197.

Hansen, H., & Mikkelsen, J. (1988). Long-term effects on serotonin transporter mRNA expression of chronic neonatal exposure to a serotonin reuptake inhibitor. *European Journal of Pharmacology*, *352*, 307-315.

Hong, S., Flashner, B., Chiu, M., ver Hoeve, E., Luz, S., & Bhatnagar, S. (2012). Social isolation in adolescence alters behaviors in the forced swim and sucrose preference test in female but not in male rats. *Physiology & Behavior, 105*, 269-275.

Hull, C. L. (1943). *Principles of Behavior.* New York, NY: Appleton.

Huot, R. L., Thrivikraman, K. V., Meaney, M. J., & Plotsky, P. M. (2001). Development of adult ethanol preference and anxiety as a consequence of neonatal maternal separation in Long Evans rats and reversal with antidepressant treatment. *Psychopharmacology, 158*, 366-373.

Jahng, J. W., Yoo, S. B., Ryu, V., & Lee, J. (2012). Hyperphagia and depression-like behavior by adolescence social isolation in female rats. *International Journal of Developmental Neuroscience, 30*, 47-53.

Janus, K. (1987). Effects of early separation of young rats from the mother on their open-field behavior. *Physiology & Behavior, 40*, 711-715.

Justel, N., Bentosela, M., Mustaca, A., & Ruetti, E. (2011). Neonatal treatment with clomipramine and depression: Review of physiological and behavioral findings. *Interdisciplinaria, 28*, 207-220.

Justel, N., Pautassi, R., & Mustaca, A. (2014). Proactive interference of open field on consummatory successive negative contrast. *Learning & Behavior, 42,* 58-68.

Justel, N., Ruetti, E., Bentosela, M, Mustaca, A., & Papini, M. (2012). Effects of testosterone administration and gonadectomy on incentive downshift and open field activity in rats. *Physiology & Behavior, 106*, 657-663.

Kalinichev, M., Easterling, K. W., Plotsky, P. M., & Holtzman S. G. (2002a). Long-lasting changes in stress-induced corticosterone response and anxiety-like behaviors as a consequence of neonatal maternal separation in Long–Evans rats. *Pharmacology & Biochemicy Behavior, 73,*131-140.

Kalinichev, M., Easterling, K. W., & Holtzman, S. G. (2002b). Early neonatal experience of long–Evans rats results in long-lasting changes in reactivity to a novel environment and morphine-induced sensitization and tolerance. *Neuropsychopharmacology, 27*, 518-533.

Kaneko, W. M., Riley, E. P., & Ehlers, C. L. (1994). Behavioral and electrophysiological effects of early repeated maternal separation. *Depression, 2*, 43-53.

Khoshaba, D. M., & Maddi, S. R. (1999). Early experiences in hardiness development. *Consulting Psychology Journal, Practical Research, 51*, 106–116.

Konorsky, J. (1964*). Integrative activity of the brain.* Chicago, IL: University Chicago Press.

Kosten, T. A., Lee, H. J, & Kim, J. J. (2007) Neonatal handling alters learning in adult male and female rats in a task-specific manner. *Brain Research, 1154*, 144-153.

Lawson, R., & Marx, M. H. (1958). Frustration: Theory and experiment. *Genetic Psychology Monographs, 57*, 393-428.

Lehmann, J., Russig, H., Feldon, J., & Pryce, C. R. (2002). Effect of a single maternal separation at different pup ages on the corticosterone stress response in adult and aged rats. *Pharmacology, Biochemistry & Behavior, 73*,141-145.

Levine, S. (1957). Infantile experience and resistance to physiological stress. *Science, 126*, 405.

Levine, S. (2005). Developmental determinants of sensitivity and resistance to stress. *Psychoneuroendocrinology, 30*, 939–946.

Levine, S., Haltmeyer, G. C., Karas, G. G., & Denenbehg, V. H. (1967). Physiological and behavioral effects of infantile stimulation. *Physiology & Behavior, 2*, 55-59.

Levine, S., & Mody, T. (2003). The long-term psychobiological consequences of intermittent postnatal separation in the squirrel monkey. *Neuroscience Biobehavioral Review, 27*, 83-89.

Lyons, D. M, Kim, S, Schatzberg, A. F, & Levine, S. (1998). Postnatal foraging demands alter adrenocortical activity and psychosocial development. *Developmental Psychobiological, 32*, 285-291.

Lyons, D. M., Martel, F. L, Levine, S., Risch, N. J, & Schatzberg, A. F. (1999). Postnatal experiences and genetic effects on squirrel monkey social affinities and emotional distress. *Hormones & Behavior, 36*, 266-275.

Maciag, D., Simpson, K., Coppinger, D., Lu, Y., Wang, Y., Lin, R., & Paul, I. (2006). Neonatal antidepressant exposure has lasting effects on behavior and serotonin circuitry. *Neuropsychopharmacology, 31,* 47-57.

Macrí, S., & Würbel, H. (2006) Developmental plasticity of HPA and fear responses in rats: a critical review of the maternal mediation hypothesis. *Hormonal Behavior, 50*, 667-680.

Maestripieri, D., Lindell, S. G., Ayala, A., Gold, P. W., & Higley, J. D. (2005). Neurobiological characteristics of rhesus macaque abusive mothers and their relation to social and maternal behavior. *Neuroscience & Biobehavioral Reviews, 29,* 51-57.

Martínez-González, D., Prospero-García, O., Mihailescu, S., & Drucker-Colın, R. (2002). Effects of nicotine on alcohol intake in a rat model of depression. *Pharmacology, Biochemistry & Behavior, 72,* 355-364.

Marx, M. H. (1956). Some relations between frustration and drive. In M. R. Jones (Ed.), *Nebraska symposium on motivation,* Lincoln, NE: University of Nebraska Press.

Matthews, S. G. (2002). Early programming of the hypothalamo–pituitary–adrenal axis. *Trends in Endocrinology & Metabolism, 13*, 373-380.

Matthews, K., & Robbins, T.W. (2003). Early experience as a determinant of adult behavioural responses to reward: the effects of repeated maternal separation in the rat. *Neuroscience & Biobehavioral Review, 27*, 45-55.

Matthews, K., Wilkinson, L., & Robbins, T. (1996). Repeated maternal separation of preweanling rats attenuates behavioral responses to primary and conditioned incentives in adulthood. *Physiology & Behavior, 59*, 99-107.

Meaney, M. J., & Aitken, D. H. (1985). The effects of early postnatal handling on hippocampal glucocorticoid receptor concentrations: temporal parameters. *Brain Research, 354*, 301-304.

Meaney, M. J., Szyf, M., & Seckl, J. R. (2007). Epigenetic mechanisms of perinatal programming of hypothalamic–pituitary–adrenal function and health. *Trends in Molecular Medicine, 13*, 269-277.

Meerlo, P., Horvath, K. M., Nag, G. M., Bohus, B., & Koolhaas, J. M. (1999). The influence of postnatal handling on adult neuroendocrine and behavioural stress reactivity. *Journal of Neuroendocrinology, 11*, 925-933.

Meinrath, A., & Flaherty, C. F. (1987). Preweanling handling influences open-field behavior, but not negative contrast or sucrose neophobia. *Animal Learning & Behavior, 15*, 83-92.

Morgan, K. N., & Tromborg, C. T. (2007). Sources of stress in captivity. *Applied Animal Behaviour Science, 102*, 262-302.

Mustaca, A. (2013). "Siento un dolor en el alma": ¿metáfora o realidad*? Revista Argentina de Ciencias del Comportamiento, 5*, 47-60.

Neumark-Sztainer, D., Wall, M., Gou, J., Story, M., Haines, J., & Eisenberg, M. (2006). Obesity, disordered eating, and eating disorders in a longitudinal study of adolescents: How do dieters fare 5 years later? *Journal of the American Dietetic Association*, *106*, 559-68.

Ortega, L. A., Daniel, A. M., Davis, J. B., Fuchs, P. N., & Papini, M. R. (2011). Peripheral pain enhances the effects of incentive downshifts. *Learning & Motivation, 42*, 203-209.

Papini, M. R., & Dudley, R. T. (1997). Consequences of surprising reward omissions. *Review of General Psychology, 1,* 175-197.

Papini, M. R., Wood, M., Daniel, A., & Norris, J. (2006). Reward loss as psychological pain. *International Journal of Psychology & Psychological Therapy, 6,* 189-213.

Parker, K. J., & Maestripieri, D. (2011). Identifying key features of early stressful experiences that produce stress vulnerability and resilience in primates. *Neuroscience & Biobehavioral Reviews, 35*, 1466-1483.

Pellegrini, S., Muzio, R., Mustaca, A., & Papini, M. (2004). Successive negative contrast after partial reinforcement in the consummatory behavior in rats. *Learning & Motivation*, *35*, 303-321.

Pellegrini, S., Wood, M., Daniel, A. M., & Papini, M. (2005). Opioid receptors modulate recovery from consummatory successive negative contrast. *Behavioural Brain Research, 164,* 239-249.

Plotsky, P. M., & Meaney, M. J. (1993). Early, postnatal experience alters hypothalamic corticotropin-releasing factor (CRF) mRNA, median eminence CRF content and stress-induced release in adult rats. *Brain Research & Molecular Brain Research*, *18*, 195-200.

Pryce, C. R., Ruedi-Bettschen, D., Dettling, A. C., Weston, A., Russig, H., Ferger, B., & Feldon, J. (2005). Long-term effects of early-life environmental manipulations in rodents and primates: potential animal models in depression research. *Neuroscience & Biobehavioral Reviews, 29*, 649-674.

Rödel, H. G., Meyer, S., Prager, G., Stefanski, V, & Hudson R. (2010). Litter size is negatively correlated with corticosterone levels in weanling and juvenile laboratory rats. *Physiology & Behaviour*, *99*, 644-650.

Rosenblum, L. A., Forger, C., Noland, S., Trost, R. C., & Coplan, J. D. (2001). Response of adolescent bonnet macaques to an acute fear stimulus as a function of early rearing conditions. *Developmental Psychobiolology, 39*, 40–45.

Rosenfeld P., Wetmore J. B., & Levine, S. (1992). Effects of repeated maternal separations on the adrenocortical response to stress of preweanling rats. *Physiology & Behavior, 52*,787-791.

Ruetti, E., Burgueño, A. L., Justel, N. R., Pirola, C. J., & Mustaca, A. E. (2013). Effect of neonatal clomipramine treatment on consummatory successive negative contrast. *Psicológica*, *34*, 25-36.

Ruetti, E., González J. A., Justel, N., Torrecilla, M., & Mustaca, A. E. (2010). Estrés neonatal y frustración. *Revista Latinoamericana de Psicología, 42,* 279-288.

Scully, J. A., Tosi, H., & Banning, K. (2000). Life event checklists: Revisiting the social readjustment rating scale after 30 years. *Educational & Psychological Measurement*, *60*, 864-876.

Seckl, J. R. (2008). Glucocorticoids, developmental 'programming' and the risk of affective dysfunction. *Programing Brain Research*, *167*, 17-34.

Shanab, M. E., & Ralph, L. (1979). Negative contrast and partial reinforcement effects as a function of crowded rearing condition in the rat. *The Journal of General Psychology*, *100*, 13-26.

Sisk, C. L., & Foster, D. L. (2004). The neural basis of puberty and adolescence. *Nature Neuroscience*, *7*, 1040-1047.

Spear, L. P. (2000). The adolescent brain and age-related behavioral manifestation. *Neuroscience & Biobehavioral Reviews*, *24*, 417-63.

Spencer, S., & Tilbrook, A. (2009). Neonatal overfeeding alters adult anxiety and stress responsiveness. *Psychoneuroendocrinology, 34*, 1133-1143.

Stacey, M., Dearden, R., Pill, R., & Robinson, D. (1970). Hospitals, children and their families: *The report of a pilot study*. London, UK: Routledge and Kegan Paul.

Stevens, H. E., Leckman, J. F., Coplan, J. D., & Suomi, S. J. (2009). Risk and resilience: early manipulation of macaque social experience and persistent behavioral and neurophysiological outcomes. *Journal of American Academy of Child & Adolescence Psychiatry, 48*, 114-127

Suomi, S. J. (1997). Early determinants of behaviour: Evidence from primate studies. *British Medical Bulletin, 53*, 170-184.

Toth, E., Avital, A., Leshem, M., Richter-Levin, G., & Braun, C. (2008). Neonatal and juvenile stress induces changes in adult social behavior without affecting cognitive function. *Behavioural Brain Research, 190*, 135-139.

Vanderschuren, L. J. M. J., Niesink, R. J. M., & Van Ree, J. M. (1996). The neurobiology of social play behavior in rats. *Neuroscience & Biobehavioral Reviews, 21*, 309-326.

Vogel, G., Neill, D., Kors, D., & Hagler, M. (1990). REM sleep abnormalities in a new animal model of endogenous depression. *Neuroscience Biobehavioral Reviews, 14*, 77-83.

Wahlstrom, D., Collins, P. White, T., & Luciana, M. (2010). Developmental changes in dopamine neurotransmission in adolescence: Behavioral implications and issues in assessment. *Brain & Cognition, 72,* 146-179.

Weiss, I. C., Domeney, A. M., Heidbreder, C. A., Moreau, J., & Feldon, J. (2001). Early social isolation, but not maternal separation, affects behavioral sensitization to amphetamine in male and female adult rats. *Pharmacology Biochemistry & Behavior, 70*, 397-409.

Williams, D. I., & Wells, P. A. (1970). Differences in home-cage-emergence in the rat in relation to infantile handling, *Psychonomic Science, 18*, 168-169.

3

Response-Outcome versus Outcome-Response Associations in Pavlovian-to-Instrumental Transfer: Effects of Instrumental Training Context

Kerry E. Gilroy, Ebony M. Everett, Andrew R. Delamater
Brooklyn College – CUNY, USA

One experiment with rats used Pavlovian-to-instrumental transfer (PIT) tests to explore potential competitive interactions between Pavlovian and instrumental processes during instrumental learning. Two instrumental response-outcome relations (e.g., left lever – grain pellets, right lever – sucrose pellets) were first trained in distinct contexts for one group of rats (Group Differential) or in each of two contexts for a second group (Group Non-Differential). Both of these groups then received training with two Pavlovian stimulus-outcome relations in a third experimental context. Selective PIT tests conducted in both the Pavlovian and instrumental contexts revealed greater selective PIT in Group Non-Differential than in Group Differential subjects. This result is discussed in terms of the roles played by context-outcome, response-outcome, and outcome-response associations during instrumental learning. The results further help us understand the nature of Pavlovian-instrumental interactions in specific PIT tasks.

The study of Pavlovian – instrumental interactions has once again become a popular and exciting area of research. Recent use of more refined behavioral tasks and neuroscience techniques has led to an explosion of interest in the neurobiological substrates of basic learning processes (e.g., Berridge, 2009; Delamater & Lattal, 2014; Fanselow, Zelikowsky, Perusini, Rodriguez Barrera, & Hersman, 2014; Honey, Iordanova, & Good, 2014; Laurent, Morse, & Balleine, 2014; McDannald, Jones, Takahashi, & Schoenbaum, 2014) and how such Pavlovian-instrumental interactions may play a role in a wide variety of circumstances (e.g., Corbit & Janak, 2007; Holland & Hsu, 2014; Holmes, Marchand, & Coutureau, 2010; Lewis, Niznikiewicz, Delamater, & Delgado, 2013; Martinovic et al., 2014; Ostlund, LeBlanc, Kosheleff, Wassum, & Maidment, 2014; Parnaudeau et al., 2014; Peciña & Berridge, 2013). It is worth briefly reviewing some of the key ideas that have arisen from the behavioral literature on the study of Pavlovian-instrumental interactions because these help identify what we take to be the central theoretical issues in this area of research.

Pavlov (1932), Konorski and Miller (1937), and Estes and Skinner (1941) were among the first to explore how these two basic learning processes might jointly contribute to affect performance. Later, Rescorla and Solomon (1967), Trapold and Overmier (1972), and Rescorla (1992) advanced the main conceptual approaches that theorists today frequently use in explaining various Pavlovian-instrumental interaction phenomena. Following Mowrer (1947; also Konorski & Miller, 1937), Rescorla and Solomon (1967) suggested that a stimulus used in Pavlovian conditioning acquires the capacity to activate a rather general central motivational state. They further assumed that activation of this central motivational state, in turn, influences instrumental responding by affecting the overall motivational substrate that supports that responding. For instance, in the case of appetitively-reinforced instrumental responding (e.g., lever pressing for food), it was assumed that activation by a stimulus of an appetitive central motivational state would

Correspondence regarding this article should be sent to Dr. Andrew Delamater. Psychology Department, Brooklyn College – CUNY. 2900 Bedford Ave, Brooklyn, NY 11210, USA. (Email: andrewd@brooklyn.cuny.edu)

enhance or energize such responding because this would further activate the appetitive motivational substrate that supports that response. In contrast, activation of an aversive motivational state by the stimulus would antagonize the appetitive state that normally supports the food-reinforced instrumental response, and the effect would be to decrease instrumental responding (see also Weiss, Thomas, & Weissman, 1996). The added value of this framework is that it makes further interesting and testable predictions for situations where the instrumental response is maintained through aversive motivational processes, such as avoidance conditioning (e.g., Overmier, Bull, & Pack, 1971; Rescorla & LoLordo, 1965).

While this approach continues to have a rather wide appeal (e.g., see Balleine & Killcross, 2006), it fails to account for more specific incentive motivational effects that a stimulus has on instrumental behavior. The most common method used today to study Pavlovian-instrumental interactions is the Pavlovian-to-instrumental transfer test (PIT). There are different variants of the PIT procedure, but a common method is to train an animal to perform two distinct instrumental responses with different outcomes, creating two response-outcome (R-O) relations (e.g., a left lever press is paired with pellets and a right lever press is paired with sucrose) in one phase of the experiment. Separately, two distinct Pavlovian stimuli are differentially paired with the two outcomes (e.g., a light is paired with pellets and a tone is paired with sucrose). And, finally, the effects of the Pavlovian stimuli on instrumental responding are assessed in a non-reinforced choice test. The usual result is that the stimulus selectively enhances, above baseline, the response with which it shares a reinforcing outcome. That is, in this example, the presentation of the light results in increased responding to the left lever and the presentation of the tone results in increased responding to the right lever (e.g., Delamater & Holland, 2008; Kruse, Overmier, & Rokke, 1983), an effect known as *outcome-specific PIT*.

Outcome-specific PIT poses a serious problem for the sort of motivational account of Rescorla and Solomon (1967), because both stimuli should activate the same central appetitive motivational state and, therefore, activate both responses, not just one. In order to explain the specific incentive motivational effect, Trapold and Overmier (1972) suggested that in addition to a stimulus activating a general central motivational state, the stimulus comes to associate with (see also Konorski, 1967) and, thus, activate, a representation of the specific sensory qualities of the reinforcer (e.g., the taste of sucrose). Further, these authors assumed that this sensory-specific *outcome expectancy* could, itself, act as a stimulus that could associate directly with the instrumental response. In the usual PIT paradigm, this outcome-response (O-R) association could be learned during the instrumental training phase of the experiment by virtue of the fact that the response is often reinforced in the presence of an expectancy of the outcome (provided, for instance, by contextual cues that have become associated with the outcome). As such, this expectancy can be seen as a discriminative stimulus for the instrumental response. If we allow for specific S-O and O-R associations to be formed in the Pavlovian and instrumental phases of the experiment, respectively, then one can see how a Pavlovian stimulus could exert a selective effect on instrumental responding during the PIT test. Namely, a given stimulus activates the specific O representation with which it was associated (S-O), and this, in turn, activates the specific R with which it was associated (O-R).

A related account – the *bidirectional hypothesis* – was put forth by Pavlov (1932) and discussed more extensively by Mackintosh and Dickinson (1979; also Colwill & Rescorla, 1985; Rescorla, 1992; Urcuioli & DeMarse, 1997). This account similarly assumes that specific S-O associations are formed during Pavlovian learning, but that R-O (rather than O-R) associations are formed during instrumental training. In order for the stimulus to selectively affect instrumental responding during a PIT test in this case, it is further assumed that the stimulus activates the outcome representation, which, in turn, activates its associated response through the forward R-O associative link that is used in the backward direction, i.e., the R-O link is, in some sense, bidirectional. In this way, the specific PIT effects that are usually found can be understood, once again, in the form of an S-O, O-R associative chain but the nature of the instrumental learning is different in the two cases.

This rather subtle difference has important implications for the control of instrumental actions. Rescorla (1992) contrasted different predictions made by these two accounts and provided evidence favoring the bidirectional R-O model. In one experiment, Rescorla (1992) taught the rat to make one instrumental response (R1) for one particular reinforcing outcome (O1) in the presence of a discriminative stimulus that otherwise signaled the non-contingent delivery of a different reinforcing outcome (O2). In this task, the animals could potentially learn an R1-O1 association (when R1 was reinforced with O1) or an O2-R1 association (because R1 was reinforced in the presence of an expectation for O2 activated by the discriminative stimulus). In a series of studies, Rescorla (1992) observed that the rats were more strongly controlled by the R-O than the O-R relations.

Another type of experiment – the so-called "stimulus-response overshadowing" experiment popular for a time in the 1970s – provides some evidence to favor the view that R-O (and not O-R) associations are learned during instrumental training. In one study, Pearce and Hall (1978; see also Williams, 1999) demonstrated with rats that learning to lever press on an intermittent reinforcement schedule was impaired when a brief visual stimulus consistently occurred just prior to the delivery of every food reinforcement. The result was understood by assuming that a Pavlovian light-pellet association was established and competed with (overshadowed) the formation of an instrumental lever press-pellet association. This interpretation quite naturally follows from the assumption that expected outcomes are less well processed and, therefore, cannot easily support new learning compared to unexpected outcomes (Kamin, 1969). If instrumental learning consists of the animals developing an O-R association, it is not so straightforward to see why presenting a light stimulus after the response but just before the outcome should have diminished O-R learning. However, one possible way to explain this is to assume that O-R learning is best accomplished when the instrumental response is trained in the presence of a strongly conditioned context (e.g., Steinhauer, Davol, & Lee, 1976). If the visual cue in this study overshadowed the context-pellet association, then this could have potentially weakened the development of an O-R association because the outcome expectancy would not have been present prior to the actual response having been made. Therefore, the outcome expectancy should not have been easily learned as a discriminative cue for the instrumental response (Trapold & Overmier, 1972).

The present study explored this issue in a somewhat different way. Half of the rats in the present experiment were first taught an R1-O1 relation in Context 1 and an R2-O2 relation in a physically distinct Context 2 (Group Differential), while the remaining rats learned both of these instrumental relations in both contexts (Group Non-Differential). If the context in which lever pressing takes place associates with the reinforcing outcomes, then according to the O-R view of instrumental learning Group Differential subjects will learn to press each of the two levers in the presence of distinct outcome expectancies. This might be expected to enhance instrumental learning and outcome-specific control over responding because of the *differential outcome effect* (e.g., Trapold, 1970; Trapold & Overmier, 1972). In contrast, according to this view Group Non-Differential subjects should learn to associate each of the two contexts with both reinforcing outcomes. But since both responses are trained in those contexts the two outcome expectancies should each associate with both instrumental responses, and this would be expected to diminish outcome-specific control over these responses.

We tested these predictions by giving differential S1-O1 and S2-O2 Pavlovian training in a third context, and then, ultimately, giving PIT tests in either the Pavlovian or instrumental training contexts. If O-R associations were learned during instrumental training and controlled performance during the PIT tests, then greater selective PIT should be seen in Group Differential than in Group Non-Differential for the reasons noted above (and related to this theory's account of the basic differential outcome effect; Trapold & Overmier, 1972).

On the other hand, the opposite prediction is made if instrumental learning results in the formation of R-O associations. Group Differential subjects would learn to make each instrumental response in the presence of a context that already predicts the reinforcing outcome. Because of the *stimulus-response* overshadowing (Pearce & Hall, 1978; Williams, 1999) and blocking (Kamin, 1969) effects, the distinct context-outcome associations in Group Differential should reduce the effectiveness of those reinforcers in supporting instrumental R-O associations (see also Rescorla & Wagner, 1972). Group Non-Differential subjects should not suffer from this competition, however, because the different instrumental responses are the most valid predictors of the different reinforcing outcomes in this situation. In this case, since both responses are trained in both contexts, the contexts become less valid than the responses, themselves, at predicting which outcome will occur at any given moment. Thus, the problem reduces to a relative cue validity one (Wagner, Logan, Haberlandt, & Price, 1968), and, as a result, the R-O associations should be more strongly conditioned in Group Non-Differential than in Group Differential. Therefore, during the PIT tests the strongest selective PIT effects should be seen in Group Non-Differential. The present study examined these contrasting hypotheses in an effort to determine which associative mechanism, R-O or O-R, underlies instrumental learning and, ultimately, mediates the selective PIT effect.

Method

Subjects

Subjects were 32 naïve male Long-Evans rats, weighing approximately 325 g at the start of the experiment. The experiment was run in two replications (n = 16 rats in each replication). The rats were housed in cages containing between two and four animals and were food restricted such that their weights were maintained at 85% of their free-feeding weight throughout the experiment. They were given free access to water at all times. The colony room in which they were housed was kept on a 14/10 hours light/dark cycle where the lights came on at 7 AM and turned off at 9 PM each day.

Apparatus

The apparatus consisted of two sets of eight identical conditioning chambers, which were encased in light and sound resistant wooden shells. The conditioning chambers were 30.5 cm long x 24.0 cm wide x 25.0 cm deep. The end walls were made from aluminum and the ceiling and the sidewalls were made from clear Plexiglas. The food magazine measured 3.0 cm long x 3.6 cm wide x 2.0 cm deep and was located at the center of one of the end walls. The outcomes (0.1 ml droplet of 20% sucrose or approximately two 45 mg food pellets (Research Diet)) were delivered into a well on the bottom of the food magazine. The floor was made from stainless steel rods (0.6 cm in diameter, 2.0 cm apart). An infrared detector and emitter were mounted on the magazine walls (and positioned at the entrance) to record magazine entries by the rat. Two response levers were presented that were 4 cm wide and were located 3 cm either side of the food magazine and 8 cm above the floor level. While both levers were permanently mounted in the chamber, access to either one could be restricted by placement of an aluminum cover over it. The cover was the same height as the chamber and was 8.1 cm wide and 3.18 cm deep. A tone CS (1500 Hz) was produced by a speaker located approximately 22 cm behind the front wall of the conditioning chamber. This tone measured 4 dB above background noise levels. A steady light CS (6-W light bulb) was mounted on the top of the sidewall of the outer chamber. Background noise and ventilation were created by a fan, which was attached to the outer shell. Background noise was measured at 78 dB. The equipment was controlled and data were recorded by a personal computer and interfacing equipment (Alpha Products) located in the same room as the experimental chambers.

To create three distinct contexts different sets of inserts were used. The two instrumental training contexts were created using either aluminum or Plexiglas inserts. In the aluminum context a flat sheet of aluminum (28.74 cm x 23.81 cm) was inserted to cover the grid floor, and a second sheet (35.56 cm x 23.5 cm) was arranged such that it sat diagonally across the chamber between the top of the wall bearing the levers and the magazine, and the floor on the opposite side of the chamber. The second instrumental context was made up of a 27.94 cm x 29.53 cm sheet of Plexiglas with 506 evenly spaced .64 cm diameter holes drilled into it. A second sheet of Plexiglas sat diagonally across the chamber so that it reached from the vertical edge of the wall bearing the levers and the magazine to the furthest corner on the opposite side of the chamber. The context used during the Pavlovian stage consisted only of the chamber itself with the levers covered by the aluminum covers. Thus, the three contexts differed in terms of their floor texture and their overall shape.

Behavioral Procedures

Magazine training. For two days hungry subjects were placed in individual conditioning chambers and were trained to approach the food magazine to receive the outcomes. All of the animals received two training sessions on each day – Context 1 was used for one of these sessions and Context 2 for the other. For Group Non-Differential, on day one, Outcome 1 was presented in Context 1 and Outcome 2 in Context 2. On the second day Outcome 1 was presented in Context 2 and Outcome 2 in Context 1. In this way both outcomes were presented in each context. The magazine training for Group Differential was very similar, except that Outcome 1 was always presented in Context 1 and Outcome 2 was always presented in Context 2. The identity of the outcomes as O1 or O2 (pellets, sucrose) was also counterbalanced across animals, as was the identity of the contexts as Context 1 or 2. The outcome was delivered 20 times during each 20 min session, and was presented on a variable time 60-s schedule. The order of presentation of the outcomes was also counterbalanced across the two days; if Outcome 1 was presented first on the first day of magazine training, then Outcome 2 was presented first on the second day. Access to the levers during these sessions was prevented by using the aluminum lever covers, and the two Pavlovian stimuli were not presented during the magazine training phase.

Instrumental training. Following completion of magazine training, the rats were given two sessions of instrumental continuous reinforcement (CRF) training. In each of these sessions, only one lever was accessible to the rat. In the first session of the day rats were presented with lever 1, so that only response 1 (R1) could be performed. Initially rats were trained on a CRF schedule, so that every time they performed R1, O1 was delivered to the magazine. During the second session of the day, lever 2 was made accessible, and lever 1 was covered. Again, animals were initially trained on a CRF schedule so that every time the rat performed R2, O2 was delivered. For the animals in Group Non-Differential, both levers were paired with their respective outcomes in both contexts, so on day 1 R1-O1 was given in Context 1 and on day 2 it was given in Context 2. The same was true of the R2-O2 pairing. For animals in Group Differential, each R-O relation was trained in only one context. That is, on both days R1-O1 was given only in Context 1 and R2-O2 only in Context 2. Animals were given instrumental training in both contexts on each day. Each subject was trained on the CRF schedule until they made 50 responses on each lever. After reaching this criterion, all subjects were trained on steadily increasing variable ratio schedules. They received VR 5 for two days and VR 10 for four days. On each of these days, subjects were given two 20-min training sessions. During one of these sessions R1 was reinforced with O1 and R2 was reinforced with O2. For animals in Group Differential, the R1 was only ever available in Context 1, and R2 in Context 2. For the animals in Group Non-Differential, as with CRF training, both pairings were given in both contexts. That is, R1 was reinforced with O1 in Context 1 and in Context 2 on an equal number of occasions. This was also true of R2 and O2. The order of training sessions was counterbalanced in a pseudorandom order so that on some days the animals were trained with R1 first and on the remaining days they were trained on R2 first. The number of responses was recorded during each session.

Pavlovian conditioning. For eight days following the completion of instrumental training, the two Pavlovian stimuli (S1 and S2) were individually paired with the two outcomes (O1 and O2). For half of the animals S1 was paired with sucrose and S2 with pellets, for the other half S1 was paired with pellets and S2 with sucrose. Each conditioning session was 79 min long, during which there occurred six S1-O1 and six S2-O2 trials. The order of the stimulus presentations was presented in a pseudorandom order with the provision that neither stimulus was presented more than three times in a row. Each stimulus lasted 90 s and the appropriate outcome was delivered within each stimulus according to a variable time 30 s schedule. The inter-trial intervals (ITIs) averaged 5 min and ranged from 2 – 8 min, and the animals were removed from the chambers 1 min following the final conditioning trial. The number of magazine approach responses was recorded 90 s before the stimulus (referred to as the pre-CS), and for the 90 s duration of the stimulus. Pavlovian conditioning took place in Context 3.

Pavlovian-instrumental transfer test. Following Pavlovian conditioning, the animals were given two further instrumental training sessions the day before the first test session, one for each response. These sessions were conducted with VR 10 reinforcement schedules. The rats received four test sessions in the Pavlovian contexts on consecutive days. Two of these tests were single response tests and two were choice tests where both of the levers were available. Half of the rats received two single response tests (one with each lever) followed by two choice tests, and the remaining rats were tested with two choice tests followed by two single response tests. Each test session lasted 30 min, with four 90 s presentations of each Pavlovian stimulus alternating with four 90 s pre stimulus periods. The tests began with a 6-min period in which no stimuli were presented to familiarize the animals with the choice procedure as well as to lower the overall levels of responding before the transfer trials began. The two stimuli were then presented in an ABBA BAAB sequence (counterbalanced across days). The number of responses on each of the levers was recorded during the 90 s immediately before stimulus onset (pre-CS) and during the 90 s presentation of the stimulus. No outcomes were delivered during these test sessions.

In order to determine if the pattern of PIT results would differ when testing occurred in the instrumental, as opposed to the Pavlovian training contexts, rats in replication 2 received an additional set of tests that were conducted following the tests described above. These rats were first given an additional six instrumental retraining sessions followed by two additional Pavlovian retraining sessions, and all of these were conducted exactly as in these original conditioning phases. Subsequently there were two choice tests like those described above, but one of these was conducted in instrumental context 1 and the other in instrumental context 2.

Statistical Analyses

The lever press data were analyzed using standard analysis of variance (ANOVA) techniques. A Type I error rate of 0.05 was adopted for all statistical tests. Magazine responding during the Pavlovian conditioning phases was not statistically evaluated because such responding could reflect a mixture of both conditioned and unconditioned effects when the outcomes were presented at random times within the 90 s stimulus.

Results

Lever press responding steadily increased over the course of instrumental conditioning in both groups (from a mean of 10.7 rpm on day 1 to 19.0 rpm on day 6 for Group Differential, and from 12.3 to 21.2 rpm for Group Non-Differential). An ANOVA applied to these data revealed a significant main effect of Session, $F(5,140) = 61.45$, but the small apparent difference between the groups was not significant.

The PIT results from the choice test sessions conducted in the Pavlovian training context can be seen in Figure 1. The data were converted to elevation scores. The elevation score was calculated by dividing the mean response rate during the stimulus presentation (A) by the sum of the response rate during the stimulus and the 90 s pre-CS (B) period (A/(A+B)). To ensure that there were no significant differences between the two replications, Replication was included as a factor in an ANOVA comparing the effects of Group (Differential or Non-Differential) and Response (the lever associated with the same outcome as the stimulus being presented or the lever associated with a different outcome). The ANOVA revealed no meaningful effects involving the Replication factor (a significant Replication x Group interaction, $F(1,28) = 8.00$, merely reflected the fact that overall levels of responding in the two groups differed in the two replications). In addition, there was a significant main effect of Response, $F(1,28) = 6.38$, as well as a significant Group x Response interaction, $F(1,28) = 6.74$, where Group Non-Differential subjects responded more to the lever that was associated with the same than different outcome as the stimulus being presented. The mean response rates per minute during the baseline pre-CS intervals (collapsed across bins) was 2.1 ($MSE = 0.35$) and 2.3 ($MSE = 0.54$) on the *same* lever for Group Differential and Non-Differential, respectively, and on the 'different lever' it was 2.5 ($MSE = 0.57$) and 2.4 ($MSE = 0.47$). These small baseline differences were not reliably different.

In the single response test sessions (data not shown) none of the main effects or interactions were significant.

The results from the PIT tests conducted in the instrumental training contexts (for replication 2 rats) are presented in Figure 2. We examined the hypothesis that Group Differential subjects may have been impaired at selective PIT when testing took place in the Pavlovian training context because they had difficulty retrieving the R-O associations at the time of test. If so, then these subjects should perform more normally when testing takes place in the instrumental training contexts, especially if the same R-O relation was retrieved at the time of test. The data were, therefore, initially segregated in Group Differential subjects in terms of whether the same R-O relation as that signaled by the test stimulus was tested in the context in which that particular R-O relation was trained (and, therefore, *retrieved*) or whether the same R-O relation was tested in the context in which it was not trained (and, thus, *not retrieved*). For instance, Group Differential rats received R1-O1 training in Context 1 and R2-O2 training in Context 2. When testing S1 in Context 1 the same R1-O1 relation would be retrieved, but when testing S1 in Context 2 the same R1-O1 relation would not be retrieved. If memory retrieval processes play a role then larger selective PIT effects would be expected when the same R-O relations were tested in their retrieved contexts.

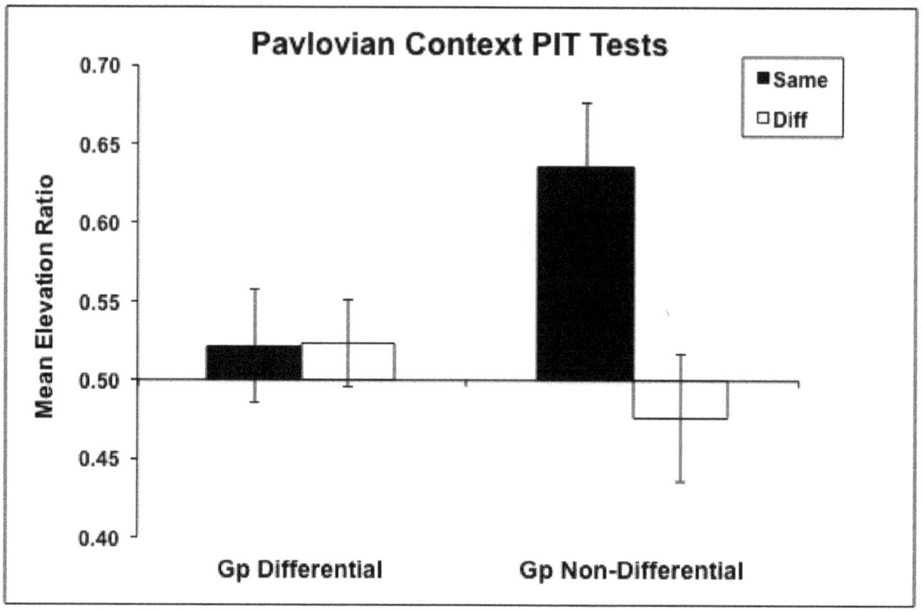

Figure 1. *Mean elevation scores during the choice tests conducted in the Pavlovian training context for responses to the same and different (Diff) lever by animals in Group Differential and Group Non-Differential.* Error bars show +/- 1 *SEM.*

The data in Figure 2 show that this was not the case. An ANOVA was performed on Group Differential subjects that compared the factors of Response (same or different) and Retrieval Context. This analysis revealed no significant main effects or interaction.

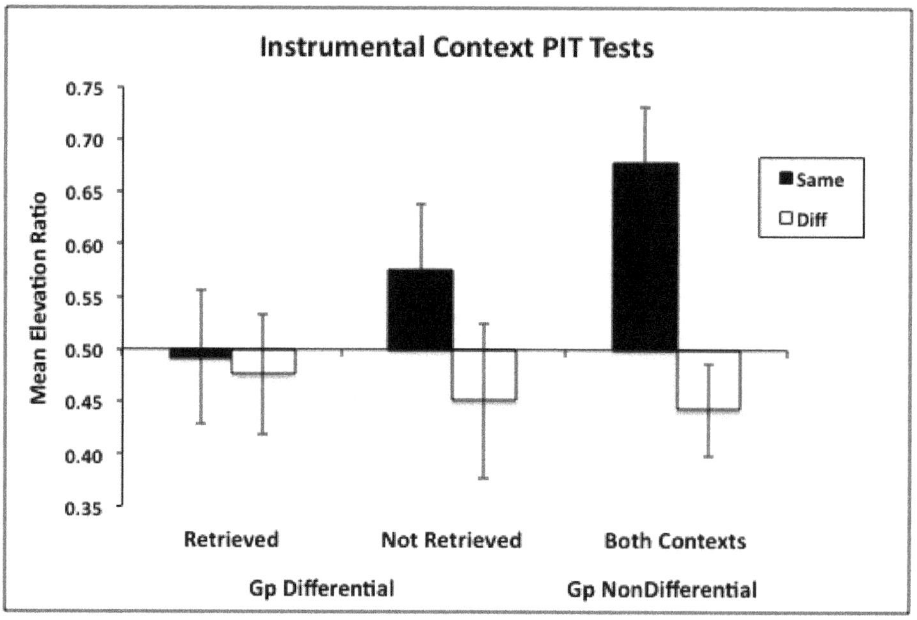

Figure 2. *Mean elevation scores during choice tests conducted in the instrumental training contexts.* Data are shown separately when "same" responses were tested in their retrieved and not retrieved contexts for animals in Group Differential, and in both contexts combined for Group Non-Differential. Error bars show +/- 1 *SEM.*

Figure 2 also shows data from these test sessions for Group Non-Differential. Since there was no effect of retrieval context in Group Differential, a second Response (same, different) x Group (Differential, Non-differential) ANOVA was conducted on the data collapsed across both instrumental contexts. Consistent with the Pavlovian context PIT data reported above, this ANOVA revealed no significant main effect of Group, a significant main effect of Response, $F(1,14) = 29.13$, and, most importantly, a significant Response x Group interaction, $F(1,14) = 8.33$. Once again, Group Non-Differential showed a greater outcome-specific PIT effect than Group Differential. The mean response rates per minute during the baseline pre-CS intervals were 4.0 ($MSE = 0.81$) and 3.1 ($MSE = 0.91$) on the *same* lever for Group Differential and Non-Differential, respectively. On the 'different' lever it was 4.3 ($MSE = 1.28$) and 3.1 ($MSE = 0.8$). None of these apparent differences were reliable.

Discussion

The main result from the present experiment is that outcome-selective PIT effects are reduced (or even eliminated) when instrumental training of two distinct R-O relations is given in two separate contexts, compared to when they are given in both of these contexts. The failure to see a strong selective PIT effect in Group Differential rats when the responses were tested in the Pavlovian context, in principle, could have been caused by an inability of these rats to retrieve their instrumental associations, rather than an inability to learn specific instrumental associations. However, further tests conducted in the instrumental training contexts were not consistent with this possibility. We reasoned that if reduced selective PIT was due to a memory retrieval deficit, then the difference between the groups should have disappeared when the same instrumental R-O relation was tested in its retrieved context. But this result was not obtained. Our findings have important implications for our understanding of Pavlovian-instrumental interactions and, more generally, of the nature of instrumental learning, and we will discuss these below.

As noted in the introduction, PIT effects have most often been understood in terms of general or specific influences of Pavlovian cues on instrumental responding. Konorski's (1967) framework has proven useful in understanding how Pavlovian stimuli might exert these general and specific effects (see also Balleine & Killcross, 2006; Wagner & Brandon, 1989). Briefly, Konorski assumed that Pavlovian stimuli enter into separate associations with the general emotional and specific sensory qualities of a reinforcing outcome. The former type of association would enable a stimulus to exert quite general effects on behavior of the sort discussed by Rescorla and Solomon (1967) because this association would result in the stimulus evoking a general motivational/emotional state capable of modulating a wide variety of activities. In contrast, when a stimulus associatively activates a sensory-specific representation of its associated outcome, such a cue would be assumed to impact instrumental responding only in a very specific manner that would require an instrumental learning structure that also directly encodes that specific outcome.

Although Konoski's framework for understanding Pavlovian learning can be usefully applied to understanding how Pavlovian stimuli might be capable of modulating instrumental behaviors in rather general or specific ways, by itself, it offers little guidance on selecting among rival mechanisms that describe the nature of the Pavlovian-instrumental interaction on performance in a PIT task. To describe selective PIT effects, for instance, we have distinguished between two different accounts. Trapold and Overmier (1972) suggested that S-O and O-R associations form during Pavlovian and instrumental training phases, respectively, whereas Pavlov (1932; also Mackintosh & Dickinson, 1979; Rescorla, 1992) suggested that S-O and R-O associations form during these phases of training and that the R-O association is used in the backward direction to enable selective PIT. Both of these models expect specific PIT to occur only to the extent that the O component in these two associations is specific in its sensory content and shared between the two. On the basis of a wide variety of studies there is little reason to question that Pavlovian conditioning can result in the development of highly specific S-O associations (e.g., Delamater, 2012). As to whether instrumental learning results in O-R or R-O associations there is less evidence available. In a series of studies Rescorla (1992) directly contrasted predictions deduced from these two views and concluded that the R-O association primarily controlled the instrumental response (see also Urcuioli & DeMarse, 1997).

Our data can also be taken to support the view that instrumental learning results in the development of highly specific R-O associations, and, by inference, that these associations are used in the backward direction during a specific PIT test. This conclusion follows from our finding that training two instrumental R-O relations in distinct contexts disrupts the ability of those responses to be modulated by Pavlovian stimuli. As noted in the introduction the O-R model predicts that training in this manner would more optimally result in learning of highly specific O-R associations than when both responses are trained in each of two contexts. As such, it fails to anticipate the results we obtained. However, the R-O model correctly anticipates our findings. According to this view, the learning of separate R-O associations should be weakened when these R-O relations are trained in distinct contexts because the contexts, themselves, signal the reinforcing outcomes and render the instrumental responses as redundant predictors of the outcomes. This would result in the context-outcome associations overshadowing the specific R-O association (see also Pearce & Hall, 1978; Williams, 1999). This overshadowing effect should not have occurred in our Group Non-Differential rats because for these rats the instrumental responses were relatively more valid predictors of the specific outcomes than were the contexts. This would mean that the R-O associations should remain strong in these rats (Wagner et al., 1968).

Our claim that context-outcome learning overshadowed R-O learning in Group Differential rats may lead one to expect that instrumental responding during the initial instrumental training phase should be lower in Group Differential than Group Non-Differential rats – a result that we did not statistically observe. However, it should be noted that our specific PIT tests allow us to target very particular aspects of learning, such as outcome-specific associations, in a way that simple instrumental responding cannot assess. It is possible, therefore, that while context-outcome associations successfully overshadowed learning of specific R-O associations, those associations may not have been able to compete with other aspects of instrumental learning, such as, acquisition of S-R associations.

If the instrumental learning we observed in Group Differential was, indeed, best described in these terms, then it follows that these responses should also be less sensitive to outcome devaluation manipulations (e.g., Colwill & Rescorla, 1985). Further work will be required to determine if this is the case, but there is a considerable amount of evidence to support the conclusion that distinct neural circuits underlie the formation of goal-oriented behaviors (reflective of R-O associations), on the one hand, and habitual behaviors (reflective of control by S-R associations), on the other hand (e.g., Coutureau & Killcross, 2003; Killcross & Coutureau, 2003). Thus, it seems highly plausible that although one aspect of instrumental learning may be undermined another aspect of learning may be fully intact with the end result being no difference in overall levels of responding.

A rather different approach to understanding PIT effects was advocated by Cohen-Hatton et al. (2013) who questioned the basic assumption that selective PIT effects occur through the operation of an S-O association learned during Pavlovian training. Instead, these investigators suggested that a mediated S-R association is learned during the Pavlovian training phase. This account assumes that during instrumental training a bidirectional R-O association is established, and, further, that when an outcome is paired with a stimulus during the Pavlovian training phase this ensures that an outcome-evoked memory of its associated response occurs in close temporal contiguity with the physically present stimulus. This contiguity results in new S-R learning and is responsible for the specific PIT effect. This view makes the somewhat radical assertion that S-O associations are either not acquired during Pavlovian learning or they play no special role in explaining selective PIT.

Our results present problems for this model. In particular, it is not clear why mediated S-R associations should have been weaker in our Group Differential rats compared to our Group Non-Differential rats. If presenting an O during the Pavlovian training phase evokes a memory of its associated R when the S is present, then it is difficult to see why this should not have occurred equally in our two groups of rats. At the very least, additional assumptions would need to be made for this account to accommodate our findings.

One further point is worth considering. While we have emphasized associative mechanisms at the intersection of Pavlovian and instrumental learning that would permit for an interaction at the levels of learning and performance, it is important to realize that there very well may be important differences, as well, in the underlying associative circuitries of Pavlovian and instrumental learning that may prevent interactions from taking place in some circumstances. For instance, in one study Corbit and Balleine (2003) trained animals to learn two instrumental responses in a heterogeneous chain to earn one outcome. Separately, the animals were trained to make two distinct Pavlovian S-O associations. In PIT tests where the rats could choose freely between both responses in the presence and absence of both Pavlovian stimuli, selective PIT was only observed with the response component of the chain that was most proximal to outcome delivery during instrumental training. In other words, the stimuli had no effect (general or specific) on the first response element of the chain. Separately, these authors found that the first response element of the chain, but not the second, was sensitive to an instrumental incentive learning manipulation. Thus, it appears that there may be important differences in the manner in which the outcome is encoded in both Pavlovian and instrumental conditioning that may limit performance interactions. The incentive learning effect requires that the distal response had, indeed, associated with a specific O, but that outcome encoding was apparently quite different from the manner in which the outcome was encoded during Pavlovian training since the Pavlovian stimulus failed to control this response.

In contrast, the proximal response element apparently did associate with an encoding of the outcome that was more similar to the Pavlovian outcome encoding since this response was influenced by the Pavlovian stimulus in an outcome-specific manner. Selective PIT, then, would only be expected to occur to the extent that the outcome encodings in both Pavlovian and instrumental associative structures were similar. Under conditions where instrumental incentive learning is expected to occur, selective PIT should not also occur and the only manner in which Pavlovian stimuli might come to modulate such responding would be through the more general processes emphasized by Rescorla and Solomon (1967). The generality of this conclusion will need to be established, but it is illuminating that distinct neural mechanisms are beginning to be uncovered in the study of Pavlovian and instrumental processes (e.g., Corbit, Muir, & Balleine, 2001; Laurent et al., 2014).

In summary, we have presented data from an experiment designed to contrast predictions made by O-R and R-O associative models of instrumental learning. We used a selective PIT task to assess which of these models more accurately describes performance after instrumental training of separate R-O relations was conducted in two separate contexts or in each of two contexts. We observed weaker selective PIT effects when animals learned each of two different R-O relations in separate contexts. Apparently, such training enables distinct context-outcome associations to overshadow the learning of specific R-O associations over the course of instrumental learning. A further inference from these findings is that selective PIT is largely controlled by an R-O association working in the backward direction, rather than by an O-R association. Overall, the data from this study shows how specific PIT paradigms can be used to answer interesting questions about the nature of Pavlovian-instrumental interactions, while also providing further information regarding the nature of instrumental learning itself.

References

Balleine, B. W., & Killcross, S. (2006). Parallel incentive processing: an integrated view of amygdala function. *Trends in Neuroscience*, *29*,272-279.

Barnet, R. C., & Miller, R. R. (1996). Second-order excitation mediated by a backward conditioned inhibitor. *Journal of Experimental Psychology: Animal Behavior Processes*, *22*, 279-296.

Berridge, K. C. (2009). 'Liking' and 'wanting' food rewards: Brain substrates and roles in eating disorders. *Physiology & Behavior*, *97*, 537-550.

Cohen-Hatton, S. R., Haddon, J. E., George, D. N., & Honey, R. C. (2013). Pavlovian-to-instrumental transfer: paradoxical effects of the Pavlovian relationship explained. *Journal of Experimental Psychology: Animal Behavior Processes, 39*, 14-23.

Colwill, R. M., & Rescorla, R. A. (1985). Postconditioning devaluation of a reinforce affects instrumental responding. *Journal of Experimental Psychology: Animal Behavior Processes*, *11*, 120-132.

Corbit, L. H., & Janak, P. H. (2007). Ethanol-associated cues produce general Pavlovian-instrumental transfer. *Alcoholism: Clinical and Experimental Research, 31*,766-774.

Corbit, L. H., & Balleine, B.W. (2003). Instrumental and Pavlovian incentive processes have dissociable effects on components of a heterogeneous instrumental chain. *Journal of Experimental Psychology: Animal Behavior Processes*, *29*, 99-106.

Corbit, L. H., & Balleine, B. W. (2011). The general and outcome-specific forms of Pavlovian-instrumental transfer are differentially mediated by the nucleus accumbens core and shell. *Journal of Neuroscience, 17*,11786-94.

Corbit, L. H., Muir, J. L., & Balleine, B. W. (2001). The role of the nucleus accumbens instrumental conditioning: Evidence of a functional dissociation between accumbens core and shell. *Journal of Neuroscience, 21,* 3251–3260.

Coutureau, E., & Killcross, S. (2003). Inactivation of the infralimbic prefrontal cortex reinstates goal-directed responding in overtrained rats. *Behavioural Brain Research, 146*, 167-174.

Delamater, A. R. (2012). On the nature of CS and US representations in Pavlovian learning. *Learning & Behavior*, *40*, 1-23.

Delamater, A. R., & Holland, P. C. (2008). The influence of CS–US interval on several different indices of learning in appetitive conditioning. *Journal of Experimental Psychology: Animal Behavior Processes*, *34*, 202–222.

Delamater, A. R., Lattal, K. M. (2014). The study of associative learning: Mapping from psychological to neural levels of analysis. *Neurobiology of Learning and Memory*, *108*, 1-4.

Estes, W. K., & Skinner, B. F. (1941). Some quantitative properties of anxiety. *Journal of Experimental Psychology*, *29*, 390-400.

Fanselow, M. S., Zelikowsky, M., Perusini, J., Rodriguez Barrera, V., & Hersman, S. (2014). Isomorphisms between psychological processes and neural mechanisms: From stimulus elements to genetic markers of activity. *Neurobiology of Learning and Memory*, *108*, 5-13.

Holland, P. C., & Hsu, M. (2014). Role of amygdala central nucleus in the potentiation of consuming and instrumental lever-pressing for sucrose by cues for the presentation or interruption of sucrose delivery in rats. *Behavioral Neuroscience*, *128*, 71-82.

Holmes, N. M., Marchand, A. R., & Couturear, E. (2010). Pavlovian to instrumental transfer: a neurobehavioural perspective. *Neuroscience and Biobehavioral Reviews*, *34,*1277-1295.

Honey, R. C., Iordanova, M. D., & Good, M. (2014). Associative structures in animal learning: Dissociating elemental and configural processes. *Neurobiology of Learning and Memory*, *108*, 96-103.

Kamin, L. (1969). Selective association and conditioning. In N. J. Mackintosh & W. K. Honig (Eds.), *Fundamental issues in associative learning* (pp. 42-89). Halifax, UK: Dalhousie University Press.

Killcross, A.S., & Coutureau, E. (2003). Coordination of actions and habits in the medial prefrontal cortex of rats. *Cerebral Cortex*, *13*, 400–408.

Konorski, J. (1967). *Integrative activity of the brain.* Chicago, IL: University of Chicago Press..

Konorski, J., & Miller, S. (1937). On two types of conditioned reflex. *Journal of Genetic Psychology*, *16*, 264-272.

Kruse, J. M., Overmier, J. B., Konz, W. A., & Rokke, E. (1983). Pavlovian conditioned stimulus effects upon instrumental choice behavior are reinforcer specific. *Learning & Motivation*, *14*, 165-181.

Laurent, V., Morse, A. K., & Balleine, B. W. (2014). The role of opioid processes in reward and decision-making. *British Journal Pharmacology*, doi: 10.1111/bph.12818. [Epub ahead of print]

Lewis, A. H., Niznikiewicz, M. A., Delamater, A. R., & Delgado, M. R. (2013). Avoidance-based human Pavlovian-to-instrumental transfer. *European Journal of Neuroscience, 38,*3740-3748.

Mackintosh, N. J., & Dickinson, A. (1979). Instrumental (Type II) conditioning. In A. Dickinson & R. A. Boakes (Eds.), *Mechanisms of learning and motivation: A memorial volume to Jerzy Konorski* (pp.143-170). Hillsdale, NJ: Lawrence Erlbaum Associates.

Martinovic, J., Jones, A., Christiansen, P., Rose, A. K., Hogarth, L., & Field, M. (2014). Electrophysiological responses to alcohol cues are not associated with Pavlovian-to-Instrumental transfer in social drinkers. *PLoS One*, *9,* e94605. doi:10.1371/journal.pone.0094605 PMCID: PMC3986108

McDannald, M. A., Jones, J. L., Takahashi, Y. K., & Schoenbaum, G. (2014). Learning theory: A driving force in understanding orbitofrontal function. *Neurobiology of Learning and Memory*, *108*, 22-27.

Mowrer, O. H. (1947). On the dual nature of learning- a re-interpretation of "conditioning" and "problem-solving." *Harvard Educational Review*, *17*, 102-148.

Ostlund, S. B., LeBlanc, K. H., Kosheleff, A. R., Wassum, K. M., & Maidment, N. T. (2014). Phasic mesolimbic dopamine signaling encodes the facilitation of incentive motivation produced by repeated cocaine exposure. *Neuropsychopharmacology, 39*, 2441-2449.

Overmier, J. B., Bull, J. A., & Pack, K. (1971). On instrumental response interaction as explaining the influences of Pavlovian CS+s upon avoidance behavior. *Learning and Motivation*, *2*, 103-112.

Parnaudeau, S., Taylor, K., Bolkan, S. S., Ward, R. D., Balsam, P. D., & Kellendonk, C. (2014). Mediodorsal thalamus hypofunction impairs flexible goal-directed behavior. *Biological Psychiatry*, pii: S0006-3223(14)00221-222.

Pavlov, I. P. (1932). The reply of a physiologist to psychologists. *Psychological Review*, *39*, 91-127.

Pearce, J. M., & Hall, G. (1978). Overshadowing the instrumental conditioning of a lever-press response by a more valid predictor of the reinforcer. *Journal of Experimental Psychology: Animal Behavior Processes*, *4*, 356-367.

Peciña, S., & Berridge, K. C. (2013). Dopamine or opioid stimulation of nucleus accumbens similarly amplify cue-triggered 'wanting' for reward: entire core and medial shell mapped as substrates for PIT enhancement. *European Journal of Neuroscience*, *37,* 1529-1540.

Rescorla, R. A. (1992). Response-outcome versus outcome-response associations in instrumental learning. *Animal Learning & Behavior*, *20*, 223-232.

Rescorla, R. A., & LoLordo, V. M. (1965). Inhibition of avoidance behavior. *Journal of Comparative and Physiological Psychology*, *59*, 406-412.

Rescorla, R. A., & Solomon, R. L. (1967). Two-process learning theory: Relationships between Pavlovian conditioning and instrumental learning. *Psychological Review*, *74*, 151-182.

Steinhauer, G. D., Davol, G. H., & Lee, A. (1976). Acquisition of the autoshaped key peck as a function of amount of preliminary magazine training. *Journal of the Experimental Analysis of Behavior*, *25*, 355-359.

Trapold, M. A. (1970). Are expectancies based upon different positive reinforcing events discriminably different? *Learning and Motivation*, *1*, 129-140.

Trapold, M. A., & Overmier, J. B. (1972). The second learning process in instrumental learning. In A. H. Black & W. F. Prokasy (Eds.), *Classical conditioning. II. Current research and theory*. New York, NY: Appleton-Century-Crofts.

Urcuioli, P. J., & DeMarse, T.B. (1997). Further tests of response-outcome associations in differential-outcome matching-to-sample. *Journal of Experimental Psychology: Animal Behavior Processes*, *23*, 171-182.

Wagner, A. R., & Brandon, S. E. (1989). Evolution of a structured connectionist model of Pavlovian conditioning (AESOP). In S. B. Klein & R. R. Mower (Eds.), *Contemporary learning theories: Pavlovian conditioning and the status of traditional learning theory* (pp. 149–189). Hillsdale, NJ: Erlbaum.

Wagner, A. R., Logan, F. A., Haberlandt, K., & Price, T. (1968). Stimulus selection in animal discrimination learning.

Journal of Experimental Psychology, *76*, 171-180.

Weiss, S. J., Thomas, D. A., & Weissman, R. D. (1996). Combining operant-baseline-derived conditioned excitors and inhibitors from the same and different incentive classes: an investigation of appetitive-aversive interactions. *Quarterly Journal of Experimental Psychology: B*, *49*, 357-381.

Williams, B. A. (1999). Associative competition in operant conditioning: Blocking the response-reinforcer association. *Psychonomic Bulletin & Review*, *6*, 618-623.

4

Alerts for Assessing "Biological Constraints" on Learning

J. Bruce Overmier[1] & Julia E. Meyers-Manor[2]

[1]*University of Minnesota, USA*
[2]*Macalester College, USA*

Many researchers have reported differential rates of learning and inferred selective associations between events reflecting adaptive specializations or biological constraints on learning that have evolved for each given species. Although we do not doubt that there are such biological constraints on learning, we suggest that some of the many claims may actually be spurious due to use of less than optimal research designs. We propose six methodological and inferential concerns that current researchers and reviewers of past research may find useful.

The psychology of learning has been dominated by the view that at least in mammals—and possibly all vertebrates—learning proceeds in much the same way and follows the same general principles and "laws" of learning. However, organisms seem to learn some relationships rather faster or to higher asymptotes than other relationships. Accounts of learning have sometimes reflected this by including in their derived equations different rate parameters or salience parameters for some events (stimuli or responses or outcomes) as opposed to others (e.g., Hull, 1950, Postulate XVIII; Wagner & Rescorla, 1972). More interestingly, however, is when the observed different rates of learning are due to particular combinations of events, typically across motivational systems, or when some responses seem not to be reinforced by known trans-situational reinforcers; these adaptive specializations (Rozin & Kalat, 1971) have commonly been referred to as *biological constraints* on learning and/or behavior. Shettleworth (1972) provided an informative analytic review in which she categorized these constraints into three classes: stimulus→reinforcer, stimulus-→response, and response→reinforcer. These classes, of course, may not all have the same underlying mechanisms. Biological constraints on behavior became a very popular and important topic in the study of learning by psychologists in the 1960s and 1970s because they were taken by some as challenges to the assumed generality of the laws of learning (e.g., Seligman, 1970).

One often cited classical experiment and important exemplar was carried out by Garcia and Koelling (1966). They reported that rats were given access to a saccharin solution from a drinking tube, and licks of the solution also caused visual and auditory cues to be presented (so-called tasty-bright-noisy water). When these exposures were followed in different groups by either electric foot-shocks or lithium induced illness, the rats came to avoid drinking the water. Tests of the separate cue-outcome combinations, however, showed that

This paper arises from a set of comments regarding a symposium at the International Congress of Comparative Psychology in Bogota, Colombia, 2014. Please send correspondence to Dr. J. Bruce Overmier, University of Minnesota, Minneapolis, MN (Email: psyjbo@umn.edu).

when the outcome was shocks, the avoidance of the water was based on the light/noise cues, but when the outcome was illness, the avoidance was based on the taste cue. This was taken as evidence for selective associations, and Garcia hypothesized an evolved biological relatedness of interoceptive tastes to illness and exteroceptive cues to pain as likely causal factors for these selective associations—although later work by Foree and LoLordo (1975) and Martin and Lett (1985) showed that in avians visual stimuli are better integrated with the appetitive behavior rather than taste. In any case, the idea of selective associations was not totally novel because Thorndike (1932) proposed a concept of *belongingness* as a determiner of whether an association could be formed between sets of events or whether some responses could be trained. Later, Kohler (1941) noted that, generally, "little attention [is given] to the *nature* of the things which become associated" (p. 153; bracket and italics added).

Importantly—but generally ignored by those who cite it—is the fact that the classic Garcia and Koelling (1966) experiment lacked a number of important controls that could have been the basis of the purported selective associations. We now know based on a number of later experiments by Garcia and associates and especially by Domjan and associates (See Domjan, 2015) that Garcia's inference of selective associations is, in fact, valid. Many other researchers have carried out quite different experiments that purport to show other selective associations that seem to challenge the generality of the laws of learning (e.g., Hinde & Stevenson-Hinde, 1973; Seligman & Hager, 1972).

Herein, we want to simply call to the readers' attention various methodological issues that plague some of the claimed demonstrations of selective associations. We will raise these methodological issues in a general form as guiding future researches and not as criticisms of specific claimed demonstrations. We leave it to the readers to consider the applicability to existing literature of the methodological issues we raise. We will call attention to the importance of six methodological and inferential concerns. These include (1) the problem of temporary or permanent shifts in an organism's state (motivations, attention, etc.), (2) the need for controls for *non-associative* learning, (3) the lack of attention to the particular behavior selected for observation, (4) the problems that arise from using behavioral baselines that are *unidirectional* – typically from zero, (5) the need to consider what law of learning is being *violated*, and (6) advantage of using the power of double dissociation experiments.

A full treatment of each of these issues is beyond the scope of this article. Therefore, we hope the readers will take the expositions below as "alerts" for things to keep in mind when reading experiments making special claims or when designing experiments intended to support special claims. Unfortunately, just to make our tasks as researchers harder, the methodological issues we raise below are not necessarily independent of one another.

Methodological Alerts and Challenges

Shifts in an Organism's State

The presentation of biologically important stimuli (e.g., unconditioned stimuli/reinforcers) may well induce sensitization, a well-known phenomenon of change in response to a repeated stimulus. Such sensitization may include shifts in attention to stimuli other than the presented biologically important stimulus, and these shifts in attention may differ for different stimuli or may manifest themselves as differences in responsivity to the different stimuli. Rescorla and Holland (1976) introduced this possibility as an explanation for observed apparent biological constraints on learning. On this view, any differences in observed learning are attributable not to differences in learning, per se, but to differences in selective attention that in turn modulate attention or responsivity to the stimuli. Miller and Domjan (1981 a, b) have indeed shown just such selective sensitization can occur, albeit a relatively short term effect in their hands. This suggests that one common control used to study biological constraints on learning, that of having a control group that receives a neutral event as a substitute for one or both of the unconditioned stimuli/reinforcers, is an inadequate control.

One other approach to this problem of control for sensitization or of non-specific behavioral activation (or non-specific behavioral suppression) is the use of the yoked control design. In this design, the experimental group gets pairings (e.g., typically of response and reinforcer 1 or response and reinforcer 2) and the yoked control group can make responses yet gets only the same reinforcers generated by the experimental animal but without specific contiguity between the two kinds of events. Such a yoked design should in principle control for sensitization—if the individual animals are equally sensitive to or activated by the reinforcer/US. But no two animals can be perfectly matched on sensitivity. So inevitably, for example, some sensitive experimental subject will be yoked to some insensitive control subject (or *vice versa*). Church (1964) has illustrated that this inability to match animals results in systematic differences in sensitized behavior and activity levels that can lead to false inferences about the cause of the differences between master and yoked animals and even whether or not some behavior has been learned. Such an inferential error combined with the assessment of qualitatively different unconditioned stimuli/reinforcers could mislead to an inference of biological constraints on behavior where it is unwarranted.

Need for Controls for *Non-associative* Learning

Controls are needed in the assessments for learning. A pseudo-conditioning group is common, but not perfect because it is subject to some of the concerns of induced temporary shifts in sensitivity noted above. Nonetheless, such a control can be critical for assessing whether the behavioral changes seen across trials are due to learning (i.e., dependent upon the contiguity between the events) or attributable to non-associative learning like pseudo-conditioning, which is changes in target responses to the CS as a result of experiencing the US but absent any CS-US signaling relation between them. This is easily illustrated by an experiment by Hollis and Overmier (1982). The *aggressive fighting* display of the Siamese fighting fish (*Betta splendens*), which is shown in Figure 1, appears as a species characteristic integrated response of erecting the gill covers (opercula) making the head appear larger and spreading all the fins. It is beautiful. They were studying whether brain lesions altered the Pavlovian conditioning of this display to a CS signal for an impending visualization of male US. They recorded the components of the display separately. Both of the major components of the display came to appear readily after the presentation of the CS in the Pavlovian conditioning treatment. As can be seen in the left panel, the erection of the gill covers was acquired only in the Pavlovian conditioning treatment and not in their pseudo-conditioning treatment (in which CS and US were presented but uncorrelated) suggesting associative learning. However, the fin spreading was different! Fin spreading was elicited by the CS in both the Pavlovian and pseudo-conditioning treatments, suggesting that it was not acquired as an associative response but acquired as a non-associative response attributable to pseudo-conditioning. This was a surprising result. Clearly, to determine whether or not a behavior change is due to a specific operation, one must have control groups that get all the same events and experiences as the experimental group except for the one thing that is being tested for—here and in most cases the contiguity of events. And, we note that the exemplar Garcia and Koelling experiment described above lacked such controls leaving them open to non-associative explanations.

What is the basis for the strong pseudo-conditioning of fin spreading in the Hollis and Overmier experiment? We cannot tell. But pseudo-conditioning can, it seems, be based on a variety of factors including things as surprising yet simple as the similarity of the onset conditions of the CS and the US. Wickens and Wickens showed this in a not-often-noticed paper back in 1942. They asked about the amount of pseudo-conditioning occurring in four groups of rats to a visual stimulus when using an escapable footshock US. The groups being compared differed only in the onset characteristics of the light and shock, the onsets of each were either gradual or abrupt, giving us a 2 x 2 factorial design as to onset combinations. Pseudo-conditioning was only observed when the onsets of both were gradual or the onsets of both were abrupt; if the onsets differed, there was no pseudo-conditioning; thus onset characteristics in common were sufficient to support pseudo-conditioning. Is it possible that the abrupt onset of the light cue and the arranged abrupt appearance of the conspecific image provide the basis for the pseudo-conditioning of the fin spreading? Beyond this possibility, Rescorla (1985) also discussed his demonstrations of the role of other similarities between events in Pavlovian conditioning as factors that might contribute to appearance of CS evoked responses.

Figure 1. Photo of a Siamese fighting fish in its full *fighting* display which appears to be an integrated response including spreading of fins, erection of the gill covers (opercula), and beating of the spread tail back and forth.

The Behavior Selected for Observation

One other point to be made from the Hollis and Overmier (1982) experiment is that that they reached different inferences about occurrence of associative Pavlovian learning or non-associative pseudo-conditioned learning depending on the response they measured (Figure 2). The methodological guidance we should take from this is that it is wise to take multiple behavioral measures even when there is no *a priori* reason to suspect a need for multiple measures. The Siamese aggressive display was always assumed to be a single integrated modal action pattern, but it turns out that is not so. Hollis and her associate were not the only people to have found merit in using concurrent multiple behavioral indices. Matzel, Schachtman, and Miller (1985) showed that taking multiple measures in their experiments that revealed that overshadowing is not a failure of

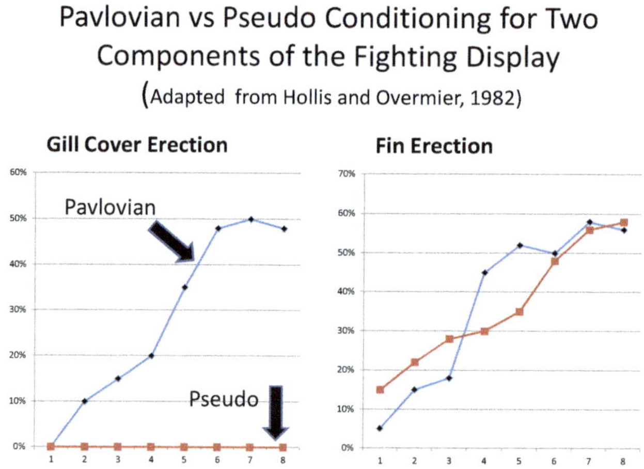

Figure 2. Sample data showing (a) that some apparently classically conditioned responses may well be pseudo-conditioned, and (b) that the components of apparently integrated action patterns may be dissociated and be differentially subject to associative and non-associative processes. Data excerpted from Hollis and Overmier (1982) and redrawn.

association but of behavioral manifestation. Dunham and Grantmyre (1982) gave us new insights into the effects of punishment on an act and related behaviors, and on how post-punishment behaviors get redistributed because they concurrently measured several behaviors during the experimental treatment. And, in the appetitive domain, Timberlake (2001) has shown us how measuring multiple responses can reveal different motivation-specific search behaviors that are dependent upon the qualities and timing of signals, reinforcers, and the structure of the environment. These revealed that multiple response behavior systems constitute rich information about biological constraints on behavior.

But, all too often we—we are guilty, too—still design our experiments with single behavior dependent variables.

The Problems of Zero-based Unidirectional Baselines

To say that one condition produces more, better, or faster learning than another group, we must compare the behavior from the two conditions. Typically we look at the performance from the beginning of the conditioning—rate of change and/or asymptote achieved. If one is higher than the other as in Figure 3 Panel A, we infer a difference in rate of learning or in the amount learned. But such a plot and inferences implicitly assumes that both CS stimuli are equivalent at the outset of learning. Frankly, we know that this is not in fact usual. So, we try to use some difference score for each CS stimulus that takes into account the differences in the unconditioned state. A couple of different approaches have been used. One is to use the first trial performance as an indicator of the baseline performance for a given CS; another is to use some control treatment that exposes the control subject to the biologically important stimulus but that is not supposed to lead to learning of associations, for example the so-called Truly Random Control (TRC). Thus, now we can compute difference scores for both CSs, as illustrated in Figure 3 Panel B. But, both of these approaches suffer from the same problem: they assume that the baseline performance is a zero value or some positive value. Yet we know that sometimes stimuli have—or acquire—inhibitory properties with respect to behaviors. And that cannot easily be detected when using a zero level baseline as is the case in most learning experiments (e.g., you cannot drink less than 0 drops of a fluid). A third approach is to design the experiment so that inhibitory effects as well as excitatory effects of stimuli can be detected. That typically requires at the outset some ongoing level of behavior that we hope to use as our dependent variable. A classic way to do this is to train a baseline of behavior and then superimpose the CS on that bidirectionally sensitive baseline. The CSs may be untrained or subject to some treatment thought not to support learning (e.g., TRC). The classic transfer of control design is useful here. In it, the dependent variable baseline is trained, the CSs are given associative or non-associative treatments, and then the CSs are presented while the animal is performing the baseline behavior. Changes from the baseline detect the stimulus specific effects for both the associative and the non-associative conditions. The differences between these for the two CSs then can be used to assess the rate of learning as separable from any differences in the asymptotic levels achieved in the associative condition. This is illustrated in Figure 3 Panel C.

In fact, Linwick, Paterson, and Overmier (1981) provided just such a demonstration as shown in Figure 3 Panel C (redrawn from their data). Had they used a design with no baseline (Panel A) or one with a unidirectionally sensitive baseline (Panel B), they might have inferred that their two stimuli (a tone CS and a light CS, each paired with footshock) were different in amount of fear learning that took place. But when they used the bidiectionally sensitive baseline to assess the TRC control treatment, we see that the non-associative effect of one of the stimuli is neutral while the non-associative effect of the other is inhibitory for that target behavior. When the *difference scores* between the non-associative reference condition and the conditioned fear detected (functionally the slope, rate, or amount of conditioned associative learning) are computed, they saw that the associative learning to the two different CSs appear equal! Although one can argue about the right index for learning, it seems that one cannot easily argue against using bidirectionally sensitive baselines (trained or natural pre-existing ones). Is it possible that the reason Cook and Mineka (1989,) in their now classic experiments on observational learning of fear, failed to find emergence of fear to flowers (flowers being so-called "fear-irrelevant") was because flowers are inherently initially inhibitory of fear responses? Their unidirectional baseline would not allow us to see that. We recognize that there are other approaches for detecting inhibitory influences like resistance to conditioning, but we believe that the bidirectionally sensitive baseline is the most straight forward approach.

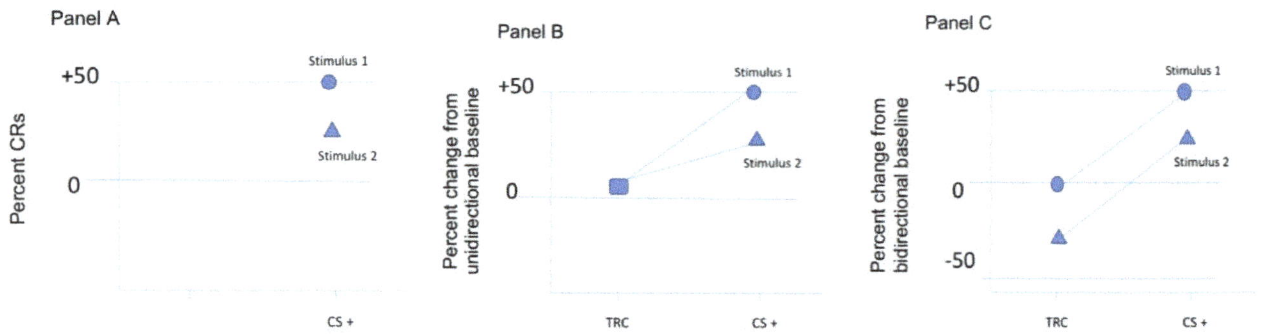

Figure 3. Different ways of evaluating obtained differences in asymptotic levels of conditioning. Panel A directly compares the asymptotic levels attained with the two CSs. Panel B compares the two CSs on the basis of the change or slope from baseline to asymptote, when the baseline is only unidirectionally modifiable. Panel C compares the conditioning to the two CSs on the basis of difference from a control treatment of the CS where all values are changes from baseline behavior where the baseline is bidirectionally sensitive to the properties of the stimuli (redrawn).

What Law of Learning is being *Violated*?

In addition to a basic demonstration of selective associations, Garcia and his associates (Garcia, Ervin, & Koelling, 1966) also demonstrated that the association of taste with illness seemed to occur over long delays—delays longer than had previously been used in associative learning tasks. This *long-delay* learning was pounced upon by theoreticians as a violation of some basic law of learning and thus evidence that there were no *general laws of learning* (e.g., Seligman, 1970). But what was this basic general law that was being violated? We presume that the referenced law is *contiguity*, that taste and illness could be associated without close temporal contiguity. The intervals in Garcia, Ervin, and Koelling over which associations were formed were in fact an hour or more. This was a surprise to many who had grown up with the paradigmatic example of classical conditioning being the conditioning of the eyeblink reflex and the usual CS onset to US onset interval was about 0.5 sec and cited in every introductory textbook. Indeed, some theorists actually argued that this 0.5 sec interval was determined by the neural system underlying learning and were likely general for all learning. Those swayed by this line of reasoning must have forgotten Pavlov's lectures (1927) wherein Pavlov routinely describes conditioning experiments on salivary conditioning with CS-US intervals of 30 sec or more!

We now know that the ratio of the CS-US interval to the ITI (or closely related values depending on the particular theory) is an important determiner of whether an association develops or not (e.g., Gibbon & Balsam, 1981). In the eyeblink experiments, the inter-trial interval (ITI) was seconds; in the salivary experiments, the ITI was several minutes; in the taste aversion learning, the ITI was day(s). It turns out that the general principle is that there exists — for each particular CS and particular US conditioning combination of a given response with a particular ITI — an optimal CS-US interval and CS-US interval values longer or shorter than that optimal value produce less effective conditioning. This is seen in a range of species conditioning different responses (e.g., McAllister, 1953 [human eyelid optimum 0.5 sec]; Noble, Gruender, & Meyer, 1959 [fish motor movement optimum 2 sec]; Noble & Adams, 1963 [pig motor movements optimum 8 sec]; Longo, Klempay, & Bitterman, 1964 [pigeon motor movements optimum 10 sec]; Paré 1967 [rats CER optimum 2 min]). The general law seems to be that amplitude of conditioning is an inverted U-shaped function of CS-US interval; the central locus of that function is characteristic for each particular CS, US, response, and ITI combination—a summary that might fit well into Shettleworth's review. For example with regard to taste aversion learning, a much overlooked experiment by Krane and Wagner (1975) is consistent with this summary. They showed that *both* light-tone compounds and tastes can become CSs for illness and that *both* light-tone compounds and tastes can become CSs for shock, but they do so at very different CS-US intervals, thus challenging any *belongingness* hypothesis. (See also Westbrook, Clarke, and Provost, 1980, and Martin & Lett, 1985, for their data, not their conclusions.)

Double Dissociation Paradigm

The Garcia and Koelling (1966) bright-noisy-tasty water aversion learning demonstration was readily accepted despite its lack of controls. This is perhaps because it used a powerful methodological design that allowed showing of a *double dissociation* in which there was a full reversal of which CS became associated with illnesses and which became associated with shocks. Double dissociation demonstrations in behavioral neuroscience are generally quite compelling and often required to show system disjunctions (Weiskrantz, 1968). And because of their compelling power, others studying adaptive specializations and biological constraints on learning have also adopted this design (Domjan & Wilson, 1972; Foree & LoLordo, 1973; Miller & Domjan, 1981). But the design in its basic form does have weaknesses, Weiskrantz (1968); describes conditions under which a double dissociation demonstration is not sufficient for validating qualitative differences in treatment effects (e.g., see pp. 418-419).

One case is illustrated in Figure 4. An apparent double dissociation can arise when performance is an inverted-U shape. One example would be in the Yerkes-Dodson Law where performance is an inverted-U shape function of level of motivation (or some other some resource function). Then, even when two different CSs stand in the same *associability* relation to each other, if the two reinforcers used place the CS contrasts at opposite sides of the inverted U-function between performance and motivation: CS2 will be greater than CS1 at low motivation and CS2 will be less than CS1 at high motivation. [Think of moving a two-tine fork along the x-axis of an inverted U-shaped function.] Thus, one could obtain the data for a double dissociation in the absence of any associative mechanism difference. Double dissociations are not typically all-or-none, and such task sensitivity then plays a role.

Additionally, double dissociation designs have typically not controlled well for differential sensitization or differential pseudo-conditioning across USs. Conditioning designs with controls that include presentation of *both* CSs and presentation of *both* USs are needed for this, and they have been developed where all subjects get all stimuli (e.g., Rescorla & Holland, 1976).

Conclusions

We accept that differential rates of learning to different stimulus-reinforcer-response event combinations occur and that these may reflect selective associations between events thus reflecting adaptive specializations and biological constraints on learning. But we think that many simple demonstrations of such differences in learning found when using different CSs or different USs are sometimes all too readily initially characterized as reflecting biological constraints on learning. That such constraints do exist does not imply that every apparent difference in learning *is* an instance of biological constraints on learning. Indeed, we think that some such inferences may be spurious. We have highlighted a few methodological and inferential concerns and challenges that current researchers going forward—and reviewers of past research—may find useful as they think about research on biological constraints on learning. In a sense, these are old methodological issues and unfortunately sometimes forgotten ones, but they are of current relevance. Our list is not exhaustive; for example, we have not discussed *between vs within subject* designs (Charnes, Gneezy, & Kuhn, 2012; Grice,

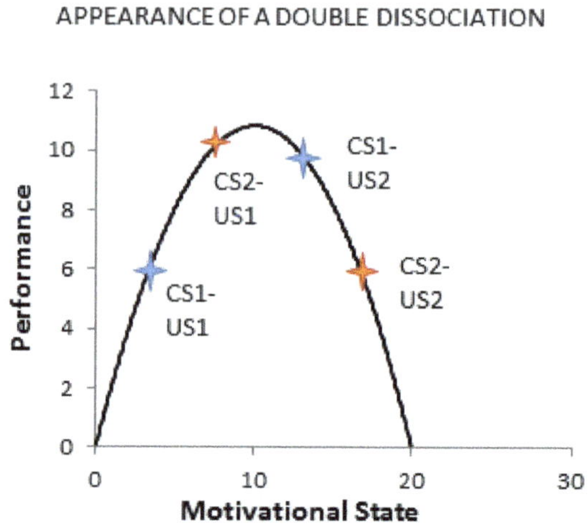

Figure 4. Shows how an experiment that pairs two different CSs with two different USs of strikingly different motivational power might lead to an appearance of a double dissociation in the absence of different associability (here CS2 > CS1) if the performance function is non-monotonic with respect to the motivational function (or other task sensitivities).

1966), but rather our list is illustrative that careful analysis and rich designs are needed as hallmarks for such demonstrations to support strong inferences and claims. We do not want to claim that heeding these various alerts will lead to successful identification of a biological constraint, but rather to do so may help us avoid erroneous inference.

We would like our note here to be in the spirit of—or better an extension of—Wesikrantz's (1968) provocative chapter "Some traps and pontifications" and Domjan and Galef's (1983) "Retrospect and prospect". If you have not read these, you should be sure to do so because (a) they, too, are relevant to what inferences we can draw from what kinds of data sets and how we sometimes get led astray, and (b) they offer guides as to ways forward in this challenging area of research.

Acknowledgments

This paper arises from a set of comments regarding a symposium at the International Congress of Comparative Psychology in Bogota, Colombia, 2014

References

Charnes, G. Gneezy, U, Kuhn, M. A. (2012). Experimental methods: Between-subject and within subject design. *Journal of Economic Behavior & Organization, 81*, 1-8.

Church, R. M. (1964). Systematic effect of random error in the yoked control design. *Psychological Bulletin, 62,* 122-131.

Cook, M., & Mineka, S. (1989). Observational conditioning of fear to fear-relevant versus fear irrelevant stimuli in rhesus monkeys. *Journal of Abnormal Psychology, 98*, 448-459.

Dunham, P. J., & Grantmyre, J. (1982). Changes in a multiple-response repertoire during response-contingent punishment and response restriction: Sequential relationships, *Journal of the Experimental Analysis of Behavior, 37*, 123-133.

Domjan, Michael. (2015). The Garcia-Koelling Selective Association Effect: A Historical and Personal Perspective. *International Journal of Comparative Psychology*, 28. Retrieved from: http://escholarship.org/uc/item/5sx993rm.

Domjan, M., & Galef. B.G. (1983). Biological constraints on instrumental and classical conditioning: Retrospect and prospect. *Animal Learning & Behavior, 11,* 151-161.

Domjan, M., & Wilson, NE. (1972). Specificity of cue to consequence in aversion learning in the rat. *Psychonomic Science, 26,* 143-145.

Foree, D. D., & LoLordo, V. M. (1973). Attention in the pigeon: Differential effects of food-getting versus shock-avoidance procedures. *Journal of Comparative and Physiological Psychology, 85*, 551-558.

Foree, D. D., & LoLordo, V. M. (1975). Stimulus-reinforcer interactions in the pigeon: The role of electric shock and the avoidance contingency. *Journal of Experimental Psychology: Animal Behavior Processes, 1*, 39-46.

Garcia, J., Ervin, F. R., & Koelling, R. A. (1966). Learning with prolonged delay of reinforcement. *Psychonomic Science, 5,* 121-122.

Garcia, J., & Koelling, R. A. (1966). Relation of cue to consequence in avoidance learning. *Psychonomic Science, 4,* 123-124.

Gibbon, J., & Balsam, P. (1981). Spreading associations in time. (219-253). In C. M. Locurto, H. S., Terrace, & J. Gibbon (Eds.), *Autoshaping and conditioning theory*. London, England: Academic Press.

Grice, R. (1966). Dependence of empirical laws upon the source of experimental variation. *Psychological Bulletin, 66,* 488–498.

Hollis, K. L., & Overmier, J. B. (1982). Effect of telencephalon ablation on the reinforcing and eliciting properties of species-specific events in *Betta splendens. Journal of Comparative and Physiological Psychology, 96,* 574-590.

Hull, C. L. (1950). Behavior postulates and corollaries-1949. *Psychological Review, 57,* 173-180.

Hinde, R. A., & Stevenson-Hinde, J. (Eds.). (1973). *Constraints on learning.* New York, NY: Academic Press.

Kohler, W. (1941). On the nature of associations. *Proceedings of the American Philosophical Society, 84*, 489-502.

Krane, R. V., & Wagner, A. R. (1975). Taste aversion learning with a delayed shock US: Implications for the "generality" of the laws of learning. *Journal of Comparative and Physiological Psychology, 88*, 882-889.

Linwick, D., Patterson, J., & Overmier, J. B. (1981). On inferring selective association: Methodological considerations. *Animal Learning & Behavior, 9*, 508-512.

Longo, N., Klempay, S., & Bitterman, M. E. (1964). Classical appetitive conditioning in the pigeon. *Psychonomic Science, 1,* 19-20.

Martin, G. M., & Lett, B. T. (1985). Formation of associations of colored and flavored food with induced sickness in five avian species. *Behavioral & Neural Biology, 43,* 223-237.

McAllister, W. R. (1953). Eyelid conditioning as a function of the CS-US interval. *Journal of Experimental Psychology, 45,* 417-422.

Miller, V., & Domjan, M. (1981a). Selective sensitization induced by lithium malaise and footshock in rats. *Behavioral and Neural Biology, 31,* 42-55.

Miller, V., & Domjan, M. (1981b). Specificity of cue to consequence in aversion learning in the rat: Control for US-induced differential orientations. Animal Learning & Behavior, 9, 339-345.

Noble, M., Gruender, A., & Meyer, D. R. (1959). *Journal of Comparative and Physiological Psychology, 52*, 236-239.

Noble, M., & Adams, C. K. (1963). *Journal of Comparative and Physiological Psychology, 56,* 215-219.

Pare, W. P. (1967). The CS-US onset interval and the acquisition of a conditioned emotional response. *Newsletter for Research in Psychology, 9,* 52.

Pavlov, I. P. (1927). *Conditioned reflexes.* New York, NY: Oxford University Press.

Rescorla, R. A., & Holland, P. C. (1976). Some behavioral approaches to the study of learning. In M. R. Rosenzweig & E. L. Bennett (Eds.), *Neural mechanisms of learning and memory* (pp. 165-192). Cambridge, MA: MIT Press.

Rescorla, R. A. (1985). Pavlovian conditioning analogs to Gestalt principles. In F. R. Brush & J. B. Overmier (Eds.), *Affect, conditioning, & cognition* (pp. 113-130). Hillsdale, NJ: Lawrence Erlbaum Associates. [Reissued by Taylor & Francis, 2014]

Rozin, P., & Kalat, J. W. (1971). Specific hungers and poison avoidance as adaptive specializations of learning. *Psychological Review, 78,* 459-486.

Seligman, M. E. P. (1970). On the generality of the laws of learning. *Psychological Review, 78,* 459-486.

Seligman, M. E., & Hager, J. L. (1972). Biological boundaries of learning. East Norwalk, CT, US: Appleton-Century-Crofts.

Shettleworth, S. J. (1972). Constraints on learning. *Advances in the Study of Behavior, 4,* 1-68.

Thorndike, E. L. (1932).*The fundamentals of learning*. New York, NY: Columbia University Bureau.

Timberlake, W. (2001). Motivational modes in behavior systems. In R. R. Mowrer & S.B. Klein (Eds.), *Handbook of contemporary learning theories* (pp. 155-209). Mahwah, NJ: Lawrence Erlbaum Associates Publishers.

Wagner, A. R., & Rescorla, R. A. (1972). A theory of Pavlovian conditioning: Variations in the effectiveness of reinforcement and nonreinforcement. In A. H. Black & W. F. Prokasy (Eds.), *Classical conditioning II: Current theory and research* (pp. 64-91, esp 76). New York, NY: Appleton Century Crofts.

Weiskrantz, L. (1968). Some traps and pontifications. In L. Weiskrantz (Ed.), *Analysis of behavior change* (pp. 415-430). New York, NY: Harper & Row.

Westbrook, R. F., Clarke, J. C., & Provost, S. (1980). Long-delay learning in the pigeon: Flavor, color, and flavor-mediated color aversions. *Behavioral & Neural Biology, 28,* 398-407.

Wickens, D. D., & Wickens, C. D. (1942). Some factors related to pseudo-conditioning. *Journal of Experimental Psychology, 31*, 518-526

5

Persistent Memory Retention of Reward Events and Proactive Interference in Reward Series Learning By Mice

Tohru Taniuchi
Kanazawa University, Japan

This study examined acquisition of a single alternating series of reward quantities in mice. Four male ICR mice, trained in a straight runway, showed deferential response to items in a 3-0-3-0-3-0-3 series, constructed from a varying number of 0.045 g food pellets under inter-trial intervals (ITI) of 30 s (Experiment 1) or 20 min (Experiment 2), by running more slowly to nonrewards than rewards. Although mice showed reliable item anticipation under 20 min ITIs, nonreward anticipation became poorer in later serial positions than in earlier positions. It is possible that gradual deterioration of nonreward anticipation in a series is caused by proactive interference from previous item memories, since the nonreward anticipation was improved when the target item was divided by a long 120 min interval from prior items that were a potential source of proactive interference (Experiment 3). In Experiment 4, mice learned to respond differentially to the second item of 5-0 and 0-5 series with an ITI of 180 min. These results suggest that mice can discriminate reward magnitudes by forming item-associations between adjacent items and retain information of a previous item for a long interval, and that proactive interference occurs among item memories in a series.

Given that events in natural or experimental settings often have sequential order, animals may predict coming events from prior events (Capaldi, 1994) and choose possible behavioral options by considering the order of events (Phelps & Roberts, 1991; Wathen & Roberts, 1994) or temporal delays from a time point to multiple serial events simultaneously (Brunner, 1999; Brunner & Gibbon, 1995). The ability to learn the order of events has been studied in the form of serial learning. Serial learning in primates and birds has been examined mainly by the simultaneous chain task method, where all of the items are presented simultaneously and animals are trained to respond to these items in a fixed order (for a review, see Terrace, 2005). However, serial learning in rodents has been typically studied in the form of reward-serial learning, where items of a series are constituted from varying amounts of 0.045 g food pellets (e.g., Hulse & Dorsky, 1977) or a varying quality of food (e.g., Capaldi & Miller, 1988b). These food items are placed in the goal box of a straight runway in a fixed order on consecutive trials. Learning is indexed by slower running to smaller rewards, especially to nonrewards, and faster running to larger rewards.

It has been demonstrated that rats learn a series with a simple structure (e.g., 14-7-3-1-0) faster than one with a more complex structure (e.g., 14-1-3-7-0; Hulse & Dorsky, 1977), transfer learning between series with the same formal structure (Hulse & Dorsky, 1979; Taniuchi, 1995), extrapolate a novel item based on series structure (Fountain & Hulse, 1981), and facilitate learning by phrasing complex series into simple sub-

This research was supported by a Grant-in-Aid for JSPS Fellows (grant number 99J06740) from the Japan Society for the Promotion of Science. I thank Mauricio R. Papini for his helpful comments on an earlier version of this article. Correspondence concerning this article should be addressed to Tohru Taniuchi, Department of Psychology, Kanazawa University, Kakuma, Kanazawa-shi, Ishikawa, Japan. (Email: tohruta@staff.kanazawa-u.ac.jp)

patterns (Fountain, Henne, & Hulse, 1984). These results were interpreted as evidence that rats encode and represent the abstract structure of the series. This rule learning view has been strongly challenged by a memory-discrimination learning theory that explains serial learning by formation of item-association and stimulus generalization among signals of the associations (Capaldi, 1994; Capaldi & Molina, 1979; Capaldi, Nawrocki, Miller, & Verry, 1986; Capaldi, Verry, & Davidson, 1980; Capaldi, Verry, Nawrocki, & Miller, 1984; Haggbloom & Brooks, 1985).

Whether rats can encode abstract rule structure is not clear (Capaldi, 1994). In contrast, formation of item-association between adjacent items and stimulus generalization among signals in item-association is clearly demonstrated for rats (Capaldi et al., 1980). Moreover, it has been shown that rats can form an association between remote items (Capaldi et al., 1983; Capaldi & Miller, 1988b; Capaldi & Verry, 1981) and utilize the whole of a series representation as a discriminative stimulus for a succeeding series (Capaldi, 1992; Capaldi, Miller, Alptekin, & Barry, 1990; Haggbloom, Birmingham, & Scranton, 1992).

Although reward serial learning in rats has been studied extensively, generality of the findings across species has not been examined, even in other rodents. In serial pattern learning, which requires animals to track signals presented in different spatial locations, temporal phrasing of complex patterns into simple sub-patterns facilitates learning in rats (Fountain & Rowan, 1995; Stempowski, Carman, & Fountain, 1999), whereas it impairs performance of mice (Fountain, Krauchunas, & Rowan, 1999). The inconsistency of the effects of temporal phrasing on rats versus mice motivated us to investigate whether the findings in rat reward serial learning generalize to other rodent species. This study examined the mouse's basic capacity to learn reward series through acquisition of single-alternation series and concurrent learning of simple two-item series.

Experiment 1

The goal of Experiment 1 was to examine the basic cognitive ability of mice to learn reward series through acquisition of a single alternation series. It has been well documented that rats could learn to anticipate a reward event on a current trial of single alteration series, utilizing the preceding reward event as a discriminative cue (Tyler, Woltz, & Bitterman, 1953). The single alternation series is one of the simplest reward series, where only two types of reward events, reward (R) or nonreward (N), are presented alternately. The ability to associate memories of a preceding reward event with a following event is critical for learning in a single alternation series. The single alternation series can be mastered by forming R'-N (apostrophe meaning "memory" of a reward event) and N'-R associations between items. In Experiment 1, mice received a 3-0-3-0-3-0-3 series, where each R-N and N-R transition occurred three times in a series presentation. The inter-trial interval (ITI) was 30 s, and mice were required to retain item information only for this short period. If mice could master the series, anticipation of reward magnitude should be displayed by running faster to reward items and slower to nonreward items.

Differential response to reward and nonreward items might also be induced for other reasons, such as a slight, transient reduction in hunger level by consumption of a food reward, possibly resulting in slower running to the following nonreward. Another possible source of differential response might be a reinforcement-omission effect, referring to an invigoration of response following a nonreward but not following a reward (e.g., Amsel, 1958; Stout, Boughner, & Papini, 2003). To check for these possibilities, mice were tested with a quasi-random series 3-3-0-0-3-0-3, after acquisition training with the single alternation series was completed. If either a transient reduction of hunger level following a reward or the reinforcement-omission effect were the main cause of differential responses to reward and nonreward trials, it would be expected that mice would run more slowly to a nonreward following a reward than on a trial after a nonreward in this quasi-random series. However, item-association learning predicts a deterioration of differential response to reward items and nonreward items in the quasi-random series because inconsistent outcomes were signaled by identical prior items, that is, R'-R and R'-N, as well as N'-R and N'-N.

Method

Subjects. The subjects were four male ICR mice approximately 150 days old. These mice had experience as intruders in a resident-intruder test for an experiment on aggressiveness in mice, but they had not participated in any discrimination learning experiments.

Apparatus. The apparatus was an enclosed straight runway, 132.0 cm long, 10.0 cm wide, and 16.0 cm high, covered by wire mesh on hinged frames. The start box and the goal box were 15.0 cm and 20.0 cm long, respectively, and could be closed off by guillotine doors. The inside of the runway was painted flat black. A digital timer started when the start door was raised and stopped when the infrared ray, located 10.0 cm into the goal box, was interrupted by a mouse. The goal door was lowered when the infrared ray was interrupted, confining the mouse in the goal box. At the end of the goal box, 0.045 g food pellets could be placed in a food cup, 1.5 cm in diameter and 0.5 cm in depth.

Pretraining. During the first fourteen days, mice were handled for 1 min per day and their ad-lib body weight was reduced to 85% by food deprivation. These body weights were maintained throughout the remainder of the experiment. On Days 8-12, each mouse was given 10 min of exploration of the runway with all the doors open and permitted to eat six food pellets scattered on the runway floor. On Days 13-14, mice were confined to the goal box with the door lowered and allowed to eat three food pellets from the food cup.

Experimental training. Acquisition training began on Day 15 and continued for 80 days. Mice were brought into the experiment room in their home cage. A 3-0-3-0-3-0-3 series was presented once per day under ITIs of 30 s. A trial began with placement of the mouse in the start box with the start door raised 5 s later. On rewarded trials, the mouse was removed to the home cage after the reward was consumed. On nonrewarded trials, the mouse was confined to the goal box with no reward for 20 s and then removed to the home cage. If a mouse failed to complete a trial in 60 sec, it was picked up by the experimenter and placed in the goal box to receive the reward scheduled for that trial with a time score of 60 s assigned for that trial. A single mouse completed all trials of the series before the next mouse was run and the order of runs was varied and counterbalanced in blocks of four days. After completion of acquisition training with the 3-0-3-0-3-0-3 single alternation series, the series was shifted to a 3-3-0-0-3-0-3 quasi-random series for four days.

Results and Discussion

Figure 1 shows running speeds on each trial of 3-0-3-0-3-0-3 series grouped in blocks of four days. With training, anticipation of reward magnitudes developed, with faster trials to a reward and slower trials to a nonreward. The data from the single alternation series were subjected to a Trials * Blocks * Subjects analysis of variance. The analysis revealed significant main effects of Trials ($F(6, 18) = 12.86, p < 0.01$) and Blocks ($F(19, 57) = 15.88, p < 0.01$), and the Trials * Blocks interaction ($F(114, 342) = 4.00, p < 0.01$). Simple effects of Trials were significant at Blocks 8-20 (Fs(6, 360) = 2.99, 5.22, 8.61, 2.49, 6.20, 8.20, 8.15, 9.12, 15.73, 11.43, 10.50, 19.20, and 19.47, $ps < 0.05$) for Blocks 8-20. Paired comparisons by t-test with a nominal significance level regulated by Ryan's method were performed over the data of the last block, Block 20. The analysis revealed that mice ran faster to all the reward items than to all the nonreward items ($ps < 0.05$), and that difference in running speeds was not significant among reward items or among nonreward items ($ps > 0.05$).

When the series was shifted to a 3-3-0-0-3-0-3 quasi-random series, slower running to nonrewards was completely eliminated. A Trials * Blocks * Subjects analysis of variance on the quasi-random series data revealed significant main effects of Trials ($F(6, 18) = 12.34, p < 0.01$) and paired comparisons by t-test with a nominal significance level regulated by Ryan's method showed that Trial 1 and Trial 2 were significantly slower than all the other trials (*ps* < 0.05) and that the difference between Trial 1 and Trial 2 was not significant.

Reliable differential response between reward and nonreward in the single alternation series was developed as a result of training, and it was completely eliminated by the series shift to a quasi-random series. In particular for the 3-3-0-0-3-0-3 quasi-random series, running speeds did not differ between the third or sixth nonreward following a reward and fourth nonreward following a nonreward. If the transient reduction of hunger level by consumption of a reward or an invigoration of response by the reinforcement-omission effect (e.g., Amsel, 1958; Stout et al., 2003) were the main cause of slower running to a nonreward, mice would be expected to run more slowly to a nonreward after a reward than to a nonreward following a nonreward. Thus, the results of the quasi-random test do not support an explanation in terms of differential hunger levels or the reinforcement-omission effect. On the contrary, item-association learning appropriately predicts such deterioration of differential response in the quasi-random series because it offers a difficult discrimination task, where different outcomes are signaled by identical prior items in the series (R'-R and R'-N or N'-R and N'-N). Therefore the results of Experiment 1 support the view that mice, as well as rats, can utilize memory of a reward event on a prior trial as a discriminative cue for a following reward event, and that they have the basic ability to learn a reward series. Although mice showed reliable nonreward anticipation on Block 8, it took about thirty presentations of the series, that is, about 90 R-N transitions, to develop a reliable anticipation of reward magnitude. While we cannot compare the present mouse performance with previous rat studies because of differences in some experimental parameters, such as reward magnitude or ITI, the performance of mice appears somewhat poorer than that of rats, which showed a clear response patterning to the single alternation series after about 50 R-N transitions (Flaherty & Davenport, 1972; Tyler et al., 1953).

Experiment 2

The results in Experiment 1 showed that mice could acquire a single alternation series and retain item information for 30 s. Several studies have shown that rats manifested anticipation of reward magnitude under considerably longer ITIs, ranging from minutes to 24 h (Capaldi & Lynch, 1966; Capaldi, Nawrocki, Miller, & Verry, 1985). Experiment 2 examined whether mice could anticipate reward events in a single alternation series with a longer ITI of 20 min versus the 30 s ITI of Experiment 1. If mice could retain item information during a 20 min ITI, the differential response to reward and nonreward items of the single alternation series must occur as in Experiment 1.

Method

Subjects. Mice that participated in Experiment 1 were used as subjects. The animals were allowed free access to food and water for 64 days after Experiment 1 was finished and then received pretraining for Experiment 2.

Apparatus. The apparatus was the same as that employed in Experiment 1.

Pretraining. During the first 12 days, mice were reduced to 85% of ad-lib body weight by food deprivation and were maintained at that body weight throughout the remainder of the experiment. On Days 1-7, mice were handled for 1 min per day. On Days 8-12, each animal was confined to the goal box with the door lowered and allowed to eat three food pellets from the food cup.

Experimental training. Training began on Day 13 and continued for 40 days. A 3-0-3-0-3-0-3 series was presented once per day under an ITI of 20 min. During a subject's ITI, trials for other subjects were conducted. The order of the running of mice was consistent each day but it varied and was counterbalanced in blocks of four days. All other aspects of the training procedure were as in Experiment 1.

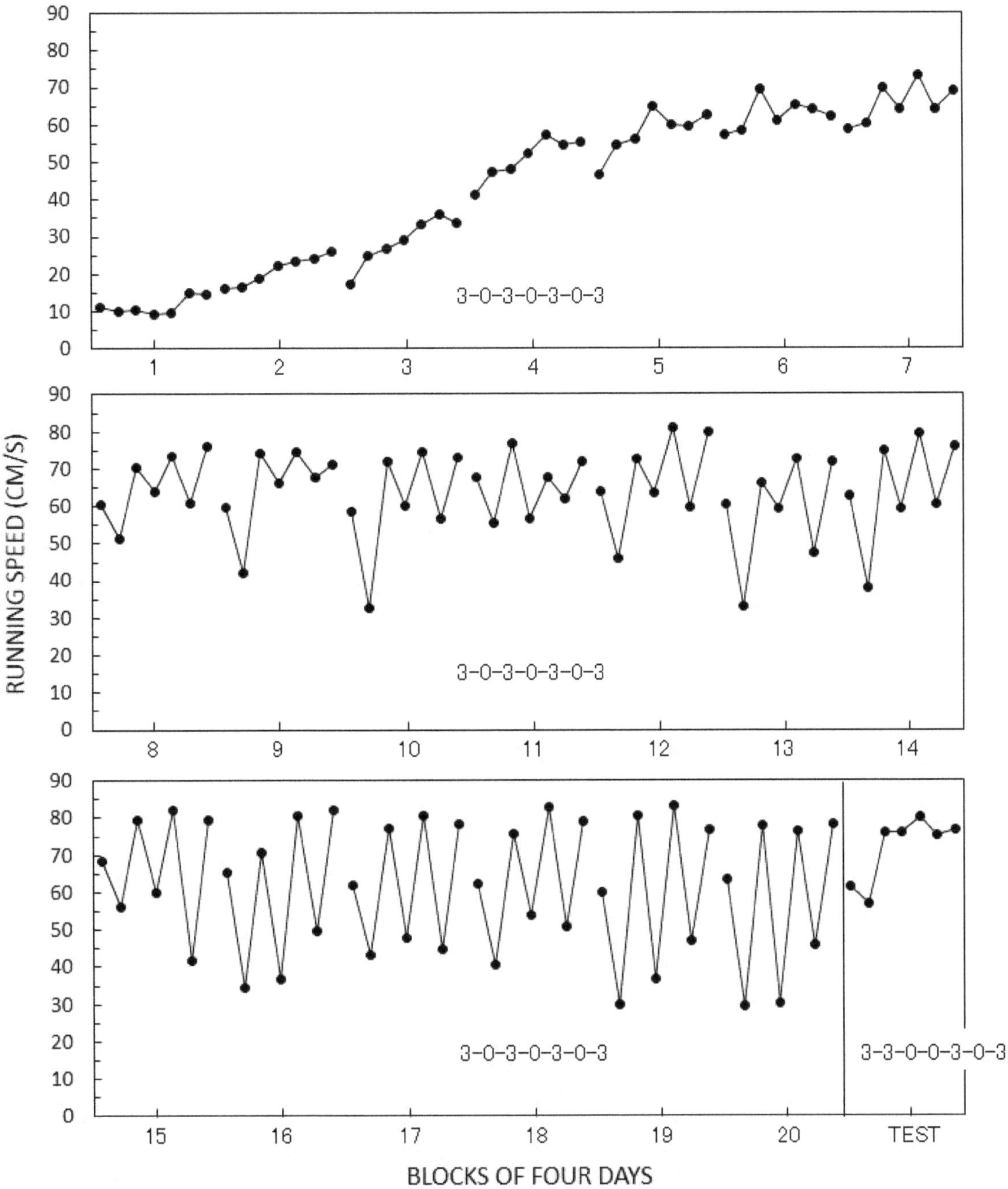

Figure 1. Running speeds on trials in a 3-0-3-0-3-0-3 series and a 3-3-0-0-3-0-3 series in blocks of four days in Experiment 1. Trials were separated by a 30 s ITI.

Results and Discussion

Figure 2 shows running speeds on each trial of the 3-0-3-0-3-0-3 series presented under a 20 min ITI in blocks of four days. With training, anticipation of reward magnitude developed again. The data shown in Figure 2 were subjected to a Trials * Blocks * Subjects analysis of variance. The analysis revealed significant main effect of Trials ($F(6, 18) = 21.81, p < 0.01$) and Trials * Blocks interaction ($F(54, 162) = 2.26, p < 0.01$). Simple effects of Trials were significant at Blocks 3-10 (Fs(6, 180) =5.74, 6.19, 11.05, 9.68, 8.41, 9.79, 11.12, and 19.28, $ps < 0.01$ for Blocks 3-10). Paired comparisons by t-test with a nominal significance level regulated by Ryan's method were performed over the data of the last block, Block 10. The analysis revealed that mice ran faster to all the reward items than all the nonreward items ($ps < 0.05$) and that running speeds did not differ reliably among the reward items ($ps > 0.05$). However, running speeds differed significantly among nonreward items of Block 10. Anticipation of nonreward on Trial 6 was inferior to Trial 2 ($p < 0.05$). Differences between Trial 2 and Trial 4 or Trial 4 and Trial 6 were not reliable ($ps > 0.05$).

Mice showed reward anticipation under a 20 min ITI. Although different sensory traces of previous R and N items may serve as discriminative stimuli in short ITI (e.g., 30 s), reward anticipation under a 20 min ITI may exclude such a sensory trace explanation and support the idea that memory processes mediate single alternation series learning.

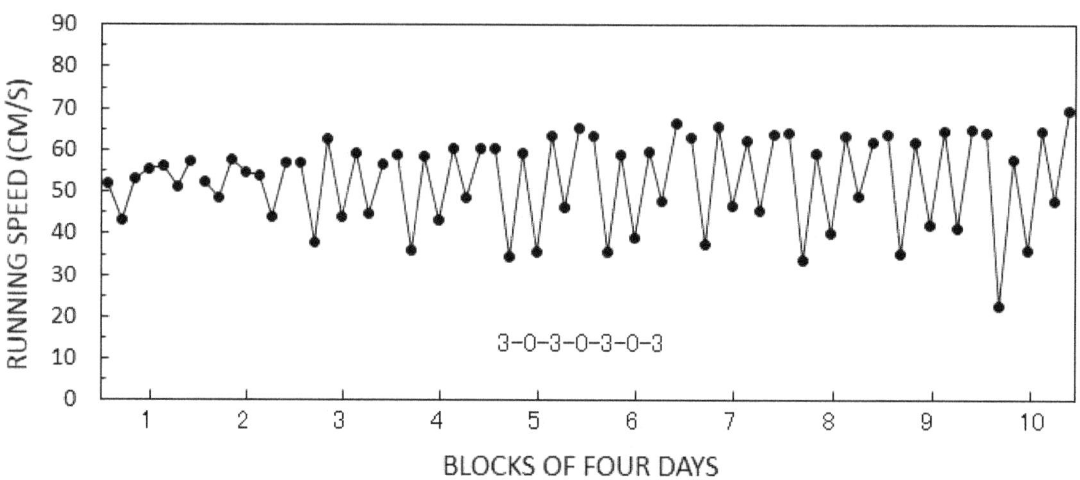

Figure 2. Running speeds on trials in a 3-0-3-0-3-0-3 series in blocks of four days in Experiment 2. Trials were separated by a 20 min ITI.

Another possible source for a discriminative cue of a forthcoming reward event is a distinctive odor that is emitted by other subjects. For example, Ludvingson and Sytsma (1967) showed that rats emitted specific odors when they encountered a reward or a nonreward and that the subjects following them could utilize it as a discriminative stimulus for a forthcoming reward event in a double alternation series of reward and nonreward in a straight runway. In Experiment 2, it is possible that mice could utilize such odor stimuli from preceding subjects to discriminate the reward event on a trial. To test for this possibility, we compared the mice's performance when they were run as the first subject versus the second to fourth subjects in daily training. Mice running after the first could possibly use the odor cue from preceding subjects. However, for the first mouse, no such odor cue on the first trial or discrepant odor cue from the fourth mouse on the immediately preceding trial should be present. Given that the order of running was varied irregularly day by day, the possible odor cue might be valid for three-fourths of the sessions for all subjects, but not valid for one-fourth of the sessions. Therefore, if an odor cue from other subjects were a dominant discriminative cue for differential running, the mice's performance should be better when they were run on the second, third, or fourth turn than on the first turn in a session. Order * Trials * Subjects analysis of variance on the last two blocks revealed a significant main effect of Trials ($F(6, 18) = 25.40$, $p < 0.01$). But the main effect of Order ($F(1, 3) = 0.13$) and the interaction of Order * Trials ($F(6, 18) = 0.74$) were not significant. Absence of significant effects related to running order in a session suggests that the odor cue emitted by other subjects was not a dominant discriminative cue for reward anticipation in Experiment 2.

This discrepancy between the present study and Ludvingson and Sytsma (1967) on the effect of the odor cue from preceding subjects might be explained by the availability of adjacent item associations. Learning a single alternation series could be regarded as a discrimination task that requires animals to discriminate a memory cue of R' (R'-N) from N' (N'-R), where memory of reward item (R') signals a following nonreward item and memory of a nonreward (N') signals a following reward item. In contrast, because the identical memory cues of R' (R'-R and R'-N) and N' (N'-R and N'-N) are followed by both reward and nonreward in a double alternation series, for example, R-R-N-N-R-R-N-N or N-N-R-R-N-N-R-R, a single item memory cue is not an effective discriminative stimulus for a following reward event. Indeed, if the odor cue from a preceding subject became ineffective by destroying a stable relationship between reward events for that preceding subject and the subject that followed, rats could not learn to anticipate reward events in a double alternation series at all (Ludvingson & Sytsma, 1967). The item memory cue might overshadow the odor cue emitted by preceding subjects when it is a good discriminative stimulus for a following reward event. Of course, the inconsistent results with regard to the effect of the odor cue might result from species differences between mice in the present study and rats in Ludvingson and Sytsma (1967). Examining discrimination learning of the odor cue from other subjects in mice would be a worthwhile topic of research.
Present results indicate that mice, like rats, can retain information of reward items for a relatively long interval. However, some deterioration of nonreward anticipation was observed on later serial positions. One possible cause of the gradual deterioration of nonreward anticipation is proactive interference. As mentioned above, learning a single alternation series could be regarded as a discrimination task of a memory cue of R' (R'-N) and N' (N'-R). If memory of a preceding nonrewarded trial (N'), which signals a reward item, is persistent in working memory during a nonreward trial following a rewarded trial, then it will interfere with memory of the reward (R') that signals a nonreward on the current trial. In a spatial working memory task using a radial maze, it was reported that rats could not reset memory of events in preceding trials and showed gradual deterioration of performance caused by proactive interference on subsequent trials (e.g., Cohen, Reid, & Chew, 1994; Roberts & Dale, 1981). The same may hold true for mice in reward serial learning. That is, if mice cannot reset their memory of prior items in a single alternation series, interference among item memories must be greater on later trials than on earlier trials.

Experiment 3

In Experiment 2, nonreward anticipation gradually deteriorated as serial position advanced. One possible explanation for this phenomenon is proactive interference produced by confusion among preceding item memories. Roberts and Dale (1981) explained the magnitude of proactive interference in rats' radial maze performance in terms of temporal discriminability. That is, in subsequent trials, rats have to discriminate event memories of preceding trials from a current trial in terms of a temporal feature determined by the time elapsed from the occurrence of those events. Thus, the temporal discriminability view predicts superior performance given a longer interval between interfering events and target events, which ensures a higher temporal discriminability of those events. Cohen et al. (1994) confirmed this prediction by showing the release of proactive interference in a radial maze task by lengthening the inter-trial interval.

Experiment 3 examined the effects of temporal discriminability among item-memories on a single alternation series performance. Procedures were similar to those of Experiment 2, where a 3-0-3-0-3-0-3-0 series was presented under ITI of 20 min, but in Experiment 3, a 60 min (Phase 1) or a 120 min (Phase 2) interval was inserted between the sixth and the seventh trial (3-0-3-0-3-0/3-0, where the slash represents the lengthened interval). The target behavior in this experiment was the anticipation of the eighth nonreward, signaled mainly by memory of the seventh reward (R'[7]-N[8]). If progressive deterioration of nonreward anticipation was caused by proactive interference among memories of reward events, insertion of the longer interval would be expected to increase discriminability between R'[7] and the preceding memory of nonreward that signaled reward, for example N'[6]-R, and improve the anticipation of N[8].

The other possible cause of progressive deterioration of nonreward anticipation is the influence of differences in hunger level. Because the mice were fed after daily training and first nonreward and last nonreward were separated by more than 120 min under the condition of a 20 min ITI, the level of hunger might have been lowest on the initial trials and highest at the end of the series. A higher hunger level may hinder mice from inhibiting their response to an unbaited goal. Thus, different hunger levels could be a cause of the progressive deterioration of nonreward anticipation. To control for this possible hunger effect, subjects received control trials in which the long interval was inserted between the second and third items (3-0/3-0-3-0-3-0). Therefore, hunger strength should be same on the target eighth nonreward trial of the experimental 3-0-3-0-3-0/3-0 trial and the control 3-0/3-0-3-0-3-0 trial because the elapsed time from the preceding day's feeding to the target eighth item was scheduled to be the same between these conditions. If anticipation of the eighth nonreward item were better on the experimental trials than on the controls, it would suggest that proactive interference among item memories is for a factor in the progressive deterioration of nonreward anticipation.

Method

Subjects. Mice from Experiments 1 and 2 were used. The mice were continuously maintained at 85% of ad-lib body weight from the start of Experiment 2 onwards.

Apparatus. The apparatus was the same as that employed in Experiments 1 and 2.

Experimental training. Phase 1 of Experiment 3 began the day after Experiment 2 finished and lasted for 20 days. A 3-0-3-0-3-0-3-0 series was presented under an ITI of 20 min once per day. A long ITI of 60 min was inserted between sixth and seventh items (3-0-3-0-3-0/3-0) of the experimental trials, whereas a long ITI was inserted between second and third items (3-0/3-03-0-3-0) of the control trials. Half of the subjects received the experimental trial on odd days and the control trial on even days. For the other half of the subjects, assignments were reversed. All of other aspects of the training procedure were the same as in Experiment 2.

Phase 2 of Experiment 3 began the day after Phase 1 finished and lasted for 20 days. In Phase 2, the long ITI was extended to 120 min. All other aspects of the training procedure were the same as in Phase 1.

Results and Discussion

The top panel of Figure 3 shows running speeds for each trial of the experimental condition (3-0-3-0-3-0/3-0) and the control condition (3-0/3-0-3-0-3-0) in Phase 1. Planned comparisons using the Dunn-Sidak method showed no reliable differences between the experimental and control conditions in all serial positions (*DS* = -0.68, -0.92, 1.75, 1.10, -0.96, 0.77, -0.46, and 1.96, *ps* > 0.05 for Runs 1-8, respectively). The data shown in the top panel of Figure 3 were subjected to a Trials * Conditions * Subjects analysis of variance. The analysis revealed a significant main effect of Trials ($F(7, 21) = 19.24$, $p < 0.01$). Paired comparisons by t-test with a nominal significance level regulated by Ryan's method revealed that running speeds were slower on all nonreward trials than on all reward trial (*p*s < 0.05). In addition, mice ran more slowly to a nonreward on Trial 2 than on Trial 6 and Trial 8 (*p*s < 0.05). These results show reliable nonreward anticipation and its progressive deterioration, but they do not suggest a recovery from the progressive deterioration of nonreward anticipation by the insertion of the 60 min interval.

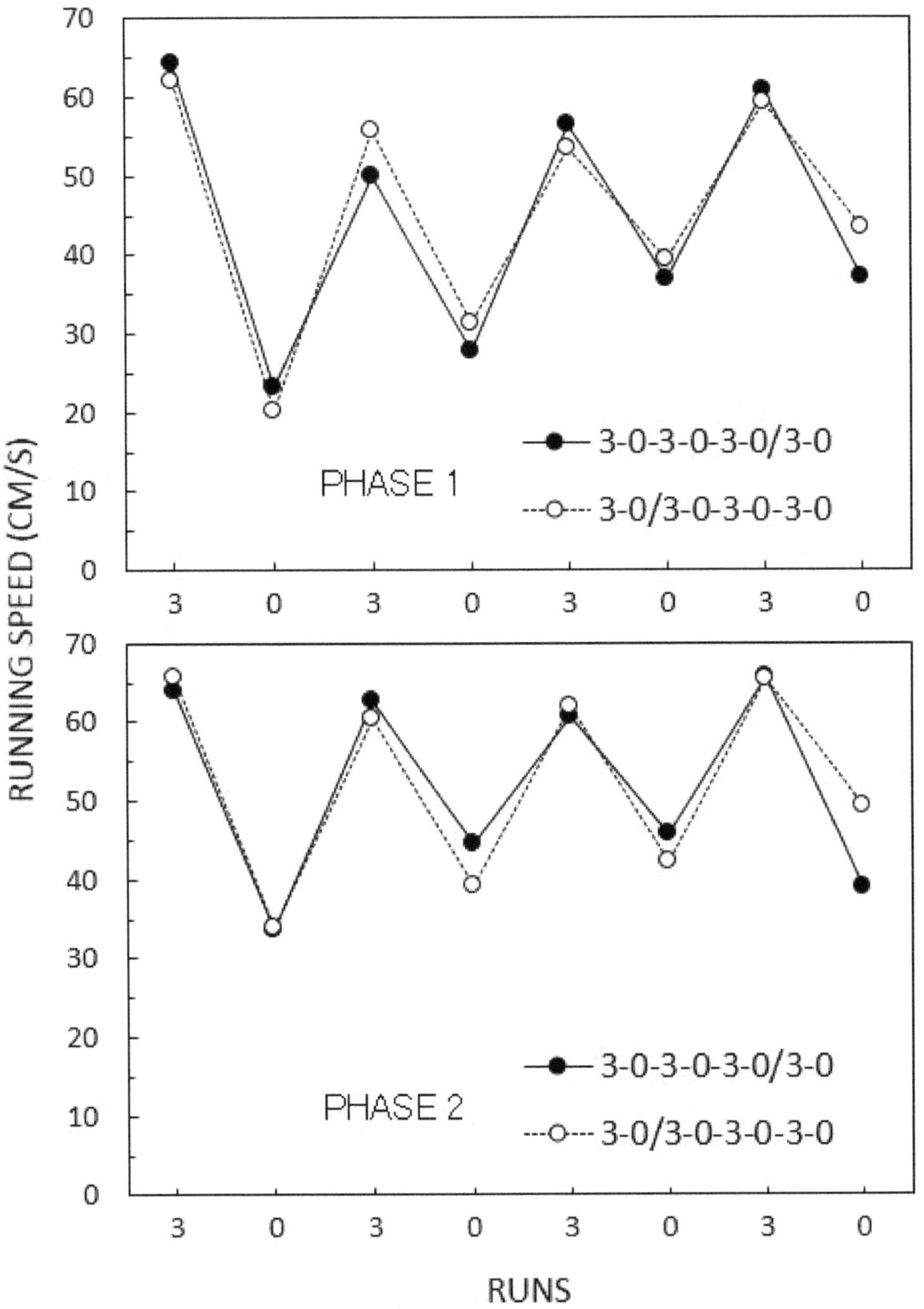

Figure 3. Running speeds on trials in a 3-0-3-0-3-0-3-0 series in Experiment 3. A 60 min (Phase 1: top panel) or 120 min (Phase 2: bottom panel) ITI was inserted between the fifth and sixth trials (3-0-3-0-3-0/3-0) or the second and third trials (3-0/3-0-3-0-3-0). Other ITIs, represented by hyphens, lasted 20 min.

Roberts and Dale (1981) predicted a lessening of proactive interference by increased temporal discriminability among events to be memorized. They did not find any decrease in the proactive interference effect in a radial maze task by extending the inter-trial interval from 1 min to 4 min. However, later studies found a complete release from proactive interference in a spatial memory task with a 120 min ITI (e.g., Cohen et al., 1994). Thus, it is probable that insertion of a 60 min interval was not adequate to provide sufficient temporal discriminability for recovery from proactive interference among memories of reward events in Phase 1. To test this possibility, the long ITI was extended to 120 min in Phase 2.

The bottom panel of Figure 3 shows running speeds in Phase 2. Planned comparisons using the Dunn-Sidak method showed that mice ran more slowly on Trial 8 of the experimental condition than on that of control condition and that running speeds did not differ significantly on all other trials ($DS = 3.10$, $p < 0.05$ for Run 8; $DS = 0.54$, 0.10, -0.70, -1.55, 0.34, -1.01, and -0.09, $p > 0.05$ for Runs 1-7, respectively). A Trials * Conditions * Subjects analysis of variance revealed a significant main effect of Trials ($F(7, 21) = 29.08$, $p < 0.01$) and interaction of Trials * Conditions ($F(7, 21) = 2.53$, $p < 0.05$). Simple effects of Conditions on each trial were significant for Trial 8 ($F(1, 24) =9.63$, $p < 0.01$) but not for the other trials ($ps > 0.13$).

Results revealed by planned comparisons and ANOVA demonstrate a reliable decrease in proactive interference by the insertion of a 120 min ITI between the signal of a target nonreward and prior items. Since appetitive motivational strength for food reward should not have differed between the experimental and control conditions, the slower running for the eighth target nonreward in the experimental condition versus the control condition may provide evidence of a decrease in proactive interference among preceding item memories. The influence of the reinforcement-omission effect (e.g., Amsel, 1958; Stout et al., 2003) does not seem to be an adequate explanation for the results of Experiment 3. First, we know that the reinforcement-omission effect occurs within a relatively short temporal interval. For example, Stout et al. (2003) reported that lengthening the interval between the sudden omission of reinforcement and the next opportunity of response from 2 s to 20 s eliminated the reinforcement-omission effect completely. Although the experimental situation and variables in the present study differ from Stout et al. (2003), it is unlikely that lengthening ITI from 20 min to 120 min decreases the possible reinforcement-omission effect substantially and affects performance on subsequent trials. Second, no apparent decrease of response invigoration on the third or seventh reward trial following the 120 min interval was observed. If insertion of the longer 120 min ITI were to decrease frustration and result in response invigoration, running speed should have decreased even on reward trials following the longer ITI. Therefore, the influence of the reinforcement-omission effect seems to be excluded as a possible explanation of slower running on the eighth nonreward trial following the longer ITI.

One may also ask why a gradual deterioration of anticipation of the reward event was observed only on the nonreward trials since proactive interference should have produced greater confusion of reward and nonreward trials, even on the later reward trials. This problem might be related to the experimental paradigm of the present study. Learning a single alternation series of reward and nonreward could be regarded as one variation of a Go/No-Go task. In the Go/No-Go discrimination paradigm, poor performance is generally characterized by an indifferent active response to No-Go negative stimuli as well as Go positive ones, whereas good performance is usually shown by the development of response suppression only on No-Go trials (e.g., Izumi, 2001). The same is true for rats' serial learning, where poor reward anticipation is generally shown by indifferent fast running to larger rewards as well as smaller or nonrewards (e.g., Capaldi et al., 1986; Hulse & Dorsky, 1977, 1979). Gradual deterioration of nonreward anticipation might not be detectable in reward trials in Experiment 3 because both good anticipation of a reward and poor discrimination of a reward event, caused by proactive interference, could lead to fast running on reward trials in a single alternation series. It would be worth reexamining proactive interference in single alternation learning using another discrimination paradigm, for example, spatial alternation learning in a T-maze, because gradual deterioration of performance on both item trials, left and right goals, could be detected correctly in such a simultaneous discrimination.

A decrease in proactive interference by increased temporal discriminability among memories has been supported by many different types of animal memory studies, such as spatial memory tasks on the radial maze (Cohen et al., 1994) or nonspatial matching to sample tasks (D'Amato, 1973). The findings in Experiment 3 confirm the further generality of effects of temporal discriminability on proactive interference in serial learning.

Another factor said to affect the strength of proactive interference is item discriminability based on item materials. In a rat spatial memory task, a change in the floor texture of arms of the radial maze decreased proactive interference (Cohen et al., 1994). A rhesus monkey study in which animals were required to memorize photographs revealed release from proactive interference by changing the categories of objects in photographs (Jitsumori, Wright, & Cook, 1989; Jitsumori, Wright, & Shyan, 1989). Examining the effects of change in item quality on proactive inference in mice reward serial learning may clarify these issues.

Experiment 4

Experiments 2 and 3 demonstrated that mice could retain item information for at least 20 min. In addition, mice run reliably faster to a reward that follows a 60 min or 120 min interval than to a nonreward. Although this faster running to a reward following to a long interval might reflect the persistent retention of a prior nonreward item by mice, it also could be interpreted as a nondifferential response caused by forgetting prior item information. It has been shown that rats can still respond differentially to reward and nonreward of a single alternation series under an ITI of 24 h (Capaldi & Lynch, 1966; Jobe, Mellgren, Feinberg, Littlejohn, & Rigby, 1977). Mice also show persistent retention of spatial information assessed by spontaneous alternation behavior in a T-maze (e.g., Jaffard, Dubois, & Galey, 1981), but there has been no previous research examining the temporal persistence of memory retention of reward events in mice. Experiment 4 investigated the ability of mice to retain reward item information over a longer interval than in Experiments 2 and 3 by examining the concurrent acquisition of a 5-0 and 0-5 series presented with a 180 min ITI. If mice could retain information about the first items for 180 min, then differentiated responses to the second items of a 5-0 and 0-5 series would be expected.

Several studies have shown that rats can utilize different levels of food deprivation as an interoceptive discriminative cue in a conditional place discrimination task (Bloomberg & Webb, 1949; Jenkins & Hanratty, 1949) or in an aversive classical conditioning situation (Davidson, Flynn, & Jarrard, 1992). Therefore, potential differential motivational levels caused by consumption of the first items of a 5-0 and 0-5 series could possibly mediate discriminative responding to second items in these series. In order to eliminate this possibility, five food pellets were delivered to the waiting cage 1 min after the completion of the first trial of a 0-5 series in Phase 2 of Experiment 4. This procedure ensured an equalization of the potential motivational level on the second trial of both series. If a differential response to second items were observed under this condition, it would strongly suggest that memories of first items of both series served as discriminative stimuli for the second items.

Method

Subjects. Mice from Experiments 1-3 were used as subjects. The body weights of the subjects were continuously maintained at the same level as Experiment 3.

Apparatus. The apparatus was the same as that employed in the previous experiments.

Experimental training. Phase 1 began on the day after Experiment 3 was finished and lasted for 40 days. Subjects received either of a 5-0 and 0-5 series once per day under an ITI of 180 min. Half of the subjects received the 5-0 and 0-5 series in random order per two-day blocks and the other half in reverse order of presentation. All other aspects of the training procedure were same as in Experiment 1.

Phase 2 began the day after Phase 1 was finished and lasted for 40 days. In Phase 2, mice received five 45 mg food pellets in the waiting cage about 1 min after the mice received the first nonreward of the 0-5 series and were placed in the waiting cage. All other aspects of the training procedure were the same as in Phase 1.

Results and Discussion

The left panel of Figure 4 shows running speeds on each trial of the 5-0 and 0-5 series under an ITI of 180 min in Phase 1. With training, a differential response developed on Trial 2. The data shown in the left panel of Figure 4 were subjected to a Series * Blocks * Trials * Subjects analysis of variance. The analysis revealed a significant main effect of Series ($F(1, 3) = 36.84$, $p < 0.01$) and Trials ($F(1, 3) = 73.72$, $p < 0.01$), and Series * Trials interaction ($F(1, 3) = 11.17$, $p < 0.05$). Simple main effects showed that running speeds of the two series were significantly differentiated on Trial 2 ($p < 0.01$) but not on Trial 1.

The right panel of Figure 4 shows running speeds in Phase 2. Although a differential response to the second item disappeared in the first block, it recovered soon with training. A Series * Blocks * Trials * Subjects analysis of variance revealed a significant main effect of Series ($F(1, 3) = 22.25$, $p < 0.02$) and Blocks ($F(3, 9) = 11.55$, $p < 0.01$), and Series * Trials interaction ($F(1, 3) = 64.85$, $p < 0.01$). Simple main effects showed that running speeds of the two series were significantly differentiated on Trial 2 ($p < 0.01$) but not on Trial 1.

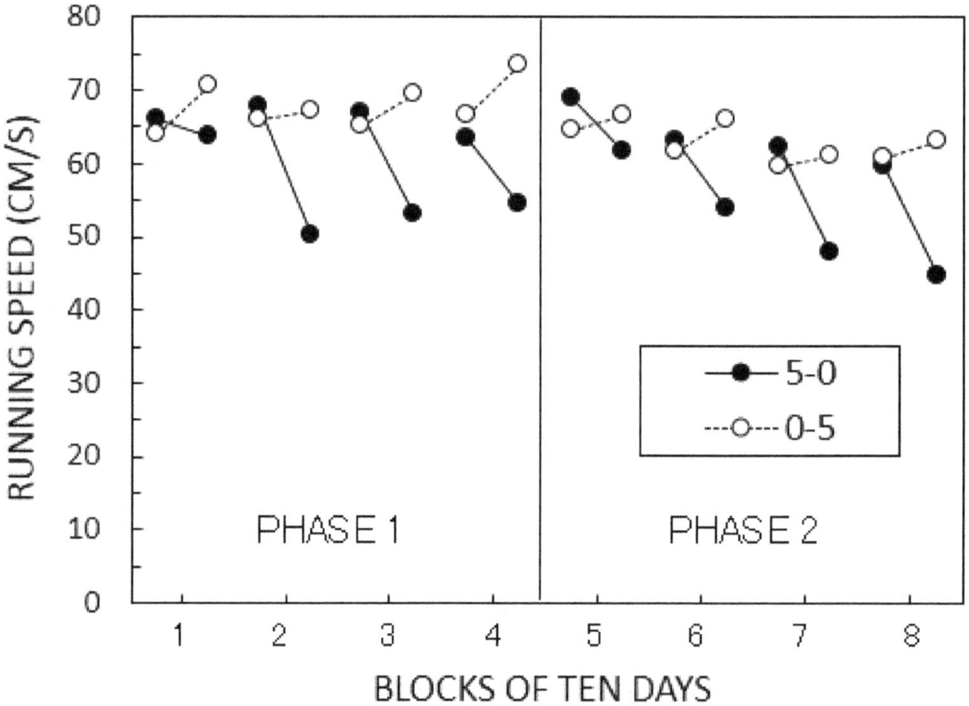

Figure 4. Running speeds on trials in a 5-0 and 0-5 series in blocks of ten days in Experiment 4. Runs were separated by a 180 min ITI. In Phase 2, five food pellets were delivered in a waiting cage 60 s after the first 0 pellet trial of the 0-5 series was presented.

On the first trial of Phase 1, mice only received food rewards in the 5-0 series, not in the 0-5 series, whereas in Phase 2, they received food rewards on the first trial of both the 5-0 series (in the goal box) and the 0-5 series (in the waiting cage). Mice showed reliable anticipation of reward magnitude under an ITI of 180 min in Phase 1, and this performance was maintained under conditions where motivational differences would not have served as discriminative stimuli in Phase 2. These findings indicate that mice can retain item information of a reward series, as well as spatial information (Jaffard et al., 1981), for long intervals.

Anticipation of the second item temporarily deteriorated when feeding control in the waiting cage was introduced in Phase 2. However, if a motivational level were utilized as discriminative stimuli during Phase 1, rapid recover of performance in Phase 2 would not be expected. Therefore, the deterioration of item anticipation at the beginning of Phase 2 might reflect some retrospective interference from the reward event that occurred in waiting cage to memory of the first item of a 0-5 series. Although it is shown that feeding during the retention period did not interfere in rat spatial memory tasks, where spatial item information and intervening reward stimulus were dissimilar (Maki, Brokofsky, & Berg, 1979), in the present study, the item event to be retained and the intervening event were quite similar. This similarity of the item event and the intervening event might produce a retrospective interference effect.

General Discussion

In rat reward serial learning, rewards delivered in a fixed order for instrumental responses have been probed as to function as sources signaling following reward events, as well as reinforcers for instrumental responses. In the present study, mice could also utilize reward events as discriminative stimuli to predict following reward events, running faster to rewards and slower to nonrewards. Moreover, such differential responses, manifested under ITIs of 20 min or 180 min, demonstrated persistent retention of item information in mice. These results are similar to those of rat studies and confirm some generality of basic cognitive capacity for reward serial learning among rodents.

Although many rat studies did not report running speed on each serial position of single alteration series, Ishida (1981) reported no gradual deterioration in anticipation of nonreward in rats. In a single alteration series of reward events, there are only two types of reward events, that is R and N. Thus, strength of proactive interference is mainly decided by the persistence of a preceding item memory and the ability to discriminate those item memories in terms of temporal information. Since it has been documented, as previously mentioned, that rats could retain item information for 24 h (Capaldi & Lynch, 1966; Jobe et al., 1977), the absence of evidence for the proactive interference effect may represent the rats' prominent ability to discriminate item memories based on the elapsed time information from the occurrence of the events. This view may be consistent with the results of Experiment 1, which showed slower learning of a single alternation series in mice compared with previous rat studies (Flaherty & Davenport, 1972; Tyler et al., 1953).

Given that there are no guarantees about the equality of experimental variables for previous rat studies and the present mouse experiments, some inconsistency might be produced by differences in effects of some experimental variables among the experiments with these two species, rather than in the cognitive capacities of rats and mice. The type of experimental paradigm might also affect single alternation series learning. As mentioned above, acquisition of a single alternation series of reward and nonreward events could be regarded as a form of the Go/No-Go task. It has been pointed out that the Go/No-Go task not only measures discrimination learning ability but also impulsivity that affects response suppression on No-Go trials (e.g., Winstanley, 2011). Therefore, species differences between rats and mice in single alternation learning in the present study may reflect not only differences in serial learning ability but also in impulsivity between these species.

In addition, the small number of subjects and their continuous participation across the four experiments might make it difficult to interpret some of the statistical results in the present study. For example, a tendency toward increasing running speeds as the series progressed was shown for reward trials in Experiment 1 and nonreward trials in Experiment 2, but this tendency was significant only for Experiment 2. Due to the small number of subjects, it may not be possible to detect some phenomena statistically in the present study. Also, as this gradually increasing tendency of running speeds was obvious on reward trials in Experiment 1, but not in Experiment 2, it is difficult to determine whether such differences can be attributed to differences in ITIs between the experiments or if the extended training of subjects from Experiment 1 to Experiment 2 produced a ceiling effect on running performance. Examination of the generality of proactive interference effects in mice across a wide range of variables and experimental paradigms with a larger number of subjects is necessary to identify possible causes for the inconsistent results between rats and mice.

Although acquisition of a single alteration series suggests that mice can utilize item information when there are only two variations in this information, which can be clearly distinguished from each other, rats have proved that they are able to learn a reward series constructed from varied food quantities, to form item associations between remote items as well as adjacent items (Capaldi & Miller, 1988b), and to utilize an integrated series chunk as a discriminative stimulus for a later series (Capaldi, 1992; Capaldi et al., 1990). Moreover, rats can choose the larger food item among four different spatial locations by anticipating it based on concurrent learning of four different reward series (Phelps & Roberts, 1991; Wathen & Roberts, 1994). As a next step for research, more complex or higher order serial learning should be examined in mice.

In addition, several cognitive processes which mediate rats' serial learning have been hypothesized. Memory-discrimination learning theory (Capaldi & Molina, 1979) assumes that rats form item-associations, and that stimulus generalization among signals of the associations and reward-signal strength of each signal, determines the strength of instrumental response to items in a series. When similar items signal dissimilar items in a series, anticipation of those items becomes difficult (Capaldi et al., 1980). SPAM (Sequential Pairwise Associative Memory), an associative model of serial learning developed by Wallace and Fountain (2002), assumes composition of item memory as a determinant of item retrieval (Fountain, 2008; Wallance & Fountain, 2002). In addition to item association, rats seem to be able to learn the serial position of items or the number of trials, in circumstances where a simple item cue could not be an effective discriminative cue for a subsequent item (Capaldi & Miller, 1988a; Taniuchi, 2000). Moreover, rats may extract the abstract relationship between adjacent items and learn the formal structure of a series. Rats can learn to anticipate a nonreward of a 14-7-3-1-0 monotonic series more easily than a 14-1-3-7-0 non-monotonic series (Hulse & Dorsky, 1977), and they learn a long series more smoothly when it is "phrased" into subpatterns with a simple formal structure (Fountain, Henne, & Hulse, 1984). Therefore, rats' serial learning suggests that it is mediated by different learning processes that require encoding of item information at various levels. However, these various phenomena and possible learning processes in reward serial learning have not been examined in other rodents.

In serial pattern learning, which requires animals to track signals presented in different spatial locations, temporal phrasing of complex patterns into simple sub-patterns facilitates learning in rats (Fountain & Rowan, 1995; Stempowski et al., 1999), whereas it impairs performance of mice (Fountain et al., 1999). This inconsistency in the effects of temporal phrasing on rats versus mice strongly suggests the necessity of examining whether we can generalize the findings in rat reward serial learning to other rodent species.

Fountain et al. (1999) suggested two possible cognitive differences between rats and mice based on different effects of phrasing in spatial serial learning. First, that rats and mice differ qualitatively in using a phrasing cue. This possibility might be related to cognitive ability in chunking multiple events. Second, rats and mice share similar cognitive abilities, but mice have less working memory capacity such that they cannot process serial events and phrasing cues concurrently. These ideas might guide our future examination of species differences between rats and mice in serial learning. That is, we may be able to compare these species by a chunking paradigm in a runway situation (Capaldi, 1992; Capaldi et al., 1990; Fountain et al., 1984), a multiple series learning paradigm (e.g., Phelps & Roberts, 1991; Wathen & Roberts, 1994), or in terms of simple working memory capacity (e.g., Cole & Chappell-Stephenson, 2003). Species differences between rats and mice have also been reported in spatial memory (Frick, Stillner, & Berger-Sweeney, 2000; Stranahan, 2011) but not in object recognition memory (Frick et al., 2000). Considering the discrepancy in results between rats and mice in phrasing effects and some memory tasks, it is obvious that the generality of a wide range of findings in rat reward serial learning and assumed learning processes should be examined in mice to identify species' differences in cognitive processes.

Acknowledgements

I thank Mauricio R. Papini for his helpful comments on an earlier version of this article.

References

Amsel, A. (1958). The role of frustrative nonreward in noncontinuous reward situations. *Psychological Bulletin*, *55*, 102-119.

Bloomberg, R., & Webb, W. B. (1949). Various degrees within a single drive as cues for spatial response learning in the white rat. *Journal of Experimental Psychology*, *39*, 628-636.

Brunner, D. (1999). Preference for sequences of rewards: Further tests of a parallel discounting model. *Behavioural Processes*, *45*, 87-99.

Brunner, D., & Gibbon, J. (1995) Value of food aggregates: Parallel versus serial discounting. *Animal Behaviour*, *50*, 1627-1634.

Capaldi, E. J. (1992). Levels of organized behavior in rats. In W. K. Honig & J. G. Fetterman (Eds.), *Cognitive aspects of stimulus control* (pp. 385-404). Hillsdale, NJ: Erlbaum.

Capaldi, E. J. (1994). The sequential view: From rapidly fading stimulus traces to the organization of memory and the abstract concept of number. *Psychonomic Bulletin & Review*, *1*, 156-181.

Capaldi, E. J., & Lynch, D. (1966). Patterning at 24-hour ITI: Resolution of a discrepancy more apparent than real. *Psychonomic Science*, *6*, 229-230.

Capaldi, E. J., & Miller, D. J. (1988a). Counting in rats: Its functional significance and the independent cognitive processes that constitute it. *Journal of Experimental Psychology: Animal Behavior Processes*, *14*, 3-17.

Capaldi, E. J., & Miller, D. J. (1988b). The rat's simultaneous anticipation of remote events and current events can be sustained by event memories alone. *Animal Learning & Behavior*, *16*, 1-7.

Capaldi, E. J., Miller, D. J., Alptekin, S., & Barry, K. (1990). Organized responding in instrumental learning: Chunks and superchunks. *Learning and Motivation*, *21*, 415-433.

Capaldi, E. J., & Molina, P. (1979). Element discriminability as a determinant of serial-pattern learning. *Animal Learning & Behavior*, *7*, 318-322.

Capaldi, E. J., Nawrocki, T. M., Miller, D. J., & Verry, D. R. (1985). An examination into some variables said to affect serial learning. *Animal Learning & Behavior*, *13*, 129-136.

Capaldi, E. J., Nawrocki, T. M., Miller, D. J., & Verry, D. R. (1986). Grouping, chunking, memory, and learning. *The Quarterly Journal of Experimental Psychology*, *38B*, 53-80.

Capaldi, E. J., Nawrocki, T. M., & Verry, D. R. (1983). The nature of anticipation: An inter- and intraevent process. *Animal Learning & Behavior*, *11*, 193-198.

Capaldi, E. J., & Verry, D. R. (1981). Serial order anticipation learning in rats: Memory for multiple hedonic events and their order. *Animal Learning & Behavior*, *9*, 441-453.

Capaldi, E. J., Verry, D. R., & Davidson, T. L. (1980). Memory, serial anticipation pattern learning, and transfer in rats. *Animal Learning & Behavior*, *8*, 575-585.

Capaldi, E. J., Verry, D. R., Nawrocki, T. M., & Miller, D. J. (1984). Serial learning, interitem associations, phrasing cues, interference, overshadowing, chunking, memory, and extinction. *Animal Learning & Behavior, 12*, 7-20.

Cohen, J. S., Reid, S., & Chew, K. (1994). Effects of varying trial distribution, intra- and extramaze cues, and amount of reward on proactive interference in the radial maze. *Animal Learning & Behavior, 22*, 134-142.

Cole, M. R., & Chappell-Stephenson, R. (2003). Exploring the limits of spatial memory in rats, using very large mazes. *Learning & Behavior, 31*, 349-368.

D'Amato, M. R. (1973). Delayed matching and short-term memory in monkeys. In G. H. Bower (Ed.), *The psychology of learning and motivation: Advances in research and theory* (Vol.7, pp. 227-269). New York, NY: Academic Press.

Davidson, T. L., Flynn, F. W., & Jarrard, L. E. (1992). Potency of food deprivation intensity cues as discriminative stimuli. *Journal of Experimental Psychology: Animal Behavior Processes, 18*, 174-181.

Flaherty, C. F., & Davenport, J. W. (1972). Successive brightness discrimination in rats following regular versus random intermittent reinforcement. *Journal of Experimental Psychology, 96*, 1-9.

Fountain, S. B. (2008). Pattern structure and rule induction in sequential learning. *Comparative Cognition & Behavior Reviews, 3*, 66-85.

Fountain, S. B., Henne, D. R., & Hulse, S. H. (1984). Phrasing cues and hierarchical organization in serial pattern learning by rats. *Journal of Experimental Psychology: Animal Behavior Processes, 10*, 30-45.

Fountain, S. B., & Hulse, S. H. (1981). Extrapolation of serial stimulus patterns by rats. *Animal Learning & Behavior, 9*, 381-384.

Fountain, S. B., Krauchunas, S. M., & Rowan, J.D. (1999). Serial-pattern learning in mice: Pattern structure and phrasing. *The Psychological Record, 49*, 173-192.

Fountain, S. B., & Rowan, J. D. (1995). Sensitivity to violations of "run" and "trill" structures in rat serial-pattern learning. *Journal of Experimental Psychology: Animal Behavior Processes, 21*, 78-81.

Frick, K. M., Stillner, E. T., & Berger-Sweeney, J. (2000). Mice are not little rats: Species differences in a one-day water maze task. *NeuroReport, 11*, 3461-3465.

Haggbloom, S. J., Birmingham, K. M., & Scranton, D. L. (1992). Hierarchical organization of series information by rats: Series chunks and list chunks. *Learning and Motivation, 23*, 183-199.

Haggbloom, S. J., & Brooks, D. M. (1985). Serial anticipation and pattern extrapolation in rats as a function of element discriminability. *Animal Learning & Behavior, 13*, 303-308.

Hulse, S. H., & Dorsky, N. P. (1977). Structural complexity as a determinant of serial pattern learning. *Learning and Motivation, 8*, 488-506.

Hulse, S. H., & Dorsky, N. P. (1979). Serial pattern learning by rats: Transfer of a formally defined stimulus relationship and the significance of nonreinforcement. *Animal Learning & Behavior, 7*, 211-220.

Ishida, M. (1981). Persistent resistance to extinction of single alternating reinforcement after long acquisition-extinction interval. *The Journal of General Psychology, 104*, 191-201.

Izumi, A. (2001). Relative pitch perception in Japanese Monkeys (*Macaca fuscata*). *Journal of Comparative Psychology, 115*, 127-131.

Jaffard, R., Dubois, M., & Galey, D. (1981). Memory of a choice direction in a T-maze as measured by spontaneous alternation in mice: Effects of intertrial interval and reward. *Behavioral Processes, 6*, 11-21.

Jenkins, J. J., & Hanratty, J. A. (1949). Drive intensity discrimination in the albino rat. *Journal of Comparative & Physiological Psychology, 42*, 228-232.

Jitsumori, M., Wright, A. A., & Cook, R. G. (1988) Long-term proactive interference and novelty enhancement effects in monkey list memory. *Journal of Experimental Psychology: Animal Behavior Processes, 14*, 146-154.

Jitsumori, M., Wright, A. A., & Shyan, M. R. (1989). Buildup and release from proactive interference in a rhesus monkey. *Journal of Experimental Psychology: Animal Behavior Processes*, *15*, 329-337.

Jobe, J. B., Mellgren, R. L., Feinberg, R. A., Littlejohn, R. L., & Rigby, R. L. (1977). Patterning, partial reinforcement, and N-length as a function of reinstatement of retrieval cues. *Learning and Motivation*, *8*, 77-97.

Ludvigson, H. W., & Sytsma, D. (1967). The sweet smell of success: Apparent double alternation in the rat. *Psychonomic Science*, *9*, 283-284.

Maki, W. S., Brokofsky, S., & Berg, B. (1979). Spatial memory in rats: Resistance to retroactive interference. *Animal Learning & Behavior*, *7*, 25-30.

Phelps, M. T., & Roberts, W. A. (1991). Pattern tracking on the radial maze: Tracking multiple patterns at different spatial locations. *Journal of Experimental Psychology: Animal Behavior Processes*, *17*, 411-422.

Roberts, W. A., & Dale, R. H. (1981). Remembrance of places lasts: Proactive inhibition and patterns of choice in rat spatial memory. *Learning and Motivation*, *12*, 261-281.

Stempowski, N. K., Carman, H. M., & Fountain, S. B. (1999). Temporal phrasing and overshadowing in rat serial-pattern learning. *Learning and Motivation*, *30*, 74-100.

Stout, S. C., Boughner, R. L., & Papini, M. R. (2003). Reexamining the frustration effect in rats: Aftereffects of surprising reinforcement and nonreinforcement. *Learning and Motivation*, *34*, 437-456.

Stranahan, A. M. (2011). Similarities and differences in spatial learning and object recognition between young male C57Bl/6J mice and Sprague-Dawley rats. *Behavioral Neuroscience*, *125*, 791-795.

Taniuchi, T. (1995). Interseries transfer and effect of retention interval in rats' serial pattern learning. *Japanese Journal of Animal Psychology*, *45*, 21-29. (In Japanese with English abstract)

Taniuchi, T. (2000). Relative memory load as a determinant of learning process in reward serial learning by rats. *Japanese Journal of Animal Psychology*, *50*, 41-48.

Terrace, H. S. (2005). The simultaneous chain: A new approach to serial learning. *Trends in Cognitive Sciences*, *9*, 202- 210.

Tyler, D. W., Wortz, E. C., & Bitterman, M. E. (1953). The effect of random and alternating partial reinforcement on resistance to extinction in the rat. *American Journal of Psychology*, *66*, 57-65.

Wallace, D. G., & Fountain, S. B. (2002). What is learned in sequential learning? An associative model of reward magnitude serial-pattern learning. *Journal of Experimental Psychology: Animal Behavior Processes*, *28*, 43-63.

Wathen, C. N., & Roberts, W. A. (1994). Multiple-pattern learning by rats on an eight-arm radial maze. *Animal Learning & Behavior*, *22*, 155-164.

Winstanley, C. A. (2011). The utility of rat models of impulsivity in developing pharmacotherapies for impulse control disorders. *British Journal of Pharmacology*, *164*, 1301-1321

6

Spatial Variability in Serial Response Learning and Performance by Pigeons (*Columba livia*)

Walter T. Herbranson, Patricia M. Xi, and Yvan T. Trinh
Whitman College, U.S.A.

Pigeons can learn structured sequences of cued responses and perform them quickly, even when random variability is later introduced into the originally learned sequence, making some cue locations unpredictable. In order to determine if initial learning shows the same tolerance of spatial variability as steady-state performance, naïve pigeons were trained on random distortions around a structured sequence without having seen the original sequence itself. Learning was possible, but accommodated less variability than did performance of the same sequence previously learned in an undistorted context. Analysis of results indicated that performance of a randomly distorted sequence is best when birds are initially trained with little or no variability, and randomness is later introduced in a gradual fashion.

Modern comparative psychology has frequently benefitted from concepts and methods imported from human cognitive psychology. While some cognitive concepts, such as awareness, are virtually impossible to study in nonhuman animals, others lend themselves quite readily to cross-species investigations. Procedural memory, for example, refers to memory for how to perform a behavior (Squire, 2004). As such, investigations of procedural memory are often easier to implement within comparative psychology, as they commonly utilize objective, performance-based measures such as response times, without needing to rely on self-report.

One classic example of a human procedural memory task is the Serial Response Time (SRT) procedure (Nissen & Bullemer, 1987). The procedure involves a participant responding to a series of cues appearing sequentially in four different locations by pressing four corresponding buttons. If the cued locations (and consequently, the required responses) appear in a perpetually repeating sequence, response times become faster as a participant learns to anticipate upcoming cues. The change in response time is due to a participant having learned about the sequence, rather than mere familiarity with the general procedure and apparatus because response times slow immediately when the sequence is later changed to a random one.

A strength of the SRT task is that the dependent variable (median response time) is performance-based, and thus can be easily adapted for use with nonhuman animal populations. Froehlich, Herbranson, Loper, Wood, and Shimp (2004), for example, had pigeons peck lighted cues that appeared on 3 different response keys in perpetually repeating nine-element sequences such as L-C-R-L-R-C-R-L-C- (where L, C, and R indicate the left, center, and right keys respectively). Their results mirrored those of a typical human SRT experiment in that response times gradually became faster when cues appeared according to a repeating sequence, and then slowed immediately when cues appeared in a random order. The difference in response times to predictable cues (in structured conditions) and to unpredictable cues (in random conditions) constitutes *global facilitation*, and is the standard measure of learning in SRT tasks.

Patricia M. Xi is now at Claremont Graduate University. Please send correspondence to Walter Herbranson, Department of Psychology, Whitman College, 345 Boyer Ave, Walla Walla, WA 99362. (Email: mherbrawt@whitman.edu)

While global facilitation is a convenient and concise measure of procedural learning, it may gloss over some details that a finer-grained analysis can reveal. Froehlich et al.'s analysis, for example, indicated that faster response times were a consequence of pigeons having learned probabilities associated with the specific key-to-key transitions that constituted a sequence. As such, some elements in a structured sequence produced faster response times than others. For example, in the sequence specified above, L appears three times, with two instances followed immediately by C, one by R. Correspondingly, the conditional probability of a target appearing on key C given a preceding response on key L is equal to two-thirds. For the same reason, the conditional probability of R given L is one-third. Response times are generally faster on keys having higher conditional probabilities. In this case, if a pigeon had just pecked L, it would respond more quickly to C than to R because the conditional probability $p(C|L)$ is greater than $p(R|L)$. One implication of this finding is that response times are not uniform across a learned sequence. Some transitions within the sequence appear more frequently, and thus contribute disproportionately to the global effect. This key-to-key effect is known as *local facilitation*.

An important consequence of parallel results from humans and pigeons is that the well-established frameworks from human cognition can provide a rich context for investigations of animal learning. For example, SRT learning can progress in humans independently of a functioning hippocampus (Nissen & Bullemer, 1987), as well as under the effects of the amnesia-inducing, anti-cholinergic drug scopolamine (Nissen, Knopman, & Schacter, 1987). These physiological characteristics provide several ready-made hypotheses for parallel manipulations of pigeon SRT learning. In addition to physiological frameworks, several cognitive frameworks simultaneously provide useful context. For example, procedural memory is one of several varieties of implicit memory, along with numerous other learning phenomena such as priming (Tulving & Schacter, 1990), habit formation (Knowlton, Mangels, & Squire, 1996), and artificial grammar learning (Reber, 1967), all of which have also been studied in nonhuman animals (Brodbeck, 1997; Bullock & Bitterman, 1962; Herbranson & Shimp, 2008). The primary characteristic that these different varieties of implicit learning all have in common is their lack of reliance on an intact hippocampus (Squire, 1992).

An additional characteristic that many implicit memory tasks share is that they support considerable variability. For example, weather prediction (Knowlton, Squire, & Gluck, 1994) and artificial grammar learning (Reber, 1967) tasks are two widely used implicit memory tasks, and both involve presentation of stimulus sets that are so complex as to have potentially infinite numbers of exemplars. While the standard SRT stands out among implicit memory tasks in that it does not involve such extreme variability (in fact, the response sequence is highly stereotyped), variability can be incorporated into the procedure and still produce similar results. Howard and Howard (1997) for example, introduced spatial variability into an SRT procedure by alternating predictable cue locations with random ones. Doing so naturally increased the number of different response sequences produced in a session. Nevertheless, even with the increased spatial variability, response time facilitation was still produced. The authors concluded that facilitation was based on learning of specific response pairs and triplets that appeared more frequently than others. This interpretation is consistent with theories about what is learned in other implicit memory tasks. Strings of characters generated by an artificial grammar, for example, may be identified because they are more likely to contain certain letter pairs (bigrams) and triplets (trigrams) than non-grammatical strings (Meulemans & Van der Linden, 1997).

Herbranson and Stanton (2011) took a similar approach to introducing spatial variability in a pigeon version of the SRT. They did so by manipulating cue validity, the likelihood that a particular cue would appear in the location dictated by the sequence. For example, with a cue validity of 0.9, each cue had a 90% chance of appearing on a specific key in accordance with the sequence, and a 10% chance of appearing on a different key, randomly selected from the remaining candidates. After learning the undistorted sequence, cue validity was reduced by 0.1 every 10 days (from 1.0 to 0.9 to 0.8 and so on). As cue validity fell, the magnitude of the global facilitation effect grew correspondingly smaller, down to a cue validity of 0.6. At values less than 0.6, there was no global facilitation effect and responses to valid cues were as slow as responses to invalid ones. Importantly, in conditions that produced significant global facilitation, response times were still based on local predictability. In this case though, local predictability reflected not just the original sequence, but also the declining cue validity parameter. The likelihood that a cue would appear in a particular location (*true* local predictability) is equal to local predictability (the conditional probability as defined above), times cue validity (the probability that the local predictability figure actually applies), and consistently predicted response times across cue validity conditions.

Herbranson and Stanton's pigeons were able to respond quickly, even when cue validity was not 100% as a consequence of having previously learned the undistorted sequence. The intact fragments of the sequence could be executed quickly because they had already been learned in a consistent, unambiguous context. Invalid (randomly distorted) fragments were executed more slowly because they violated the content of that previous learning. When the proportion of intact fragments was high, the global facilitation effect was slightly diminished, but still strong because the majority of targets were valid. In contrast, when cue validity was low and a larger proportion of transitions had been distorted, there were not enough intact transitions to maintain a strong global facilitation effect. Those local transitional probabilities that underlie SRT learning however, might or might not have been learned in the first place had they been obscured by random variability all along.

There are some reasons to expect that it might be possible to learn a response sequence by performing random distortions of that sequence. For example, the original, undistorted sequence might play a role similar to that played by a prototype in categorization. In a classic study, Posner and Keele (1968) had participants learn categories consisting of randomly distorted dot patterns. Later, when shown the original prototype dot pattern from which training exemplars had been generated, its category membership was more easily classified than the actual training stimuli. Huber and Lenz (1996) showed a similar prototype effect with pigeons, training them on exemplar stimuli that varied across multiple dimensions. Later, pigeons produced enhanced responding to previously unseen stimuli that were near the central tendency of the learned category. In the context of categorization, it seems that both humans and pigeons are able to extract regularly occurring features and use those extracted features to classify prototypical stimuli. If a similar process is at work in serial response learning, then one might see a response time equivalent of a prototype effect: a drop in response times to a previously unseen prototype sequence following training on random distortions of that sequence.

The following experiment introduces spatial variability into a serial response time task in the manner of a category learning experiment: by incorporating variability during the acquisition phase. If learning is able to accommodate variability and pigeons can extract the prototype sequence, then we should see global and local facilitation effects in proportion to cue validity, down to a cue validity value of about 0.6. On the other hand, if acquisition is not as tolerant of variability as performance, then birds might only show learning at higher cue validity values, might show a weakened form of response time facilitation, or might not show response time facilitation at all.

Method

Animals

Twelve white Carneau pigeons were purchased from Double T Farm (Glenwood, IA). Each was maintained at 80-85% of free-feeding weight to approximate the condition of healthy wild pigeons (Poling, Nickel, & Alling, 1990). Birds were housed in individual cages in a colony room with a 14:10 hour light: dark cycle, and had continuous access to water and grit. The 12 birds were arbitrarily assigned to four groups of three, designated as: 90% cue validity, 80% cue validity, 70% cue validity, and 60% cue validity.

Apparatus

Four identical BRS/LVE operant chambers were used. Each had three circular response keys (2.5 cm in diameter) located in a horizontal row in the front wall, and a food hopper located directly below the center key. A houselight located on the front wall, directly above the center key was illuminated for the duration of each experimental session.

Procedure

All birds were pretrained in sessions consisting successively of habituation, magazine training, and autoshaping (Brown & Jenkins, 1968) until consistent responding was achieved on each of the three response keys. Stimuli during autoshaping were white key lights.

A daily experimental session consisted of 1,000 trials (gradually increased from 10 over the first 10 days of the experiment). Each trial consisted of a response-to-stimulus (RS) interval of 0.5 s, illumination of one of the three response keys with white light (the *target key*), a peck to the illuminated target key, and (on a random 5% of trials) a reinforcement interval. Illuminated keys remained lit until pecked, and there were no programmed consequences for pecks to unlit keys. A single peck to any lit key either initiated a reinforcement interval of approximately 3 s (durations varied slightly between birds in order to maintain individual running weights), or else passed directly to the RS interval for the next trial. The first trial of a daily session began with the illumination of the target key (without an RS interval), and the rest of the trial progressed as normal.

Target locations for each trial in a session were based on the same fixed nine-element sequence used by Herbranson and Stanton (2011): L-C-R-L-R-C-R-L-C-. Local predictability for individual items in the sequence were either 0.33 (Positions 1, 5, and 6) or 0.67 (Positions 2, 3, 4, 7, 8, and 9). The starting point in the sequence was randomly determined at the beginning of each session. Upon reaching the final element in the sequence, it restarted at the beginning and continued to repeat until the entire 1,000 pecks for a session had been made. The end of one sequence and the beginning of the next were not indicated in any way.

Blocks of training. The experiment consisted of three blocks of sessions. The first block lasted for 35 days, and each daily session during that block consisted of a mix of valid and invalid trials, according to the designated cue validity parameter for each group. Birds in the 90% cue validity group saw 90% valid cues and 10% invalid cues. Similarly, birds in the 80%, 70%, and 60% cue validity groups saw 80%, 70%, and 60% valid cues respectively, with the remainder of cues being invalid. The second block of sessions lasted for 15 days, and consisted entirely of valid cues, regardless of group. The third block of trials lasted for 10 days, and was otherwise identical to the first block, with mixed validity trials presented to each group according to its cue validity parameter (90%, 80%, 70%, or 60%).

During the first and third blocks, sequences deviated from the one specified above based on cue validity, the probability that the target key would be the one specified by the fixed nine-item sequence. Thus, a session with cue validity of 100% (as in Block 2) would consist exclusively of validly cued targets, and precisely match the sequence specified above. A session with imperfect cue validity (any value other than 100%) would consist of both validly cued and invalidly cued targets, and thus differ from the original. For example, in a 90% cue validity condition, each target appeared in the location specified by the sequence with $p = 0.9$, and in one of the other two possible locations (randomly chosen) with $p = 0.1$. Thus, 90% of trials presented validly cued targets, whose locations could be predicted on the basis of the preceding trials. The remaining 10% of trials presented invalidly cued targets, whose locations were inconsistent with the preceding trials. The probabilities applied individually to each and every cue presented during a session. Thus, depending on random variation, each iteration of the sequence might have a larger or smaller percentage of valid trials. Position within the sequence during mixed validity blocks was always preserved, even when invalid targets were presented. For example, the undistorted sequence L-C-R-L-R-C-R-L-C might appear as L-*R*-R-*C*-R-C-R-L-C, if the second and fourth (italicized) elements in the sequence were invalid. Note that the remaining valid targets have retained their original relative positions. Each peck to a lit response key had a 5% chance of resulting in reinforcement, regardless of its location and whether or not it was a valid target.

Results

Average Response Times

Figure 1 displays the average daily median response time for each of the four groups across the entire experiment. Notice that response times for all groups were initially slow (600 ms or more), and dropped to a consistent level of around 400 ms over the first 10 days of training. By the end of Block 1 (35 days), response times for each group were relatively consistent from day to day. During the 15 days that constituted Block 2, there appears some notable separation between groups, and that separation remains through the 10 days of Block 3. The source of the between-groups separation appears to be steadily decreasing response times for the 90% (b = -4.55, $p < 0.01$) and 80% (b = -5.48, $p < 0.01$) cue validity groups during Block 2. The 70% (b = 0.31, p = 0.68) and 60% (b = -0.17, p = 0.88) cue validity groups had slopes that were not significantly different from zero during the same block.

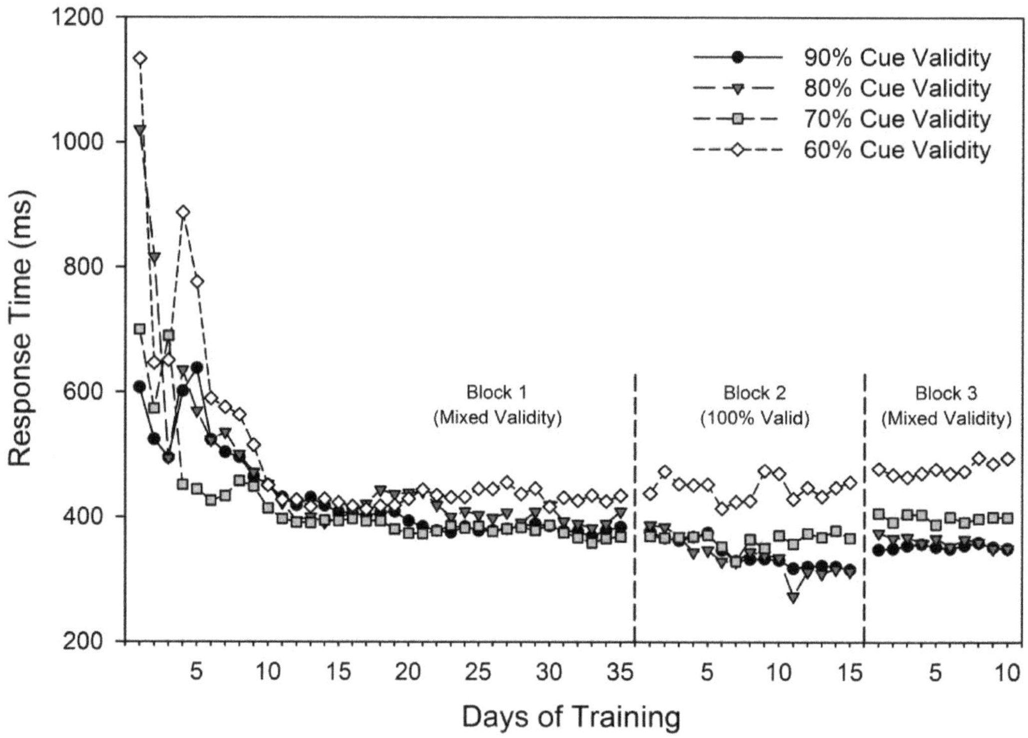

Figure 1. Average daily median response time for each cue validity group across the three blocks of the experiment.

In order to statistically assess the effects of the two independent variables (blocking and cue validity), we ran a 3 (block: mixed validity, 100% valid, mixed validity) x 4 (cue validity condition: 90%, 80%, 70%, 60%) mixed ANOVA on daily median response times from the final 10 days of each block. Block was a repeated-measures factor and condition was a between-groups factor. Averages for each combination of block and cue validity are shown in Figure 2. There was a main effect of blocks indicating that birds performed differently across the three blocks that constituted the experiment ($F(2, 72) = 112.60$, $p < 0.01$, partial $\eta^2 = 0.76$). There was a main effect of cue validity condition, indicating that birds performed differently depending on which of the four conditions they had been arbitrarily assigned to ($F(2, 36) = 405.35$, $p < 0.01$, partial $\eta^2 = 0.97$). Finally, there was an interaction between block and cue validity ($F(6, 72) = 36.16$, $p < 0.01$, partial $\eta^2 = 0.75$). These ANOVA results are consistent with the interpretation that cue validity did influence response times, and confirms some instances of prototype effects. Recall that a prototype effect would be indicated by enhanced responding when shown an undistorted pattern (Block 2) after initial training on distortions of that pattern (Block 1). A post-hoc Tukey test confirmed two prototype effects, as there were significant differences between Blocks 1 and 2 for the 90% and 80% cue validity groups ($p < 0.01$ with Bonferroni correction; marked by asterisks), but not for either of the other two groups.

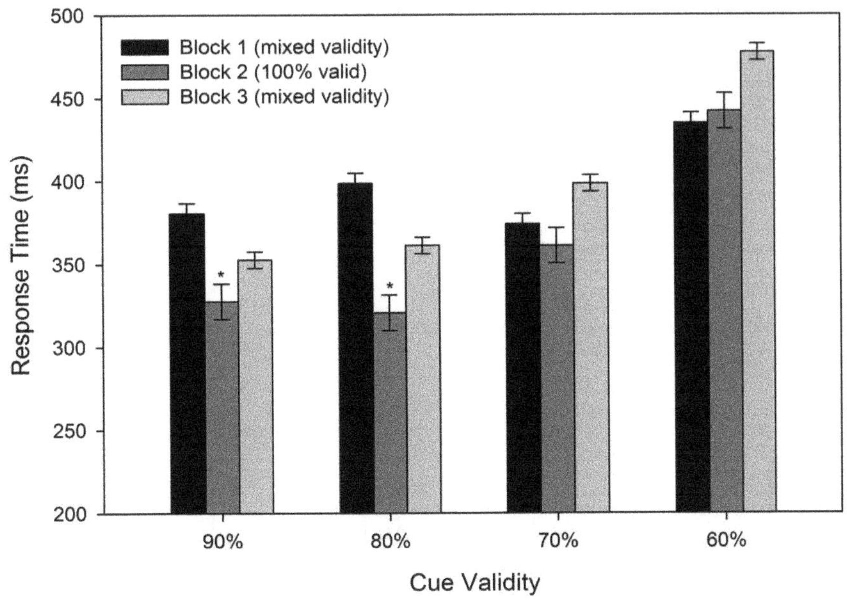

Figure 2. Response times for each cue validity group during Blocks 1, 2, and 3. Significantly reduced response times from Block 1 to Block 2 constitute *prototype effects*, and are designated by asterisks.

Because cue validity condition was a between-groups factor, we cannot confidently attribute differences between cue validity groups to cue validity itself. That is, birds in some groups may have been faster than others to begin with. If so, then we risk misattribution of response time differences between groups to a cue validity effect. Therefore, in order to isolate a possible cue validity effect, we must instead look to additional statistical analyses, presented below.

Cue Validity Effect (Global Facilitation)

Figure 3 shows the effect of cue validity during mixed-validity Blocks 1 (black bars) and 3 (grey bars). This basic measure of global response time facilitation is computed by subtracting the median response time for validly cued targets from the median response time for invalidly cued targets. In this way, general speed differences between birds are factored out under the assumption that they should affect both types of trials in the same manner. This difference could not be computed for Block 2 because it consisted entirely of validly cued targets. During Block 1, the only group to show a significant cue validity effect was the 90% cue validity group, as its 95% confidence interval does not encompass zero (no difference between valid and invalid trials). The remaining groups were approximately as fast to respond to invalidly cued targets as they were to validly cued targets. On Block 3, the cue validity effect for the 90% cue validity group remained significant, and in fact was considerably stronger than it was on Block 1. Furthermore, the 80% cue validity group showed a small but significant cue validity effect during Block 3, while the remaining groups continued to show no effect. Both mixed-validity blocks from the current experiment show a marked contrast with the data from Herbranson & Stanton (2011; white bars) where there is a significant effect at all four cue validity values.

In order to statistically confirm these observations, we ran a 2 (block: 1, 3) x 4 (cue validity condition: 90%, 80%, 70%, 60%) mixed ANOVA on response time facilitation. Block was a repeated-measures factor and condition was a between-groups factor. There was a main effect of block indicating a stronger facilitation effect during Block 3 ($F(1, 36) = 45.65$, $p < 0.01$, partial $\eta^2 = 0.56$). There was a main effect of cue validity indicating that higher cue validity values produced stronger response time facilitation ($F(3, 36) = 94.21$, $p < 0.01$, partial $\eta^2 = 0.89$). There was also a significant interaction between block and cue validity, ($F(3, 36) = 8.44$, $p < 0.01$, partial $\eta^2 = 0.41$).

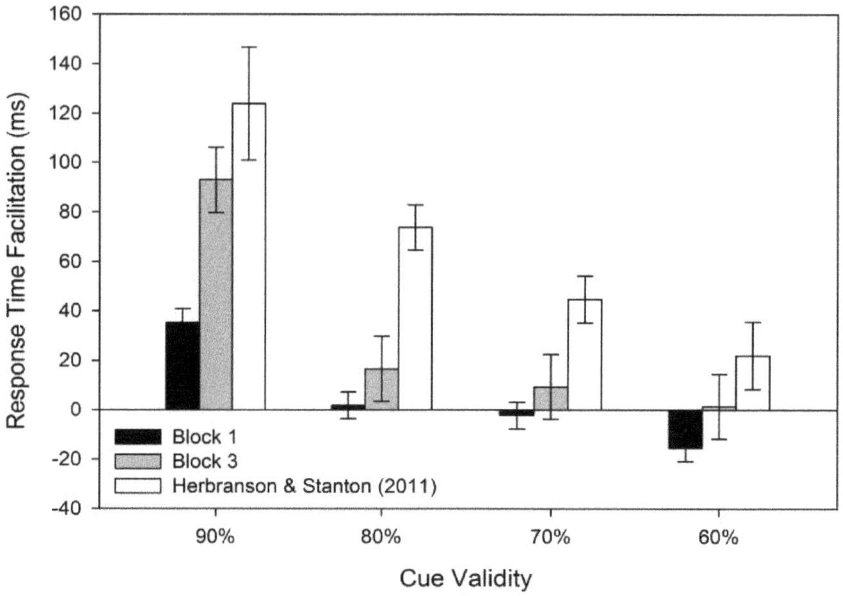

Figure 3. Global response time facilitation (response time to invalid cues minus response time to valid cues) on Blocks 1and 3. For comparison, white bars show the same measure from birds in Herbranson & Stanton (2011). Error bars depict 95% confidence intervals.

Local Predictability

Figure 4 shows data pertaining to local predictability, a possible basis for global response time facilitation. Recall that local predictability is the conditional probability that a target will appear in a particular location, given the most recent response, and that targets in the sequence used could take on two possible values: 0.33 (hereafter referred to as *low predictability* targets) and 0.67 (hereafter referred to as *high predictability* targets). Figure 4 shows that during Block 1, the only group to show a local facilitation effect, whereby birds responded to high predictability targets more quickly than low predictability targets, was the 90% cue validity group, and this finding is consistent with the previous analysis of cue validity (global facilitation). For the remaining groups, birds were just as fast to respond to low predictability targets as they were to respond to high predictability targets. During Block 2, when all four groups saw the undistorted sequence (100% cue validity), all four groups showed a local predictability effect, indicating that they were capable of learning something about the sequence. Finally during Block 3, all four groups continued to show a local predictability effect, even when cue validity was no longer 100%.

To statistically confirm these observations, we ran a 3 (block: mixed validity, 100% valid, mixed validity) x 2 (local predictability: low, high) x 4 (cue validity condition: 90%, 80%, 70%, 60%) mixed ANOVA on median response times across the final 10 days of each condition. Block and local predictability were repeated measures factors and condition was a between-groups factor. Even though they did not all pertain to hypothesized effects, all of the main effects and interactions were statistically reliable. There were significant main effects of block ($F(2, 72) = 80.57$, $p < 0.01$, partial $\eta^2 = 0.69$), local predictability ($F(1, 36) = 985.37$, $p < 0.01$, partial $\eta^2 = 0.97$) and cue validity ($F(3, 36) = 867.95$, $p < 0.01$, partial $\eta^2 = 0.99$).

There were significant two-way interactions between block and local predictability ($F(2, 72) = 187.36$, $p < 0.01$, partial $\eta^2 = 0.84$), between block and cue validity ($F(6, 72) = 23.67$, $p < 0.01$, partial $\eta^2 = 0.66$) and between local predictability and cue validity ($F(3, 36) = 59.55$, $p < 0.01$, partial $\eta^2 = 0.83$). Finally, there was a significant three-way interaction between block, local predictability, and cue validity ($F(6, 72) = 4.54$, $p < 0.01$, partial $\eta^2 = 0.28$).

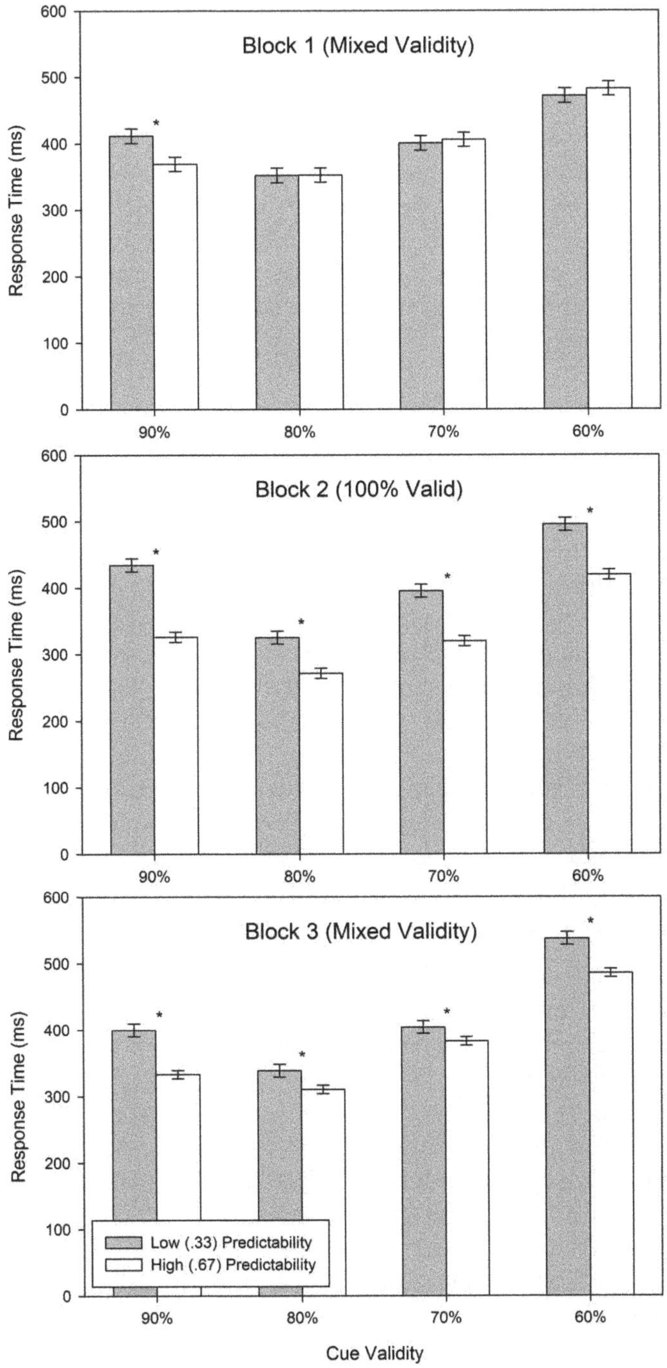

Figure 4. Response times as a function of local predictability during the final 10 days of each condition. Error bars depict 95% confidence intervals. Asterisks indicate significant differences between pairs of bars having high and low local predictability values for a given condition and block.

The significant 3-way interaction is essential, as the critical pairwise comparisons pertaining to local facilitation are between low and high local predictability means for a given block and cue validity condition (paired bars in Figure 4). We tested for these 12 possible differences using a post-hoc Tukey test. There were significant differences for all four cue validity groups during Blocks 2 and 3, and for only the 90% cue validity group during Block 1 (all $ps < 0.01$ with Bonferroni correction). These significant differences are indicated in Figure 4 by asterisks.

The results of this ANOVA confirm previously presented analyses, and are what one would expect to see if the global facilitation effect shown in Figure 3 were due to local predictability. The one group that showed global facilitation during Block 1 was also the only group to show a local predictability effect during that same block. The difference between groups that did and did not show global facilitation during Block 1 however, was not due to an inability of the lower cue validity groups to learn transitional probabilities because each showed local facilitation during Block 2. Neither was it due to the inability of the lower cue validity groups to apply knowledge of response transitions (once learned) to a distorted sequence, as each group showed local facilitation during Block 3 after having learned the undistorted sequence during Block 2.

True Local Predictability

The previous two analyses indicated that response times during Blocks 1 and 3 were influenced by two factors: cue validity and local predictability. Presumably, these two factors both had their effects by influencing how consistently upcoming targets could be predicted. The two factors logically combine in that local predictability (whether high or low) is proportionally diluted by imperfect cue validity (the probability that cue validity applies and a target can actually be predicted by previous responses). Therefore, one can define *true* local predictability as the combined effect of these two factors: local predictability times cue validity. Figure 5 displays response times as a function of true local predictability. Notice that plotted true local predictability values along the x-axis are different for each group because each group's local predictability is modified by a different cue validity parameter. If birds' response times are a function of their ability to successfully predict the location of an upcoming target, then higher true local predictability should yield greater response time facilitation (again defined as the difference between response times to invalidly cued targets and validly cued targets).

During Block 1, the only group that showed either global facilitation or local facilitation was the 90% cue validity group. Figure 5 shows that this same group was the only one for which there was greater facilitation for the higher true local predictability value (indicated by a line with a positive slope). The other groups produced slopes that were essentially flat (in fact, slightly negative), indicating that response time facilitation did not increase with true local predictability. During Block 3 all four groups showed a positive slope, indicating that facilitation increased with true local predictability. The bottom panel in Figure 5 shows the same analysis for the data from Herbranson & Stanton (2011), and the same pattern emerges. While the data from Herbranson and Stanton are more tightly clustered, note that all of their data came from the same birds (cue validity was a within-groups factor) whereas our birds were divided into different cue validity groups (a between-groups factor). The most important pattern is that in both cases, response time facilitation was greater in a given condition when true local predictability was higher.

Cue Repetition

Notice in Figure 5 that there are negative response time facilitation values (see the data points representing birds in the 60% and 70% cue validity conditions of the present experiment). This is initially curious, because negative values indicate that birds were actually faster to respond to invalid targets than to valid ones. Consider though, that given the sequence used, consecutive valid targets could not appear in the same location, whereas an invalid target creates such a possibility. Consequently, a bird that is unable to effectively anticipate upcoming target locations, and instead simply monitors the display for a target in any location, might be especially fast to respond to certain invalid targets – specifically those that result in consecutive targets on the same key (and after only a 500 ms ISI), if only because the necessary movement is minimized.

Given the above pattern, it would seem that one specific type of local predictability that could be especially important is repetition of consecutive targets. Because the original, undistorted sequence did not contain any two consecutive targets in the same location, a bird that has learned the sequence would, in part, be anticipating a lack of immediate repetitions (consecutive cues in the same location). Imperfect cue validity (i.e., any value less than 100%) on the other hand, creates the possibility of repetition, and as cue validity declines, repetitions would become proportionally more probable. To assess the importance of cue repetition, we separately calculated median response times to repeated targets (those appearing in the same location as the previous target) and non-repeated targets (those appearing in a different location) during Block 3. Birds in the 90% cue validity group were considerably faster to respond to non-repeated targets (M = 352.23, SD = 4.84) than to repeated targets (M = 475.17, SD = 23.30) (t (9) = 14.99, p < 0.01). Note that response times to repeated targets were slower despite the fact that by definition they require a bird to move a shorter distance. The other three groups all showed differences of less than 7 ms, indicating that they responded approximately as quickly to repeated and non-repeated targets (all ps > 0.25).

Discussion

The experiment duplicated the methods of Herbranson and Stanton (2011), using the same sequence and cue validity values, but with one critical difference: Herbranson and Stanton's pigeons were initially trained on the undistorted sequence and only later introduced to variability, whereas our pigeons saw variable sequences from the beginning. These differences in training had a profound influence over performance, as Herbranson and Stanton's pigeons showed significant response time facilitation with cue validities as low as 60%, whereas our pigeons only showed global facilitation if cue validity was 90% (and even then the effect was considerably weakened). After exposure to the undistorted sequence, the performance of our pigeons improved, but still fell short of the results from Herbranson and Stanton, as significant global facilitation was produced only down to 80% cue validity, and when produced was weaker in magnitude. We believe that the differences between the present results and those of Herbranson and Stanton are primarily attributable to the effects of variability during early training. Birds in both experiments were the same strain, experimentally naïve, tested in the same operant chambers, and received the same amount of initial training (35 days).

While all of our birds appeared to have reached steady levels of performance by the end of Block 1, it is also true that birds in different cue validity groups would have seen different numbers of valid trials during those 35 days. Thus, in some sense, they can be said to have received different amounts of training. However, consider that analysis of local predictability indicated that birds in all four groups learned the undistorted sequence within the 15 days that constituted Block 2 (a total of 15,000 valid trials). By comparison, birds in the 90%, 80%, 70% and 60% cue validity groups would have accumulated 15,000 valid trials in approximately 16.67, 18.75, 21.43, and 25.00 days of mixed validity training, respectively. In each case, the 35 day duration of Block 1exceeded that number of trials, and birds in the 80% and below groups still displayed no traces of either global or local facilitation.

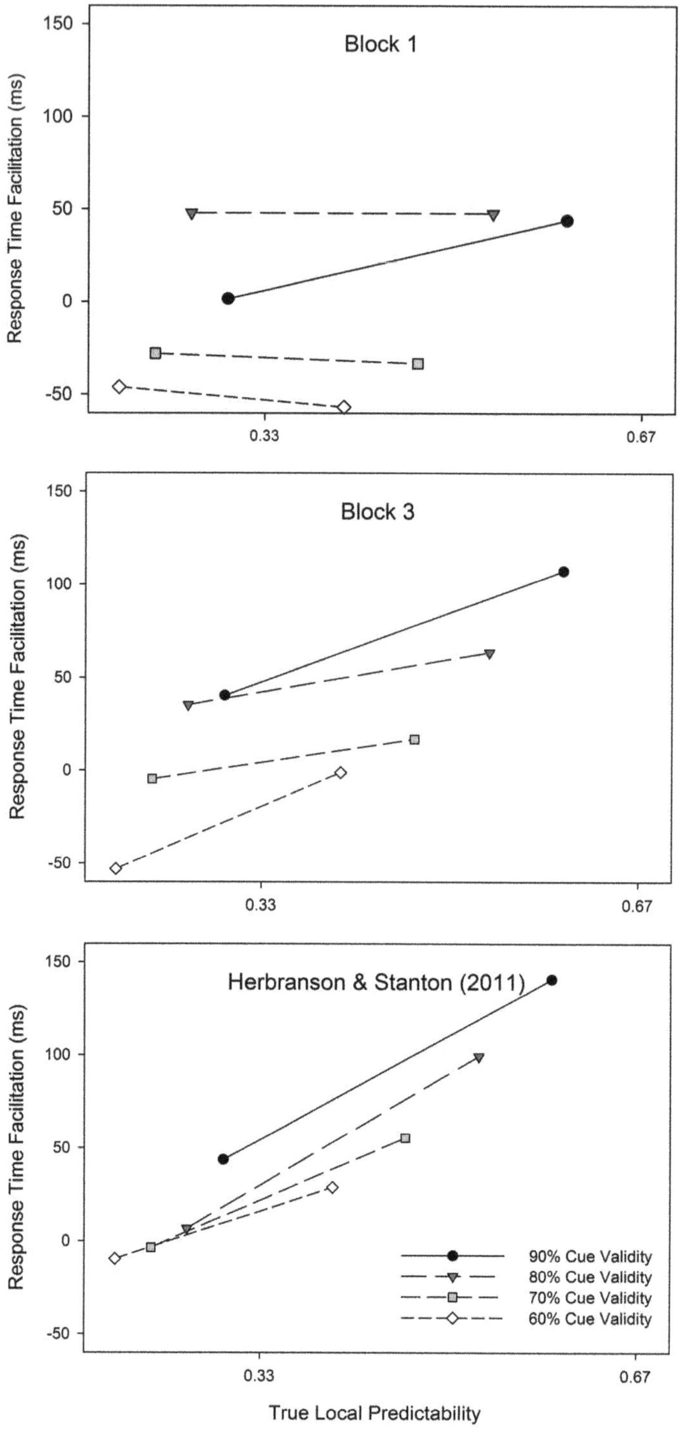

Figure 5. Response time facilitation as a function of true local predictability from the mixed validity Blocks 1 (top panel) and 3 (middle panel) and from Herbranson & Stanton (2011; bottom panel).

When interpreting the present results, it is important to remember that the design is somewhat different from a prototypical SRT, in which the critical comparison is between consecutive blocks of trials that are structured (i.e., predictable) and random (i.e., unpredictable). In the present experiment, the critical comparison is between predictable and unpredictable targets within the same block. Similar approaches have been used previously by Herbranson and Stanton (2011) and by Howard and Howard (1997), and bear the advantage of avoiding comparisons across blocks (introducing possible sequencing effects or history confounds) or across groups (making individual differences a concern). Nevertheless, the present approach might be strengthened by including a random control group that is presented with nothing but random targets throughout each block. This control condition would provide for potentially informative comparisons as it would involve the simplest of all strategies (search for any lit key and peck it), stripped of any possible local predictability effects.

Results from the current experiment and from Herbranson and Stanton (2011) both indicated that pigeons can skillfully *perform* variable response sequences with cue validities down to about 60%. The present results however, indicate that learning is less accommodating of spatial variability and that a response sequence can be reasonably *learned* only if cue validity during acquisition is no less than about 90%. Cognitive psychologists have long made a distinction between encoding and retrieval as distinct memory processes (e.g., Tulving & Thompson, 1973), and the present results would indicate that a similar distinction may also be relevant to pigeons' procedural memory, as acquisition and performance are not affected in the same way by variability. While encoding and retrieval are more commonly used in reference to explicit (or declarative) memory, recent neuropsychological evidence has revealed some striking parallels, both physiological and cognitive between implicit and explicit processes for both encoding (Turk-Browne, Yi, & Chun, 2006) and retrieval (Schott et al., 2005).

These results seem to show a loose parallel with those from classic research on categorization (Posner, 1968). That is, our pigeons showed the equivalent of a prototype effect, in which responding to an undistorted prototype is enhanced following training on random distortions around that prototype. In this case though, the prototype was not for a perceptual category, but for a motor response pattern. Despite the name of the effect, note that there is debate over whether individuals actually extract a complete representation of the prototype (see Medin & Smith, 1984). In the present case for example, it appears that pigeons learned about the probabilities of the various response transitions that made up the sequence (local transitional probabilities) rather than extracting a complete intact prototype sequence. While these results mirror the basic pattern of a prototype effect as seen in categorization research, there are some potentially important differences. First, prototype effects in categorization experiments can usually be seen upon first exposure to an undistorted stimulus, whereas the effect shown here did not appear immediately upon exposure to the undistorted sequence (compare the final day of Block 1 with the first day of Block 2 in Figure 1). The effect here refers only to the difference between the stable performance levels achievable under distorted and undistorted conditions. Second, in categorization experiments, one can ensure that the undistorted prototype is not presented until after training is complete. That was not possible in the present experiment. Because we introduced variability via cue validity, it is quite possible that pigeons (especially those in the high cue validity groups) at some point during training saw a sequence of nine consecutive valid targets. Such a chain of responses might or might not be comparable to exposure to an undistorted prototype. That is, the prototype sequence in the present experiment is ongoing and perpetually repeating with no defined beginning or end. Posner's (1968) prototypes on the other hand, were much more precisely defined. Nevertheless, these constitute potentially important differences and should not be overlooked when referring to results from the present experiment as prototype effects.

On a methodological note, these results demonstrate that different measures of performance on a single task can show markedly different sensitivities to learning. For example, our measure of global response time facilitation (Figure 3) by itself would indicate that the 70% and 60% cue validity groups showed no evidence of learning at any point in the experiment, and that even the 80% cue validity group only showed weak facilitation during Block 3. In contrast, our measure of local predictability (shown in Figures 4 and 5) indicates that all four cue validity groups learned something about the sequence by the end of the experiment. It would thus appear that local predictability is a more sensitive measure of response sequence learning than is global facilitation. Local facilitation, however, may not tell the entire story either. While true local predictability does provide an orderly account of the results, we must also consider the possibility that birds in different conditions learned different things. For example, our analyses indicated that birds in the 90% cue validity condition learned transitional probabilities, including the special case that repetitions were rare (one specific kind of local transition). Birds in other conditions did not appear to be as sensitive to target repetitions, but did still show local predictability effects, indicating that other transitional probabilities were learned.

We believe that these results have important consequences for the training of behaviors in a variety of contexts. In the case of SRT learning, it seems that there is a limit to the amount of variability that can be accommodated during training, and consistency is particularly important during early training of a response sequence. Once the sequence is established, variability can be incorporated, but is best incorporated gradually (as in Herbranson & Stanton, 2011). Despite eventual exposure to the undistorted sequence, our pigeons did not show the same magnitude of facilitation as Herbranson and Stanton's pigeons that were not exposed to variability until after the sequence had been learned. Thus, it would seem that the introduction of variability too early might retard learning, and possibly even prevent eventual performance at a level that would have been attainable had an undistorted (or less distorted) sequence been learned initially. Schwartz (1981) showed a similar effect in an experiment where pigeons had to produce a sequence of responses across keys to earn reinforcement. If progress through the sequence was indicated by systematic changes in a matrix of stimulus lights, pigeons developed stereotyped and efficient response sequences. If, however, the matrix light changed randomly, birds failed to develop those efficient response sequences. More importantly, when later exposed to the systematically changing display those birds that had initially seen the randomly changing light matrix failed to develop efficient response sequences. In other words, randomness during initial training prevented the acquisition of an efficient response sequence. This effect of randomness during initial training, however, is not necessarily universal. In humans, for example, it has been well established that variable practice conditions can actually enhance learning of motor skill relative to constant training (Coelho, Nusbaum, Rosenbaum, & Fenn, 2012; Wulf, 1997).

Finally, we believe that these results may reflect general learning processes that pertain to a variety of natural behaviors grounded in procedural memory (locomotion, foraging, social interaction, etc.). Exactly how our cue validity parameter translates into real-world variability is at this point unclear, but it is important to note that variability influences both learning and performance, and that these two processes apparently do not operate in perfect parallel. Specifically, learning appears to require considerably more consistency than does performance. Nevertheless, the natural world is highly variable, and so any useful learning process would almost certainly need to include some factor that can accommodate an appreciable (though not unlimited) degree of variability.

References

Brown, P. L., & Jenkins, H. J. (1968). Autoshaping of the pigeon's keypeck. *Journal of the Experimental Analysis of Behavior, 11*, 1–8.

Brodbeck, D. R. (1997). Picture fragment completion: Priming in the pigeon. *Journal of Experimental Psychology: Animal Behavior Processes, 23*, 461-468.

Bullock, D. H., & Bitterman, M. E. (1962). Habit reversal in the pigeon. *Journal of Comparative and Physiological Psychology, 55*, 958-962.

Coelho, C. J., Nusbaum, H. C., Rosenbaum, D. A., & Fenn, K. M. (2012). Imagined actions aren't just weak actions: Task variability promotes skill learning in physical practice but not in mental practice. *Journal of Experimental Psychology: Learning, Memory, and Cognition, 38*, 1759-1764.

Froehlich, A. L., Herbranson, W. T., Loper, J. D., Wood, D. M., & Shimp, C. P. (2004). Anticipating by pigeons depends on local statistical information in a serial response time task. *Journal of Experimental Psychology: General, 133*, 31–45.

Herbranson, W. T., & Shimp, C. P. (2008). Artificial grammar learning in pigeons. *Learning and Behavior, 36*, 116-137.

Herbranson, W. T., & Stanton, G. L. (2011). Flexible serial response learning in pigeons and humans. *Journal of Comparative Psychology, 125*, 328-340.

Howard, J. H., Jr., & Howard, D. V. (1997). Age differences in implicit learning of higher-order dependencies in serial patterns. *Psychology and Aging, 12*, 634–656.

Huber, L., & Lenz, R. (1996). Categorization of prototypical stimulus classes by pigeons. *The Quarterly Journal of Experimental Psychology, 49B*, 111-133.

Knowlton, B. J., Mangels, J. A., & Squire, L. R. (1996). A neostriatal habit learning system in humans. *Science, 273*, 1399 – 1402.

Knowlton B., Squire L., & Gluck, M. (1994). Probabilistic classification learning in amnesia. *Learning and Memory, 1*, 106–120.

Medin, D. L., & Smith, E. E. (1984). Concepts and concept formation. In M. R. Rosenzweig (Ed.), *Annual Review of Psychology. Vol. 35*. (pp. 113-138). Palo Alto, CA: Annual Reviews.

Meulemans, T., & Van der Linden, M. (1997). Associative chunk strength in artificial grammar learning. *Journal of Experimental Psychology: Learning, Memory, & Cognition, 23*, 1007-1028.

Nissen, M. J., & Bullemer, P. (1987). Attentional requirements of learning: Evidence from performance measures. *Cognitive Psychology, 19*, 1–32.

Nissen, M. J., Knopman, D. S., & Schacter, D. L. (1987). Neurochemical dissociation of memory systems. *Neurology, 37*, 789–794.

Poling, A., Nickel, M., & Alling, K. (1990). Free birds aren't fat: Weight gain in captured wild pigeons maintained under laboratory conditions. *Journal of the Experimental Analysis of Behavior, 53*, 423–424.

Posner, M. I., & Keele, S. W. (1968). On the genesis of abstract ideas. *Journal of Experimental Psychology, 77*, 353–363.

Reber, A. S. (1967). Implicit learning of artificial grammars. *Journal of Verbal Learning and Verbal Behavior, 6*, 855–863.

Schott, B. H., Henson, R. N., Richardson-Klavehn, A., Becker, C., Thoma, V., Heinze, H. J., & Düzel, E. (2005). Redefining implicit and explicit memory: The functional neuroanatomy of priming, remembering, and control of retrieval. *Proceedings of the National Academy of Sciences, 102,* 1257–1262.

Squire, L. R. (1992). Memory and the hippocampus: A synthesis from findings with rats, monkeys, and humans. *Psychological Review, 99*, 195-231.

Squire, L. R. (2004). Memory systems in the brain: A brief history and current perspective. *Neurobiology of Learning and Memory, 82*, 171–177.

Tulving, E., & Schacter, D. L. (1990). Priming and human memory systems. *Science, 247*, 301–306.

Tulving, E., & Thompson, D. M. (1973). Encoding specificity and retrieval processes in episodic memory. *Psychological Review, 80*, 352-373.

Turk-Browne, N.B., Yee, D, & Chun, M.M. (2006). Linking implicit and explicit memory: Common encoding factors and shared representations. *Neuron, 49*, 917-927.

Wulf, G. (1997). Variability of practice and implicit motor learning. *Journal of Experimental Psychology: Learning, Memory, and Cognition, 23*, 987-1006.

7

Evocation of Behavioral Change by the Reinforcer is the Critical Event in Both the Classical and Operant Procedures

John W. Donahoe
University of Massachusetts, USA

By definition, in a Pavlovian (classical) procedure a stimulus is presented prior to an eliciting stimulus whereas in an operant procedure a response occurs prior to the eliciting stimulus. In spite of the different contingencies implemented by the two procedures, some behavior necessarily precedes the eliciting stimulus in the Pavlovian procedure and some stimulus necessarily precedes the eliciting stimulus in the operant procedure. If conditioning depends on the momentary relation of environmental and behavioral events to an eliciting stimulus, then the two procedures must engage a common conditioning process. The cumulative effects of that common process may be different, however, because of differences in the frequency with which specific environmental and behavioral events are contiguous with the eliciting stimulus (and its elicited response). The view that the critical reinforcing event is the evocation of a change in ongoing behavior evoked by the eliciting stimulus provides the basis for an interpretation of the conditioning process that encompasses the effects of both procedures.

Within 10 years of the publication in English of Pavlov's Conditioned Reflexes (1927) American psychologists began to differentiate between Pavlovian, or classical, conditioning and operant, or instrumental, conditioning. Others had recognized the distinction (e.g., Schlosberg, 1937), but the difference was most fully appreciated by B. F. Skinner (1935, 1937). Two primary differences were emphasized. First, the nature of the contingency that defined the operant and Pavlovian procedures differed: "There are two fundamental cases: in one the reinforcing stimulus is correlated temporally with a response and in the other with a stimulus" (Skinner, 1937, p. 272). Second, whereas the Pavlovian procedure primarily changed only the stimulus that controlled a response already evoked by another stimulus, the operant procedure potentially brought a wide range of behavior under the control of the stimulus. As a Pavlovian example, the ticking sound of a metronome acquired control of salivation after the sound had been followed by food, a stimulus that already elicited salivation. As an operant example, an auditory stimulus presented to a rat would acquire control of lever-pressing, chain-pulling, or running depending on which response preceded food. The response that preceded the food was designated an operant to indicate that it operated on the environment to produce food.

A close reading of Skinner's early writings (e.g., Skinner, 1938) on the classical-operant distinction indicates that he viewed the difference as primarily one of procedure, not process. To wit, Skinner acknowledged without dissent that "…'reinforcement' is essentially the same process in both [procedures]" (citing Hilgard, p. 111) and that conditioning "...may eventually be reduced to a single formula" (citing Mowrer, p. 111). In spite of Skinner's early willingness to consider the possibility that the two procedures engaged the same conditioning process, different conceptions of the conditioning process increasingly arose.

Please send correspondence to Dr. John Donahoe, Department of Psychological and Brain Sciences, Tobin Hall, University of Massachusetts, Amherst, MA 01003 (Email: jdonahoe@psych.umass.edu).

The differing conceptions were fostered, in part, by the use of different technical terms to designate analogous events manipulated and monitored in the procedures. The technical terms employed in the classical procedure followed Pavlov's usage. The environmental event that preceded the elicited response was termed the conditioned stimulus, the eliciting stimulus the unconditioned stimulus, and the elicited response the unconditioned response. The monitored response that ultimately came under control of the conditioned stimulus was termed the conditioned response. *Conditioned* was used to indicate that the control exerted by the conditioned stimulus was not innate, but conditional upon – that is, dependent upon – its presentation within the Pavlovian procedure.

The technical terms used to designate the corresponding events in the operant procedures did not follow Pavlov's usage. The environmental events prior to the operant were simply described in general physical terms (the characteristics of the conditioning chamber) or in terms of their specific properties (the wavelength of light, the frequency of sound, and so on). One of Skinner's major contributions was to demonstrate that behavior could display orderly properties without identifying the environmental events if the precise relation of behavior to its consequences was specified (Ferster & Skinner, 1957; cf., Donahoe, Palmer, & Burgos, 1997). Skinner did not deny that operants were under environmental control but asserted that their specification was often unnecessary. Indeed, under appropriate experimental arrangements the precise stimuli that controlled the operant could be identified and, in such cases, these stimuli were termed discriminative stimuli. In fact, Skinner maintained that "...it is the nature of [operant] behavior that ... discriminative stimuli are practically inevitable" (Skinner, 1937, p. 273). Note, however, that in the operant procedure the temporal relation of a discriminative stimulus to an eliciting stimulus (e.g., food) could be comparable to the temporal relation of the conditioned stimulus to the unconditioned stimulus in the classical procedure. Thus, stimuli bearing similar temporal relations to the eliciting stimulus were designated by different technical terms. Next, consider the terms used to designate the eliciting stimulus. As previously noted, the eliciting stimulus is called an unconditioned stimulus in the classical procedure. In an operant procedure, the eliciting stimulus is called a reinforcer if the operant increases in frequency but a punisher if it decreases. Once again, different technical terms are applied to the same physical event when it appears in the two procedures. Finally, the behavior monitored in the procedures clearly differs. In the classical procedure, a response similar to that evoked by the eliciting stimulus is typically measured (e.g., salivation occasioned by the conditioned stimulus). In the operant procedure, the operant is monitored but the response corresponding to the conditioned response in the classical procedure almost always goes unmeasured even though it may be occurring. (There are a few notable exceptions in which both the operant and the conditioned response are measured, e.g., Shapiro, 1962.)

The fact that analogous events are designated by different technical terms in the two procedures and that the behavior monitored also differs has encouraged the conclusion that different conditioning processes are engaged by the two procedures. This conclusion is revisited in the next section.

Two Conditioning Procedures, but One Conditioning Process?

Let us examine afresh the events that occur in the classical and operant procedures. In both procedures the organism is immersed in a succession of environmental stimuli in which a stream of responses is occurring (cf., Schoenfeld, 1972). Also, in both procedures an eliciting stimulus (or elicitor) is introduced into that environment (see Figure 1). What differs between the procedures, as Skinner observed, is whether the elicitor follows an environmental stimulus, in which case it is a classical procedure, or follows a behavior, in which case it is an operant procedure. Note, however, that at the moment the reinforcer occurs, there is no detectable difference between the two procedures (Donahoe, Burgos, & Palmer, 1993). In the classical procedure, some behavior has inevitably occurred prior to the reinforcer, although that behavior may change from moment-to-moment. Similarly, in the operant procedure, some stimulus must have been detected immediately prior to the reinforcer, although that stimulus may also vary from moment-to-moment. If conditioning involves processes that are engaged on a moment-to-moment basis, then at the moment when the reinforcer occurs there can be no difference in the processes engaged by the two procedures. The undeniable difference in the behavioral effects of the procedures emerges over time – the conditioned response in the classical case and the operant as well as the conditioned response in the operant case. In the classical procedure, the behavior occurring during the moment prior to the reinforcer varies, whereas in the operant procedure it is the stimulus occurring during that moment that varies. The stimulus-reinforcer relation is constant in the classic procedure; the response-reinforcer relation is constant in the operant procedure. This difference in the event temporally correlated with the reinforcer has encouraged different conceptions of the conditioning process in the two procedures.

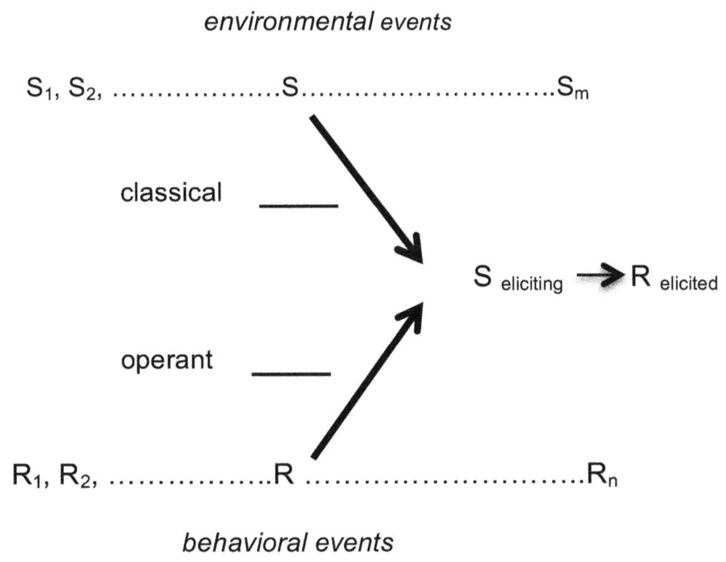

Figure 1. *A stream of environmental events (S) and accompanying behavioral events (R) into which a reinforcing eliciting stimulus* ($S_{eliciting}$) *and its elicited response are introduced.* A Pavlovian procedure is implemented when the eliciting stimulus is introduced after a stimulus (S), but note that some response (R) must also be occurring. An operant procedure is implemented when the eliciting stimulus is introduced after a response (R), but note that some stimulus (S) must also be occurring.

Moment-to-Moment Versus Molar Conceptions of the Conditioning Process

For Skinner, conditioning was consistently viewed as a moment-to-moment process. Contingency was defined by the temporal relation between an individual stimulus or response and an individual elicitor, not by the correlation between these events over extended periods of time. Perhaps the clearest examples of a moment-to-moment conception come from experimental demonstrations of what Skinner called "superstitious" behavior. When a stimulus is presented at varying times independent of on-going behavior, that stimulus can nevertheless acquire control of behavior when some response in its presence was – by chance – followed by a reinforcer such as food. This control persisted until – again, by chance – another stimulus happened to occur when the response was followed by the reinforcer (Morse & Skinner, 1957). Similarly, in an environment in which no stimulus was presented by the experimenter, if a reinforcer occurred independent of on-going behavior but – by chance – appeared immediately after some response, then that response increased in frequency, particularly when it was compatible with the behavior evoked by the elicitor (Skinner, 1948, cf., Staddon & Simmelhag, 1971). Based on such experiments, Skinner concluded: "To say that a reinforcement is contingent upon a response may mean nothing more than that it follows the response" (Skinner, 1948, p. 168). Causation was reduced to temporal coincidence, a very Humian (Hume, 1748) conception.

The conclusion that contiguity of a stimulus, in the classical case, or a response, in the operant case, with a reinforcer is sufficient to produce conditioning was directly challenged by findings in the 1960s and 70s. Experiments with both the classical procedure (Kamin, 1968, 1969) and the operant procedure (Vom Saal & Jenkins, 1970) demonstrated that an eliciting stimulus did not function as a reinforcer when it was presented in an environment in which conditioning with that same elicitor had already taken place. The ability of the elicitor to function as a reinforcer was said to be *blocked.* Given these findings, some theorists proposed that conditioning was not the result of moment-to-moment contiguities of an elicitor with a stimulus and/or a response, but of the overall correlation of these events with the elicitor. Such proposals are known as molar theories because contingency is defined, not by the moment-to-moment relation between events, but by the correlation between events over extended periods of time, such as the duration of an experimental session. As an example of a molar view with a classical procedure, if elicitors are more common during periods of time when putative conditioned stimuli are frequent than when they are uncommon, then conditioning occurs (Rescorla, 1967), supposedly independent of individual stimulus-reinforcer contiguities. Given such findings, molar theories were developed for both the classical (Rescorla, 1967) and operant (Baum, 1973) procedures. However, subsequent experimental and theoretical research has found that the molar relations observed in these studies could arise as the cumulative product of individual stimulus-reinforcer and response-reinforcer contiguities. This was found for both the classical procedure (e.g., Ayres, Benedict, & Witcher, 1975; Rescorla & Wagner, 1972) and the operant procedure (e.g., Crowley & Donahoe, 2004; MacDonall, 2009, McDowell, 2004; and see Donahoe, 2012 for a brief review of the molar-molecular issue).

An Alternative Momentary Conception of Conditioning

Although a molar conception of the reinforcement process appears not to be required, the question remained as to what produced the blocking phenomenon. Blocking demonstrated that contiguity of either a stimulus or a response with a putative reinforcing stimulus would not produce conditioning if some other stimulus were simultaneously present that was previously contiguous with that reinforcer. Something beyond contiguity with a reinforcing stimulus was required for conditioning.

A candidate for the critical factor arises from the realization that when an eliciting stimulus is presented an elicited response also occurs: Contiguity of a stimulus or response with a reinforcing stimulus also produces contiguity with a reinforcer-elicited *response.* (Apparent exceptions in conditioned drug responses are resolved when the unconditioned response is properly identified as the immediate neural response to the elicitor and not the more delayed behavioral response; Eickelboom & Stewart, 1982.) From an evolutionary perspective it seems plausible that natural selection would be more sensitive to the behavior of an organism in response to a stimulus than to the perception of the stimulus alone. A very few theorists using the classical procedure explicitly recognized the potential importance of contiguity of the conditioned stimulus with the reinforcer-elicited response instead of the eliciting stimulus (Gormezano & Kehoe, 1981; Guthrie, 1935). The elicited response was generally ignored altogether in the operant procedure because the elicited response was rarely monitored. (Stimulus sampling theory developed by Estes (1950), a former student of Skinner, is an exception.) More recently, an experimental preparation was developed that allowed the question of whether contiguity with the reinforcing stimulus or with the reinforcer-elicited response was crucial for conditioning (Donahoe & Vegas, 2004). Using a liquid-elicited swallowing response that has a latency of several hundred milliseconds and duration of several seconds, the temporal relation of the conditioned stimulus to the elicited response was varied independently of its relation to the eliciting stimulus. With this preparation, conditioning occurred whenever the conditioned stimulus preceded or overlapped the reinforcer-elicited *response* independent of its temporal relation to the eliciting stimulus. The neural mechanisms of conditioning naturally selected by the environment appear more attuned to the occurrence of the elicited response than to the perception of the eliciting stimulus. Thomas Huxley's maxim (1887) endures: "The great end of life is not knowledge but action."

The current proposal is that the critical reinforcing event in both the classical and operant procedures is more closely correlated with the evocation of a change in behavior induced by the reinforcing stimulus than with the presentation of that stimulus itself. In experimental analyses conducted at the behavioral level, the change in behavior induced by the reinforcer is apparent and may be directly measured, as with salivation induced by food in the mouth. However, once the neural mechanisms correlated with changes in behavior have been naturally selected, those same mechanisms could become exploited by other stimuli, such as conditioned reinforcers whose direct behavioral effects are less apparent. As an example, liquid introduced into the mouth of a monkey evokes activity in dopaminergic neurons of the ventral tegmental area and very similar neural activity is produced by a formerly neutral stimulus after it had reliably preceded the liquid (Schultz, 1997). As noted elsewhere (Donahoe & Vegas, 2004),

> It has long been recognized that the behavioral expression of the UR [the reinforcer-elicited response] is not necessary for conditioning as demonstrated by cases in which the behavioral UR is prevented (as when transmission at the neuromuscular junction is blocked; e.g., Solomon & Turner, 1962) or by cases in which the CS does not support expression of the UR (as when an auditory CS is paired with food for the pecking response of the pigeon; e.g., Leyland & Mackintosh, 1978). However, if the behavioral expression of conditioning were not highly correlated with the neural mechanisms that mediate conditioning, then those mechanisms could never have been naturally selected. As E. O. Wilson has observed, "Learning is the pacemaker of evolution" (Wilson, 1975, p. 156). Nevertheless, once these mechanisms have been naturally selected, their behavioral expression is not necessary for the environment to engage them. (p. 31)

From the perspective that the evocation of the reinforcer-elicited response is the critical event in conditioning, blocking may be interpreted as follows: Blocking occurs when the environment present when the reinforcing stimulus occurs already evokes the conditioned response previously established with that reinforcer. When these circumstances obtain, the reinforcer no longer evokes a change in behavior because the conditioned response is already occurring. Without a change in behavior evoked by the reinforcer, conditioning does not occur. Research using computer-simulations with biologically informed neural networks demonstrates that only an elicitor that evokes a behavioral change functions as a reinforcer and that this conception of reinforcement applies equally to conditioning with the classical and operant procedures (Donahoe et al., 1993). A unified conception of selection by reinforcement appears viable. Note that a unified conception of conditioning is not simply a claim that classical conditioning affects operant conditioning but that the different outcomes of both procedures are expressions of a common conditioning process.

Conditioning and its Neural Mechanisms

A unified conception of conditioning is also not a claim that the neural mechanisms ultimately engaged by the two procedures are totally the same. Instead, it is a claim that the events sensed by the organism are identical at the moment of reinforcement and, for that reason, all the neural processes relevant to both procedures must be engaged at that moment. The cumulative effect of reinforcement on the conditioning process differs because the events that are most reliably contiguous with the reinforcing behavior differ, most prominently the response that precedes the reinforcer in the operant procedure.

An elaboration of the differences in the neural processes engaged by the two procedures is beyond the scope of this discussion but two obvious ones merit mention. First, in the operant procedure the entire behavioral repertoire of the organism is a potential candidate for selection. In mammals, this necessarily involves cortical structures whereas many responses that are conditionable with the classical procedure can be mediated by subcortical structures alone (e.g., Oakley & Russell, 1972). Second, there is typically a greater delay between the occurrence of the operant and the reinforcer-elicited response in the operant procedure than between the conditioned stimulus and the reinforcer-elicited response in the classical procedure. For example, the time between bar pressing and the ingestion of food in Skinner's procedure is generally greater than between hearing a tone and injecting acid into the mouth in Pavlov's procedure. In Skinner's first studies with the operant procedure, he addressed this temporal asynchrony by first pairing the sound of the operation of the feeder with the ingestion of food and then later presented this sound immediately after a bar press had occurred. Computer simulations using neural networks have demonstrated that without additional neural systems to bridge the temporal gap between the operant and the reinforcer, conditioning fails to occur (Donahoe & Burgos, 2005).

References

Ayres, J. J. B., Benedict, J. O., & Witcher, E. S. (1975). Systematic manipulation of individual events in a truly random control in rats. *Journal of Comparative and Physiological Psychology*, *88*, 97–103

Baum, W. M. (1973). The correlation–based law of effect. *Journal of the Experimental Analysis of Behavior, 20*, 137–15.

Crowley, M. A., & Donahoe, J. W. (2004). Matching: Its acquisition and generalization. *Journal of the Experimental Analysis of Behavior*, *82*, 143–1593.

Donahoe, J. W. (2012). Origins of the molar-molecular divide. *European Journal of Behavior Analysis*, *19*, 196-200.

Donahoe, J. W., & Burgos, J. E. (2005). Selectionism: Complex outcomes from simple processes. *Behavioural and Brain Sciences*, *28*, 397-468.

Donahoe, J. W., Burgos, J. E., & Palmer, D. C. (1993). A selectionist approach to reinforcement. *Journal of the Experimental Analysis of Behavior*, *60*, 17-40.

Donahoe, J. W., Palmer, D. C., & Burgos, J. E. (1997) The S-R issue: Its status in behavior analysis and in Donahoe & Palmer's *Learning and Complex Behavior*. *Journal of the Experimental Analysis of Behavior*, *67*, 193-211.

Donahoe, J. W., & Vegas, R. (2004). Pavlovian conditioning: The CS-UR relation. *Journal of Experimental Psychology: Animal Behavior Processes*, *30*, 17-33.

Eickelboom, R., & Stewart, J. (1982). Conditioning of drug-induced physiological response. *Psychological Review*, *89*, 507-528.

Estes, W. K. (1950). Toward a statistical theory of learning. *Psychological Review*, *57*, 94-107.

Gormezano, I., & Kehoe, E. J. (1981). Classical conditioning and the law of contiguity. In P. Harzem & M. D. Zeiler (Eds.), *Predictability, correlation, and contiguity* (pp. 1-45). New York, NY: Wiley.

Guthrie, E. R. (1935). *The psychology of learning*. New York, NY: Harper & Row.

Hume, D. (1748/1955). *Philosophical essays concerning human understanding*. Indianapolis, IN: Bobbs-Merrill.

Huxley, T. H. (1877/1964). Technical education. In T. H. Huxley and J. Priestly (Eds.), *Science and education.* New York, NY: Philosophical Library.

Kamin, L. J. (1968). Attention-like processes in classical conditioning. In M. R. Jones (Ed.), *Miami symposium on the prediction of behavior: Aversive stimulation* (pp. 9-31). Coral Gables, FL: University of Miami Press.

Kamin, L. J. (1969). Selective association and conditioning. In N. J. Mackintosh & F. W. K. Honig (Eds.), *Fundamental issues in associative learning* (pp. 4-64), Halifax, Canada: Dalhousie University Press.

Leyland, C. M., & Mackintosh, N. J. (1978). Blocking of first- and second-order autoshaping in pigeons. *Animal Learning & Behavior*, *6*, 392-394.

MacDonall, J. S. (2009). The stay/switch model of concurrent choice. *Journal of the Experimental Analysis of Behavior*, *91*, 21–39.

McDowell, J. J. (2004). A computational model of selection by consequences. *Journal of the Experimental Analysis of Behavior, 81*, 297-317.

Morse, W. H., & Skinner, B. F. (1957). A second type of superstition in the pigeon. *American Journal of Psychology, 70*, 308–311.

Oakley, D. A., & Russell, I. S. (1972). Neocortical lesions and Pavlovian conditioning. *Physiology & Behavior, 8*, 915-926.

Pavlov, I. P. (1927). *Conditioned reflexes.* (Translated by G. V. Anrep). London, UK: Oxford University Press.

Rescorla, R. A. (1967). Pavlovian conditioning and its proper control procedures. *Psychological Review, 74*, 71–80.

Rescorla, R. A., & Wagner, A. R. (1972). A theory of Pavlovian conditioning: Variations in the effectiveness of reinforcement and nonreinforcement. In A. H. Black & W. F. Prokasy (Eds.), *Classical conditioning: Current research and theory* (pp. 64-99). New York, NY: Appleton-Century-Crofts.

Schlosberg, H. (1937). The relationship between success and the laws of conditioning. *Psychological Review, 44*, 379-394.

Schoenfeld, W. N. (1972). *Stimulus schedules: The t-T systems.* Oxford, England: Harper & Row.

Schultz, W. (1997). Appetitive dopaminergic neurons report the appetitive value of environmental stimuli. In J. W. Donahoe & V. P. Dorsel (Eds.), *Neural-network models of cognition: Biobehavioral foundations* (pp. 317-335). New York, NY: Elsevier Science Press.

Shapiro, M. H. (1962). Temporal relationship between salivation and lever pressing with differential reinforcement of low rates. *Journal of Comparative and Physiological Psychology, 55*, 567-571.

Skinner, B. F. (1935). Two types of conditioned reflex and a pseudo type. *Journal of General Psychology, 12*, 66-77.

Skinner, B. F. (1937). Two types of conditioned reflex: A reply to Konorski & Miller. *Journal of General Psychology, 16*, 272-279.

Skinner, B. F. (1938). *The behavior of organisms.* New York, NY: Appleton-Century-Crofts.

Skinner, B. F. (1948). “Superstition” in the pigeon. *Journal of Experimental Psychology, 38*, 168-172.

Solomon, R. L., & Turner, L. H. (1962). Discriminative classical conditioning in dogs paralyzed by curare can later control conditioned avoidance responses in the normal state. *Psychological Review, 69*, 202-219.

Staddon, J. E., & Simmelhag, V. L. (1971). The 'superstition' experiment: A reexamination of its implications for the principles of adaptive behavior. *Psychological Review, 78*, 3-43.

Vom Saal, W., & Jenkins, H. M. (1970). Blocking the development of stimulus control. *Learning and Motivation, 1*, 52-64.

Wilson, E. O. (1975). *Sociobiology.* Cambridge, MA: Harvard University Press.

8

The Development of Strain Typical Defensive Patterns in the Play Fighting of Laboratory Rats

Stephanie M. Himmler, Jena M. Lewis, & Sergio M. Pellis

Department of Neuroscience, University of Lethbridge, Lethbridge, Alberta, Canada

During play fighting, rats attack and defend the nape, which if contacted is nuzzled with the snout. While all strains of rats use the same suite of defensive tactics to protect the nape, different strains use some tactics more frequently. This study tests two hypotheses for this strain difference: (1) each strain has a preference for using particular tactics and (2) strain differences in defense are a byproduct of strain differences in patterns of nape attack. Juvenile Long-Evans (LE) and Sprague-Dawley (SD) males, raised in same strain quads from shortly after weaning to the early juvenile period (i.e., 24-31 days), were tested with unfamiliar same-strain and different-strain partners (Experiment 1) and LE and SD males raised in mixed LE-SD quads were tested with both familiar (Experiment 2) and unfamiliar same-strain and different-strain partners. If hypothesis (1) were true, they would maintain strain-typical defense patterns irrespective of the strain of the attacking partner, whereas if hypothesis (2) were true, it would vary with the strain of the attacking partner. Hypothesis (1) was supported in the first experiment; all the rats maintained their strain-typical patterns regardless of the partner's strain. However, Experiments 2 and 3 supported neither hypothesis, as each animal displayed strain-divergent behavior when playing with partners of either strain. Given that in Experiments 2 and 3, subjects were reared in mixed-strain groups, it is possible that, during the early juvenile period, play fighting experiences shape strain-typical patterns of use of defensive tactics.

Play fighting is one of the most commonly studied forms of play behavior in mammals with laboratory rats being one of the most studied species (e.g., Bolles & Woods, 1964; Meaney & Stewart, 1981; Panksepp, Siviy, & Normansell, 1984; Pellis & Pellis, 1998; Vanderschuren, Niesink, & Van Ree, 1997). However, there are many different strains of laboratory rats that are used in experimental research and these have been shown to differ in many features of their behavior (e.g., Pisula, Gonzalez Szwacka, & Rojek, 2003; Pisula, Turlejski, Stryjek, Nalecz-Tolak, Grabiec, & Djavadian, 2012; Prusky, Harker, Douglas, & Whishaw, 2002), including aspects of their play behavior (e.g., Reinhart, Pellis, & McIntyre, 2004; Siviy, Baliko, & Bowers, 1997; Siviy, Love, DeCicco, Giordano, & Seifert, 2003; Siviy, Crawford, Akopian, & Walsh, 2011). Moreover, laboratory strains of rats are domesticated versions of wild rats and domestication is known to change many aspects of physiology and behavior (e.g., Castle, 1947; Coppinger & Coppinger, 2001; Lockard, 1968; Pisula et al., 2012; Takahashi & Blanchard, 1982).

A recent pair of papers used a standardized testing and scoring scheme (B. T. Himmler, Pellis & Pellis, 2013a) to compare the play behavior of four domestic strains to that of a strain of wild rats (B. T. Himmler, Stryjek, Modlinska, Derksen, Pisula, & Pellis, 2013b; S. M. Himmler, Modlinska, Stryjek, Himmler, Pisula, & Pellis, 2014). In both domesticated and wild rats, play fighting involves competition for access to the partner's nape of the neck, which if contacted, is gently nuzzled with the snout (B. T. Himmler et al., 2013b; S. M. Himmler et al., 2014; Pellis & Pellis, 1987; Siviy & Panksepp, 1987).

Competition for the nape not only involves attacking the nape but also the recipient defending its nape from such contact (Pellis & Pellis, 1987). There are two main types of defense that rats can employ when defending against an attack, (a) evasion and (b) facing defense. Evasion involves the defender moving its nape away from its attacker by running, leaping, or pivoting away, and, in so doing, turning its face away from the attacker. Facing defense involves the defending animal turning to face its attacker, while simultaneously withdrawing the nape. In turn, facing defense can take one of two forms: rotating around its longitudinal axis or rotating around a vertical axis. Moreover, rotation around the longitudinal axis can also take one of two forms: rotating fully until the rat is lying supine, or partially, in which the forequarters are rotated toward its

Correspondence concerning this article should be sent to Stephanie M. Himmler (Email:s.derksen@uleth.ca).

partner, with one or both of its hind feet planted on the ground (B. T. Himmler et al., 2013a). When rotating around the vertical axis, the defender maintains ground contact with all four paws. Rotation around the vertical axis and partial rotation around the longitudinal axis can end in the same configuration if the rats rear up onto their hind feet and face one another (B. T. Himmler et al., 2013a). Facing defenses, especially full rotation to supine, increase the occurrence and duration of body-to-body contact as the animals wrestle one-another, while evasion decreases body contact as the defender withdraws from the attacker.

Like domesticated rats, wild rats use all these tactics during play fighting (B. T. Himmler et al., 2013b; S. M. Himmler et al., 2014). However, wild rats use evasion more frequently and supine defense less frequently than do the domestic strains, but the domestic rats differ from one another in how they differ to the wild rats. The largest strain difference in defensive tactics among the strains compared was between Sprague-Dawley (SD) and Long-Evans (LE) rats. SD used evasion more frequently than facing defense and LE used facing defense more frequently than evasion. Also, when engaging in facing defense, LE used the full rotation to supine tactic more often than SD. Two hypotheses that could account for the strain differences in the use of defense tactics are tested in this paper.

The first hypothesis posits that different strains have a strain-typical bias for using some tactics more frequently than others. An analogy would be with sex-typical behavior. In rats, females are less likely to mount and more likely to exhibit lordosis than males, which exhibit the opposite pattern. The male-typical pattern is established by perinatal hormonal influences on the neural mechanisms that regulate these behaviors (Baum, 1984). The same mechanism of sexual differentiation has been shown to account for the sex-typical differences the frequency of play fighting, with males usually engaging in more play (Meaney, Stewart, & Beatty, 1985). That there may be strain-typical preferences for using certain defense tactics is supported by findings that differences in neural function have been correlated with some aspects of the differences in the play between some strains (e.g., Siviy et al., 2011). Moreover, the bias to use the full rotation to supine defense in LE has been shown to be dependent on a specific area of the brain. Removal of the motor cortex selectively reduces the frequency of rotating to supine (Kamitakahara, Monfils, Forgie, Kolb, & Pellis, 2007). The rats with motor cortex damage attack and defend at the same frequency as intact controls, and like intact LE rats, use facing defense more frequently than evasion. The motor cortex damage-induced change selectively decreases the frequency of using supine defense and increases the frequency of partial rotation. With regard to facing defense, cortex damaged LE rats are like intact SD rats (B. T. Himmler et al., 2013b; S. M. Himmler et al., 2014). Therefore, it is possible that the strain-typical differences in the use of supine defense and evasion in LE and SD may be due to differences in strain-typical neural biases. This is the brain-bias hypothesis.

The second hypothesis does not focus on brain mechanisms regulating the selection of preferred defensive tactics, but rather, on possible differences in the conditions that create the opportunity to use different tactics by different strains. For example, compared to wild rats, domestic strains of rats are less acrobatic and tolerate closer proximity when attacked (B. T. Himmler et al., 2013b, S. M. Himmler et al., 2014). It remains to be determined whether these differences arise from differences in rearing, caging and feeding patterns or from genetic differences. Regardless of their origin, subtle differences in sensorimotor capabilities can have an impact on the execution of behavior patterns in various contexts (e.g., Berridge, 1990; Whishaw, Gorny, Foroud, & Kleim, 2003). The differences between LE and SD rats may make the attack of an LE rat contextually different enough to that of an attack by an SD rat to make supine defense in the former and evasion in the latter the more effective tactics. There is precedent for such sensory and biomechanical factors influencing choice of defense tactics.

During serious fighting, short-bodied species, like hamsters, are more likely to use a rotation to supine tactic to block a bite to the rump, while long-bodied species, like voles, are more likely to use a rotation around a vertical axis (Pellis, 1997). The number of body movements and the time taken to block a bite in these species show that supine defense is faster and more efficient in short-bodied rodents and vertical rotation is more efficient in long-bodied rodents (Pellis, 1997). A sensorimotor difference affecting the successful use of some defense tactics used during play has been found between male and female LE rats. When attacked directly from the rear, rats are likely to use the vertical axis rotation tactic, but in this attack configuration, females begin to rotate to face when the attacker is further away than do males. This difference in timing of initiation means that females are more successful in facing the attacker before contact is made and so can block the attack in a face-to-face orientation. In contrast, the males, by beginning to turn later, give the attacker time to close the distance and pounce on the back and so contact the nape with the snout, leading the male to turn to supine to withdraw the nape (Pellis, Pellis, & McKenna, 1994). That is, the successful execution of particular tactics may depend on biomechanical factors arising from small sensorimotor differences (Blumberg, 2005), such that attacks by members of a particular strain are more likely to create the context for particular kinds of defensive tactics to be used. This is the biomechanical hypothesis.

In order to test which of these two hypotheses may best explain strain differences in defensive tactics, the present study compared how SD and LE rats defended when attacked by either SD or LE partners. This was done in two ways. First, rats were housed in same-strain quads and then tested in the standard play paradigm (B. T. Himmler et al., 2013a) with unfamiliar partners of the same-strain and the opposite strain (Experiment 1). Second, rats were housed in mixed-strain quads and then tested with either familiar (Experiment 2) or unfamiliar (Experiment 3) same-strain and opposite-strain partners. If the brain hypothesis were correct, then irrespective of the rearing and testing paradigm, all rats should have used strain-typical patterns of defense. If the biomechanical hypothesis were correct, then rats should have used the strain-typical pattern of defense when attacked by same strain partners and some modified version when attacked by opposite strain partners. However, it is possible that rats could undergo experience-based learning, which would enable them to modify their pattern of defense to deal with the idiosyncrasies of the attacks by partners of the opposite strain better. Experiments 2 and 3 should detect such experience-based modifications. Nonetheless, while this modified brain hypothesis would account for experience-based changes in defending against an opposite strain attacker, it would still predict that when defending against a same-strain attacker, the pattern of defense should remain strain-typical. The modification should only occur when rats have had prior experience with opposite strain partners, especially familiar ones.

Method

Subjects

A total of 96 male rats (48 LE and 48 SD) were used. The rats were obtained from Charles River Laboratories (St. Constant, Quebec) around 23 days of age and housed at the Canadian Centre for Behavioral Neuroscience. All subjects were randomly housed in quads with two animals in each serving as the experimental subjects. The quad design was used to allow for a comparative measurement of the experimental animals playing with a partner of the same strain and a partner of the different strain (see below). The rats were maintained at a constant 21-23°C on a 12:12-hour light-dark cycle and were kept in 46cm X 25cm X 20cm polyethylene tubs, with processed corncob bedding. Food and water were provided *ad libitum*. All animals were handled and cared for in accordance with the Canadian Council for Animal Care regulations.

Procedure

Play was tested between 31 and 35 days, which is within the peak period for play behavior in rats (Thor & Holloway, 1984) but before the age at which dominance hierarchies begin to form in males (Pellis & Pellis, 1991; Takahashi & Lore, 1983). For 3 days before play testing, all animals were habituated, in their quads, to the testing enclosure for 30 minutes each day. Short periods of social isolation preceding testing increases the frequency of play fighting (Niesink & van Ree, 1989; Panksepp & Beatty, 1980); the present study used 24 hours of social isolation (B. T. Himmler et al., 2013a). Rats were tested twice, with a 24-hour rest period between the two test days in order to avoid having animals socially isolated longer than 24 hours. Test trials lasted for 10 minutes each, providing enough time to capture most aspects of playful interactions (B. T. Himmler et al., 2013a). Both habituation and testing occurred in complete darkness as it has been shown that social behaviors such as play increase when in the dark compared to light conditions (B. T. Himmler et al., 2013a).

Experiment 1: Same-Strain Rearing and Play with Unfamiliar Partners

Forty-eight rats were divided in 12 quads with each quad composed of rats of the same strain. Two of the rats from each quad were designated the experimental subjects and were tested with unfamiliar rats from other quads – one from the same strain and one from the opposite strain. In this way, one experimental rat from each quad was tested with a same strain partner and one experimental rat was tested with an opposite strain partner. That is, no rat was exposed to the unfamiliar partner more than once, ensuring that the behavior of the rats was not influenced by previous experience with those partners. Three groups were tested with the same strain first, and then a day later with the opposite strain partner, and the other three experimental subjects were tested in the reverse order, so counter-balancing for any order or age effects.

Experiment 2: Mixed-Strain Rearing and Play with Familiar Partners

Twenty-four rats were divided in six quads with each quad composed of two LE and two SD rats. One LE and one SD from each quad were designated the experimental subjects and were tested with the other two quad members. In this way, each experimental rat was tested with an LE and an SD partner. As in Experiment 1, the testing of the quads was counter-balanced.

Experiment 3: Mixed-Strain Rearing and Play with Unfamiliar Partners

Twenty-four rats were divided in six quads with each quad composed of two LE and two SD rats. One LE and one SD from each quad were designated the experimental subjects and were tested with two members from a different quad. In this way, each experimental rat was tested with an LE and an SD partner. As in Experiments 1 and 2, the testing of the quads was counter-balanced.

Equipment

Play trials occurred in a 50cm X 50cm X 50cm plexiglass box encased in a soundproofed chamber (61cm X 61cm X 84cm). The inside of the plexiglass box was filled with 1-2cm of CareFresh® bedding. A DVD103 Sony Handycam was used to film all play trials at a 45° angle using the night-shot option to film in the dark.

Behavioral Analysis

Playful interactions were scored for attack and defense (Pellis & Pellis, 1987). A playful attack was scored when the tip of the snout of one partner was either in contact with its partner's nape or when one partner made a targeted movement towards the nape of the other. The recipient of the attack could either respond to the attack using one of many defenses or simply ignore the attack. Playful defense of the nape could take one of two major forms: (a) evasion, which involves the defender moving its nape away from its attacker and does so by running, jumping, or pivoting away, and (b) facing defense, in which the defender moves its nape away by turning to face its attacker in order to block access to its nape by opposing its teeth between its partner and its own nape. Facing defense can take one of three forms: (a) complete rotation, which involves the defender rolling completely over onto its back, (b) partial rotation, which involves the defender rotating its forequarters while maintaining contact with the ground with one or both of its hind feet, and (c) other, which involves rotations or other movements in other dimensions. The first 2-3 video frames were used to determine the type of defensive tactic first attempted by the defending rat rather than recording the eventual outcome of an attack (Himmler et al., 2013a).

To assess possible cross-strain effects on overall playfulness, the frequency of nape attacks and probability of defense against attacks was recorded (B. T. Himmler et al., 2013a). To test the predictions arising from the two hypotheses, the probability of evasive defense as a proportion of total defense and the probability of supine defense as a proportion of total facing defense was calculated (B. T. Himmler et al., 2013b; S. M. Himmler et al., 2014).

Statistical Analysis

The data were analyzed from both experiments using a two-way analysis of variance (ANOVA), with identity of experimental subject (LE or SD) and identity of the play partner (LE or SD) as independent factors; for significant analyses of variance, the Least Significant Difference test with the Bonferroni correction was used for subsequent pair wise comparisons. Differences were considered significant for p values of ≤ 0.05. For graphical representation of the data, values are given for group means and standard error.

Validation of Testing Protocols and Behavioral Analyses

The experimenter (Himmler) who performed the behavioral analysis for this study had previously scored with a high degree of inter-observer reliability in two previous studies (B. T. Himmler et al., 2013b; S. M. Himmler et al., 2014). Given the consistency across studies in inter-observer reliability, it can be concluded that any significant differences in the current study were due to differences in manipulation of rearing rather than inconsistent behavioral scoring.

Results

Experiment 1

For all analyses of variance, three factors were compared, the identity of the performer, the identity of the partner and their interaction. A 2 X 2 ANOVA for the frequency of launching nape attacks revealed a significant effect for identity of attacker ($F(1, 20) = 5.780$, $p = 0.026$), but not for the identity of the partner; nor was there a significant interaction. SD rats launched more nape attacks than LE rats irrespective of the partner's identity (Figure 1a). There were no main effects for the probability of defense ($F(1, 20) = 2.816$, $p = 0.095$) (Figure 1b).

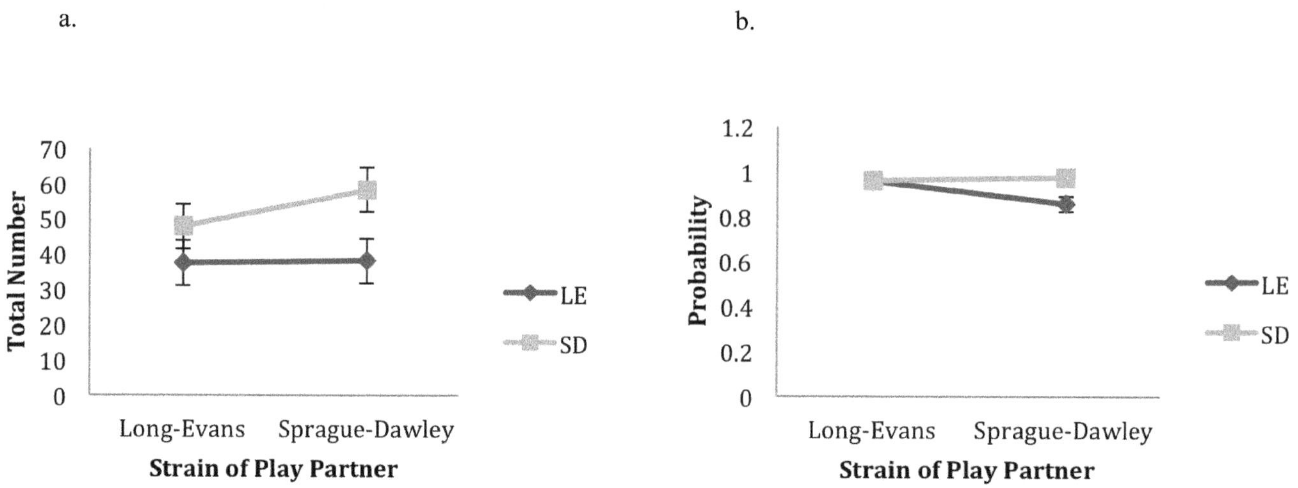

Figure 1. (a). The total number of playful attacks per 10 minute play trial. (b). The probability of defense against a playful attack.

A 2 X 2 ANOVA for the probability that a defending rat would use the complete rotation tactic revealed a significant difference for the identity of the defender ($F(1, 20) = 47.115$, $p = 0.0001$), but not for the identity of the partner, nor was there an interaction. LE rats were more likely to use the complete rotation tactic than SD rats irrespective of partner (Figure 2a). For the probability that the defending rat would use the evasion tactic there was a significant difference for the identity of the defender ($F(1, 20) = 90.658$, $p = 0.0001$), and for the identity of the partner ($F(1, 20) = 12.674$, $p = 0.002$), but there was no significant interaction. SD rats were more likely to use evasive tactics than LE rats irrespective of the identity of the partner (Figure 2b). Moreover, Bonferroni corrected pairwise comparisons showed that being attacked by an SD partner was more likely to lead to evasive defense in both LE and SD rats ($p < 0.05$).

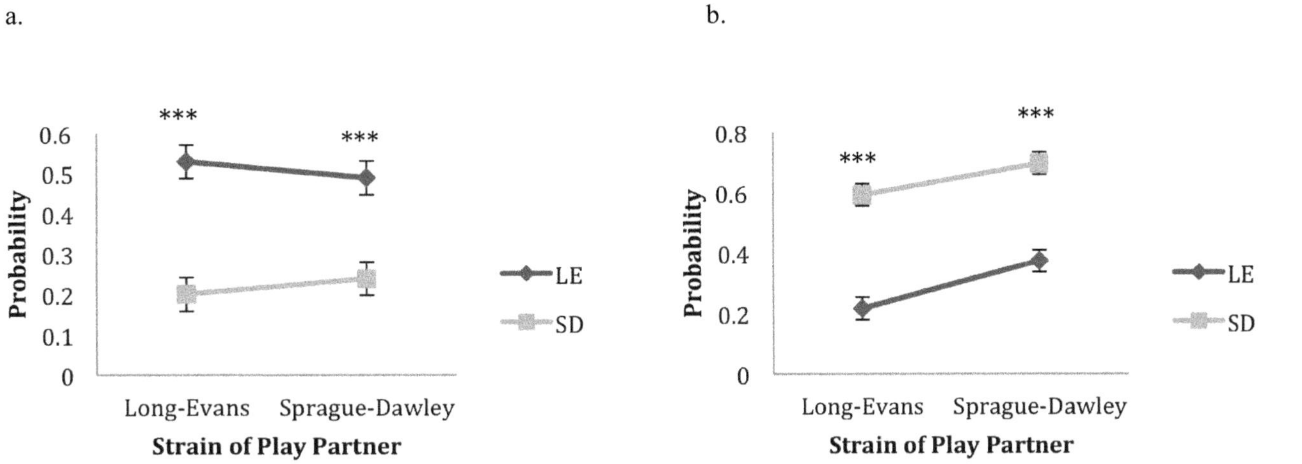

Figure 2. (a). The probability of using the complete rotation defense in response to a playful attack. (b). The probability of using evasive defense tactics in response to a playful attack.

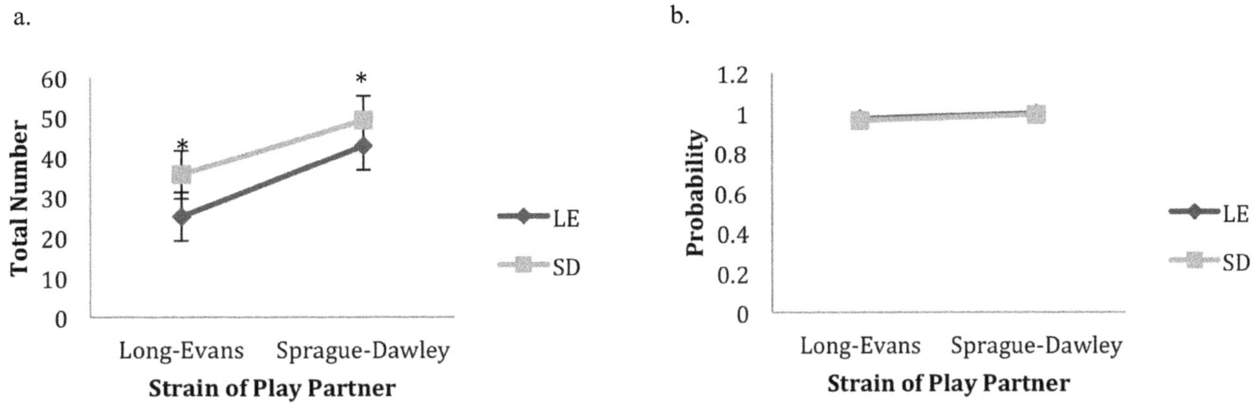

Figure 3. (a). The total number of playful attacks per 10 minute play trial. (b). The probability of defense against a playful attack.

Experiment 2

A 2 X 2 ANOVA for the frequency of launching nape attacks revealed a significant difference for the identity of the attacker ($F(1, 20) = 6.617$, $p = 0.018$), but not for the identity of the partner; nor was there a significant interaction. SD rats launched more nape attacks irrespective of the identity of the partner (Figure 3a). There were no main effects for the probability of defending against nape attacks ($F(1, 20) = 0.017$, $p = 0.897$) (Figure 3b).

Similarly, there were no significant differences for the probability that a defending rat would use either the complete rotation tactic ($F(1, 20) = 1.075$, $p = 0.312$) (Figure 4a) or evasion ($F(1, 20) = 0.173$, $p = 0.682$) (Figure 4b).

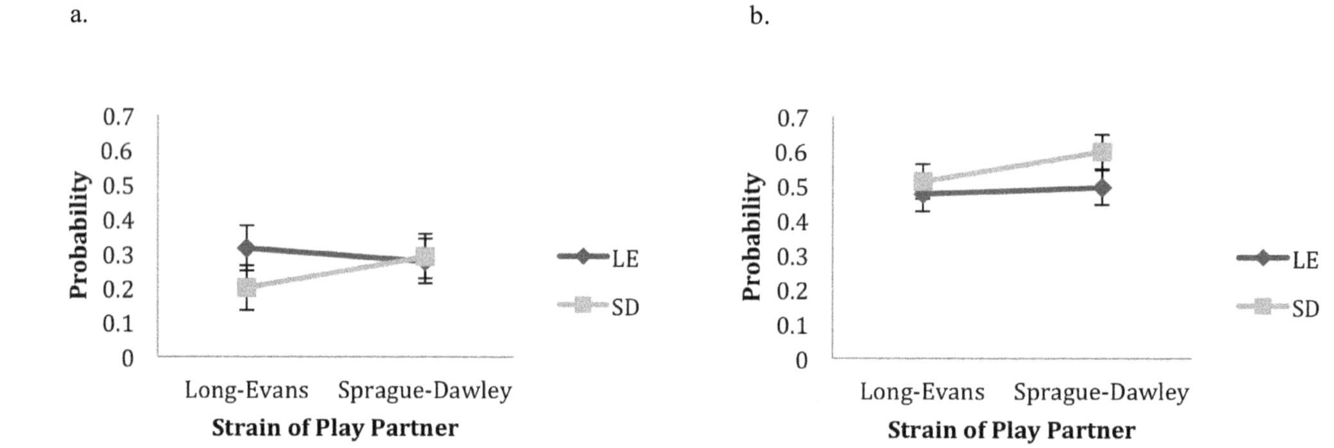

Figure 4. (a). The probability of using the complete rotation defense in response to a playful attack. (b). The probability of using evasive defense tactics in response to a playful attack.

Experiment 3

A 2 X 2 ANOVA for the frequency of launching nape attacks revealed a significant difference for the identity of the attacker ($F(1, 20) = 12.629$, $p = 0.002$), but not for the identity of the partner; nor was there a significant interaction. SD rats launched more nape attacks irrespective of the identity of the partner (Figure 5a). A 2 X 2 ANOVA for the probability of defending against nape attacks revealed a significant difference for the identity of the attacker ($F(1, 20) = 6.942$, $p = 0.016$), but not for the identity of the partner, nor was there a significant interaction. SD rats were more likely to defend against a playful attack from either strain of partner (Figure 5b).

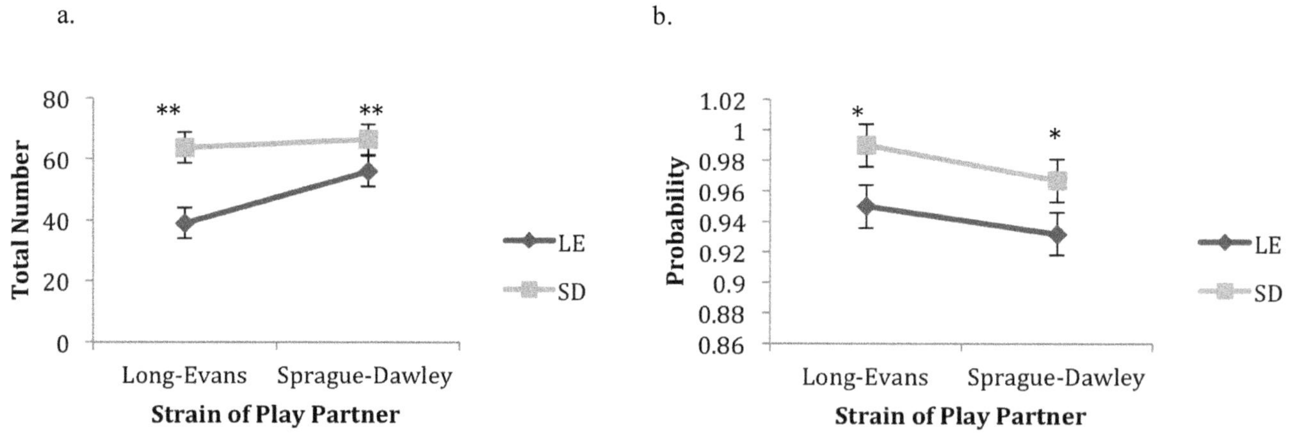

Figure 5. (a). The total number of playful attacks per 10 minute play trial. (b). The probability of defense against a playful attack.

There were no significant differences for the probability that a defending rat would use either the complete rotation tactic ($F(1, 20) = 0.285$, $p = 0.600$; Figure 6a) or evasion ($F(1, 20) = 1.957$, $p = 0.177$; Figure 6b).

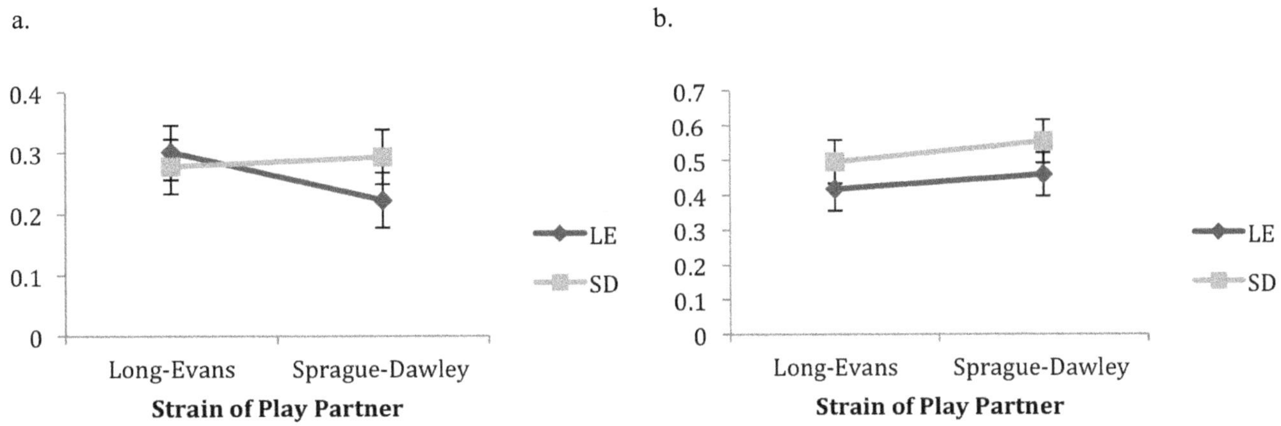

Figure 6. (a). The probability of using the complete rotation defense in response to a playful attack. (b). The probability of using evasive defense tactics in response to a playful attack.

Discussion

The present study was designed to test whether the strain-typical patterns of playful defense in rats is fixed by strain-typical brain mechanisms or arises from strain differences in how partners attack. For motivation to initiate play, as measured by the frequency of nape attacks (Panksepp, 1981; Thor & Holloway, 1983), there were no rearing and testing differences, in all cases SD rats launched more attacks than LE rats. For defensive responses to such attacks, SD rats tended to defend more frequently in all cases, with the difference reaching significance in Experiment 3. Thus, irrespective rearing experience and strain of the partner, with regard to attack and defense, the rate was higher in SD rats as shown in previous studies (B. T. Himmler et al., 2013b; S. M. Himmler et al., 2014). It is how the rats defended themselves that specifically tested whether type of defense is based on a strain-typical preference or a byproduct of how different strains attack.

The findings from Experiment 1 were consistent with the brain hypothesis as all animals maintained their strain-typical patterns of playful defense regardless of the strain of the attacking partner. Although LE rats showed an increase in evasive tactics when playing with an SD partner, this frequency of evasion was not as high as in SD rats. This suggests that, while subtle differences in patterns of attack by different strains may have a small influence on some tactics, the biomechanics of attack is not sufficient to affect the strain-typical preference for using particular defensive tactics. Indeed, the values for percentages of using evasion and supine defense are in the strain-typical range established in previous studies (B. T. Himmler et al., 2013b, S. M. Himmler et al., 2014). This being the case, it would mean that the diversification of defensive tactics among strains following domestication (B. T. Himmler et al., 2013b, S. M. Himmler et al., 2014) would likely have involved differential changes in the neural mechanisms that regulate different facets of play behavior (e.g., Kamitakahara et al., 2007; Siviy et al., 2011). That is, strain differences in defense involve differing biases for use of the different tactics of defense, with the neural mechanisms regulating those biases being changed accordingly. While the results from Experiment 1 clearly support this conclusion, the results from Experiments 2 and 3 suggest that more complex developmental processes in producing strain-typical patterns are involved.

The findings from the second and third experiments were not consistent with either the brain hypothesis or the biomechanical hypothesis. The biomechanical hypothesis predicted that, if strain differences are due to differences in attack styles, then these rats, just like those in Experiment 1, would defend in the strain-typical manner when tested with a same strain partner, but in a modified form when playing with an opposite strain partner. Given that Experiment 1 was consistent with the brain hypothesis, any change in behavior when defending against opposite strain partners in Experiments 2 and 3 would be more consistent with a modified brain hypothesis – prior experience with the play of the opposite strain modifies how rats defend against strain discordant partners. Thus, defending in a strain-typical way with same strain partners and in non-strain typical ways with opposite strain partners could be consistent with both hypotheses. Yet the changes in defense seen in Experiments 2 and 3 were not predicted by any version of the two hypotheses.

In Experiments 2 and 3, the rats had eight days of cohabitation experience with both same and opposite strain partners before being tested, so providing them with experience of the differences in play typical of the two strains. Yet, while SD rats maintained the higher frequency of attacks and probability of defense compared to LE rats as was seen in same strain reared animals, rats from neither strain maintained their strain-typical patterns of defense. When playing with an LE or SD partner, LE rats displayed lower frequencies of complete rotation and higher frequencies of evasion than seen in LE rats from Experiment 1 and from the previous studies (B. T. Himmler et al., 2013b; Kamitakahara et al., 2007; Pellis & Pellis, 1987). Similarly, when playing with either a LE or SD partner, SD rats displayed higher frequencies of complete rotation and lower frequencies of evasive tactics than SD rats from Experiment 1 and from a previous study (S. M. Himmler et al., 2014).

For Experiments 2 and 3, defensive behavior patterns in both same-strain and different-strain pairings were not strain-typical, but rather, the playful defense of both LE and SD subjects converged at a level intermediate between the two strains (Experiment 1; B. T. Himmler et al., 2013b, S. M. Himmler et al., 2014). This convergence was present whether the rats were tested with familiar (Experiment 2) or unfamiliar (Experiment 3) partners, increasing the likelihood that the difference with the results from Experiment 1 and from previous studies (B. T. Himmler et al., 2013b; S. M. Himmler et al., 2014) was due to the effects of being housed with partners of both strains. These findings suggest that the strain-typical biases for using particular tactics can be modified by social experiences in the first week of the juvenile period.

For LE and SD rats, the strain typical pattern of defense emerges whether housed in same sex pairs, quads or whole, mixed sex litters (e.g., Experiment 1 in this study; B. T. Himmler et al., 2013b, S. M. Himmler 2014; Pellis & Pellis, 1987, 1990, 1997). The critical difference between the rats in Experiments 2 and 3 compared to Experiment 1 appears to be that those rats experienced living with and interacting with rats of both strains from 24-31 days of age. Play fighting begins to emerge in the week preceding weaning at about 16-17 days of age (Bolles & Wood, 1964; Pellis & Pellis, 1997) and reaches its peak frequency of occurrence between 30-35 days of age (Meaney & Stewart, 1981; Panksepp, 1981; Pellis & Pellis, 1990; Thor & Holloway, 1984). Even though playful interactions begin as early as 16 days of age, they do not reach the fully strain-typical pattern until about 30 days of age. In LE rats, patterns of facing defense leading to supine are favored, with the strain-typical pattern of infrequent evasion and highly frequent complete rotation gradually maturing through the weaning to the early juvenile period (Pellis & Pellis, 1997). The early post-weaning period, when the rats were formed in mixed strain quads for Experiments 2 and 3, represents an age when the juvenile-typical pattern of play is still maturing and so may be susceptible to novel social experiences.

The juvenile period is critical for brain and behavioral development, making animals in this stage of life particularly sensitive to a variety of experiences, especially social ones (e.g., Baarende, Counotte, O'Donnell & Vanderschuren, 2013; Einon & Morgan, 1977; Einon, Morgan, & Kibbler, 1978; Hall, 1998; Van den Berg, Hol, Van Ree, Spruijt, Everts, & Koolhaas, 1999; Von Frijtag, Schot, van den Bos, & Spruijt, 2002). A series of studies on the effects of social isolation at different times during post-weaning development not only supports the view that the juvenile period is critical for neurobehavioral development, but that the first week of post-weaning is particularly critical for the development of social behavior (Arakawa, 2002, 2003, 2007a,b). In addition, Meaney and Stewart (1981) compared the play behavior of adult rats reared in mixed sex social groups compared to same sex groups as juveniles. The behavior of the females remained relatively consistent across rearing conditions, whereas that of the males differed. The males reared in mixed sex groups had a bigger age-related decrease in play than did those reared in same sex groups. In combination, these studies suggest that the type of partners experienced during the juvenile period can affect the development of social behavior and that the early phase of post-weaning is likely a highly critical time for these experiences to affect brain and behavior.

Conclusions

Strain differences in play behavior appear to be determined by brain mechanisms that control preferences for particular patterns of defense, as animals that have been reared with animals of the same strain will exhibit their strain-typical patterns of play regardless of the strain of the partner (Experiment 1). However, brain mechanisms regulating strain differences appear to be vulnerable to change during the early juvenile period - indeed, so much so, that living with a different strain during the early juvenile period produces atypical strain behavior during play (Experiments 2 and 3), further supporting that, during the juvenile period, behavior is modifiable by novel social experiences. Thus, while it can be concluded that strain differences in playful defense do not arise from biomechanical differences but from brain mechanisms regulating biases in tactics used, it is possible that playful experience with same strain partners is necessary for those brain biases to be established.

Acknowledgments

We thank Vivien Pellis for her comments on the paper.

References

Arakawa, H. (2002). The effects of age and isolation period on two phases of behavioral response to foot-shock in isolation-reared rats. *Developmental Psychobiology*, *41*, 15-24.

Arakawa, H. (2003). The effects of isolation rearing on open-field in male rats depends on developmental stages. *Developmental Psychobiology*, *43*, 11-19.

Arakawa, H. (2007a). Age-dependent change in exploratory behavior of male rats following exposure to threat stimulus: Effect of juvenile experience. *Developmental Psychobiology*, *49*, 522-530.

Arakawa, H. (2007b). Ontogeny of sex differences in defensive burying behavior in rats: Effect of social isolation. *Aggressive Behavior*, *33*, 38-47.

Baarende, P. J. J., Counotte, D. S., O'Donnell, P., & Vanderschuren, L. J. M. J. (2013). Early social experience is critical for the development of cognitive control and dopamine modulation of prefrontal cortex function. *Neuropsychopharmacology*, *38*, 1485-1494.

Baum, M. J. (1984). Hormonal control of sex differences in brain and behavior of mammals. In D. Crews (Ed.), *Psychobiology of Reproductive Behavior* (pp. 231-257). Englewood Cliffs, NJ: Prentice-Hall.

Berridge, K. C. (1990). Comparative structure of action: rules of form and sequence in the grooming patterns of six rodent species. *Behaviour*, *113*, 21-56.

Blumberg, M. S. (2005). *Basic instinct. The genesis of behavior*. New York, NY: Thunders' Mouth Press.

Bolles, R. C., & Woods, P. J. (1964). The onotogeny of behavior in the albino rat. *Animal Behaviour*, *12*, 427-441.

Castle, W. E. (1947). The domestication of the rat. *Proceedings of the National Academy of Sciences, 33,* 109-117.

Coppinger, R., & Coppinger, L. (2001). *Dogs: A startling new understanding of canine origin, behavior and evolution*. New York, NY: Scribner.

Einon, D. F., & Morgan, M. J. (1977). A critical period for social isolation in the rat. *Developmental*

Psychobiology, 10, 123–132.

Einon, D. F., Morgan, M. J., & Kibbler, C. C. (1978). Brief periods of socialization and later behavior in the rat. *Developmental Psychobiology, 11*, 213–225.

Hall, F. S. (1998). Social deprivation of neonatal, adolescent, and adult rats has distinct neurochemical and behavioral consequences. *Critical Reviews in Neurobiology, 12*, 129-162.

Himmler, B. T., Pellis, V. C., & Pellis, S. M. (2013a). Peering into the dynamics of social interactions: Measuring play fighting in rats. *Journal of Visualized Experiments, 71*, e4288, 1-8.

Himmler, B. T., Stryjek, R., Modlinska, K., Derksen, S. M., Pisula, W., & Pellis, S. M. (2013b). How domestication modulates play behavior: A comparative analysis between wild rats and a laboratory strain of *Rattus norvegicus*. *Journal of Comparative Psychology, 127*, 453-464.

Himmler, S. M., Modlinska, K., Stryjek, R., Himmler, B. T., Pisula, W., & Pellis, S. M. (2014). Domestication and diversification: A comparative analysis of the play fighting of brown Norway, Sprague-Dawley, and Wistar strains of laboratory rats. *Journal of Comparative Psychology,(Washington, DC: 1983)* doi: 10.1037/a0036104.

Holloway, K. S., & Suter, R. B. (2004). Play deprivation without social isolation: Housing controls. *Developmental Psychobiology, 44*, 58-67.

Kamitakahara, H., Monfils, M. H., Forgie, M. L., Kolb, B., & Pellis, S. M. (2007). The modulation of play fighting in rats: Role of the motor cortex. *Behavioral Neuroscience, 121*, 164-176.

Lockard, R. B. (1968). The albino rat: a defensible choice or a bad habit? *American Psychologist, 23*, 734-742.

Meaney, M. J., & Stewart, J. (1981). A descriptive study of social development in the rat (*Rattus norvegicus*). *Animal Behaviour, 29*, 34-45.

Meaney, M. J., Stewart, J., & Beatty, W. W. (1985). Sex differences in social play: The socialization of sex roles. *Advances in the Study of Behavior, 15*, 1-58.

Niesink, R. J., & Van Ree, J. M. (1989). Involvement of opioid and dopaminergic systems in isolation-induced pinning and social grooming of young rats. *Neuropharmacology, 28*, 411-418.

Panksepp, J. (1981). The ontogeny of play in rats. *Developmental Psychobiology, 14*, 327-332.

Panksepp, J., & Beatty, W. W. (1980). Social deprivation and play in rats. *Behavioral & Neural Biology, 30*, 197-206.

Panksepp, J., Siviy, S. M., & Normansell, L. A. (1984). The psychobiology of play: Theoretical and methodological perspectives. *Neuroscience & Biobehavioral Reviews, 8*, 465-492.

Pellis, S. M. (1997). Targets and tactics: the analysis of moment-to-moment decision making in animal combat. *Aggressive Behavior, 23,* 107-129.

Pellis, S. M., Hastings, E., Shimizu, T., Kamitakahara, H., Komorowska, J., Forgie M. L., & Kolb, B. (2006). The effects of orbital frontal cortex damage on the modulation of defensive responses by rats in playful and non-playful social contexts. *Behavioral Neuroscience*, 120, 72-84.

Pellis, S. M., & Pellis, V. C. (1987). Play-fighting differs from serious fighting in both target of attack and tactics of fighting in the laboratory rat *Rattus norvegicus. Aggressive Behavior, 13*, 227–242.

Pellis, S. M., & Pellis, V. C. (1990). Differential rates of attack, defense, and counterattack during the developmental decrease in play fighting by male and female rats. *Developmental Psychobiology, 23*, 215-231.

Pellis, S. M., & Pellis, V. C. (1991). Role reversal changes during the ontogeny of play fighting in male rats: Attack vs. defense. *Aggressive Behavior, 17,* 179-189.

Pellis, S. M., & Pellis, V. C. (1997). The pre-juvenile onset of play fighting in laboratory rats *Rattus norvegicus. Developmental Psychobiology, 31*, 193–205.

Pellis, S. M., & Pellis, V. C. (1998). Play fighting of rats in comparative perspective: A schema for neurobehavioral analyses. *Neuroscience & Biobehavioral Reviews, 23*, 87–101.

Pellis, S. M., Pellis, V. C., & Mckenna, M. M. (1994). Feminine dimension in the play fighting of rats (*Rattus norvegicus*) and its defeminization neonatally by androgens. *Journal of Comparative Psychology, 108,* 68-73.

Pisula, W., Gonzalez Szwacka, A. & Rojek, E. (2003). Juvenile play fighting and adult investigatory responses in male rats. *Polish Psychological Bulletin, 34*, 47-49.

Pisula, W., Turlejski, K., Stryjek, R., Nałęcz-Tolak, A., Grabiec, M., & Djavadian, R.L. (2012). Response to novelty in the laboratory Wistar rat, wild-captive WWCPS rat, and the short-tailed opossum. *Behavioral Processes, 91,* 145-151.

Prusky, G. T., Harker, K. T., Douglas, R. M., & Whishaw, I. Q. (2002). Variation in visual acuity within pigmented, and between pigmented and albino rat strains. *Behavioural Brain Research, 136*, 339-348.

Reinhart, C. J., Pellis, S. M., & McIntyre, D. C. (2004). Development of play fighting in kindling-prone (FAST) and kindling-resistant (SLOW) rats: How does the retention of phenotypic juvenility affect the complexity of play? *Developmental Psychobiology, 45*, 83-92.

Siviy, S. M., Baliko, C. N., & Bowers, K. S. (1997). Rough-and-tumble play behavior in Fischer-344 and Buffalo rats: Effects of social isolation. *Physiology & Behavior, 61*, 597-602.

Siviy, S. M., Crawford, C. A., Akopian, G., & Walsh, J. P. (2011). Dysfunctional play and dopamine physiology in the Fischer 344 rat. *Behavioural Brain Research, 220,* 294-304.

Siviy, S. M., Love, N. J., DeCicco, B. M., Giordano, S. B., & Seifert, T. L. (2003). The relative playfulness of juvenile Lewis and Fischer-344 rats. *Physiology & Behavior, 80*, 385-394.

Siviy, S. M., & Panksepp, J. (1987). Sensory modulation of juvenile play in rats. *Developmental Psychobiology, 20,* 39-55.

Takahashi, L. K., & Blanchard, R. J. (1982). Attack and defense in laboratory and wild Norway and black rats. *Behavioral Processes, 7,* 49-62.

Takahashi, L. K., & Lore, R. K. (1983). Play fighting and the development of agonistic behavior in male and female rats. *Aggressive Behavior, 9*, 217-227.

Thor, D. H., & Holloway, W. R., Jr. (1983). Play solicitation behavior in juvenile male and female rats. *Animal Learning & Behavior, 11*, 173-178.

Thor, D. H., & Holloway, W. R., Jr. (1984). Developmental analysis of social play behavior in juvenile rats. *Bulletin of the Psychonomic Society, 22,* 587–590.

Van den Berg, C. L., Hol, T., Van Ree, J. M., Spruijt, B. M., Everts, H., & Koolhaas, J. M. (1999). Play is indispensable for an adequate development of coping with social challenges in the rat. *Developmental Psychobiology, 34*, 129-138.

Vanderschuren, L. J. M. J., Niesink, R. J. M., & Van Ree, J. M. (1997). The neurobiology of social play behavior in rats. *Neuroscience & Behavioral Reviews, 21,* 309-326.

Varlinskaya, E. I., Spear, L. P., & Spear, N. E. (1999). Social behavior and social motivation in adolescent rats: Role of housing conditions and partner's activity. *Physiology & Behavior, 67*, 475-482.

Von Frijtag, J. C., Schot, M., van den Bos, R., & Spruijt, B. M. (2002). Individual housing during the play period results in changed responses to and consequences of a psychosocial stress situation in rats. *Developmental Psychobiology, 41*, 58-69.

Whishaw, I. Q., Gorny, B., Foroud, A., & Kleim, J. A. (2003). Long-Evans and Sprague-Dawley rats have similar skilled reaching success and limb representations in motor cortex but different movements: some cautionary insights into the selection of rat strains for neurobiological motor research. *Behavioural Brain Research, 145*, 221-232.

9

Exploring Potential Mechanisms Underlying the Lack of Uncertainty Monitoring in Capuchin Monkeys

Bonnie M. Perdue[1], Barbara A. Church[2], J. David Smith[2], & Michael J. Beran[3]

[1]Department of Psychology, Agnes Scott College, USA
[2]Department of Psychology, University at Buffalo, The State University of New York, USA
[3]Language Research Center and Department of Psychology, Georgia State University, USA

In a widely used animal-metacognition paradigm, monkeys are positively reinforced with food for correct classifications of stimuli as sparse or dense and punished with timeouts for incorrect responses, but they also have access to an *uncertainty* response that moves them to the next trial without either of these forms of feedback. Rhesus monkeys use this uncertainty response most often for trials on which they are at greatest risk for making an error, suggesting that they are monitoring their ability to make these classifications. Capuchin monkeys do not succeed to the same degree on these tasks – conceivably as a result of differential contingencies in place in all existing studies between the sparse/dense responses (food delivery or timeout) and the uncertainty response (avoidance of a timeout but also no chance for food reward). Here, we used a novel variation of this task in which the outcomes of the three response classes (sparse, dense, uncertain) were functionally equivalent. All responses simply determined the delay interval before presentation of a second task (matching-to-sample), and that task yielded potential food rewards. Overall, capuchin monkeys used the dense and sparse responses appropriately, including some animals that had no prior experience in performing this classification task. However, none used the uncertainty response appropriately even when it was placed on the same contingency plane as the dense and sparse responses. This suggests that the failure of capuchin monkeys to use an uncertainty response is not the result of that response producing a qualitatively different outcome compared to the dense and sparse responses.

Humans are metacognitive – often expressed as an explicit, declarative awareness of their states of learning and knowing. Metacognition is a late developmental achievement (Balcomb & Gerken, 2008) and it might be uniquely human (Metcalfe & Kober, 2005). Accordingly, there has been sharp interest in this cognitive capacity (e.g., Hertzog & Dunlosky, 2004; Koriat, Goldsmith, & Pansky, 2000; Koriat & Levi-Sadot, 2001; Nelson & Dunlosky, 1991). Given the potential adaptive significance of metacognition, it would not be surprising to find that nonhuman animals share some form of metacognitive abilities, and many empirical studies and theoretical debates have emerged in recent years to address this question (e.g., Carruthers, 2008, 2009; Crystal & Foote, 2009; Hampton, 2009; Jozefowiez, Staddon, & Cerutti, 2009; Smith, 2009; Kornell, 2009, 2013; Le Pelley, 2012; Smith, Beran, Couchman, & Coutinho, 2008).

Please send correspondence to Dr. Bonnie Perdue, Agnes Scott College, 141 E. College Avenue, Decatur, GA 30030. (Email: bperdue@agnesscott.edu)

The uncertainty-monitoring task is a prevalent paradigm for assessing metacognition in nonhuman animals. Subjects typically make a dichotomous classification of a stimulus presented on the screen (e.g., determining if a pixelated square is *sparse* or *dense*). If correct, subjects hear a melodic tone and receive a food pellet. If not, a timeout begins and the screen is blank until the next trial. Sometimes a third response option – typically a *?* on the screen – allows subjects to opt out of a trial (all stimuli disappear from the screen) with no direct reward (e.g., the food reward) and no direct punishment (e.g., the penalty timeout for an error). The next trial simply begins. Rhesus macaques (*Macaca mulatta*) often selectively opt out of more objectively more difficult trials, as defined by proximity to the objective midpoint of the continuum. They choose the uncertainty response most often for exactly those trials where they are at greatest risk for making an error (see Smith, 2009). They do this in a wide variety of tasks and circumstances, including perceptual classification tasks with deferred feedback (Smith, Beran, Redford, & Washburn, 2006), same-different assessments (Shields, Smith, & Washburn, 1997), numerical judgments (Beran, Smith, Redford, & Washburn, 2006), and when they perform as many as four different tasks at the same time (Smith, Redford, Beran, & Washburn, 2010). However, there is not a consensus about the mechanisms underlying these performance patterns, and many empirical reports have been conducted to better understand the mechanism(s) underlying uncertainty responding by rhesus monkeys. Often, human participants are given the same tasks as monkeys, and perform similarly in terms of their use of the uncertainty response (and even say that they use it when they are not sure how to otherwise respond), but this does not mean that the same mechanism – metacognition – underlies the performance of both species. Thus, the debate continues about the proper interpretation of data from this test paradigm (Carruthers, 2008, 2009; Crystal & Foote, 2009; Hampton, 2009; Kornell, 2009, 2013; Le Pelley, 2012; Jozefowiez et al., 2009; Smith, 2009; Smith et al., 2008).

Capuchin monkeys (*Cebus apella*) – a New World primate species – do not show the use of the uncertainty response that is clearly expressed by apes and macaques (e.g., Beran, Smith, Coutinho, Couchman, & Boomer, 2009). The latter species commonly select the uncertainty response and use it most often when trials are objectively most difficult. Capuchin monkeys rarely do so, even when there are extremely long penalty timeouts for incorrect classification responses (e.g., Beran et al., 2009). This might suggest that capuchin monkeys lack whatever metacognitive monitoring capacity exists for rhesus monkeys. Recently, however, we have shown that capuchins can make appropriate uncertainty responses if one sharply reduces their probability of being correct by chance guessing (Beran, Perdue, & Smith, 2014). This suggests a species difference in risk tolerance between the capuchins and macaques. And if there are differences across species in the sensitivity to contingencies like risk, there might also be differences across species in the sensitivity to other contingencies that are present in the uncertainty monitoring task.

More specifically, an important aspect of the uncertainty-monitoring paradigm is that use of the uncertainly response need not be positively reinforced (though in some studies it has been, see discussion in Smith et al., 2008). Generally, in research with macaques, a food reward is not delivered for making that response. Instead, the uncertainty response avoids a potential timeout, and moves to the next trial (which may be harder or easier). But, choice of the uncertainty response also eliminates any chance for food reward. This is a critical aspect to its function, but one that is also sometimes forgotten. Monkeys must know what trials are best for using the uncertainty responses (e.g., those with high degrees of risk of error) rather than to use it indiscriminately because then many easy trials that should produce food reward will be lost.

With regard to avoiding timeouts, the function of the uncertainty response can be seen as providing the subject with negative reinforcement because its selection avoids a potentially aversive stimulus (the long timeout that is given only for incorrect responses). One possibility is that avoidance learning could be shaping the use of the uncertainty response as follows. Some stimuli (i.e., the most difficult stimuli near the breakpoint of the discrimination) could serve as discriminative stimuli indicating that the uncertainty response will lead to the avoidance of an otherwise likely timeout if a primary response is made. Thus, over time, the behavior of selecting the uncertainty response might increase in the presence of those stimuli because of negative reinforcement (choice of the uncertainty response takes away the negative timeout stimulus). This type of learning has been demonstrated in many species and, if this is in fact occurring with the perceptual judgment task, perhaps capuchin monkeys do not use uncertainty responses not because they cannot monitor their own capacity for classifying stimuli, but because they are not as sensitive to negative reinforcement relative to positive reinforcement, and so the value of the uncertainty response is not the same for them as it is for rhesus monkeys. Thus, guessing incorrectly (but, with a 50% chance of still being correct given that there are only two classes of stimulus denseness) is viewed as a better outcome than avoiding a timeout but with a 100% cost of also eliminating any chance for a food reward. As noted earlier, there is some evidence that capuchin monkeys may be more risk tolerant than macaques in these contexts (Beran et al., 2014), and so we attempted to assess this aspect of the temporal contingencies of the uncertainty monitoring task.

We presented capuchin monkeys with a new variation of the dense-sparse task to explore whether differential sensitivity to temporal contingencies might account for the previous failure of these monkeys to use an uncertainty response. We used an uncertainty-monitoring task in which correctly made primary discrimination responses (i.e., sparse/dense responses) *and* the uncertainty response all resulted in the same kind of contingency. Monkeys still performed a box density classification, and could still label a box as sparsely pixelated, densely pixelated, or could select the uncertainty response. Now, however, for the first time these three response classes generated the same qualitative outcome, but to quantitatively different degrees. In all cases, the outcomes of these choices dictated the temporal delay until a second task was presented, and it was this task that afforded the monkeys the opportunity to earn potential food rewards. This second task was a matching-to-sample (MTS) task, in which monkeys viewed a sample on the screen and then selected a match choice that was identical to the sample from an array of possible matches. If they selected correctly *then and only then* did they receive a food reward. For the density discrimination task there was no chance to receive food rewards. Rather, correct primary classification (Dense/Sparse) led to nearly immediate presentation of the MTS task. Incorrect classifications led to a long temporal delay before the MTS trial was presented, and the uncertainty response led to an intermediate delay until presentation of the MTS trial.

It is critical to note that appearance of the sample for the MTS trial was not differentially probable on the basis of the density classification. It always appeared whether the monkey was correct, incorrect, or chose the uncertainty response, and thus could not operate as a secondary reinforcer that selectively reinforced certain choices in the density discrimination task. And, it is critical to note that the monkeys then still had to accurately perform the MTS trial to get any food reward. If they were wrong, they sat through another timeout. Thus, reward was entirely contingent on performing the MTS task well, and had nothing to do with performance on the density discrimination task. The only impetus for doing well at the density classification (and perhaps learning when to use the uncertainty response) was to minimize the delay that otherwise existed before the MTS trial could be performed.

If capuchin monkeys were unable to learn and perform even the basic density discrimination task under these newly established contingencies, it would suggest that differential sensitivity to negative reinforcement (i.e., removing the time delay until the MTS trial was presented) is a viable explanation for capuchin monkey responses patterns, and one that is different from a claim that these monkeys lack access to metacognitive signals that underlie uncertainty monitoring. In our view, this is an important issue in further understanding the nature of the uncertainty response as it is experienced by capuchin monkeys, and in better defining the role of stimulus control in these kinds of tasks. However, if capuchin monkeys learned the basic sparse-dense discrimination proficiently, but still did not use the uncertainty response, this would allow us to discount the hypothesis that the different behavioral profiles seen in the two species in uncertainty-monitoring tasks is the result of capuchin monkeys lacking sensitivity to the value of minimizing temporal delays in tasks that also produce food rewards.

Experiment 1

Sparse/dense trials involve the presentation of a pixelated box in the middle of the computer screen in which the number of pixels could range from sparsely to densely pixelated on a continuum. Subjects select a *S*, *D*, or *?* icon on the screen to classify the pixelated box (see method section for more details). We presented capuchin monkeys with a task in which a trial began with this sparse/dense judgment before monkeys were presented with a matching-to-sample (MTS) trial, and it was only the MTS trial that afforded the monkey a chance to obtain food reward. This modification from the standard task was made to ensure that the responses on the sparse/dense task were never directly positively reinforced. Rather, they led to a separate, distinct task that could potentially yield food reinforcement depending on the accuracy of the response.

For the sparse/dense judgment task, three response options were available on the screen during each trial (*S* for sparse stimuli, *D* for dense stimuli, and *?* as the uncertainty response). A correct response in classifying a stimulus as dense or sparse led to the immediate presentation of a MTS task but no food reward or other tangible positive reinforcer. An incorrect sparse or dense response led to a 30 s delay before presentation of the MTS task. The *?* response led to a 6 s delay before the onset of the MTS task. Thus, correct responses on the sparse/dense judgment allowed the subject to entirely avoid longer delays to another task, but were never directly positively reinforced. Similarly, the *?* response avoided a longer delay that could have occurred with an incorrect response but still added a longer delay than would have occurred for a correct response. The uncertainty response also was not directly reinforced.

Once the MTS trial was presented, a correct matching response led to a food reward whereas an incorrect response led to another timeout period before the next sparse/dense trial was presented. Thus, the only way to earn positive reinforcement in the form of food reward was through correct matching. It is critical to note that this MTS trial always appeared. Thus, the presence of a sample in the middle of the screen could not operate as any kind of conditioned reinforcer of responses made to specific density boxes in the first component of the task, because the presence of a sample always happened.

Given capuchin monkeys' limited use of the uncertainty response in past tasks with this design (e.g., Beran et al., 2009), their performance in this experiment allowed insight into what mechanisms might underlie uncertainty responding in this type of task. More specifically, this experiment presented an opportunity to test the alternative hypothesis that capuchin monkeys previously failed to produce adaptive patterns of uncertainty responding in this density discrimination task because they are less sensitive to the temporal contingencies of these tasks than other species. There were three possible outcomes of interest:

1. Capuchin monkeys fail to learn to use any of the discrimination responses. This would include failing to maintain sparse, dense, or uncertainty responses appropriately.

This finding would suggest that capuchin monkeys are not proficient at learning in general through the use of presenting or removing time delays that slow eventual access to food rewards. This would also suggest that some uncertainty-monitoring paradigms used with macaques may not be fair tests when used with capuchins because of this differential learning sensitivity.

2. Capuchin monkeys succeed in using all three responses appropriately (sparse, dense, uncertainty).

This finding would suggest that capuchin monkeys are sensitive to the negative contingencies (removal of time delays), and that the uncertainty response may have failed to emerge in capuchins in previous studies because the primary and uncertainty responses were learned under different contingencies (i.e., positive reinforcement for the dense and sparse responses, negative reinforcement for the uncertainty response). This would suggest that uncertainty monitoring in capuchin monkeys requires an equivalent reinforcement (and punishment) structure across the response classes.

3. Capuchin monkeys successfully use the primary discrimination responses under negative contingencies, but do not use the uncertainty response when appropriate.

This finding would suggest that capuchin monkeys are sensitive to negative contingencies in this kind of perceptual judgment task because they can make responses that solely operate to remove time delays. When the temporal contingencies are all placed on the same plane within the task, the monkeys can judge density, but still do not anticipate and respond to difficult trials that risk making errors. This finding would argue against the hypothesis that species differences in uncertainty responding can be explained by species differences in sensitivity to negative reinforcement, but would leave open the question of whether capuchin monkeys lack metacognitive monitoring abilities or are constrained by other aspects of the task demands that are not directly relevant to metacognitive monitoring.

Method

Subjects. Ten adult capuchin monkeys between the ages of 5 and 13 years were tested. Five of these monkeys had participated in the previous Beran et al. (2009) study (three males - Logan, Liam, and Griffin, and two females – Wren and Nala) whereas the other five monkeys were naïve with regard to this computerized task (two males – Nkima and Drella, and three females - Gambit, Widget, and Lily). Although these monkeys were naïve to the sparse/dense task, they already had learned and were highly proficient with MTS tasks, how to respond to computer-generated stimuli, and how to engage those tasks using the joystick. All monkeys were housed in social groups of six individuals, and these monkeys spent the majority of the days in these social groups with access to outdoor yards and continuous access to water. Monkeys voluntarily separated into individual test boxes that allowed them to access a dedicated computer system for assessing various cognitive capacities (e.g., see Beran, 2008; Beran, Evans, Klein, & Einstein, 2012; Beran & Parrish, 2012; Smith et al., 2012). These test sessions typically lasted between 2 and 4 hours, and then monkeys returned to the larger social group.

Apparatus. The monkeys were tested using the Language Research Center's Computerized Test System. This system consisted of a personal computer, digital joystick, color monitor, and pellet dispenser (Evans, Beran, Chan, Klein, & Menzel, 2008; Richardson, Washburn, Hopkins, Savage-Rumbaugh, & Rumbaugh, 1990). Monkeys manipulated the joystick with their hands to produce isomorphic movements of a small cursor somewhere on the computer screen. Contacting stimuli with the cursor sometimes resulted in the delivery of 45-mg banana-flavored chow pellets (Bio-Serv, Frenchtown, NJ) via a pellet dispenser that was connected to the computer. The task program was written in Visual Basic 6.0.

Design and procedure. We presented monkeys with a task in which a trial began with a sparse/dense judgment that monkeys could make or could avoid by choosing the uncertainty response. A correct sparse or dense response led to the immediate presentation of an MTS task. An incorrect sparse or dense response led to a 30 s delay before presentation of the MTS task. The uncertainty response led to a 6 s delay before presentation of the MTS task. Thus, correct responses on the sparse/dense judgment allowed the subject to avoid longer delays to another task, but were never directly positively reinforced. Similarly, the uncertainty response avoided the long delay of an incorrect response but still gave a longer delay than a correct response. It was not directly reinforced.

Density discrimination. On each trial, monkeys saw a 185 X 185-pixel box in the screen's top center. The box was filled with a varying number of randomly placed white pixels presented on a black background. Sixty stimulus levels could be presented (Levels 1-60). Each level's pixel count was given by the formula pixels = round (base pixels x 1.036^{Level}) where the base pixel number was 400. This formula gave the continuum a logarithmic character, with each density step a constant percentage increase in pixels and not a constant absolute increase in pixels. Half of the trials were objectively defined by the program as being sparse (Levels 1-30) and half were dense (Levels 31-60). Approximately 30% of the trials were restricted to only the central third of the range (Levels 21-40) whereas the other 70% were sampled from the full continuum (Levels 1-60; note that Level 21-40 trials also were possible as part of this second sampling method).

Capuchin monkeys touched an *S* or *D* icon located at left center and right center of the screen to classify the pixelated box as sparse or dense, respectively. Correct responses immediately led to the presentation of the MTS trial (see description below). When an *S* or *D* response was made incorrectly, there was a 30 s interval with a blank screen, and then the MTS trial was presented. Choice of the uncertainty response (the *?* at the bottom center) led to a 6 s blank screen followed by presentation of the MTS trial. Thus, there was no positive reinforcement presented for correct responses. Rather, those responses were negatively reinforced by removing any delay to the MTS part of the trial. Incorrect responses were positively punished (as in past research using this paradigm), and uncertainty responses operated to alleviate some of the delay to the MTS part of the trial (i.e., were negatively reinforced but to a smaller degree than correct primary responses).

Matching-to-sample (MTS) task. In the MTS task, a sample image first appeared in the center of the screen. This image was randomly selected from a large library of distinctive clip art images. Monkeys made an observing response to this sample by moving the cursor into contact with it. Then, one identical matching stimulus and three non-matching comparison stimuli appeared randomly assigned in the four corners of the computer screen. Monkeys had to choose the comparison stimulus that was identical to the sample. There was no memory demand as the sample remained onscreen with the match choices, and thus the task was very easy for the monkeys (they typically performed at 90-100% accuracy on these trials). Correct responses led to a melodic tone and delivery of a food pellet whereas incorrect responses led to a buzz tone and a 30 s timeout during which the screen remained blank. Following either of these outcomes, a 1 s inter-trial interval occurred, and then the next density discrimination was presented.

Because monkeys worked at their own pace, they completed variable numbers of trials within experimental sessions and across the whole experiment. We first examined performance when the trial count for a monkey was approximately 4,000 trials. If subjects only used one response during the density discrimination task (i.e., chose the sparse stimulus 80% or more of the trials, or conversely selected the dense stimulus on 80% or more of trials) after these approximately 4,000 trials, participation in the task was stopped. All other subjects continued in the experiment until all monkeys had completed approximately 10,000 trials or more. Some monkeys exceeded this number substantially because they tended to perform many more trials per session than other monkeys. One monkey, Wren, was not regularly engaging this task during the time period of this study, and so we discontinued testing her given this low motivation level to engage the task but still included her data in analyses. Thus, her lower data count reflects her choice to not participate as often as the other monkeys. Trial counts are provided in Table 1.

Table 1

Trial counts for Experiments 1 and 2

Monkey Name	Trials	
Capuchin Monkeys	Experiment 1	Experiment 2
Drella	4,138	19,505
Gambit	6,510	9,737
Lily	8,528	5,278
Griffin	22,663	6,258
Wren	3,991	2,553
Logan	26,497	9,140
Nala	9,911	9,975
Nkima	9,975	12,410
Liam	9,974	9,977
Widget	9,661	---
Gabe	---	9,560

Data analysis. Group level (see Figure 1) and individual (see Figure 2) plots of the sparse, dense and uncertainty responses were made. For the purpose of statistical analysis, the stimulus levels were collapsed into bins. To approximate an equal number of trials in each bin, 2-level bins were created for the middle region (because this was oversampled in the task) and 4-level bins were created for the ends. For the sparse and dense response, the percent correct was calculated for each bin. For the uncertainty response, the overall percent of trials in which it was used was calculated for each bin. Subjects that showed an 80% or greater biased selection of one response (Drella, Gambit and Lily, see Figure 2) were excluded from the analysis. We used three separate repeated-measures analysis of variance (ANOVA) tests to assess the effect of bin level on the sparse, dense and uncertainty response. For a more conservative statistical approach, we used the Huyhn-Feldt correction (Huyhn & Feldt, 1976).

Results

Subjects were highly proficient in the MTS task – typically ranging between 90% and 100% correct. Three (out of 10) monkeys (Drella, Gambit, Lily) did not succeed on the density discrimination task and primarily (80% or more) used one of the response options for the majority of trial levels. Participation by those monkeys was discontinued after approximately 4,000 trials. These three monkeys were three of the five that were naïve to the sparse/dense discrimination task at the onset of the experiment. In general, not all monkeys used the uncertainty response in previous experimental tasks (e.g., Smith et al., 2006; Smith et al., 2010), suggesting that this is a challenging task and it is not entirely surprising that some naïve monkeys did not initially learn the task. The other seven monkeys, including two naïve subjects, showed primary discrimination curves that nicely approximated the expected responses based on the perceptual continuums. Specifically, as supported by visual inspection of the data shown in Figure 1, we expected sparse responses to decrease, and dense responses to increase, as the level increased. There was a significant effect of bin on proportion of sparse responses, $F(3.7, 22.3) = 366.73$, $p < 0.001$, and dense responses, $F(3.7, 22.3) = 366.73$, $p < 0.001$. However, bin level did not have any effect on the use of the uncertainty response, $F(4.2, 25.3) = 2.05$, $p = 0.115$ (Figure 1), suggesting that subjects did not use the uncertainty response in a manner that suggested uncertainty monitoring, with an increase in UR use as objective trial difficulty increased. These monkeys all showed clear discrimination of the sparse and dense regions even though the responses in classifying those stimuli as sparse or dense were never directly reinforced with food pellets in this experiment.

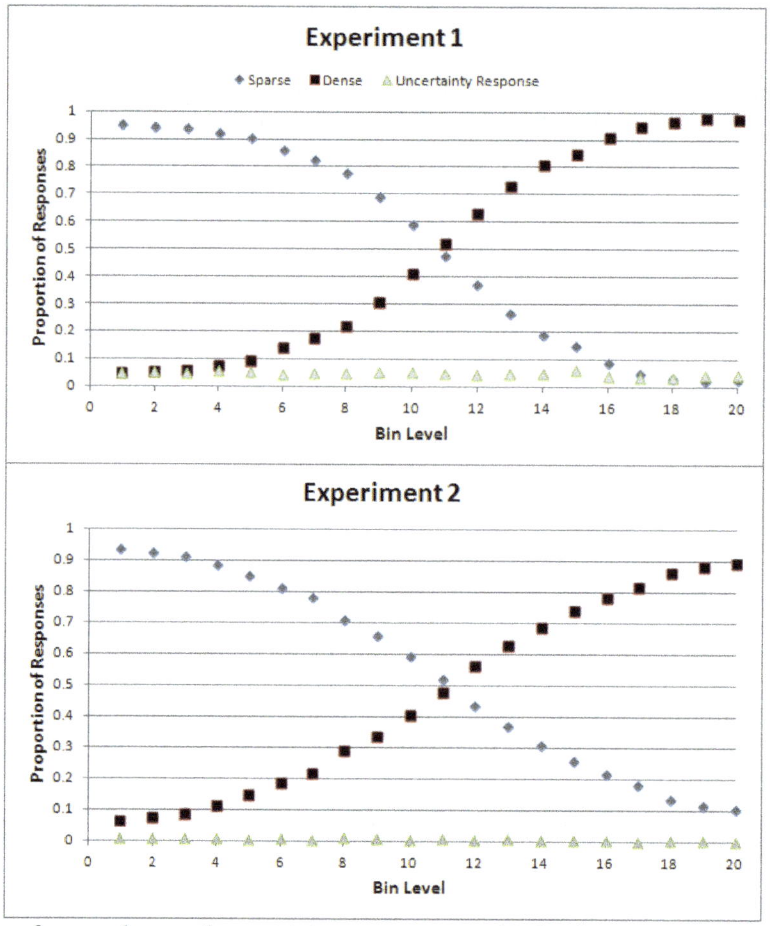

Figure 1. Average proportion of sparse, dense and uncertainty responses across bin levels.

In terms of our potential outcomes, the results are mostly in line with the third potential outcome that stated that monkeys could learn the primary discrimination in a perceptual judgment task via negative reinforcement, but not integrate proficient use of the uncertainty response. This finding suggests that in this type of perceptual judgment task, capuchin monkeys are capable of learning the appropriate task responses via negative reinforcement contingencies for those responses, but they still do not produce adaptive uncertainty monitoring curves even when all response classes are similar in nature. We can reject the idea that capuchins are not capable of learning through negative reinforcement (potential Outcome 1) or that they learn all response classes when placed under the same contingencies (potential Outcome 2).

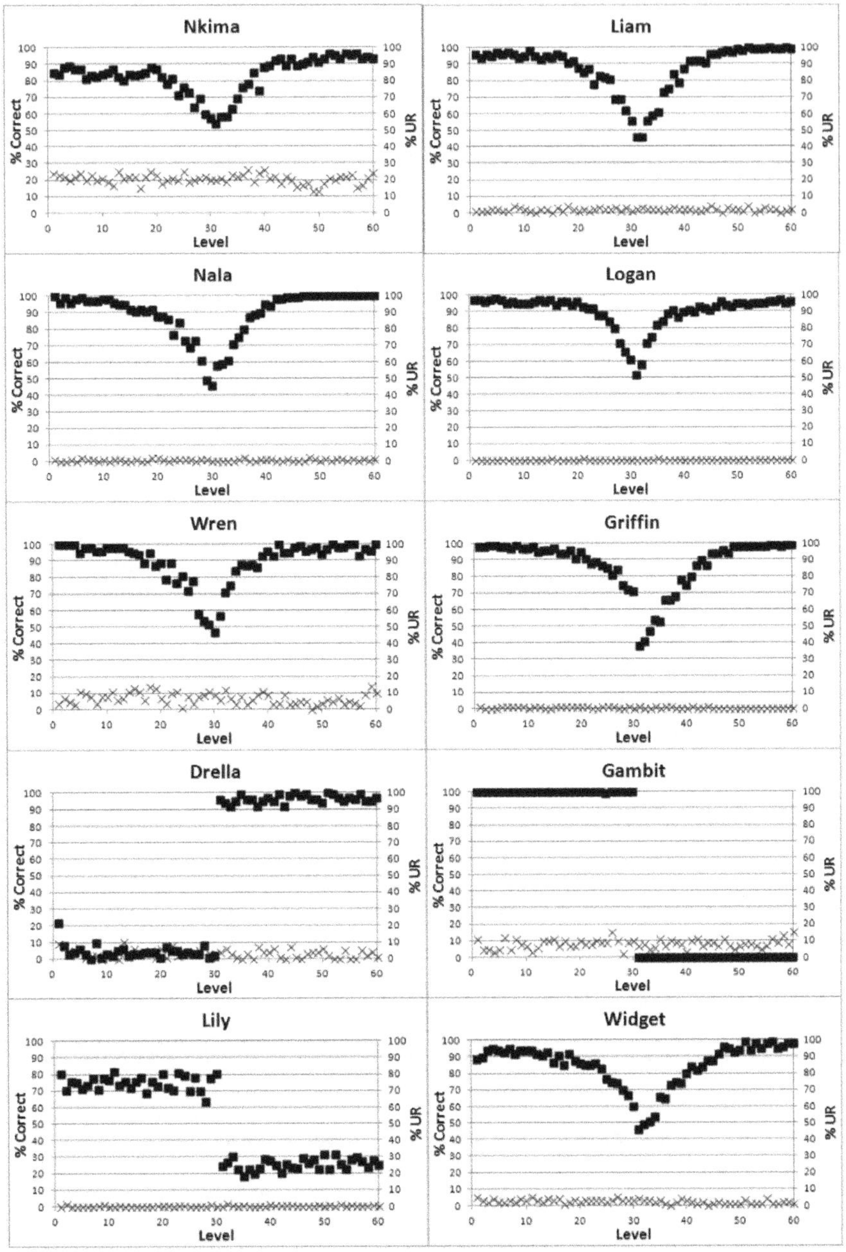

Figure 2. Capuchin monkey performance (% Correct – black squares; % Uncertainty Response – gray hatched marks) in Experiment 1 as a function of trial level.

Discussion

This experiment was designed so that primary discrimination responses yielded the same type of outcome (determining the delay to another task) as the uncertainty response. The majority of capuchin monkeys were capable of learning and performing a perceptual discrimination task under these conditions. Unlike previous studies, they were never positively rewarded for a correct sparse or dense response. Instead, a correct response avoided a timeout to another task that did provide positive reinforcement for correct responses. Given these contingencies, seven out of 10 monkeys discriminated sparsely and densely pixelated images from one another.

However, these monkeys still did not use the uncertainty response adaptively to avoid the most difficult trials. To the capuchins, this third response in the task was somehow meaningfully different, even though all three responses acted only to determine the temporal delay until the MTS task was presented. Thus, one cannot attribute the failure of capuchins to respond uncertain in the previous study (Beran et al., 2009) to their insensitivity to avoiding time outs. For most monkeys, their sensitivity was fine when it came to perceptual-discrimination responses. Instead, capuchins exhibited a selective failure to use the uncertainty response in particular. One must seek another behavioral or psychological explanation for this selective failure, and we return to this issue in the General Discussion.

Crucially, we tested five naïve animals that had not been in the Beran et al. (2009) study, although one of these monkeys (Drella) had some experience classifying pixel boxes (but not using uncertainty responses) as part of a pilot study for the Beran et al. (2009) study. The other four monkeys had no experience classifying pixel boxes as sparse or dense. Although Drella, Lily, and Gambit showed strong response biases and seemed to have some difficulty in learning the classification categories under these contingencies, Widget and Nkima did learn the primary discrimination, but these monkeys failed to show any proficient uncertainty responding.

The perceptual discriminations used in Experiment 1 were objectively easier than those used in previous experiments (e.g., Beran et al., 2009). The changes in density level to level were larger than typically used. This was intentionally done to motivate participation in a task that did not in and of itself yield positive reinforcement. However, it is possible that the capuchin monkeys opted not to use the uncertainty response because the sparse and dense responses were subjectively easy to make (even if they were not always accurate), and this could account for the pattern of uncertainty responding in Experiment 1 (E1). Experiment 2 (E2) addressed this issue.

Experiment 2

Method

Subjects and apparatus. Nine of the same capuchin monkeys were tested as in Experiment 1. We added one new male (Gabe) and removed Widget from Experiment 2 due to her limited availability during the project. Even monkeys that were excluded from E1 analyses based on performance patterns were included again at the start of this new phase. The apparatus was identical to that in Experiment 1.

Design and procedure. All aspects of the task were the same except for the following:

Although 60 stimulus levels again could be presented (Levels 1-60), each level's randomly placed pixel count now was given by the formula pixels=round (base pixels x 1.018^{Level}) where the base pixel number was 689. This formula again gave the continuum a logarithmic character, with each density step a constant percentage increase in pixels and not a constant absolute increase in pixels. This change in base pixel number and multiplier value made the task objectively more difficult as each level was closer in comparison to its neighbors than had been the case in Experiment 1. Monkeys again performed variable numbers of trials as a result of individual differences in productivity within individual test sessions. Trial counts for each monkey are provided in Table 1.

Results

All subjects were highly proficient on the MTS task – typically ranging between 90% and 100% correct.

Three out of 10 capuchin monkeys (Gambit, Lily and Nkima) did not succeed on the primary discrimination and were excluded from the statistical analysis. The other seven monkeys showed primary discrimination curves that nicely approximated the expected responses (as detailed in E1) to sparse stimuli,

$F(1.4, 8.2) = 58.59, p < 0.001$, and dense stimuli, $F(1.4, 8.2) = 58.59, p < 0.001$; however, they did not use the uncertainty response, $F(3.9, 23.6) = 1.06, p = 0.398$, in a selective manner (see Figures 1 and 3).

We also assessed whether the objective difficulty changes made to the program led to differences in performance. For the animals that learned the primary discrimination in both experiments, performance was significantly better in E1 ($M = 88.79$, $SD = 1.04$) than in E2 ($M = 80.89$, $SD = 3.72$), $t(4) = 6.08, p = 0.004$.

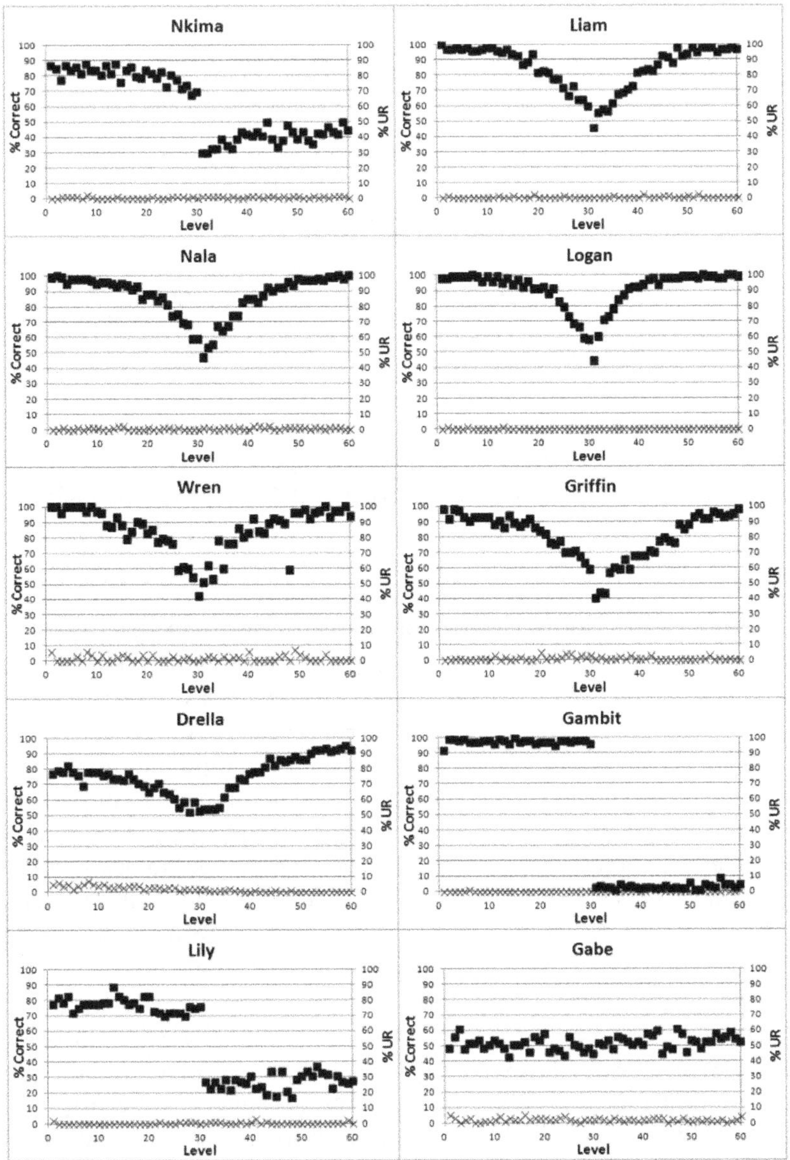

Figure 3. Capuchin monkey performance (% Correct – black squares; % UR – gray hatched marks) in Experiment 2 as a function of trial level.

Discussion

Experiment 2 systematically tightened the psychophysical discrimination, adding in more objective task difficulty by presenting more trials that were closer to the Sparse-Dense divide than in Experiment 1, plausibly increasing capuchins' motivation to use the uncertainty response adaptively to decline the most difficult trials (or, interpreted associatively: to avoid the most error-causing stimuli). The density discrimination part of the experiment was still run with no positive reinforcement for the sparse, uncertain, and dense responses. The result was the same as in Experiment 1. Capuchin monkeys were capable of performing the more difficult perceptual discrimination task and still did not use the UR. However, these monkeys still did not respond by using the uncertainty response to avoid longer delays on the most difficult trials. One cannot explain this result using the ease of the task in Experiment 1.

General Discussion

The findings of the present work suggest that a potential lack of, or limitation in learning via negative reinforcement is *not* a likely reason that capuchin monkeys do not succeed on uncertainty responding tasks. Thus, the data support our third outcome of interest described earlier while not supporting the first two outcomes that were noted. There has been the fairly consistent finding that capuchin monkeys fail to produce the adaptive response patterns of rhesus monkeys in uncertainty monitoring tasks as well as other tasks that are proposed to assess metacognition across species. Rhesus monkeys efficiently seek information about where food might be hidden (Basile, Hampton, Suomi, & Murray, 2009), but capuchin monkeys do not (Paukner, Anderson, & Fujita, 2006). Rhesus monkeys search for specific kinds of needed information during computerized memory tests whereas capuchin monkeys do not (Beran & Smith, 2011). And in tasks such as the one used in this experiment, macaques use the uncertainty response most often when they encounter difficult discriminations, whereas capuchin monkeys do not (e.g., Beran et al., 2009; but see Beran et al., 2014). One possible explanation for the apparent species difference on these tasks is that capuchins indeed lack metacognitive abilities present in some other primate species. However, it is critical to assess the possibility that researchers have yet to determine the correct situations in which such capacities might manifest in capuchin monkeys. Failures on the existing tasks should be carefully assessed to determine if an explanation other than lack of metacognition might explain differences in performance.

Typically, in uncertainty monitoring tasks monkeys are rewarded for correct classifications (positive reinforcement) and punished for incorrect classifications, but use of the uncertainty response simply moves to the next trial. This simplicity, however, does not necessarily extend to a straightforward interpretation of exactly what an uncertainty response is for the subject. Here, we have addressed the concern that it might operate as a form of negative reinforcement in the sense that if the animal was about to suffer an error, and receive a penalty, that penalty was avoided by making the uncertainty response. Below, we discuss this possibility in more detail. However, it is critical to remind the reader that uncertainty responses also *cost* the subject the chance at a reward. There is no way to receive positive outcomes (food pellets) when using an uncertainty response that simply erases the trial. Thus, the uncertainty response perhaps causes the combined feelings of avoiding a possible timeout and giving up a possible reward – and what the sum of the two motivations is for the subject is unknown, particularly for nonverbal subjects.

Furthermore, the concern that capuchin performance might differ as a function of positional biases or differential sensitivity to delay has been addressed in previous work. Capuchin monkeys did not use the UR in Beran et al. (2009), but they did frequently and appropriately use the Middle response that was in the same location on the screen as the UR was located, but in a different trial type. And, some monkeys did use the UR located at the bottom of the screen in Beran et al. (2014). Thus, we can discount a bias to not move downward in discrimination tasks, and we note that monkeys will select the *?* stimulus in some contexts. Capuchin monkeys are as sensitive to different delay levels as other primates. For example, we have conducted numerous delay discounting tasks with these specific monkeys, and they showed consistent within-subjects degrees of delay discounting that also were similar to those seen in rhesus monkeys (e.g., Evans, Perdue, Parrish, & Beran, 2014).

The primary goal of this article was to explore whether subjects could learn a psychophysical discrimination task when the outcome contingencies for all three response classes were qualitatively similar (they all impacted delay to the MTS task, which was the only part of the experiment in which food reward could be earned). This discrimination task was not designed to promote the strongest and clearest use of the uncertainty response, but rather to contrast performance on this task with that of previous assessments with capuchin monkeys. In the current task, the uncertainty response actually led to a timeout period before the MTS trial appeared. The uncertainty response here served more as a "plea bargain" response that would allow subjects to endure a shorter timeout than an incorrect response would yield. The majority of the capuchins learned and maintained the primary classifications (sparse and dense) in this task, but still never appropriately used the uncertainty response. Capuchin monkeys were sensitive to temporal contingencies that determined how soon the next trial can appear and be completed. However, the monkeys only were successful in making the sparse and dense responses under these contingencies, whereas the uncertainty response, even when equated to the other responses in terms of its qualitative effect to dictate the delay interval, remained unused or used without any clear relation to objective trial difficulty. Thus, the search for uncertainty responding in capuchin monkeys remains ongoing, but one potential non-metacognitive reason for differential performance of this species compared to macaques now can be dismissed.

Acknowledgments

This research was funded by NIH grants HD061455 and HD060563 and by NSF grant BCS0956993.

References

Basile, B. M., Hampton, R. R., Suomi, S. J., & Murray, E. A. (2009). An assessment of memory awareness in tufted capuchin monkeys (*Cebus apella*). *Animal Cognition, 12*, 169-180.

Beran, M. J. (2008). Capuchin monkeys (*Cebus apella*) succeed in a test of quantity conservation. *Animal Cognition, 11,* 109-116.

Beran, M. J., Evans, T. A., Klein, E. D., & Einstein, G. O. (2012). Rhesus monkeys (*Macaca mulatta*) and capuchin monkeys (*Cebus apella*) remember future responses in a computerized task. *Journal of Experimental Psychology: Animal Behavior Processes, 38,* 233-243.

Beran, M. J., & Parrish, A. E. (2012). Sequential responding and planning in capuchin monkeys (*Cebus apella*). *Animal Cognition, 15,* 1085-1094.

Beran, M. J., Perdue, B. M., & Smith, J. D. (2014). What are my chances? Closing the gap in uncertainty monitoring between rhesus monkeys (*Macaca mulatta*) and capuchin monkeys (*Cebus apella*). *Journal of Experimental Psychology: Animal Learning and Cognition, 404,* 303-316.

Beran, M. J., & Smith, J. D. (2011). Information seeking by rhesus monkeys (*Macaca mulatta*) and capuchin monkeys (*Cebus apella*). *Cognition, 120*, 90-105.

Beran, M. J., Smith, J. D., Coutinho, M. V. C., Couchman, J. J., & Boomer, J. (2009). The psychological organization of "uncertainty" responses and "middle" responses: A dissociation in capuchin monkeys (*Cebus apella*). *Journal of Experimental Psychology: Animal Behavior Processes, 35*, 371-381.

Beran, M. J., Smith, J. D., Redford, J. S., & Washburn, D. A. (2006). Rhesus macaques (*Macaca mulatta*) monitor uncertainty during numerosity judgments. *Journal of Experimental Psychology: Animal Behavior Processes, 32*, 111-119.

Call, J. (2010). Do apes know that they could be wrong? *Animal Cognition, 13*, 689-700.

Call, J., & Carpenter, M. (2001). Do apes and children know what they have seen? *Animal Cognition, 4*, 207-220.

Carruthers, P. (2008). Meta-cognition in animals: a skeptical look. *Mind and Language, 23*, 58-89.

Carruthers, P. (2009). How we know our own minds: The relationship between mindreading and metacognition. *Behavioral and Brain Sciences, 32*, 121-182.

Crystal, J. D., & Foote, A. L. (2009). Metacognition in animals: Trends and challenges. *Comparative Cognition and Behavior Reviews, 4*, 54-55.

Evans, T. A., Beran, M. J., Chan, B., Klein, E. D., & Menzel, C. R. (2008). An efficient computerized testing method for the capuchin monkey (*Cebus apella*): Adaptation of the LRC-CTS to a socially housed nonhuman primate species. *Behavior Research Methods, 40,* 590-596.

Evans, T. A., Perdue, B. M., Parrish, A. E., & Beran, M. J. (2014). Working and waiting for better rewards: Self-control in two monkey species (*Cebus apella* and *Macaca mulatta*). *Behavioural Processes, 103,* 236-242.

Fujita, K. (2009). Metamemory in tufted capuchin monkeys (*Cebus apella*). *Animal Cognition, 12*, 575-585.

Hampton, R. R. (2001). Rhesus monkeys know when they remember. *Proceedings of the National Academy of Sciences, 98*, 5359-5362.

Hampton, R. R. (2009). Multiple demonstrations of metacognition in nonhumans: Converging evidence or multiple mechanisms? *Comparative Cognition and Behavior Reviews*, *4*, 17-28.

Hertzog, C. & Dunlosky, J. (2004). Aging, metacognition, and cognitive control. In B. H. Ross (Ed.), *The psychology of learning and motivation: Advances in research and theory* (p. 215 – 251). San Diego, CA:Academic Press.

Huynh, H., & Feldt, L. S. (1976). Estimation of the Box correction for degrees of freedom from sample data in randomised block and split-plot designs. *Journal of Educational Statistics*, *1*, 69-82.

Jozefowiez, J., Staddon, J. E. R., & Cerutti, D. T. (2009). Metacognition in animals: How do we know that they know? *Comparative Cognition and Behavior Reviews, 4*, 29-39.

Koriat, A., Goldsmith, M., & Pansky, A. (2000). Toward a psychology of memory accuracy. *Annual Review of Psychology, 51,* 481-537.

Koriat, A., & Levy Sadot, R. (2001). The combined contributions of the cue-familiarity and accessibility heuristics to feelings of knowing. *Journal of Experimental Psychology: Learning, Memory, and Cognition, 27,* 34-53.

Kornell, N. (2009). Metacognition in humans and animals. *Current Directions in Psychological Science, 18*, 11-15.

Kornell, N. (2013). Where is the "meta" in animal metacognition? *Journal of Comparative Psychology*, *128*, 143-149. doi:10.1037/a0033444

Le Pelley, M. E. (2012). Metacognitive monkeys or associative animals? Simple reinforcement learning explains uncertainty in nonhuman animals. *Journal of Experimental Psychology. Learning, Memory, and Cognition, 38*, 686-708.

Nelson, T. O., & Dunlosky, J. (1991). When people's judgments of learning (JOL) are extremely accurate at predicting subsequent recall: The delayed-JOL effect. *Psychological Science, 2,* 267-270.

Paukner, A., Anderson, J. R., & Fujita, K. (2006). Redundant food searches by capuchin monkeys (*Cebus apella*): A failure of metacognition? *Animal Cognition, 9*, 110-117.

Richardson, W. K., Washburn, D. A., Hopkins, W. D., Savage-Rumbaugh, E. S., & Rumbaugh, D. M. (1990). The NASA/LRC Computerized Test System. *Behavior Research Methods, Instruments, and Computers, 22,* 127-131.

Shields, W. E., Smith, J. D., & Washburn, D. A. (1997). Uncertain response by humans and rhesus monkeys (*Macaca mulatta*) in a psychophysical same-different task. *Journal of Experimental Psychology: General, 126,* 147-164.

Smith, J. D. (2009). The study of animal metacognition. *Trends in Cognitive Sciences, 13*, 389-396.

Smith, J. D., Beran, M. J., Couchman, J. J., & Coutinho, M. V. C. (2008). The comparative study of metacognition: Sharper paradigms, safer inferences. *Psychonomic Bulletin and Review, 15,* 679-691.

Smith, J. D., Beran, M. J., Redford, J. S., & Washburn, D. A. (2006). Dissociating uncertainty responses and reinforcement signals in the comparative study of uncertainty monitoring. *Journal of Experimental Psychology: General, 135*, 282-297.

Smith, J. D., Coutinho, M. V. C., Church, B. A., & Beran, M. J. (2013). Executive-attentional uncertainty responses by rhesus macaques (*Macaca mulatta*). *Journal of Experimental Psychology: General, 142,* 458-475.

Smith, J. D., Crossley, M. J., Boomer, J., Church, B. A., Beran, M. J., & Ashby, F. G. (2012). Implicit and explicit category learning by capuchin monkeys (*Cebus apella*). *Journal of Comparative Psychology, 126,* 294-304.

Smith, J. D., Redford, J. S., Beran, M. J., & Washburn, D. A. (2010). Rhesus monkeys (*Macaca mulatta*) adaptively monitor uncertainty while multi-tasking. *Animal Cognition, 13*, 93-101.

10

Modulation of Variation by Response-Reward Spatial Proximity

Kenneth J. Leising & Chad M. Ruprecht
Texas Christian University, U.S.A.

W. David Stahlman
University of Mary Washington, U.S.A.

There has been a recent surge in the experimental investigation of the control of behavioral variability. Currently, it is understood that variability in behavior is predictably modulated by reinforcement parameters (e.g., a probability of reward delivery and reward magnitude). In two experiments, we investigated how spatial proximity between response and reward locations impacts the production of behavioral variability in both response rate and lever press duration. Rats were trained to lever press on two levers in a standard operant chamber that only differed from one another in their proximity to a food niche (i.e., Near vs. Far); a second experimental factor, the probability of reward, was signaled by an auditory cue. In Experiment 1, trials with a high-probability stimulus terminated with reward on 100% of trials, while trials with a low-probability stimulus terminated with reward 25% of the time. We used a similar procedure in Experiment 2, but reduced the likelihood of reward on low-probability trials to 10% and collected data in a post-acquisition extinction test. Overall, proximity and probability were inversely related to variation of response rate, whereas only the probability factor affected variation in lever press duration. Proximity also interacted with probability to influence variation in response rate. These findings extend the factors modulating behavioral variability to include the spatial proximity between a response and reward.

The degree of behavioral variability during periods in which an expected reward was omitted (i.e., an extinction trial) has been the focus of much previous research (e.g., Antonitis, 1951; Balsam, Deich, Ohyama, & Stokes, 1998; Devenport, 1984; Eckerman & Lanson, 1969; Herrick & Bromberger, 1965; Morgan & Lee, 1996; Millenson & Herwitz, 1961; Neuringer, Kornell, & Olufs, 2001; Notterman, 1959; Stebbins & Lanson, 1962). During extinction trials, response variability (e.g., in the rate of lever pressing) has been shown to be higher relative to that observed during acquisition. However, response rate also decreases during extinction trials, thus limiting the amount of data that can be collected without retraining.

Many studies of reward-expectation induced variability have utilized steady-state procedures as alternatives to extinction. During steady-state procedures, response rates are stable and variability can be measured across many sessions of training (e.g., Stahlman, Roberts, & Blaisdell, 2010a). For example, Gharib, Gade, and Roberts (2004) trained rats that two signals, high-probability and low-probability, ended with food with a probability of 100% or 25%, respectively. Over 31 sessions of training, rats emitted hundreds of responses each day. Interresponse times (IRTs) and lever press durations (DURs) during the low-probability signal demonstrated greater variability as compared to the high-probability signal. Because the delivery of reward during steady-state instrumental procedures is contingent solely upon a lever press, additional dimensions (e.g., IRT or Duration) of the response (related to the expected density of reward) are free to vary. These results supported a rule proposed by Gharib et al. (2001): a reduction in the expectation of reward increases variation of behavioral form (see also Roberts & Gharib, 2006).

All experimental procedures were done in correspondence with the relevant ethical guidelines and were approved by TCU's Institutional Animal Care and Use Committee. Please send correspondence to Kenneth J. Leising, Department of Psychology, Texas Christian University, 2800 S. University Dr., Box 298920, Fort Worth, TX 76129. (Email: k.j.leising@tcu.edu)

More recent results have supported this rule. Stahlman and Blaisdell (2011b) manipulated both the magnitude of the reward and the temporal delay to reward with pigeons pecking to a visual stimulus displayed on a touchscreen-equipped monitor. Presenting a reward of lower magnitude instantiated higher amounts of behavioral variability (e.g., standard deviation of IRTs and standard deviation of X, Y coordinates); similarly, the insertion of a delay between pecking and the delivery of the reward increased variability of behavior. These results suggest that probability and magnitude of reward, as well as the temporal proximity of the response to reward modulated the pigeons' expectation of reward, and that lower expectations of reward led to greater variation in behavior (Stahlman & Blaisdell, 2011b). Previous research investigating the production of temporal and spatial behavior has found similar psychophysical principles governing each (see Cheng, 1992 for a review). These findings raise the question of whether manipulations of the spatial proximity between response and reward would impact variation in the same manner as temporal proximity.

Pecoraro, Timberlake, and Tinsley (1999) reported increases in the variability of sampling behavior within a plus-maze associated with a decrease in reward quality, which is another factor that modulates reward expectation. On an elevated plus maze, rats were trained to seek out a beaker of 32% sucrose solution always located on one arm of the maze. Rats in a downshift-group (32%/4%) then received trials in which the sweet solution was switched to a considerably less sweet sucrose solution; importantly, these rats decreased consummatory behavior, and increased their nose-down locomotion, location entries, and sampling of alternatives in comparison to an unshifted (4%/4%) group. Thus, in the spatial domain, drops in reward quality spur variable behavior (see Wiegmann & Smith, 2009, for a similar demonstration in honeybees).

More relevant to signaled manipulations of reward probability, Stahlman and Blaisdell (2011a) trained rats to use landmarks to search for food buried within a 4 x 4 array of response locations. On separate trials, the two landmarks were paired with a hidden food reward with similar spatial relations, but they differed in the probability (HI = 100%, LO = 20%) that reward would be found at the expected reward location. Foraging variability was considerably higher during trials with the LO landmark, as measured by the standard deviation of search frequencies. These results suggest that spatial variability in foraging is also modulated by reward probability.

Figure 1. A diagram of the interior of the experimental apparatus. The food niche is on the right-hand side of the image in the center of the chamber. The near lever is adjacent to the food niche. The far lever is positioned on the opposite wall of the chamber from the food niche. Both levers are shown in the active position (i.e., inserted), but during experimental trials only one lever was active. This image is drawn to scale.

One factor that has not yet been studied is how the spatial proximity of the response to the reward influences the production of variability. Classic models of response learning state that responses, such as pressing a lever for food, strengthen as a function of their proximity (spatial and/or temporal) to reward (Hull,

1943; Silva, Timberlake, & Gont, 1998; Staddon & Horner, 1989). According to classic optimal foraging theory (MacArthur & Pianka, 1966) successful foragers are sensitive to shifting environmental contingencies. In general, animals are required to behave flexibly, varying their responses to accommodate changes in reward probability, as well as conservatively, minimizing travel time and energy expenditure by favoring proximal response locations over distal response locations (Kacelnik & Todd, 1992). However, it is unclear how spatial proximity will influence reward expectation, and consequently, response variation. Therefore, the current research investigated whether the spatial proximity of the response location (a lever) to the food niche would influence temporal variation in the behavior of rats. We also sought to examine how reward probability and spatial proximity interact to modulate reward expectation.

In two experiments, rats were trained to lever press on two levers in a standard operant chamber; one lever was positioned adjacent to the food niche (i.e., Near), while the other was placed on the opposite side of the chamber (i.e., Far, see Figure 1). During discrimination training, rats were given separate trials of the Near and Far lever paired with one auditory cue associated with a High (100%) probability of reward and the other a Low (i.e., 25% in Experiment 1 and 10% in Experiment 2) probability. In Experiment 2, all subjects were also tested during post-acquisition extinction sessions. We expected to replicate prior findings of higher variability with decreased reward expectation, manifest as less temporal variation in lever press IRTs and DURs on the Near lever compared to the Far lever. Furthermore, based on the results of Stahlman and Blaisdell (2011b), we predicted that reward probability and spatial proximity would interact to control variability. We conducted the procedures and analyses below to conform closely to prior published work (e.g., Gharib et al., 2004).

Experiment 1

Method

Subjects. The subjects were 12 female hooded Long-Evans rats bred in the TCU vivarium from parents obtained from Harlan Laboratories (Indianapolis, IN). Subjects were pair-housed in translucent plastic tubs with a substrate of wood shavings in a vivarium maintained on a 12 hr dark/12 hr light cycle. All experimental manipulations were conducted during the light portion of the cycle. A progressive food restriction schedule was imposed over the week prior to the beginning of the experiment, until each rat received 15 g of food each day. All animals were maintained at 85% of their free-feeding weight. The rats weighed, on average, 270 grams and were six months old at the start of the experiment. All animals were handled daily for 30 s, during the week prior to the initiation of the study.

Apparatus. Figure 1 displays the experimental chamber. Each of six experimental chambers measuring 30 cm x 25 cm x 20 cm (l x w x h) was housed in a sound and light-attenuating environmental isolation chest (Med Associates). The walls and ceiling of the chamber were constructed of clear Plexiglas and the floor was constructed of stainless-steel rods measuring 0.5 cm in diameter, spaced 1.5 cm center-to-center. One wall of the chamber was equipped with a dipper that delivered a 16% sucrose solution. When in the raised position, a small well (0.05 cc) at the end of the dipper arm protruded up into the food niche. An infrared photo-detector was positioned across the entrance to the feeding niche. The near lever was positioned on the same wall as the food niche, at a distance of 12 cm center-to-center. The far lever was positioned on the wall opposite the food niche, at a distance of 25 cm center-to-center.

A ventilation fan in the enclosure and a white-noise generator on a shelf outside of the enclosure provided a constant 74-dB (A) background noise. One speaker on the outside walls of the chamber could deliver a high-frequency tone (3000 Hz) 8 dB(A) above background and the other a white noise (N) stimulus 8 dB (A) above background. The tone and white noise served as discriminative stimuli and were counterbalanced across groups. A diffuse houselight was located 13 cm above the floor on the wall opposite the food magazine.

Procedure.

Pretraining. Pretraining consisted of 10 sessions. All rats were initially trained to drink sucrose from the feeding niche. Once available, a disruption in the infrared beam in the feeding niche would initiate a 10-s access period before the lever retracted. This was also true for non-differential and discrimination training. Rats were then trained to respond on the levers in the near and far positions. On each trial, one of the two levers was randomly selected to be inserted into the chamber. Initially, responses on the lever were reinforced according to a continuous reinforcement schedule, followed by variable-ratio 2 (VR-2), VR-4, and then random-ratio 4

(RR-4) schedules of reinforcement. All trials were separated by a 60 s inter-trial interval (ITI). All sessions were 90 minutes in length. Rats were advanced together to the next reinforcement schedule only after all of them lever pressed at least 50 times in a session.

Non-differential training. All rats were given separate trial types of two stimuli (tone and noise), each paired equally often with the near and far levers (i.e., Near-Tone, Far-Tone, Near-Noise, Far-Noise). Trial type was chosen randomly without replacement, such that the number of trials per trial type would be roughly equal within each session. Each trial began with simultaneous insertion of a lever and onset of a discriminative stimulus. All trials terminated according to a RR-4 schedule and the probability of sucrose reward following trial termination was 100%. All trials were separated by a 60 s ITI and sessions were 90 minutes in length. Non-differential training consisted of 4 sessions. One rat failed to show reliable bar pressing after 4 additional sessions and so training for that rat was discontinued.

Discrimination training. In this phase, the probability of reward at a trial's termination for one of the two auditory stimuli was lowered from 100% to 25% for all subjects. Which stimulus was paired with the reduction in reward probability was counterbalanced across subjects. Each stimulus was presented equally often with the near or far lever and reinforced with the assigned probability irrespective of which lever was present. All trials were separated by a 60 s ITI. The manipulation of probability and proximity resulted in four within-subject trial types – High-Near, High-Far, Low-Near, and Low-Far. Trial type was chosen randomly without replacement in blocks with all four trials represented in each block. All sessions were 90 minutes in length. Discrimination training consisted of 30 sessions.

Measures.

Individual durations were measured to an accuracy of 20 msec. The duration from the onset of the discriminative stimulus until the first response (pre-response time, PRT) and subsequent interresponses times (IRTs) were recorded. The duration (DUR) of each lever press was also recorded. Because IRT and DUR were strongly positively skewed, we performed a log transform of the data to normalize it prior to statistical analysis (cf. Gharib et al., 2004). We then calculated the standard deviation of log IRT and log DUR within session as our measures of temporal variation. This is a common transformation of these kinds of data and has been employed in a number of recent reports (e.g., Stahlman & Blaisdell, 2011b).

PRTs and IRTs have been shown to exhibit different patterns of variability (Gharib, Gade, & Roberts, 2004; Stahlman et al., 2010a; Stahlman et al., 2010b). Differences between PRTs and IRTs would likely result in differences between DURs of the first vs. subsequent lever press as well. Consequently, we analyzed the PRTs and DURs from first responses separately from the IRTs and DURs from subsequent responses.

The number of discrimination training sessions and the probability of reward for the low and high-probability stimuli were chosen to match those reported in Gharib et al. (2004). As in previous reports (Gharib et al., 2004; Stahlman et al., 2010a), we were interested in the effects of probability and contiguity following the acquisition of steady-state responding. Consequently, we analyzed the last 20 sessions of discrimination training.

Results and Discussion

One subject failed to reach the requisite number of lever presses within four additional sessions of non-differential training, thus analyses were conducted with the remaining subjects (n = 11). The standard deviations of the first responses (PRTs and DURs) are reported followed by the same measures (IRT and DUR) collected from subsequent responses. All of the statistical results from Experiments 1 and 2 can be found in Table 1. Figure 2 shows the standard deviation of PRTs (left panel) and DURs (right panel) as a function of probability (High vs. Low) and proximity (Near vs. Far) during the last 20 sessions of training. Though the differences appear small, Figure 2 indicates that both low-probability trials (Near-Low and Far-Low) produced higher levels of variation in PRT than those with the high-probability stimulus. This observation was supported by a repeated-measures ANOVA conducted on PRTs with Probability (High vs. Low) and Proximity (Near vs. Far) as factors, which found a main effect of Probability, $F(1,10) = 16.86$, $p = 0.002$, and a marginally non-significant interaction of Proximity x Probability, $F(1,10) = 4.51, p = 0.06$. To determine the source of the near-interaction, we conducted separate post-hoc Scheffe tests. These tests revealed greater temporal variation during Far-Low than either trial type with the high-probability stimulus (Far-High and Near-High), $ps < .04$, but no reliable difference between the two low-probability trial types (see Figure 2), $p = 0.86$. Near-Low also produced higher levels of variation than Far-High, $p = 0.005$. For the

DUR of first responses (see Figure 2, right-panel), we conducted the same analysis but found no reliable main effects or the interaction, Fs(1,10) < 3.45, ps > 0.09.

The data from subsequent responses (IRT and DUR) are also shown in Figure 2. Small differences in the low- vs. high-probability trial types are noticeable in IRT and DUR, but particularly in the DUR measure. These observations were again supported by separate repeated measures ANOVAs with Probability (High vs. Low) and Proximity (Near vs. Far) as factors revealing a main effect of Probability in both IRTs, $F(1,10) = 5.17$, $p = 0.05$, and contrary to the results with first responses, the DUR of subsequent responses, $F(1,10) = 12.33$, $p = 0.006$.

The results of the last 20 sessions of discrimination training provide evidence of increased variation of PRTs/IRTs with a lower probability of reward. Experiment 1 also provided evidence for a marginally-nonsignificant interaction of probability and proximity, but only on PRTs. With respect to temporal variation in DURs, the standard deviations provided evidence only for increased variation with a lower probability of reward.

Table 1
F values and effect sizes from ANOVAs in Experiments 1 and 2

	IRT				DUR			
	First		Subsequent		First		Subsequent	
	F	η_p^2	F	η_p^2	F	η_p^2	F	η_p^2
Experiment 1								
Proximity (Prox)	.37	.04	.21	.02	3.49	.26	3.41	.25
Probability (Prob)	16.86**	.63	5.17*	.34	3.45	.26	12.33**	.55
Prox * Prob	4.51	.31	1.28	.11	.01	.01	.06	.01
Experiment 2								
Post-Acquisition								
Prox	12.55**	.56	3.97	.38	.01	.01	1.46	.13
Prob	18.08**	.64	6.11*	.38	.87	.08	8.80*	.47
Prox * Prob	15.62**	.61	6.17*	.28	.10	.01	.01	.01
Post-Acq vs. Extinction								
Prox	28.20***	.74	11.35**	.53	2.34	.19	3.24	.24
Prob	20.67**	.67	11.42**	.53	.03	.01	7.37*	.42
Prox * Prob	1.58	.14	4.02	.29	.29	.03	.02	.01
Treatment	16.27**	.62	16.86**	.63	27.51***	.73	9.38**	.48
Treatment *Prox	.01	.14	3.54	.26	.55	.05	1.57	.14
Treatment *Prob	6.31*	.39	11.59**	.54	.01	.01	1.23	.11
Treatment *Prox*Prob	3.12	.24	.35	.03	.77	.07	.85	.08

Note. Exact p-values are provided in the text. *$p < 0.05$, **$p < 0.01$, ***$p < 0.001$.

Experiment 1 failed to provide evidence for the proximity of the response-reward spatial relationship to increase the standard deviation of response rate (i.e., IRTs) and lever press DURs. Furthermore, we report only weak evidence of an interaction between proximity and probability. In Experiment 2, we decreased the probability of reward associated with the low-probability stimulus, extended the number of sessions in both non-differential and discrimination training, and included post-acquisition extinction sessions. The first two manipulations have been employed before in the investigation of reward probability and its relationship to variability in behavior (e.g., Gharib et al., 2004). Extending the number of sessions allowed us to analyze temporal variation during a period of time following a greater number of discrimination training sessions. Lastly, we included extinction training to detect how both factors (i.e., proximity and probability) would influence temporal variation in the absence of reward.

Experiment 2

Method

Subjects. The subjects were 12 experimentally-naïve female hooded Long-Evans rats bred in the TCU vivarium from parents obtained from Harlan Laboratories (Indianapolis, IN). All subjects were housed and handled as in Experiment 1. The rats weighed, on average, 265 grams and were approximately four months old at the start of the experiment.

Apparatus. The apparatus was the same as that used in Experiment 1.

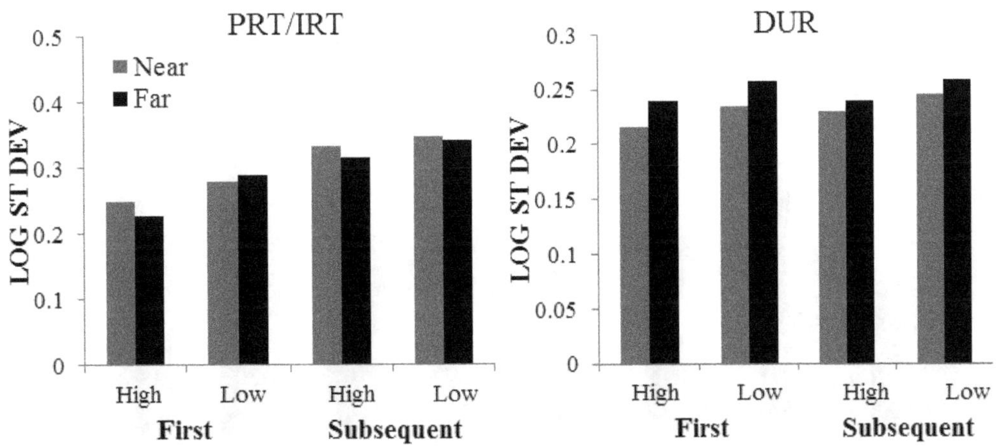

Figure 2. Left panel: The standard deviation of log PRTs and log IRTs from the last 20 sessions of discrimination training in Experiment 1. Right panel: Log DURs from the same period of training. The data from the first and subsequent responses on a trial are displayed separately for each trial type. *Far* and *Near* refer to the location of the lever relative to the food niche, and *High* (100%) and *Low* (25%) refer to the probability that a trial will terminate in reward. All units are measured in seconds.

Procedure. Pretraining and non-differential training were the same as in Experiment 1, with the exception that non-differential training in this experiment continued for 15 sessions.

Discrimination training. Discrimination training was similar to that of Experiment 1, but the probability of reward at a trial's termination for the low-probability auditory stimulus was reduced to 10% and discrimination training continued for 45 sessions. Each stimulus was again presented equally often with the near or far lever and reinforced with the assigned probability irrespective of which lever was present. The manipulation of probability and proximity resulted in four within-subject trial types – High-Near, High-Far, Low-Near, and Low-Far.

Extinction. In this phase, all sessions and trials were identical to that of Discrimination training, except that no responses were reinforced irrespective of discriminative stimulus or lever position. Extinction continued for 6 sessions.

Measures. The measures were the same as those used in Experiment 1.

Results and Discussion

Discrimination Training

One subject died during discrimination training; the analyses below were conducted with the remaining subjects (n = 11). We again report the standard deviations from the first response (PRT and DUR) followed by the same measures (IRT and DUR) collected from subsequent responses (see Table 1 for effect sizes). Figure 3 displays data from the last 20 sessions of discrimination training for first and subsequent responses. Large group differences appear in the IRT measure of variation, with the greatest variation always in Group Far-Low. To evaluate differences in the first response, we conducted a repeated measures ANOVA with Probability (High vs. Low) and Proximity (Near vs. Far) as factors on PRTs and found significant main effects of Proximity, $F(1,10) = 12.55$, $p = 0.005$, Probability, $F(1,10) = 18.08$, $p = 0.002$, and the interaction of Proximity x Probability, $F(1,10) = 15.62$, $p = 0.003$. Separate post-hoc tests revealed variability during Far-Low ($M = 0.36$, $SD = 0.13$) and Near-Low ($M = 0.26$, $SD = 0.08$) were greater than all other trials types, $ps < .03$, but variation on Far-Low trials was also reliably greater than Near-Low, $p = 0.0001$. Separate tests also indicated no reliable difference between Far-High ($M = 0.21$, $SD = 0.04$) and Near-High ($M = 0.19$, $SD = 0.04$), $p = 0.89$. A similar analysis conducted on DURs of first responses revealed no main effects or interactions, $Fs(1,10) < 1.0$.

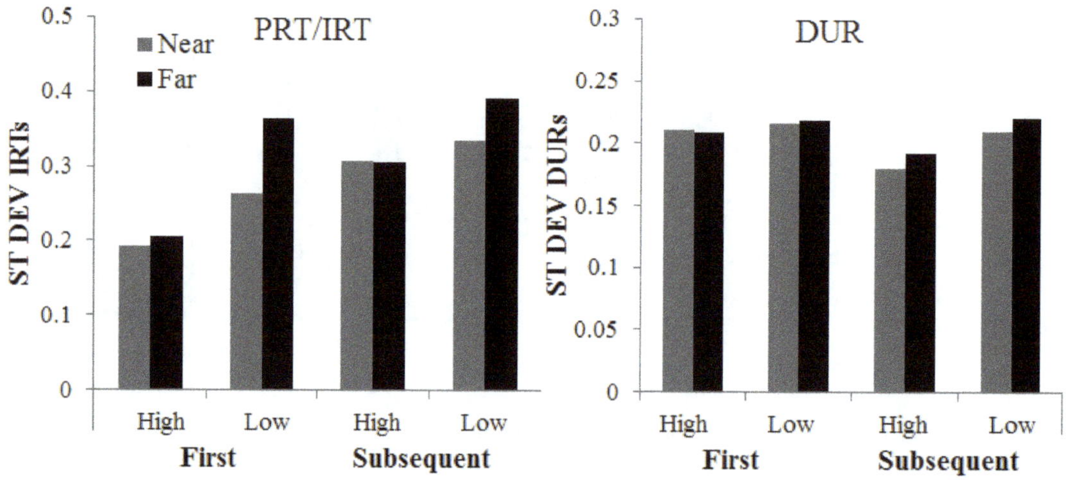

Figure 3. Left panel: The standard deviation of log PRTs and log IRTs from the last 20 sessions of discrimination training in Experiment 2. Right panel: Log DURs from the same period of training. The data from the first and subsequent responses on a trial are displayed separately for each trial type. "Far" and "Near" refer to the location of the lever relative to the food niche, and "High" (100%) and "Low" (10%) refer to the probability that a trial will terminate in reward. All units are measured in seconds.

Similar group differences appear in Figure 3 for subsequent responses. These differences were confirmed by a repeated-measures ANOVA with Probability (High vs. Low) and Proximity (Near vs. Far) as factors conducted on IRTs which revealed a main effect of Probability, $F(1,10) = 6.11$, $p = 0.03$, a significant Probability x Proximity interaction, $F(1,10) = 6.17$, $p = 0.03$, as well as a marginally non-significant main effect of Proximity, $F(1,10) = 3.97$, $p = 0.07$. Separate post-hoc tests revealed that variability during Far-Low (M = 0.39, SD = 0.08) was greater than all other trials types, $ps < 0.05$ (M = 0.39, SD = 0.02), which did not reliably differ from one another, $ps > 0.43$. Contrary to the results with DUR of first responses, analysis of subsequent responses found a main effect of Probability, $F(1,10) = 8.80$, $p = 0.01$, but no other main effects or the interaction, $Fs(1,10) < 1.46$.

The results of the last 20 sessions of discrimination training provide strong evidence for increased variation of PRTs/IRTs with a lower probability of reward and a greater distance between response and reward (i.e., proximity). Additionally, probability and proximity interacted to further modulate temporal variation in PRTs/IRTs. With respect to temporal variation in DUR, however, we again have evidence only for increased variation with a lower probability of reward. These results support and extend previous research. Researchers investigating the relationship between reward probability and variation of behavior have reported greater variation in IRTs for pigeons and rats on trials with a low-probability stimulus (Gharib, Derby, & Roberts, 2001; Gharib, Gade, & Roberts, 2004; Stahlman et al., 2010a; Stahlman et al., 2010b; Stahlman et al., 2011b). Variation in IRTs has also been shown to be sensitive to manipulations of reward expectation other than probability of reward, including the temporal proximity of a response to reward and the magnitude of reward.

Variation in response DURs, however, was not found with pigeons and has thus far only been shown to be sensitive to reward probability in rats. Gharib et al. (2001) suggests that IRT and DUR reflect different neural mechanisms which control the decision to respond and the form of the response, respectively. In support, they refer to prior research demonstrating the independence of IRT and DUR (e.g., Roberts, 1987). The implication of this is that treatments that change IRT may leave DUR unchanged, and vice versa. In the current research, proximity and probability influence the decision to respond (IRT), whereas, response form is only affected by the probability of reward signaled by the stimulus. These results support the claim by Gharib et al. (2001) of the independence of IRTs and DURs.

Extinction Training

In order to evaluate whether extinction interacts with one or both factors (probability and proximity), we compared responding from the last 5 sessions of discrimination training with those conducted during extinction (see Figure 4). For first responses, Figure 4 indicates that the differences between trials with a High- or Low-probability discriminative stimulus appear exaggerated during extinction. Our observations were supported by a repeated-measures ANOVA conducted on PRTs with Treatment (Discrimination training vs. Extinction), Proximity (Near vs. Far) and Probability (High vs. Low) as factors which revealed significant main effects of Treatment, $F(1,10) = 16.27$, $p = 0.002$, Proximity, $F(1,10) = 28.20$, $p = 0.0003$, Probability, $F(1,10) = 20.67$, $p = 0.001$, and importantly, an interaction of Treatment x Probability, $F(1,10) = 6.31$, $p = 0.03$. Separate post-hoc tests of the Treatment x Probability interaction revealed that variation between High-probability and Low-probability trials differed reliably during both discrimination and extinction, $ps < .01$. However, variation on the Low-probability trials (Near-Low and Far-Low) was greater during extinction (M = 0.43, SD = 0.14) than discrimination training (M = 0.32, SD = 0.10), $p < 0.01$, while variation during High-probability trials (Near-High and Far-High) did not differ reliably from training to extinction, $p > 0.10$ (see Figure 4). A similar analysis conducted on DURs of responses revealed only a main effect of Treatment, $F(1,10) = 27.51$, $p = 0.0003$, but no other main effects or interactions, $Fs(1,10) < 2.34$, $ps > 0.16$.

Figure 4 indicates a similar pattern of results during the IRTs and DURs of subsequent responses. This observation is supported by a repeated-measures ANOVA conducted on IRTs for subsequent responses, which revealed effects of Treatment, $F(1,10) = 16.86$, $p = 0.002$, Proximity, $F(1,10) = 11.35$, $p = 0.007$, Probability, $F(1,10) = 11.42$, $p = 0.007$, and the interaction of Treatment x Probability, $F(1,10) = 11.59$, $p = 0.007$. Separate post-hoc tests of the Treatment x Probability interaction revealed variation during the Low-probability and High-probability trial types did not differ reliably during discrimination training, $p > 0.10$, but did support greater variation on Low-probability trials during extinction, $p < 0.001$. The analysis of DURs for subsequent responses again found a main effect of Probability, $F(1,10) = 7.37$, $p = 0.02$, and Treatment, $F(1,10) = 9.38$, $p = 0.01$.

Recent research on variability as a function of reward expectation has either reported measures of variation during a steady-state procedure or during extinction. This is the first report, of which we know, that examines temporal variation during extinction following a steady-state procedure. It is unlikely that extinction would influence variation uniformly throughout each session [e.g., considering factors such as the rate of extinction during a session, the magnitude of recovery at the beginning of each extinction session, and the rate of change of this magnitude over consecutive sessions (see Bouton, 2004)]. Nevertheless, we can make some general conclusions regarding the comparison of data during steady-state responding and across the six sessions of extinction. Not surprisingly, the most robust finding during extinction was an increase in variation for all trial types. However, when an exception occurred (e.g., PRTs in extinction), it was due to no change in temporal variation on Near-High trials; during which both factors (near lever and high probability) supported lower baseline levels of variation. We reported Treatment x Probability interactions for both PRTs and IRTs, indicating a larger effect of probability than proximity on temporal variation during extinction. Temporal variation in DURs was again affected only by the probability of reward.

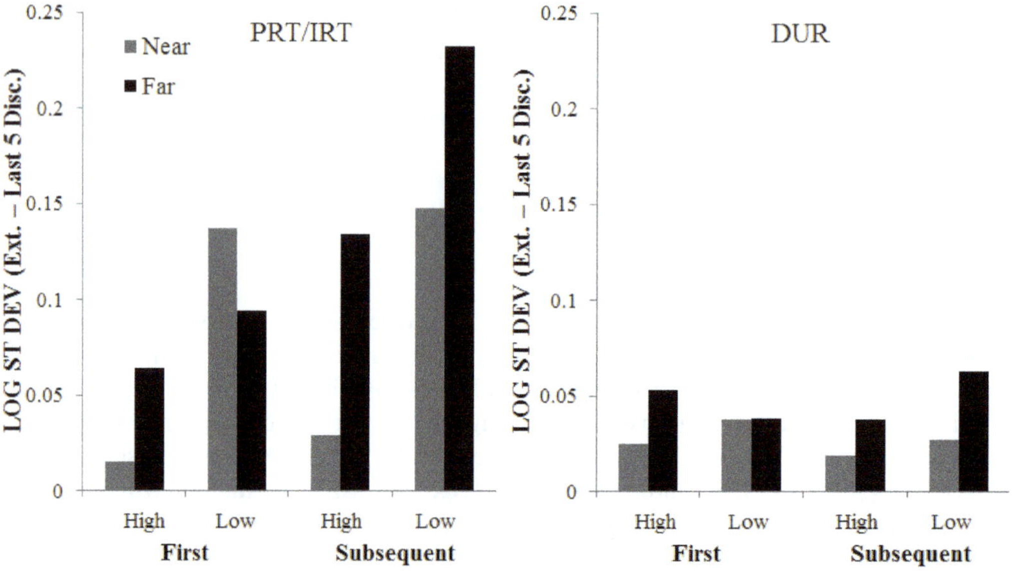

Figure 4. Difference score of the standard deviation of log PRTs, log IRTs, and log DURs during extinction minus the mean for those values over the last five sessions of discrimination training in Experiment 2. The data from the first and subsequent responses on a trial are displayed separately for each trial type. "Far" and "Near" refer to the location of the lever relative to the food niche, and "High" (100%) and "Low" (10%) refer to the probability that a trial will terminate in reward. All units are measured in seconds.

General Discussion

On the whole, our results support and extend prior work on the control of behavioral variability by associative features. On the basis of recent research, we had predicted that the variability of rats' lever pressing would increase with a decreased proximity of the lever to the goal and with a decreased reward probability, and that these factors should interact with each other to produce variation in operant behavior. Our results largely support our predictions.

The Effects of Proximity and Probability

In Experiment 1, we found that the standard deviation of IRT and DUR scores was greater with decreased probability of reward at the termination of trials. This factor weakly interacted with spatial proximity between the lever and reward, such that the effect of reduced probability increased with reduced proximity.

We conducted Experiment 2 to examine the effect of increasing the amount of training and of increasing the discrepancy between the levels of reward probability. As expected, we found that proximity and reward probability both modulated behavioral variability, and that the factors interacted to produce their effects. Specifically, in multiple instances, lever pressing behavior on Low-Far trials was more variable than behavior exhibited on the other three trial types; it is as though the combination of reduced proximity to the goal location and reduced probability of reward crosses a threshold that triggers higher amounts of variability in behavior. These findings corroborate those of Stahlman et al. (2011b), who found that a similar interaction between low levels of multiple associative factors (e.g., probability, magnitude of reward) produced an increase in variability that was not realized when either of the factors was low by themselves. In other instances (Experiment 1, PRTs), temporal variation on Far-Low was greater than all other trials types, whereas Near-Low did not differ reliably from Far-High, but variation was greater than Near-High. This suggests that in some cases, the effects of increased proximity and low probability of reward produce similar levels of variability, which are greater still than that observed during Near-High.

Of course, we cannot identify whether the additional sessions of non-differential and discrimination training or increasing the discrepancy between levels of the reward probability in Experiment 2 resulted in the reliable interaction of proximity by probability on PRTs and IRTs. There is reason to believe both manipulations would contribute to stronger effects in Experiment 2. More training in Experiment 2 would result in more reliable differences during the last 20 sessions of discrimination training, but increasing the discrepancy between levels of probability may exceed the previously mentioned threshold for higher amounts of variability during Low-Far trials.

The Impact of Extinction

In Experiment 2, we followed our training procedures with an extinction test. Prior research has typically found that extinction produces an increase in behavioral variability (e.g., Antonitis, 1951; Neuringer et al., 2001). We corroborated these findings, with variability generally greater during extinction than it was during training. We found that the variability of both lever press PRTs and IRTs was modulated by the proximity and by the probability of stimuli ending with reward during training. Interestingly, probability interacted with treatment for PRTs/IRTs and durations of subsequent responses, but we did not find any effects of probability, proximity, or an interaction with treatment on the durations of first responses. This dissociation is not unprecedented; for example, Stahlman et al. (2010a) found that the variation of pre-response times for pigeons' operant pecking behavior was modulated by reward probability, but only for responses subsequent to the initial peck. It is probable that there are distinct processes that contribute to the form of the response, depending on whether the response is the first or a subsequent response in a sequence. These processes appear to be differentially impacted by factors contributing to expectation (e.g., reward probability).

A final result was that at least two differences in behavior (in variation of both IRT and DUR across trial types) only became evident during the extinction procedure in Experiment 2, after being non-existent during the training period. This further suggests that behavior does not conform to reinforcement parameters linearly, but instead that there is a functional calculation of reward expectation that is compared to a threshold that determines whether the animal will respond with relatively large or small amounts of variability in behavior. The parameters that contribute to this calculation have been shown to be, at minimum: the probability (Gharib et al., 2004; Stahlman et al., 2010a), magnitude (Stahlman et al., 2011b), and quality (Flaherty et al., 1979) of reward, the proximity (spatial and temporal) of the reward to the location of the response (Stahlman et al., 2011b), and almost certainly the strength of the animal's relevant motivational state (Stahlman et al., 2010b). At present, the relative weights of these factors in the determination of variability in behavior are unknown, but it is evident that each holds some sway in the production of variability. Determining the functional relationship of these factors with respect to each other and with respect to behavioral variability remains an important set of questions to be answered in the future[1].

[1] It is highly likely that the value of reinforcement parameters with respect to variability production is going to be species-specific, at minimum. For example, there are data that suggest that reducing reward probability to 25% from 100% in lever-pressing rats is enough to engender consistent and enduring increases in behavioral variability (e.g., Gharib et al., 2004), but that a similar decrease in reward probability is insufficient to increase operant key-pecking variability in pigeons (e.g., Stahlman et al., 2010b).

One Potential Limitation

One possible interpretation of our experimental design and results is that the spatial relationship between the operant location and the reward location is merely an incidental factor that is not, in fact, in control of behavioral variability. After all, our manipulation of the spatial relationship between response and reward is confounded with the temporal proximity between these events. If our effects were driven by temporal proximity this study would, in essence, replicate with rats the temporal proximity effect demonstrated in pigeons (Stahlman & Blaisdell, 2011b) and extend previous results by also reporting differences during a post-acquisition extinction test. Of course, it is difficult to know which of the two possible factors (i.e., temporal vs. spatial proximity) is the controlling factor, or indeed, whether either is solely in control of behavioral variability. Future experiments that explicitly manipulate either the spatial or temporal proximity between response and reward could certainly illuminate the nature of the causal relationship that controls behavioral variability in tasks such as these.

Conclusions and Future Directions

These data strengthen the case that elements of an expected reward modulate the production of behavioral variability. A reduction in expectation, as instantiated by a reduction in probability and/or spatiotemporal proximity of response and reward, is sufficient to increase behavioral variability as compared to conditions with comparatively higher levels of reward expectation. This general finding has been replicated and verified numerous times using a variety of measures, suggesting that it is in fact a common process by which animals engage with the world around them. Future studies should focus on empirically determining the functional aspects of the relationship between expectation and variability – how does it benefit the organism to modify respondent variability in the face of fluctuations in reward expectancy?

References

Antonitis, J. J. (1951). Response variability in the white rat during conditioning, extinction, and reconditioning. *Journal of Experimental Psychology, 42*, 273-281.

Balsam, P. D., Deich, J. D., Ohyama,T., & Stokes, P. D. (1998). Origins of new behavior. In W. O'Donohue (Ed.), *Learning and behavior therapy* (pp. 403-420). Boston: Allyn & Bacon.

Bouton, M. E. (2004). Context and behavioral processes in extinction. *Learning & Memory, 11,* 485-494.

Cheng, K. (1992). Three psychophysical principles in the processing of spatial and temporal information. In W. K. Honig & J. G. Fetterman (Eds.), *Cognitive aspects of stimulus control* (pp. 69-88). London, England: Erlbaum.

Devenport, L. D. (1984). Extinction-induced spatial dispersion in the radial arm maze: Arrest by ethanol. *Behavioral Neuroscience, 98,* 979–985.

Eckerman, D. A., & Lanson, R. N. (1969). Variability of response location for pigeons responding under continuous reinforcement, intermittent reinforcement, and extinction. *Journal of the Experimental Analysis of Behavior, 12,* 73-80.

Flaherty, C. F., Powell, G., & Hamilton, L. W. (1979). Septal lesion, sex, and incentive shift effects on open field behavior of rats. *Physiology & Behavior, 22,* 903-909.

Gharib, A., Derby, S., & Roberts, S. (2001). Timing and the control of variation. *Journal of Experimental Psychology: Animal Behavior Processes, 27,* 165-178.

Gharib, A., Gade, C., & Roberts, S. (2004). Control of variation by reward probability. *Journal of Experimental Psychology: Animal Behavior Processes, 30*, 271-282.

Herrick, R. M., & Bromberger, R. A. (1965). Lever displacement under a variable ratio schedule and subsequent extinction. *Journal of Comparative & Physiological Psychology*, 59, 392-398.

Hull, C. L. (1943). *Principles of behavior*. New York, NY: Appleton-Century-Crofts.

Kacelnik, A., & Todd, I. A. (1992). Psychological mechanisms and the marginal value theorem: Effect of variability in travel time on patch exploitation. *Animal Behaviour, 43,* 313-322.

MacArthur, R. H., & Pianka, E. R. (1966). On optimal use of a patchy environment. *The American Naturalist, 100,* 603-609.

Morgan, D. L., & Lee, K. (1996). Extinction-induced response variability in humans. *Psychological Record, 46,* 145–159.

Neuringer, A., Kornell, N., & Olufs, M. (2001). Stability and variability in extinction. *Journal of Experimental Psychology: Animal Behavior Processes, 27,* 79-94.

Notterman, J. M. (1959). Force emission during bar pressing. *Journal of Experimental Psychology, 58*, 341-347.

Pecoraro, N. C., Timberlake, W. D., & Tinsley, M. (1999). Incentive downshifts evoke search repertoires in rats. *Journal of Experimental Psychology: Animal Behavior Processes, 25,* 153-167.

Roberts, S. (1987). Evidence for distinct serial processes in animals: The multiplicative-factors method. *Animal Learning and Behavior, 15,* 135-173.

Roberts, S., & Gharib, A. (2006). Variation of bar-press duration: Where do new responses come from? *Behavioral Processes, 75,* 215–223.

Silva, F. J., Timberlake, W., & Gont, R. S. (1998). Spatiotemporal characteristics of serial CSs and their relation to search modes and response form. *Animal Learning & Behavior*, 26, 299-312.

Staddon, J. E. R., & Horner, J. M (1989). Stochastic choice models: A comparison between Bush-Mosteller and a source-independent reward-following model. *Journal of the Experimental Analysis of Behavior, 52*, 57-64.

Stahlman, W. D., & Blaisdell, A.P. (2011a). Reward probability and the variability of foraging behavior in rats. *International Journal of Comparative Psychology, 24,* 168-176.

Stahlman, W. D., & Blaisdell, A. P. (2011b). The modulation of operant variation by the probability, magnitude, and delay of reinforcement. *Learning & Motivation, 42,* 221-236.

Stahlman, W. D., Roberts, S., & Blaisdell, A. P. (2010a). Effect of reward probability on spatial and temporal variation. *Journal of Experimental Psychology: Animal Behavior Processes, 36*, 77-91.

Stahlman, W. D., Young, M. E., & Blaisdell, A.P. (2010b). Response variability in pigeons in a Pavlovian task. *Learning & Behavior, 38,* 111-118.

Stebbins W. C., & Lanson, R. N. (1962). Response latency as a function of reinforcement schedule. *Journal of the Experimental Analysis of Behavior, 5*, 299–304.

Wiegmann, D. D., & Smith, B. H. (2009). Incentive relativity and the specificity of reward expectations in honey bees. *International Journal of Comparative Psychology*, 22, 141-152.

11

Variability of Manual Dexterity Performance in Non-human Primates (*Macaca Fascicularis*)

Mélanie Kaeser*, Pauline Chatagny*, Anne-Dominique Gindrat, Julie Savidan, Simon Badoud, Michela Fregosi, Véronique Moret, Christine Roulin, Eric Schmidlin[#] and Eric M. Rouiller[#]

Domain of Physiology, Department of Medicine and Fribourg Center for Cognition, University of Fribourg, Chemin du Musée 5, CH-1700 Fribourg, Switzerland.

The goal of this study was to quantify the inter-individual and intra-individual variability of manual (digits) skill in adult macaque monkeys, over a motor learning phase and, later on, when motor skills were consolidated. The hypothesis is that several attributes of the stable manual dexterity performance can be predicted from learning characteristics. The behavioral data were collected from 20 adult *Macaca fascicularis*, derived from their dominant hand, defined as the hand exhibiting a better performance than the other. Two manual dexterity tasks were tested: (i) the "modified Brinkman board" task, consisting in the retrieval of food pellets placed in 50 slots in a board, using the precision grip (opposition of the thumb and index finger); (ii) the "reach and grasp drawer" task, in which the grip force and the load force were continuously monitored while the monkey opened a drawer against a resistance, before grasping a pellet inside the drawer. The hypothesis was verified for the performance of manual dexterity after consolidation, correlated with the initial score before learning. Motor habit, reflected by the temporal order of sequential movements executed in the modified Brinkman board task, was established very early during the learning phase. As mostly expected, motor learning led to an optimization of manual dexterity parameters, such as score, contact time, as well as a decrease in intra-individual variability. Overall, the data demonstrate the substantial inter-individual variability of manual dexterity in non-human primates, to be considered for further pre-clinical applications based on this animal model.

In the common language, some people are described as clumsy whereas others have recognized talents to practice challenging motor tasks with great manual (digits) dexterity, such as musicians, top sports performers, as well as in some professional activities requiring high degree of precision in motor control (e.g., handmade watchmakers). Such inter-individual variability of motor skill is accompanied by some degree of intra-individual variability as the manual dexterity of a human being is subjected to variations from one day to the next, as well as to improvement resulting from motor practice. Manual dexterity corresponds to the skill to control independently and precisely each finger. From an evolutionary point of view, exquisite manual dexterity is largely considered as a prerogative of primates, as other mammalian orders do not exhibit such a high degree of manual dexterity, in spite of some recent findings providing evidence in favor of some manual skill in rodents for instance (see e.g., Sacrey, Alaverdashvili, & Whishaw, 2009; Whishaw, Whishaw, & Gorny, 2008; Whishaw, Travis, Koppe, Sacrey, Gholamrezaei, & Gorny, 2010; but see also Klein, Sacrey, Whishaw, & Dunnett, 2012). The specialty of primates for manual dexterity is based on the specific anatomical organization of the primate motor system, comprising the direct cortico-spinal projection called the cortico-motoneuronal (CM) system (see Lawrence & Hopkins, 1976; Lawrence, Porter, & Redman, 1985;

* shared first authorship, [#] shared senior authorship

Please send correspondence to Prof. Eric M. Rouiller, Domain of Physiology, Department of Medicine and Fribourg Center for Cognition, University of Fribourg, Chemin du Musée 5, CH-1700 Fribourg, Switzerland, (Email: eric.rouiller@unifr.ch)

Lemon, 2008). The progressive evolution of the CM system across mammalian species is correlated with an increasing manual skill (see e.g., Courtine et al., 2007). Consequently, the non-human primates represent a unique animal model to study mechanisms involved in manual dexterity, which are also applicable to human subjects. For instance, monkeys have been used extensively to investigate experimentally the consequences on manual dexterity of various types of lesions affecting the motor system (e.g., Bashir et al., 2012; Beaud et al., 2008; Beaud et al., 2012; Bihel et al., 2010; Brinkman, 1984; Brinkman & Kuypers, 1973; Dancause & Nudo, 2011; Dancause et al., 2005; Dancause et al., 2006; Darling et al., 2009; Darling et al., 2010; Darling et al., 2011; Darling et al., 2013; Eisner-Janowicz et al., 2008; Friel & Nudo, 1998; Friel, Heddings & Nudo, 2000; Frost, Barbay, Friel, Plautz & Nudo, 2003; Galea & Darian-Smith 1997; Glees & Cole, 1950; Hoogewoud et al., 2013; Kaeser et al., 2010; Kaeser et al., 2013; Liu & Rouiller 1999; Marshall et al., 2003; McNeal et al., 2010; Murata et al., 2008; Nishimura et al., 2007; Nudo & Milliken, 1996; Nudo, Wise, SiFuentes, & Milliken, 1996; Ogden & Franz, 1917; Passingham, Perry, & Wilkinson, 1983; Pizzimenti et al., 2007; Roitberg et al., 2003; Rouiller et al., 1998; Sasaki & Gemba, 1984; Schmidlin, Wannier, Bloch, & Rouiller, 2004; Schmidlin et al., 2005; Schmidlin et al., 2011; Travis, 1955; Wannier, Schmidlin, Bloch, & Rouiller, 2005) and, in some cases, also to test the potential of various treatments after such lesions (e.g., Freund et al., 2006; Freund et al., 2007; Freund et al., 2009; Hamadjida et al., 2012; Kaeser et al., 2011; Plautz et al., 2003; Sugiyama et al., 2013; Wyss et al., 2013).

Numerous studies shed light on the anatomical, physiological and developmental aspects underlying manual dexterity in monkeys (e.g., Alstermark et al., 2011, Alstermark & Isa, 2002, 2012; Armand, Edgley, Lemon, & Olivier, 1994; Armand, Olivier, Edgley, & Lemon, 1997; Borra, Belmalih, Gerbella, Rozzi, & Luppino, 2010; Bortoff & Strick, 1993; Darian-Smith, Galea, & Darian-Smith, 1996; Darian-Smith et al., 1996; Darian-Smith, Burman, & Darian-Smith, 1999; Flament, Hall, & Lemon, 1992; Galea & Darian-Smith, 1994, 1995; Iwaniuk, Pellis, & Whishaw, 1999; Kinoshita et al., 2012; Lacroix et al., 2004; Lemon, Johansson, & Westling, 1996; Lemon, 1999; Maier et al., 2002; Manoel & Connolly, 1995; Ogihara & Oishi, 2012; Olivier, Edgley, Armand, & Lemon, 1997; Padberg et al., 2007; Rathelot & Strick, 2009; Rouiller, Moret, Tanné, & Boussaoud, 1996; Sasaki et al., 2004). Furthermore, various aspects linked with manual dexterity were studied, such as manual coordination and strategies, handedness and tool use, as well as phylogenetic characteristics (e.g., Chalmeau, Visalberghi, & Gallo, 1997; Chatagny et al., 2013; Christel & Billard, 2002; Costello & Fragaszy, 1988; Falk, Pyne, Helmkamp, & DeRousseau, 1988; Fragaszy & Adams-Curtis, 1997; Gash et al., 1999; Fragaszy, 1998; Iwaniuk & Whishaw, 1999, 2000; King, 1986; King & Landau, 1993; Lacreuse & Fragaszy, 1999; Leca, Gunst, & Huffman, 2011; Lemon & Griffiths, 2005; Lindshield & Rodrigues, 2009; Nahallage & Huffman, 2007; Pouydebat, Laurin, Gorce, & Bels, 2008; Pouydebat, Gorce, Coppens, & Bels, 2009; Pouydebat, Reghem, Borel, & Gorce, 2011; Van Schaik, Deaner, & Merrill, 1999; Spinozzi, Castorina, & Truppa, 1998; Spinozzi, Truppa, & Lagana, 2004; Spinozzi, Lagana, & Truppa, 2007; Wiesendanger, 1999; Zhao, Hopkins, & Li, 2012).

In the present study, our goal was to use two complementary manual dexterity tasks, namely the *modified Brinkman board* task and the *reach and grasp drawer* task, to quantify the inter-individual variability of manual skill in adult macaque monkeys, as well as the intra-individual variations along a motor learning phase and, later on, during motor skills consolidation. More specifically, our main hypothesis is that manual dexterity performance and variability in the modified Brinkman board task, when acquired, can be predicted from the duration of the learning phase, and/or from the learning slope and/or from the initial score before any training took place. For the two tasks, it is also expected that the learning phase contributes: (i) to significantly reduce the intra-individual variability of manual skills, when a plateau of performance is reached; (ii) to optimize several attributes of manual dexterity, underlying the better motor performance reached at plateau. Nevertheless, in line with the principle of motor equivalence (see Lashley, 1930), the same motor goals with comparable levels of performance can be achieved using highly different motor strategies, as reflected by a wide inter-individual variability in manual skill parameters exhibited by adult macaque monkeys.

Method

Subjects

The behavioral experiments were conducted on 20 adult macaque monkeys (see Table 1 for individual parameters related to sex, weight, age, etc). Detailed information about the detention conditions of the monkeys, the veterinary authorizations, reward procedures and inclusion of the monkeys in previous studies can be found in the supplementary Methods and Results. As illustrated previously in the form of a video sequence (Schmidlin et al., 2011), the first experimental step (lasting 1-3 months) was to habituate the monkeys to be transferred into a primate chair, without direct manipulation of the animals by the experimenters, a procedure reducing the stress on the animals and the risks for the experimenters. Placed in the primate chair, the monkeys were weighed, and then transferred to the behavioral set-up in the laboratory.

Procedure

On each behavioral session (3-5 days a week), the monkeys systematically performed the modified Brinkman board task (derived from the initial task of Brinkman & Kuypers, 1973; Brinkman, 1984), representing the basic manual dexterity task on which the present data are based. In addition, shifting from one session to the next, the monkeys performed additional tasks (rotating Brinkman board task; Brinkman box task; reach and grasp drawer task; as illustrated in Schmidlin et al., 2011). In the present report, only the reach and grasp drawer task is considered as an additional behavioral test to the modified Brinkman board task and in a subgroup of the monkeys only as this quantitative test was introduced fairly recently.

Taking advantage of two separate windows in front of the primate chair, each hand was tested separately and the first hand tested was alternated at each session. Typically, a daily behavioral session lasted about one hour, to test separately each hand. All behavioral tests were videotaped for off-line analysis. The present report is however restricted to data derived from the **dominant hand**, defined as the hand exhibiting the highest score in the modified Brinkman board task at plateau, to be distinguished from the preferred hand defined as the hand preferably chosen to perform a task when the monkey had the choice to use one or the other hand, irrespective of the performance (see Chatagny et al., 2013).

Materials and Measures

The modified Brinkman board task requires the precision grip (opposition of thumb and index finger) to grasp food pellets from 50 slots dug in a perspex board (see Schmidlin et al., 2011), placed in front of the monkey (see also Figure 5D). The 50 slots are divided into 25 vertically oriented slots and 25 horizontally oriented slots, randomly distributed on the board. Banana flavor 45 mg pellets were used (*Bio-Serv, US and Canada: www.bio-serv.com)*.

As previously reported (Schmidlin et al., 2011), the following 4 parameters were analyzed in the modified Brinkman board task: i) the **score** (number of food pellets retrieved during the first 30 seconds); ii) the **contact time** (CT = duration in seconds of contact between the fingers and the food pellets in the slot), determined for the first 5 vertical slots and the first 5 horizontal slots; iii) the **temporal sequence** followed by the monkey's hand to visit the 50 slots of the board; iv) the **types of movements** and **strategies** used to retrieve the pellets from the slots, as well as the quantification of errors of grasping.

The reach and grasp drawer task also measures the ability to unimanually catch a food pellet in a well, but this action is preceded by the opening of a drawer, requiring to counteract a variable resistance opposing the pulling. The test thus allows quantifying via sensors the force applied to hold the knob of the drawer in between the thumb and the index finger (grip force), as well as the load force (applied to pull the drawer). Moreover, several other sensors allow quantifying distinct consecutive phases of the task (Figure 6A; Schmidlin et al., 2011). In the reach and grasp drawer task, emphasis was put on aspects not covered by the modified Brinkman board task, namely the ability of the monkey to generate different levels of force to counteract the resistances opposing the opening of the drawer (load force), while precisely controlling the grip force between the thumb and index finger to prevent the loss of contact with the drawer knob (see Schmidlin et al., 2011). The following parameters were specifically analyzed in the reach and grasp drawer task: i) the **maximal grip force**; ii) the **maximal load force**; iii) the **duration of the grip force** application; iv) the **duration of the load force** application. The load force is believed to be initiated only when the grip force has reached a sufficient level to prevent sliding of the fingers on the knob due to the resistance opposing the opening of the drawer. Further details about the behavioral set-ups were described earlier (Schmidlin et al., 2011).

The behavioral data were represented graphically and analyzed statistically using the Sigmaplot 12.0 software package (*www.sigmaplot.com*). Accordingly, group comparisons were based on parametric tests (paired or unpaired t-tests) when the normality criteria were satisfied or, if not, on non-parametric tests (Wilcoxon rank-sum test or Mann-Whitney U test). Relationships between two behavioral parameters were assessed based on the Pearson correlation test.

Results

Modified Brinkman Board Task

The modified Brinkman board task is largely intuitive in the sense that an experimentaly-naïve monkey placed in front of the board rapidly starts to grasp flavored food pellets, thus representing a fairly *natural* motor task. However, as a result of practice, the performance measured by the number of pellets retrieved in 30 seconds (score) increased from one session to the next, during the learning phase (Figure 1 and Supplementary Figure 1). The use of the precision grip to perform the task is also naturally adopted by all monkeys, although there may be subtle variations in the prehension pattern itself (see below). Furthermore, as there is no time constraint imposed to visit the 50 slots, the monkeys perform the task at their own pace depending on their motivation, a task thus assimilated to a voluntary behavior. In absence of strong constraints imposing a learning schedule and a level of performance on the monkeys, there is the possibility to assess the inter-individual variability related to manual skill, both during the learning phase and the plateau phase. The data will be first, and mainly, described based on the total score.

Learning phase: Total score. The learning phase of the modified Brinkman board task appeared quite variable from one animal to the next. A unique case is Mk-RO (Figure 1), exhibiting more a substantial decrease in variability along the 146 days of practice than a true increase in performance (modest regression line slope; see also Table 1). Another particular case is Mk-MO (Figure 1), with an impressive score from beginning, maintained during more than 100 days, before a moderate enhancement of score taking place at day 110, considered as the end of the learning phase. The regression line with a slightly negative slope is meaningless (Table 1), reflecting the absence of progressive improvement of score during the first 110 days.

All other monkeys exhibited a progressive increase in score, although the slope and the duration of the corresponding learning period were highly variable across animals (see Figure 1 and Supplementary Figure 1; Table 1). Four monkeys were characterized by a very steep learning slope (Figure 2 panel A; Table 1): Mk-AT (see also Figure 1), Mk-DI (see also Supplementary Figure 1), Mk-WI and Mk-CE. In the rest of the monkeys, the learning slope ranged from low to medium values (Figure 2 panel A), as illustrated for instance by Mk-JO (Figure 1; Table 1).

Another parameter of interest in relation to the learning phase is the intercept of the learning regression line with the y-axis (score), yielding an estimate of the initial performance at the onset of the training. As shown in Figure 2 (panel B: filled circles), the intercept values are quite variable from one monkey to the next, without however forming separate clusters. In Figure 1, three monkeys illustrate a low initial value (Mk-AN), a medium initial score (Mk-JA) and a high initial value (Mk-MO), respectively.

Highly variable also was the duration of the learning phase (Figure 2 panel C). With the exception of Mk-RO (as discussed above), the end of the learning phase was defined using the following criterion (as already used in a recent study on hand dominance/preference: Chatagny et al., 2013): when the progressive increase in score approached a plateau perceived by visual inspection, as observed in most monkeys, the first score value considered as the onset of the plateau is the score which is not exceeded by another value among the five next score values. Consequently, the end of the learning phase, indicated by the vertical dashed line in

Table 1

List of monkeys and relevant parameters for the modified Brinkman board task

	Sex+	Weight*	Age*	Learning phase (days)&	Plateau (days)&	First score value& ç	Median plateau value&	Mean plateau value&	*SD* plateau value&	Slope learning phase&	Score plateau# Comparison H vs V slots	Median contact time at plateau V slots	Median contact time at plateau H slots	Mean errors (learning; plateau)
Mk-AN	f [1,b]	3.2	6	151	44	8.894	22	21.889	1.987	0.0795	H>V	0.32	0.48	5; 0 (c)
Mk-AT	f [1,b]	3.4	7	32	129	18.266	30	29.507	3.521	0.418	**V>H (W)**	0.16	0.26	4.5; 1.2 (c)
Mk-CA	f [1,b]	3.7	7	210	30	12.177	28	26.875	4.303	0.0598	**V>H (t)**	0.2	0.36	3.8; 2.1 (e)
Mk-LO	f [1,b]	3	7	97	92	12.302	22	21.528	2.408	0.0827	**V>H (t)**	0.32	0.8	2.3; 0.4 (c)
Mk-MA	f [1,b]	3.2	7	89	133	17.416	33	33.179	2.984	0.176	**V>H (t)**	0.24	0.2	16; 0.7 (c)
Mk-MI	f [1,b]	3.1	7	86	85	19.846	26	25.465	3.397	0.0611	**V>H (t)**	0.2	0.36	9.8; 1.4 (c)
Mk-TH	f [1,b]	3.9	6	101	26	16.77	31.5	30.938	4.389	0.15	**V>H (t)**	0.2	0.32	7; 0.5 (c)
Mk-DI	f [1,b]	3.4	7	41	109	20.516	31	31.154	3.294	0.410	**H>V (W)**	0.2	0.2	4.8; 1 (c)
Mk-EN	m [3,a]	4.2	5	213	216	27.816	33	32.78	2.339	0.0095	**V>H (W)**	0.2	0.32	2; 0.4 (c)
Mk-AV	m [2,b]	3.2	3	31	120	20.132	31	30.35	2.854	0.198	H>V	0.24	0.44	0; 0 (d)
Mk-JO	m [2,b]	3.2	3	63	34	24.52	34.5	34.25	2.817	0.121	**V>H (W)**	0.16	0.28	1; 0.7 (d)
Mk-JA	m [2,b]	2.5	3	163	60	22.75	28	28.2	2.783	0.0199	**V>H (t)**	0.333	0.867	0; 0.7 (d)
Mk-WI	m [2,b]	2.7	3.5	16	234	30.116	35	34.95	3.306	0.409	**V>H (W)**	0.24	0.32	3.8; 0.2 (c)
Mk-VA	m [2,a]	3.4	3.5	64	404	24.12	26.5	26.875	4.463	0.0937	**V>H (W)**	0.333	0.6	2.3; 0 (c)
Mk-BI	m [2,a]	3.7	4.5	163	142	29.567	34.5	33.817	3.362	0.0336	**V>H (W)**	0.18	0.32	0.7; 0.3 (d)
Mk-MO	m [2,a]	4	4.5	110	114	33.318	35	34.424	2.681	-0.00370	**V>H (t)**	0.133	0.267	1; 0.5 (c)
Mk-GE	f [2,a]	3.5	5	70	447	17.751	21	20.955	4.817	0.0516	**V>H (t)**	0.34	0.56	1.9; 0.1 (c)
Mk-RO	m [2,a]	3.7	3	146	181	23.651	28	27.667	2.087	0.0288	**V>H (W)**	0.44	0.52	6.1; 0.9 (c)
Mk-CE	m [2,a]	3.5	4	21	77	21.75	25.5	23.5	4.468	0.274	**V>H (t)**	0.667	0.8	0.8; 0.9 (d)
Mk-DG	m [3,a]	5.2	4	107	64	20.58	31	31.68	4.13	0.119	**V>H (t)**	0.23	0.32	2.3; 1.8 (e)

Notes. + f = female; m = male. The following number ([1], [2] or [3]) indicates the housing conditions: 1 = 45 m^3 housing facility; 2 = 15 m^3 facility; 3 = transfer from 15 m^3 to 45 m^3 (data acquired however after transfer). The following letter ([a], [b]) indicates whether the animal has been subjected to preliminary habituation to the behavioral set-up (a) or not (b), before data collection.

* at beginning of training (age rounded 0.5).

& established for total score in the modified Brinkman board task (all monkeys).

ç intercept of regression line with y-axis in score plot.

Bold characters are for statistically significant differences between H (horizontal slots) and V (vertical slots): paired t-test **(t)** or Wilcoxon **(W)** test; see also text for learning phase. In the rightmost column, c, d and e correspond to three different error profiles (see text).

Figure 1 and Supplementary Figure 1, precedes the first score value defined as the onset of the plateau. Mk-AV is representative of a very quick learning (Supplementary Figure 1), with a plateau reached after only 31 days. At the other extremity, Mk-EN exhibited a very long learning phase, with a weak slope, completed after 213 days (Supplementary Figure 1). An average duration of learning phase is illustrated by Mk-MA (Supplementary Figure 1), with a plateau reached after about 3 months.

The difference between the average score at plateau and the initial score before training yields an estimate of the score enhancement obtained during the learning phase. This value is represented for the total score by crosses in Figure 2 (panel B). As one might have expected, there is a trend towards a larger improvement of score during the learning phase in the monkeys with a low initial score as compared to those with a higher initial score characterized by a limited score progression. The two (interdependent to some extent) parameters of initial score and score improvement during learning appear to present a difference with respect to sex. As shown in Figure 2 panel B, the nine females (identified by "f" the x-axis) exhibit lower initial values than most males. The average initial score was 15.99 pellets in 30 seconds in females (*SD* = 3.95) whereas, in males, it was 25.3 pellets in 30 seconds (*SD* = 4.3). This difference between females and males is statistically significant ($p < 0.001$; unpaired t-test). Consequently, females exhibited a larger margin of score progression during learning (average 10.84 pellets in 30 seconds; *SD* = 4.23) than males (average 5.47 pellets in 30 seconds; *SD* = 3.42); this difference related to sex is also statistically significant ($p = 0.006$; unpaired t-test). The other two parameters related to learning (learning slope and duration of training) did not differ between the sex groups (Figure 2 panels A and C).

Plateau phase: Total score. As illustrated in Figure 1 and Supplementary Figure 1, the plateau phase starts after the vertical dashed line. The average and median score values reached at plateau were also variable among monkeys, ranging from 21 to 35 pellets (Figure 2 panels E and F; Table 1). A relevant parameter at plateau is the intra-individual variability from one daily session to the next, estimated by the standard deviation (*SD*) of the score values during the entire plateau phase (Table 1). The *SD* was highly variable across monkeys (Figure 2 panel D), ranging from 1.99 to 4.82. A "typical" monkey is represented by Mk-AN (Figure 1), whereas a monkey exhibiting an atypical performance at plateau is illustrated by Mk-MI (Supplementary Figure 1).

To assess whether the performance reached at plateau (score and variability) depends on learning properties, such as the duration of the learning phase, the slope of the learning regression line or the initial score before training, the average score at plateau and its *SD* were plotted for the 20 monkeys as a function of the corresponding learning parameters (Supplementary Figure 2). There was correlation neither between the learning duration (in days) and the average score at plateau, nor between the learning duration and the *SD* of the score at plateau (top two panels in Supplementary Figure 2). The same absence of correlations was found during the first five learning sessions. Similarly, the speed of learning, estimated by the slope of the learning regression line, was not correlated with the manual performance at plateau (score or *SD*; bottom two panels in Supplementary Figure 2). In contrast, the initial score before training was to some extent a predictor of the score at plateau, as there was a statistically significant correlation between these two parameters (top right panel in Figure 3; Pearson correlation test). On the other hand, there was no correlation between the initial score before training and the variability (*SD*) of the score at plateau (middle right panel in Supplementary Figure 2).

Both the inter-individual and intra-individual variations of the total score can be better visualized when displayed in the form of box and whisker plots (Figure 3 top left panel). Some animals exhibited a fairly small variability of their total score at plateau, from one daily session to the next (Mk-AN, Mk-CA, Mk-LO, Mk-JO and Mk-RO). In these monkeys, the distance between the 25 and 75 percentiles was equal to or smaller than

3.6 pellets. At the other extreme, some monkeys were characterized by a large variability across daily sessions (Mk-GE and Mk-WI), with a distance between the 25 and 75 percentiles equal to or larger than 10 pellets.

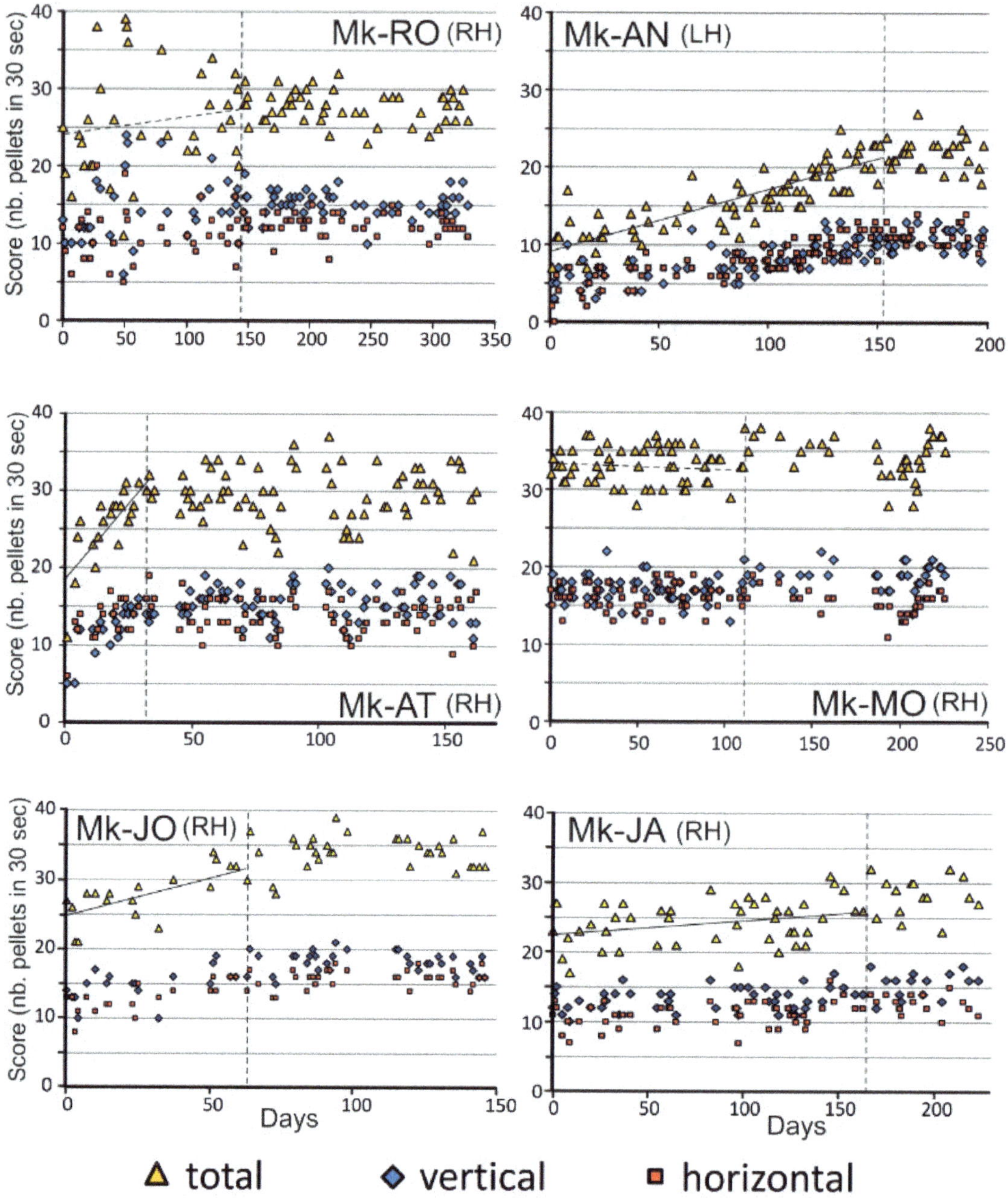

Figure 1. Plots showing the score obtained by 6 monkeys (Mk-RO, Mk-AT, Mk-JO, Mk-AN, Mk-MO, MK-JA) in the modified Brinkman board task for the dominant hand (RH=right hand; LH=left hand). Yellow triangles represent the total score, whereas the separate scores in vertical and horizontal slots are displayed by blue diamonds and purple squares, respectively. The time in days from the first day of testing is represented on the x-axis. For instance, in absence of test during the weekend, there is a delta of 3 days between tests conducted on Friday and then on next Monday. The vertical dashed lines represent the end of the learning phase and consequently the onset of the plateau phase (see text). A learning regression line on the total score is displayed for each animal (see text). The regression lines for Mk-RO and Mk-MO are represented with dashed lines as they are special cases (see text).

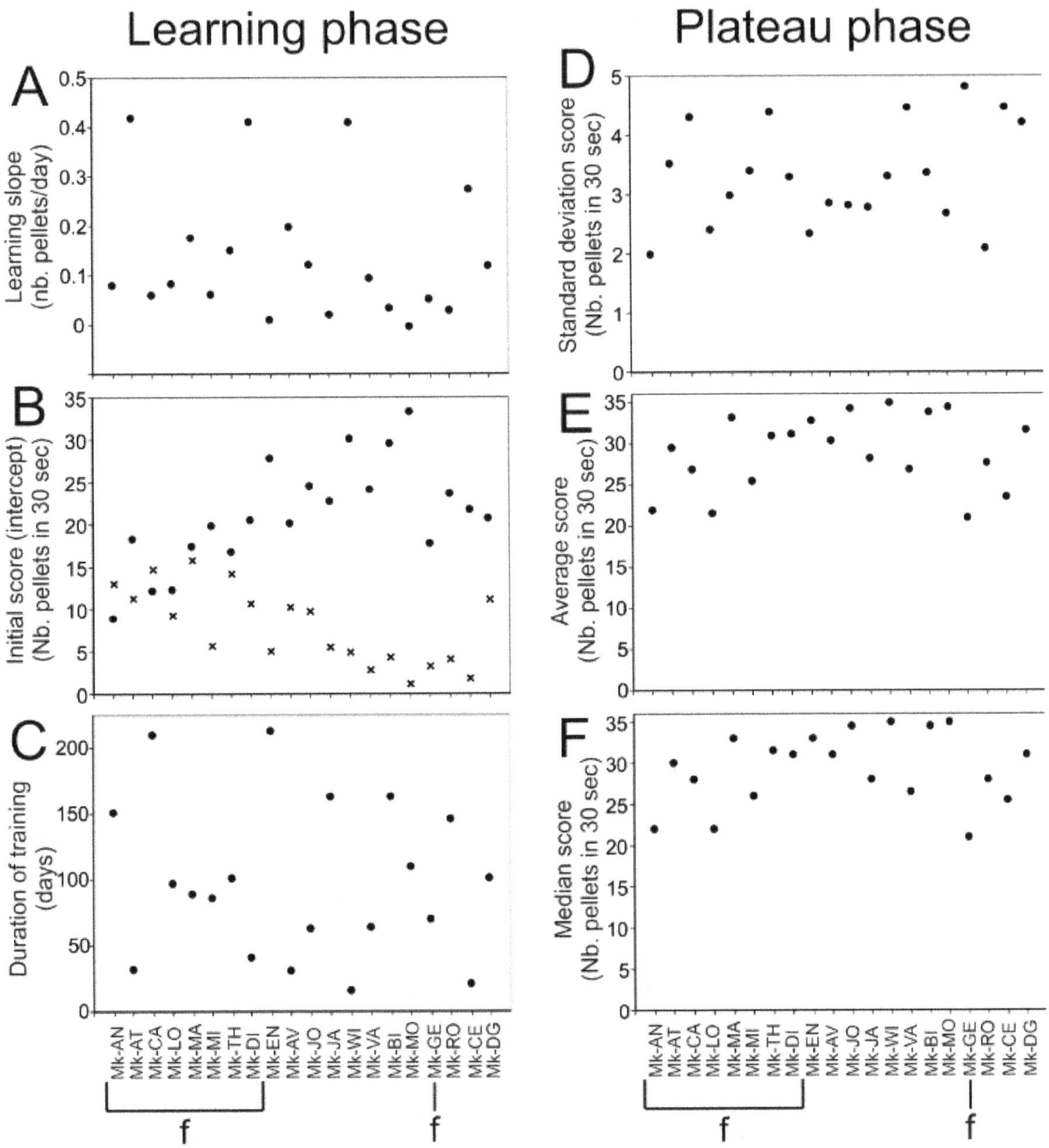

Figure 2. Plots showing relevant parameters for motor performance by all monkeys during the learning phase and the plateau phase of the modified Brinkman board task. The data concern the total score. The ID name of the monkeys appears below each bottom graphs. The 9 females monkeys are identified by "f" below the ID names. The other 11 monkeys are males. In panel B, crosses represent the progress of score obtained during the learning phase: it is the average score at plateau minus the initial score (also expressed as a number of pellets in 30 seconds; see text).

Score in vertical and horizontal slots. Pellet retrieval from the horizontal slots is more challenging than from the vertical ones (see Chatagny et al., 2013; Freund et al., 2009; Hoogewoud et al., 2013; Schmidlin et al., 2011), as the precision grip is usually accompanied by a deviation of the wrist/arm, not necessary for the vertical slots, corresponding either to an ulnar deviation or a radial deviation (see below, Variable Patterns of

Food Pellet Grasping). Below, the data are presented first at plateau, where they are more stable, and then, for comparison, during the learning phase.

At plateau, the scores were in most cases lower in the horizontal slots than in the vertical slots (Figure 1 and Supplementary Figure 1; Table 1): this difference was statistically significant in 17 monkeys ($p < 0.001$ in 15 monkeys; $p = 0.016$ in Mk-CE and $p = 0.011$ in Mk-TH; see Table 1). In contrast, in three monkeys, the horizontal scores were higher than the vertical scores, but the difference was not statistically significant ($p > 0.05$) in two monkeys (Mk-AN, see Figure 1; Mk-AV, see Supplementary Figure 1). In the third monkey (Mk-DI), the horizontal score was significantly higher than the vertical score ($p < 0.001$; see Supplementary Figure 1 and Table 1). At the plateau phase, there was no statistically significant difference between females and males in the median score for the vertical and horizontal slots taken separately, as well as for the variability of both of them (Figure 3).

The variability of the scores at plateau taken separately for the horizontal and the vertical slots can be visualized when the scores are displayed in the form of box and whisker plots (Figure 3 bottom two panels). In this way, the 20 monkeys can be distributed in three subgroups. First, in eight monkeys the variability of scores at plateau was comparable for both slot orientations. Second, the variability of scores at plateau was lower in the vertical slots in six monkeys. Third, it was the other way around in six monkeys with a lower variability in the horizontal slots.

In the learning phase, there was a positive correlation between vertical and horizontal mean scores ($r = 0.79$), indicating that the learning performance for one slot orientation is consistent with that for the other orientation. Nevertheless, no significant correlation appeared neither between vertical and horizontal *SD*s, nor between mean and *SD* for both slots orientations. However, differences between the scores observed in the vertical slots and in the horizontal slots at plateau were already visible during the learning phase (see all monkeys illustrated in Figure 1 and Supplementary Figure 1, except Mk-AT). In the three monkeys (Mk-AN, Mk-AV and Mk-DI) with a higher score in the horizontal slots at plateau, this difference was already present during the learning phase. However, it was only a trend as the differences were not statistically significant ($p > 0.05$, paired t-test or Wilcoxon rank-sum test). In the 17 monkeys exhibiting higher scores in the vertical slots at plateau, this difference was already present and statistically significant in 13 of them during the learning phase ($p < 0.05$, paired t-test or Wilcoxon rank-sum test test); it was only a trend in two monkeys (Mk-CE and Mk-EN; $p > 0.05$, paired t-test or Wilcoxon rank-sum test); there was a statistically non-significant trend towards a better score in the horizontal slots during learning in Mk-GE ($p > 0.05$, paired t-test); surprisingly, in Mk-AT, there were statistically better scores in the horizontal slots during the learning phase ($p = 0.023$, Wilcoxon rank-sum test), whereas this was the opposite at plateau (Figure 1).

Contact time (CT). The score data of the modified Brinkman board task described above involve motor components that are not purely part of the precision grip itself, such as the time of transport of the arm first towards and then away from the board. The contact time (CT) represents the time interval used by the monkey's hand to retrieve the pellets from the slots (see Method). As the precision grip movement is different with respect to slot orientation, the CT was measured separately in the horizontal and in the vertical slots in all 20 monkeys during the plateau phase (Figure 4; same plateau phase as defined for the score data). As expected, in the vast majority of monkeys ($n = 18$), the median CT at plateau was shorter in the vertical slots than in the horizontal slots (Table 1). The median CT was equal in both slot orientations in Mk-DI (0.2 second), and it was shorter in the horizontal slots in Mk-MA (Table 1). At plateau, the median CTs ranged from 0.13 sec to 0.67 sec across the 20 monkeys in the vertical slots and from 0.20 sec to 0.87 sec in the horizontal slots (see Table 1 and left panels of Figures 4A and B). The variability of the CTs at plateau (Figure 4) was greater for the horizontal slots in all monkeys. Three monkeys (Mk-CE, Mk-JA and Mk-RO) exhibited consistent highly variable CTs at plateau in both horizontal and vertical slots (Figure 4).

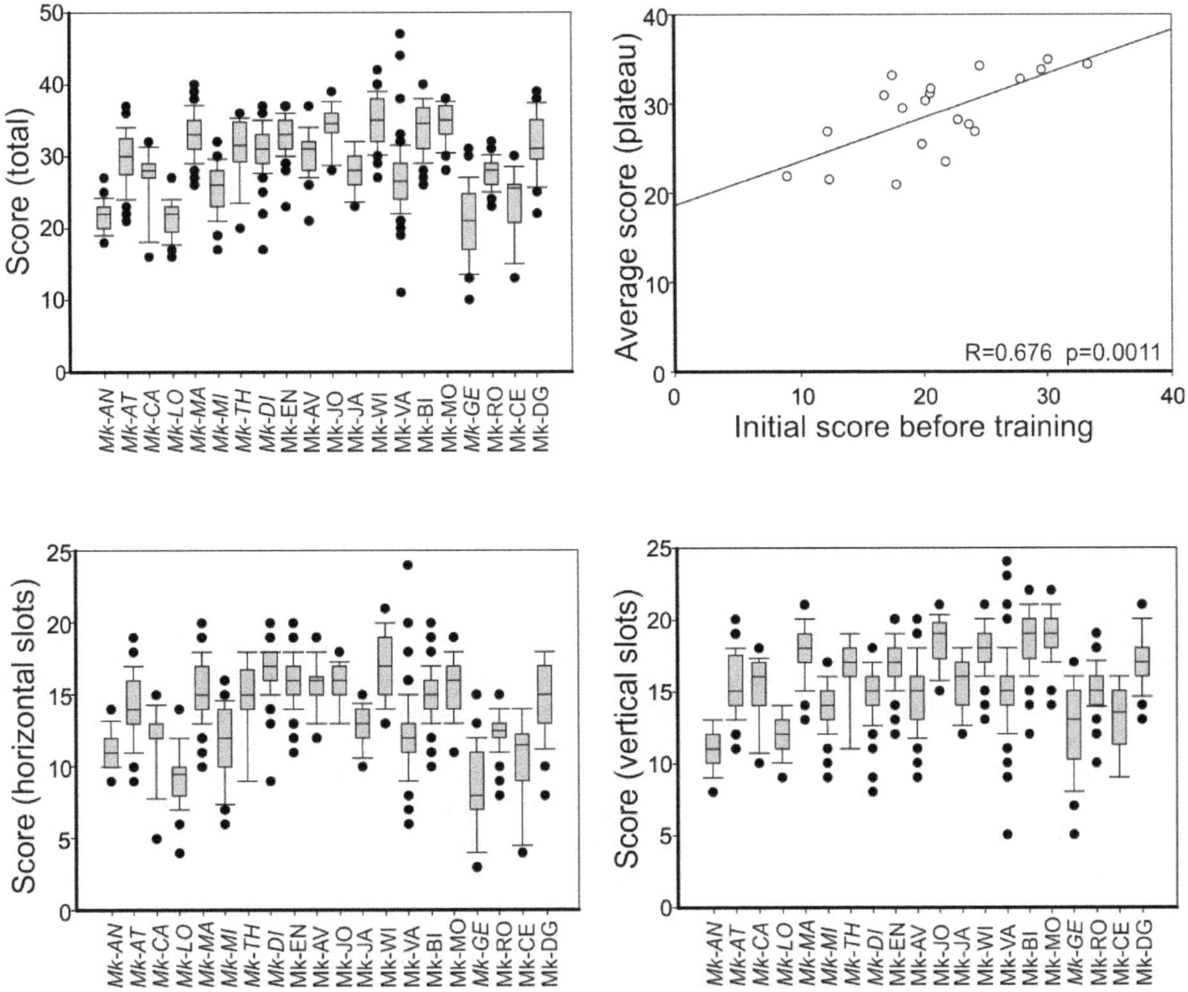

Figure 3. Scores obtained by all monkeys at **plateau phase** in the modified Brinkman board task, represented in the form of box and whisker plots. The horizontal line in the boxes represents the median value. The top and bottom of the boxes are for the 75 and 25 percentiles, respectively. The top and bottom of the whiskers represent the 90 and 10 percentiles, respectively. Black dots are for individual values above and below the 90 and 10 percentiles. The top left graph displays the total score, whereas the scores in the horizontal and vertical slots are shown in the bottom left and bottom right graphs, respectively. The ID names of females are shown in italics. The plot on the top right shows the statistically significant correlation between the average total score at plateau and the initial score before training, with the regression line. The corresponding coefficient of correlation (R) is given at the bottom right of the plot, followed by the p value (Pearson correlation test).

The CTs established at plateau were compared with those at the onset of the learning phase. The CT was assessed during the first four daily behavioral sessions (right panel in Figures 4A and B, for the horizontal and vertical slots, respectively), based on previous evidence that individual differences and intra-individual variations are greatest during the first four practice trials during motor learning (e.g., Carron & Leavitt, 1968; Marteniuk, 1974). The median CT values at onset of learning are clearly longer than those measured at plateau (Figure 4), reflecting a decrease in CT during the learning phase, corresponding to an enhancement of precision grip performance. An in-depth comparison of CTs at plateau with those at onset of learning is presented in the supplementary Methods and Results, together with supplementary Figure 3. Moreover, how the CTs progressively decrease during the first four days of learning is also reported in the supplementary Methods and Results.

Temporal sequence of grasping (motor habit). As the modified Brinkman board task is a voluntary motor task, there was no constraint on the monkey on how to perform the task, for instance in which temporal order to visit the 50 slots. However, as previously reported (Kaeser et al., 2013; Schmidlin et al., 2011), most monkeys did not visit the 50 slots randomly at plateau, but they generally adopted a preferential temporal sequence, for instance starting to empty the slots at one extremity of the board (right side for instance) and then scanning the board progressively and systematically towards the opposite extremity (left side in this example), as illustrated by the bottom inset in Figure 5A.

Such preferential temporal sequence, generally maintained at plateau from one daily session to the next, was considered as a **motor habit** and was found to be affected by a unilateral lesion of the dorsolateral prefrontal cortex (Kaeser et al., 2013; as assessed in five monkeys). In the present study, these data were extended by investigating variability of motor habit across 20 monkeys and by assessing whether the motor habit was already introduced at the beginning of the learning phase.

Overall, the comparison of the temporal sequence at the beginning of the learning phase with that at plateau yielded a distribution of the monkeys into four profiles (Figure 5 panels A and B). Profile 1, illustrated by Mk-AV, is characterized by variable temporal sequences to visit the 50 slots across daily sessions, without significant difference between the learning phase and the plateau phase. Several monkeys (n = 10 including Mk-AV) exhibited a similar sequence pattern (Mk-AT, Mk-BI, Mk-EN, Mk-GE, Mk-LO, Mk-MA, Mk-MI, Mk-RO, Mk-TH). Profile 2, illustrated by Mk-MO, is shared by three monkeys (Mk-AN, Mk-CE, Mk-MO) also exhibiting variable daily temporal sequences to visit the 50 slots but, in addition to a daily variability, the general pattern during the learning phase appears different from the one adopted during the plateau phase. Profile 3 includes four monkeys (Mk-JA, Mk-JO, Mk-VA, Mk-WI), and is characterized by a systematic temporal sequence to visit the 50 slots, present already during the learning phase and maintained during the plateau phase (illustrated by Mk-JA in Figure 5A). Finally, Profile 4 comprises three monkeys (Mk-CA, Mk-DG, Mk-DI), in which there was also a systematic daily temporal sequence to visit the 50 slots, but the sequence was significantly different during the learning phase from the one during the plateau phase (illustrated by Mk-DG in Figure 5A). The four profiles of motor habit are illustrated quantitatively in Figure 5B, where the positions of the 50 slots were given increasing numbers going from the left extremity of the Brinkman board to the right. Then, these numbers were subtracted from the temporal order (first slot visited, second, third, etc), cumulating their absolute values yielded a low cumulative value for a systematic scan from left to right; on the contrary, a systematic scan from right to left yielded a high cumulative value.

In the above four profiles of temporal sequences to visit the 50 slots, Profiles 1 and 3 exhibited comparable patterns at both learning phase and plateau phase, corresponding quantitatively to an absence of statistically significant difference between the two phases (*ns* in Figure 5B for Mk-AV and Mk-VA for instance). In contrast, the other two profiles (2 and 4) exhibited statistically significant differences in patterns of temporal sequences between the learning phase and the plateau phase (Figure 5B, *stars*, Mk-MO and Mk-DG for instance; see legend for a description of the statistical tests used).

Variable patterns of food pellet grasping. Although the monkeys generally used the standard precision grip (opposition of thumb and index finger) to grasp the food pellets in the modified Brinkman board task, there was some subtle variability in the precise pattern of grasping. For instance, already at the beginning

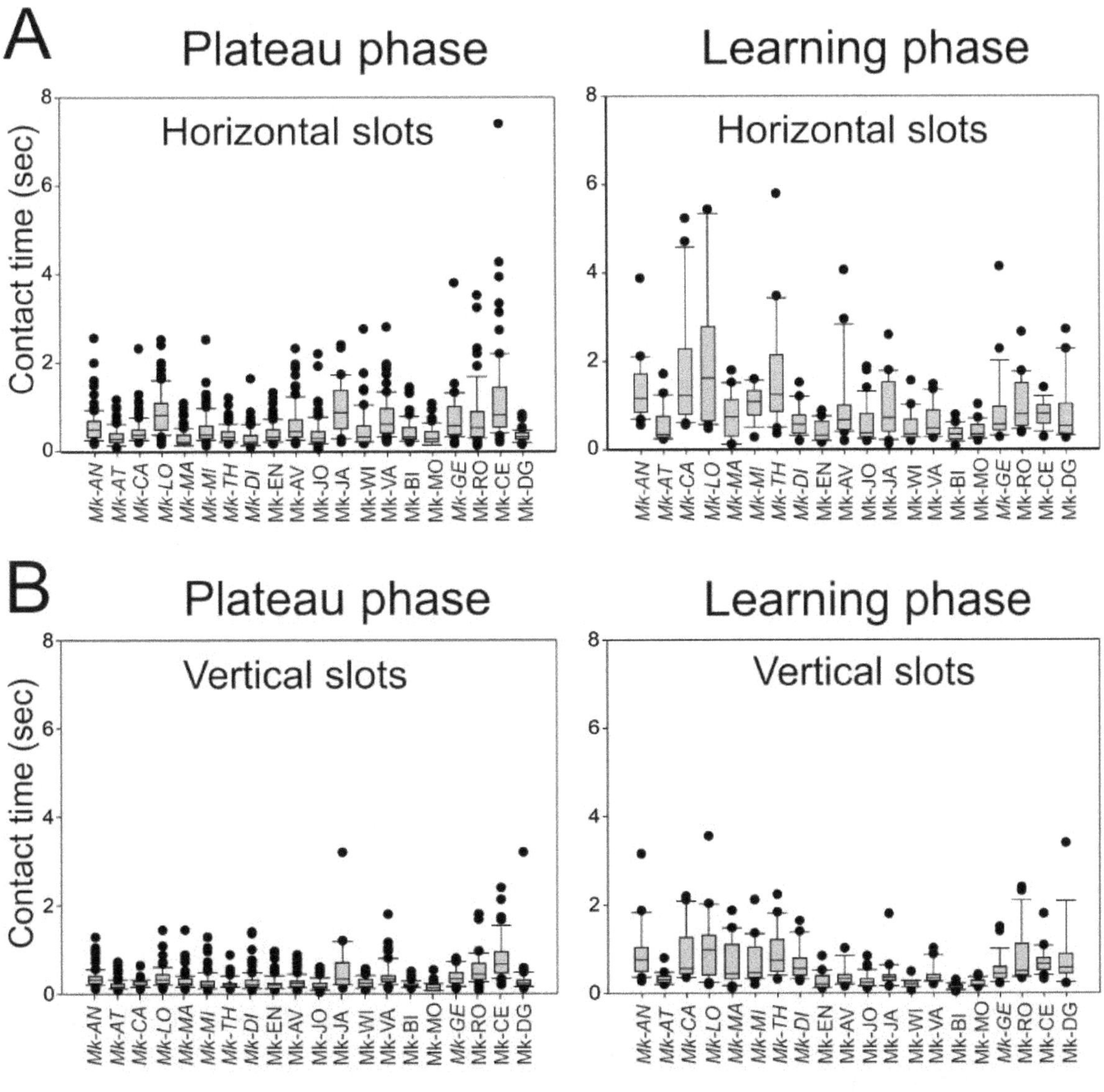

Figure 4. Contact times measured at **plateau phase** and at the **onset of the learning phase** for all monkeys in the modified Brinkman board task, in the horizontal (panel A) and vertical (panel B) slots, represented in the form of box and whiskers plots. The ID names of females are shown in italics. Same conventions as in Figure 3.

of practice, Mk-EN did not grasp a single food pellet with the left hand at a time to bring it to the mouth, as seen in the other monkeys, but grasped a first pellet, stored it in the palm of the hand, and then grasped a second pellet, before transporting both of them together to the mouth (see video sequence at http://www.unifr.ch/neuro/rouiller/ijcp/fr0.html). Conversely, single pellets were transported to the mouth with the right hand at the beginning of the learning phase. After about 10 months of practice, Mk-EN adopted frequently the strategy to collect two pellets at the same time with the left hand (Figure 5C). At the same time point, this strategy was also present for the right hand, but less systematically than for the left hand. Later, after two years of practice, Mk-EN systematically exhibited the prehension of two pellets at the same time with the left hand, extending it even to the grasping of three pellets together on a few trials (http://www.unifr.ch/neuro/rouiller/ijcp/fr0.html). This strategy to collect two pellets at the same time was also observed in few other monkeys, but more occasionally, for instance in Mk-JO and Mk-WI (Figure 5C) during the plateau phase only, and in Mk-AV and Mk-JA, both during the learning phase and the plateau phase.

The standard grasping from the vertical slots (one single pellet after the other) was highly stereotyped among the monkeys with the use of the standard precision grip (opposition of thumb and index finger). The temporal sequence of movement was such that the monkeys first established contact between the index finger and the pellet, moved the pellet toward the bottom extremity of the vertical slot and finally put the thumb in contact with the pellet to perform the retrieval itself from the slot.

The pattern of grasping was more variable for the horizontal slots. The first contact might be performed with the index finger first (as for the vertical slots) but also sometimes with the thumb first (see a few examples in Mk-EN at http://www.unifr.ch/neuro/rouiller/ijcp/fr0.html). Seven monkeys used the strategy to contact the pellet only with index finger first (Mk-BI, Mk-CA, Mk-GE, Mk-JO, Mk-LO, Mk-MO, Mk-VA). Episodic first contacts with the thumb were observed in six monkeys (Mk-AV, Mk-CE, Mk-EN, Mk-JA, Mk-MI, Mk-WI). Finally, first contacts with the thumb were frequent in seven monkeys, amounting to about 30% of trials in Mk-DG, Mk-RO and Mk-TH; in the other four monkeys, first contact established with the thumb were as frequent (Mk-AN) or even more frequent (Mk-AT, Mk-DI, Mk-MA) than with the index finger. In two of these seven monkeys with frequent first contacts with the thumb, this behavior appeared only at the plateau phase (Mk-MA, Mk-TH), whereas for the other five monkeys it was present already during the learning phase, with increasing frequency of occurrence over time.

To retrieve pellets from the horizontal slots, in part depending on their position on the Brinkman board, the monkeys performed the precision grip with the wrist/arm either in a radial deviation posture or in an ulnar deviation posture (Figure 5D; nomenclature derived from Hoffman and Strick, 1986). In 11 monkeys, the ulnar deviation was highly predominant (Mk-AN, Mk-AT, Mk-BI, Mk-GE, Mk-LO, Mk-MA, Mk-MI, Mk-MO, Mk-RO, Mk-TH, Mk-WI; see Figure 5E for Mk-LO). In one of them, the wrist/arm in radial deviation posture occurred only during the learning phase (Mk-MA), whereas in Mk-MI and Mk-RO the radial deviation posture was observed only at the plateau phase. In the other nine monkeys, ulnar and radial deviation postures of the wrist/arm were mixed with usually fewer radial deviations (ranging mostly from 20 to 40%) than ulnar deviations in eight of them (Mk-AV, Mk-CA, Mk-DG, Mk-DI, Mk-EN, Mk-JA, Mk-JO, Mk-VA; Figure 5E for Mk-JA and Mk-DG), whereas radial deviations were as frequent as ulnar deviations in Mk-CE. Overall, in the nine monkeys using a mix of radial and ulnar deviation postures, this behavior was in most cases already present during the learning phase (Figure 5E).

Errors of food pellet grasping. In the modified Brinkman board task, the monkeys made episodic errors in the form of unsuccessful trials, for instance when the pellet was ejected from the slot instead of being grasped, or when the pellet was dropped before transport to the mouth. Three profiles were identified among the 20 monkeys. The first profile (in 13 monkeys; see (c) in the rightmost column of Table 1) is defined by a progressive decrease in the number of errors from one day to the next during the few days at onset of learning followed by a further decrease at plateau, as expected. The second profile was observed in five monkeys (see (d) in Table 1), with a surprising constant and low number of errors both at onset of the learning phase and at plateau. The third profile included two monkeys (see (e) in Table 1), in which the errors occurred randomly (low to moderate number of errors), irrespective of the phase (onset of learning or plateau). As shown in Table 1, the mean number of errors at the onset of the learning phase ranged across monkeys from 0 to 16 and at plateau from 0 to 2. There was no correlation between the mean number of errors at onset of learning and the mean number of errors at plateau.

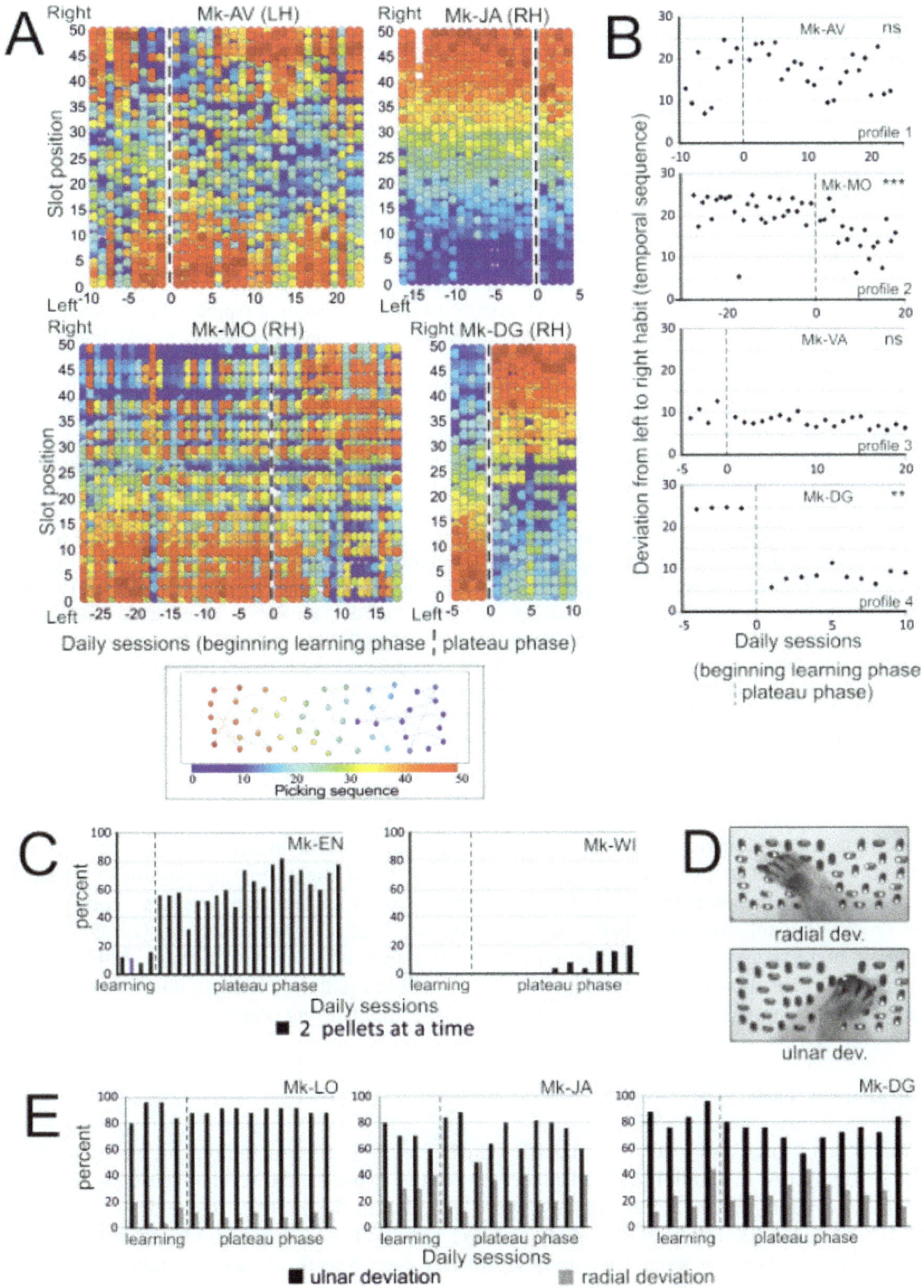

Figure 5. **Panel A:** Temporal sequence used by the monkeys to visit the 50 slots in the modified Brinkman board task. The picking sequence is shown by a color scale in the bottom inset, in which the first-visited slots are represented in blue, whereas the last visited

ones are represented in red (board scanning from right (blue slots) to left (red slots) in this example). In the top and middle displays, the temporal sequence was established for 4 monkeys, each representative of a behavioral profile (see text), both during the beginning of the learning phase (negative session numbers) and the plateau phase (positive session numbers). The x-axis displays the time in daily sessions, irrespective of the time interval (in days) between two consecutive sessions (different from the time scale in Figures 1 and Supplementary Figure 1). Each vertical column corresponds to a daily session of the modified Brinkman board task. Along each column, dots at the bottom are for slots located at the left extremity of the board, whereas dots at the top are for slots at the right extremity. RH=Right hand; LH=Left hand. **Panel B**: Quantitative assessment of the temporal sequence used to visit the 50 slots in the modified Brinkman board task for four monkeys, representative of the four profiles reported in the text. An index of systematic motor sequence (habit) was computed, indicating the extent of deviation from a systematic sequence starting from the left extremity of the board and terminating at its right extremity (corresponding to a low value for this precise sequence), and plotted in the y-axis as a function of behavioral daily sessions. The mirror sequence (systematic right to left scan) yields a high value. A small variability from one daily behavioral session to the next, indicating a reproducible motor sequence, reflects motor habit. The temporal sequence is shown qualitatively for the same monkeys Mk-AV, Mk-MO and Mk-DG in panel A. See text for detailed description of the results. The index of motor sequence was compared between the learning phase and the plateau phase with the non-parametric Mann-Whitney U test. The result of the statistical comparison is indicated at the top right of each graph: ns = statistically non-significant difference ($p > 0.05$); ** is for $p \leq 0.01$; *** is for $p \leq 0.001$. **Panel C**: Percentage of grasping patterns (at the beginning of learning and at plateau) in which two pellets were retrieved at the same time instead of a single one, in the modified Brinkman board task. In other words, the monkey grasped two pellets before transport to the mouth. In the other trials, the monkey retrieved a single pellet and brought it to the mouth. For this analysis, the vertical and horizontal slots were cumulated. **Panel D**: Usually, to retrieve pellets from the horizontal slots and depending on their position in the modified Brinkman board, the monkeys used a precision grip movement associated with a complementary wrist/arm movement. As illustrated for a right hand, on the left part of the Brinkman board, there was a trend to perform a radial deviation of the wrist/arm (top picture) whereas, on the right part of the Brinkman board, the trend was in favour of an ulnar deviation (bottom picture). **Panel E**: The distribution of wrist/arm radial deviation and ulnar deviation postures for pellet retrieval from the horizontal slots is illustrated for three monkeys over consecutive daily sessions, at the beginning of the learning phase and at plateau. For each daily session, the black bar and the gray one indicate the percentage of ulnar deviations and radial deviations, respectively. The sum of the radial and ulnar deviations is 100% in each daily session. Mk-LO is representative of 11 monkeys exhibiting a clear prevalence of ulnar deviations, during both the learning phase and the plateau phase. Mk-JA and Mk-DG also preferred ulnar deviations, but to a lesser extent.

Based on multiple correlation analyses (not shown), it turned out that the mean number of errors both at onset of the learning phase and at plateau was correlated with none of the following parameters: learning duration, slope of learning regression line, initial score value at onset of learning, median score value at plateau, *SD* of score at plateau, difference between the initial score at learning onset, or average score at plateau. Nevertheless, there was a positive correlation between the gain of score performance during practice and the mean number of errors at onset of learning ($p = 0.029$): monkeys with larger mean numbers of errors at onset of learning exhibited a larger gain of performance provided by the learning phase.

Reach and Grasp Drawer Task

Typical traces of grip force and load force recorded during a single trial of the reach and grasp drawer task are illustrated in Figure 6A, in parallel to the displacement of the drawer and discrete events, such as *touch knob*, *open onset*, *full open* and *picking*. Four monkeys were included in the analysis of the drawer task (Mk-LO, Mk-TH, Mk-DI and Mk-AT). Based on five daily sessions recorded both at the beginning of the learning phase and at plateau, the maximal grip force was measured for five correct trials at each resistance tested (R1 = 0 Newton, R2 = 1.25 N, R3 = 2.75 N, R4 = 5N) and plotted in the form of box and whisker plots (Figure 6C). Two of the monkeys (Mk-DI and Mk-TH) exhibited a systematic and statistically significant increase in the maximal grip force applied on the drawer knob when the task was performed at plateau as compared to the learning phase (Mann-Whitney U test). A comparable result was obtained in Mk-LO for the lowest two resistances, whereas there was no statistically significant difference between the learning and plateau phases at higher resistances (R3 and R4). A reverse behavior was found in Mk-AT, exhibiting in contrast a lower maximal grip force at plateau than during the learning phase at R1, R2 and R3, although the difference was statistically significant at R2 only (Figure 6C). At R4, Mk-AT used a statistically higher maximal grip force at plateau than during the learning phase, as Mk-TH.

The maximal load force was measured from the same trials, as shown in Figure 7A, and no difference between the learning and plateau phases appeared in Mk-AT and Mk-TH with the exception in the latter of the resistance R2, at which the maximal load force was significantly higher at plateau. Mk-DI used a lower maximal load force at plateau as compared to the learning phase (Figure 7A), but the difference was statistically significant only at the resistances R2 and R3. Mk-LO presented a more variable behavior, with a higher maximal load force at plateau at R1 and R2, but statistically significant at R1 only and a lower maximal load force at plateau as compared to the learning phase at R3 and R4, but statistically significant at R4 only. As illustrated for Mk-AT and for Mk-LO (Figure 7B), in the four monkeys enrolled in the reach and grasp drawer task the transition from the learning phase to the plateau phase was accompanied by a statistically significant decrease in both the grip force duration and the load force duration (Figure 7B), except at the highest level of resistance (R4). In Mk-TH, at resistance R4 as well, both durations were also statistically shorter at plateau than at the beginning of the learning phase.

The difference in grip force (solid lines in Figure 6B left column) and in load force (solid lines in Figure 6B right column) between the beginning of the learning phase and the end of the plateau phase is illustrated in Mk-DI, together with their variability (dashed lines representing plus and minus *SDs*). These data are representative of the observation (Figure 6C) that grip force was usually stronger at plateau phase than at the beginning of the learning phase, except in Mk-AT. However, variability was clearly larger at the onset of the learning phase than at the end of the plateau. Duration of grip application was shorter at plateau phase (as seen in Figure 7B). There was less difference between the two phases in the amplitude of the load force (Figure 6B right column), as compared to the grip force. However, load force duration was shorter and less variable at the end of the plateau than at onset of the learning phase, as shown in Figure 7B (right panel).

Discussion

Survey of the Main Results

Our main hypothesis that acquired manual (digits) dexterity performance and variability can be predicted from the duration of the learning phase, from the learning slope and from the initial score before any training was not verified for the most part, based on the modified Brinkman board data. Indeed, both performance and variability of manual dexterity, precision grip in the present case, were not related to the duration of training and to the slope of the learning regression line (Supplementary Figure 2). Only the performance of manual dexterity at plateau was correlated with the initial score before learning, the higher the initial score before training, the better the score at plateau (Figure 3, top right panel). On the other hand, the initial score of manual dexterity before learning was a poor predictor of intra-individual variability at plateau (Supplementary Figure 2).

As mostly expected, motor learning led to an optimization of manual dexterity parameters in the modified Brinkman board task, such as score, CT, as well as a substantial decrease in intra-individual variability, especially for the CT (Figures 1, 4 and Supplementary Figures 1, 3), in line with current theories (see e.g., Marteniuk 1974). The present study also demonstrates the considerable inter-individual variations in precision grip skills, reflected across monkeys both by wide ranges of motor parameters (score, CT, learning properties) and disparate qualitative characteristics of grasping patterns (e.g., grip type, hand posture, strategy, motor habit). Such large inter-individual variability is in line with the theory of motor equivalence claiming that a given motor goal can be achieved via multiple strategies. In relation to motor habit, reflected by the temporal order in which sequential movements were executed in the modified Brinkman board task, the data (Figure 5A and B) support the notion that motor habit is established very early during the learning phase in most animals. These data suggest that macaque monkeys, as most human subjects would do, adopt motor habits early, reflecting the capability to organize motor sequences following a strategy perceived as optimal, as opposed to a random scan of the board augmenting the probability of neglecting a slot and requiring more attention to detect yet unvisited slots. The early emergence of a preferential prehension sequence is present also in children (3-5 years old), as observed in the Pegboard with 12 pegs test (Kakebeeke, Caflisch, Chaouch, Rousson, Largo & Jenni, 2013; T. Kakebeeke, personal communication). In adult human subjects performing the modified Brinkman board task, a preferential prehension sequence is most often already present at first trial and then maintained over 10 repetitions of the test (data derived from Chatagny et al., 2013).

In the reach and grasp drawer task, the expectation that the monkeys would use exaggerated maximal grip and load forces to make sure to open the drawer during learning phase, then reduced at plateau to just exceed the minimal forces required, representing an energy conservation and behavioral optimization, was not verified, at least in three out of four monkeys tested (Figures 6 and 7: Mk-LO, Mk-TH and Mk-AT). This principle of optimization was observed only in one monkey (Mk-DI), for the load force but not for the grip force. On the other hand, the duration of application of both the grip force and load force was reduced at plateau as compared to the learning phase (Figure 7), as expected.

Methodological Considerations and Limitations

In the present study, emphasis was put on an individual analysis of 20 adult macaques. This individual (*differential*) strategy was prompted by the notion that "averaging data over participants (the *experimental* approach) can mask the actual individual participant and trial functions of change, as well as it can also produce learning curves that are not representative of any single individual in the group" (Adi-Japha, Karni, Parnes, Loewenschuss & Vakil, 2008; Newell, Liu & Mayer-Kress, 2001; Schmidt & Lee, 2011: Chapter 9). These concerns emitted in relation to the learning curves apply also most likely to the motor performance at plateau. Indeed the data shown in all Figures of the present study emphasize the considerable inter-individual variability of manual dexterity performance across our population of 20 macaque monkeys, although they were housed for many years in groups in the same environment and performed the same motor tasks in well controlled and reproducible laboratory conditions.

Our study presents weaknesses in the data gathering due to variations in the experimental protocol, inherent to this type of non-human primate study and its related constraints. First, as expected for a study conducted over a long period of time (15 years), several conditions changed from one animal to the next. One example is the size of the housing facility and its degree of enrichment (Table 1), adapted over the years according to changes in the legislation dealing with the protection of animals involved in scientific research. A second confounding factor is the supervision of the monkeys by different experimenters: a given experimenter is devoted to the very same monkeys every day and therefore cannot supervise more than two monkeys daily.

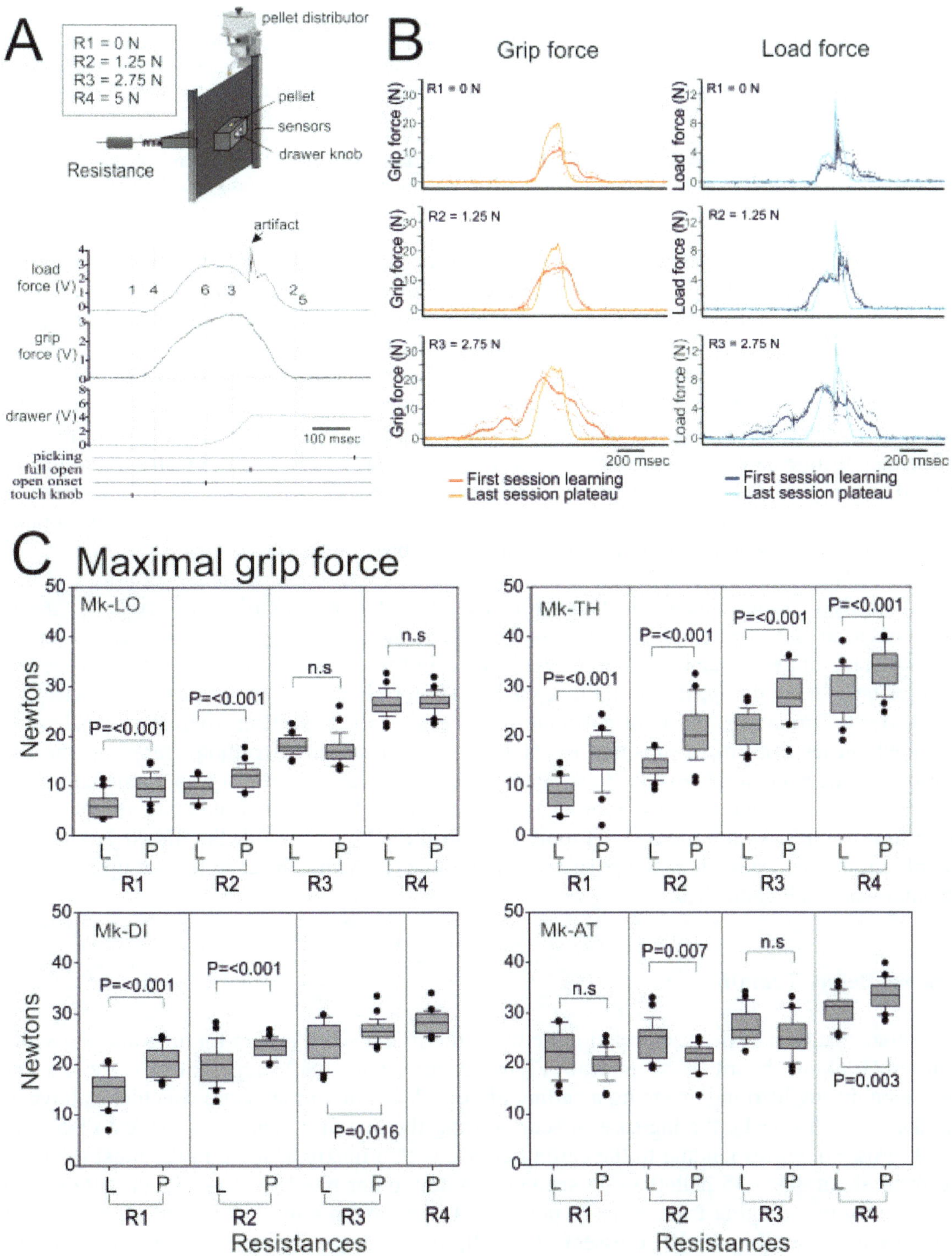

Figure 6. **Panel A**: Typical traces of the load force, grip force and drawer displacement as a function of time (from top to bottom) when a monkey executed a trial in the reach and grasp drawer task. The time occurrence of four discrete events is shown below (vertical tics). A schematic representation of the drawer set-up is shown on the top, with the four increasing resistances opposing the opening of the drawer (R1 to R4). The vertical dashed lines with numbers correspond to: *onset of grip force* (1), *offset of grip force* (2), *maximal grip*

force (3), *onset of load force* (4), *offset of load force* (5) and *maximal load force* (6). An artifact in the load force trace occurred when the drawer was blocked at its maximal opening. **Panel B**: Average traces (over 5 trials) and their variability (+/- 1 *SD*) in Newtons (N) for the grip force (left column) and load force (right column), recorded in Mk-DI. In each column, the two colors distinguish traces obtained at the beginning of the learning phase and at the end of the plateau phase. The traces are shown for three levels of resistances (R1, R2, R3; see panel A). For each curve, the variability is represented by the envelope in dashed lines. **Panel C**: Box and whisker plots (same conventions as in Fig. 3) of the maximal grip force recorded during the learning phase (L) and during the plateau phase (P), in the four monkeys involved in the reach and grasp drawer task, as a function of 4 increasing resistance levels opposing the opening of the drawer (R1, R2, R3, R4). The results of the statistical comparison between "L" and "P" are given with the corresponding p value or n.s when statistically non-significant ($p > 0.05$). Note that Mk-DI performed the task at resistance level R4 only during the plateau phase, after learning.

Moreover, the duration of the entire experiment on a given monkey may last up to two to three years and may consequently be conducted by several successive experimenters. Equally important, each experimenter develops his/her own approach to train each animal, depending also on the *personal* traits of the latter. In particular, some monkeys required a longer preliminary habituation phase than others before being actively involved in the experiment, before collecting the behavioral data for subsequent analysis (Table 1). Over the years, the monkeys originated from different sources, such as our own breeding colony (before 2010) or from different authorized suppliers (China, Mauritius Island, Vietnam), via various quarantine European centers. In spite of these multiple parameters influencing our monkey data, which cannot be strictly controlled over a 15 year period, it remains that they have most likely less impact than the even more numerous confounding factors associated with human studies, such as genetic variability, socio-cultural background, education, economical status, motivation, professional occupation, hobbies and so on.

The vast majority of lesion studies dealing with manual dexterity in non-human primates (see introduction) provide behavioral data restricted to two time points, namely before a lesion of the motor system (after reaching a plateau of performance) and after the lesion. In these studies, the data related to the learning phase of the motor tasks were rarely, if not at all, reported. The originality of the present study was to compare the manual dexterity properties of adult macaque monkeys at their plateau (before subsequent lesion) with those derived earlier from the acquisition of manual performance for two motor tasks, in the same animals. Furthermore, as the behavioral sessions took place three to five days a week, it was possible to precisely follow progressive changes in each monkey in order to assess intra-individual and inter-individual variability over a very long time frame. As the motor tests took place in the laboratory with the monkeys sitting in a primate chair, confounding factors such as the position of the monkeys with respect to the set-up and the separate use of each hand were well controlled.

Initial Score Before Training

The statistically significant correlation between the initial score before training and the score reached in the modified Brinkman board task at plateau (Figure 3, top right panel) suggests that there is a limited margin of progression during learning, meaning a ceiling effect. When the initial score was high (above 25 pellets; in four monkeys, see Table 1), the increase in score during the learning phase was modest (1-5 pellets at most; Figure 2B: crosses), corresponding to the ceiling effect, with a maximal score in the most dexterous monkeys ranging from about 30 to 35 pellets in 30 seconds. A few other monkeys ($n = 5$), in spite of a lower initial score before training (ranging from 18 to 24 pellets), also exhibited a limited gain of score during the learning phase (below 6 pellets; Figure 2B: crosses). Overall, 10 monkeys improved relatively modestly during the learning phase. In the other 10 monkeys, the margin of score progression during learning was more prominent (ranging from 9 to 16; Figure 2B: crosses). The latter monkeys were predominantly females (7 out of 10). In comparison with human subjects performing the modified Brinkman board task in 10 consecutive sessions on

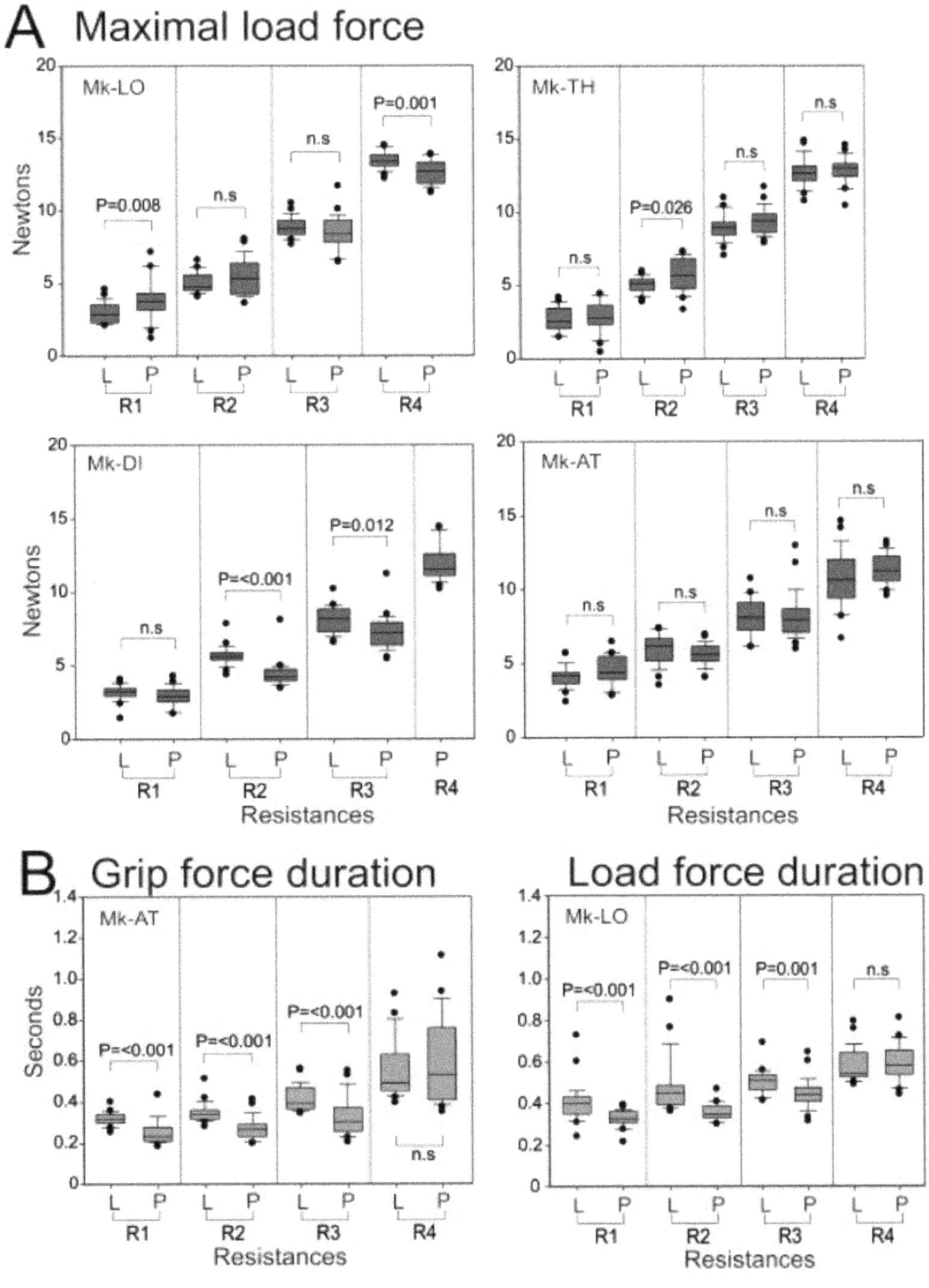

Figure 7. **Panel A**: Box and whisker plots (same conventions as in Fig. 3) of the maximal load force during the learning phase (L) and during the plateau phase (P), in the same four monkeys as in Figure 6. Same conventions as in Figure 6. **Panel B**: Grip force duration and load force duration measured in 2 animals during the learning phase (L) and the plateau phase (P), as a function of the resistance levels opposing the opening of the drawer (R1, R2, R3, R4). Same conventions as in Figure 6.

the same day, the training effect was less prominent than in monkeys (Chatagny et al., 2013), suggesting that humans started closer to the ceiling of performance.

The statistically significant lower scores in females than males (Figure 2B) is consistent with the lack of a few habituating sessions before collecting data in females, as opposed to the majority of males (Table 1). Moreover, other confounding factors might have played a role in this sex difference as well (e.g., size of housing facility, degree of enrichment; see Table 1). However, later on, when females were more familiar with the new environment and the tasks, their score increased more than in males so that the two groups exhibited largely overlapping mean or median scores at plateau (Figure 2, panels E and F). The absence of sex difference for the score at plateau in the macaque monkeys enrolled in the present study contrasts with the significantly better performance observed in women than in men in a human adapted version of the modified Brinkman board task (Chatagny et al., 2013).

Application to Lesion Studies

The large inter-individual variability of the average score at plateau (Table 1) may be considered as an inconvenience in comparing two groups of monkeys subjected to a lesion, one group receiving a treatment and the other not. Nevertheless, this drawback is actually attenuated because, in such studies and in contrast to clinical trials (see e.g., Kaeser et al., 2010), the most relevant comparison is made within the same monkey, between the pre-lesion score and the post-lesion score at plateau after functional recovery (usually incomplete; see e.g., Freund et al., 2009; Hamadjida et al., 2012). Thus, the comparison between two groups of animals is based on the percentage of functional recovery individually determined for each animal (see e.g., Freund et al., 2009; Hamadjida et al., 2012; Hoogewoud et al., 2013; Kaeser et al., 2010, 2011), which is less affected by inter-individual variability than group comparisons in clinical trials.

Learning Curves

As reviewed by Newell and collaborators (2001), the forms of the learning curves, defined as "plots of the outcome performance as a function of practice", can be highly variable: "learning curves of almost every conceivable shape can and have been found", corresponding to various mathematical functions, such as exponential, power law, S-shaped, hyperbolic, accelerating functions, etc. In the present case, one would have intuitively expected an exponential rise of performance (score) to a maximum (ceiling; see Schmidt & Lee, 2011: Chapter 10, their Figure 10.8). As illustrated in Figure 1 and Supplementary Figure 1 however, the majority of monkeys (n = 16 out of 20) exhibited a progression of performance during the learning phase that was rather better approximated by a regression line than by an exponential function. The exceptions are Mk-RO (Figure 1), Mk-DI, Mk-LO (Supplementary Figure 1) and Mk-TH (not shown). This linear learning progression observed here may be specific to the modified Brinkman board task, as well as to each monkey, in line with the proposition that the "learning rate is individual and task dependent" (Newell et al., 2001). In the same line, unlike recent studies in humans (e.g., Rosenblatt, Hurt, Latash, & Grabiner, 2014 in locomotor tasks; Wu et al., 2014 in arm movements tasks) demonstrating that a greater variability at the beginning of practice allows a faster learning rate, no such correlation was found in our monkeys performing unconditioned voluntary tasks requiring fine manual dexterity. Individual differences in motor skill learning are likely to be related to variations in the function and structure of specific brain regions, such as prefrontal, premotor and parietal cortices, as well as basal ganglia and cerebellum (Tomassini et al., 2011).

An important parameter here is the time scale when attempting to characterize the change in behavior resulting from motor learning (Newell et al., 2001). In most cases, especially in human subjects, the time range of observation of the learning phase was narrow (an hour to a single day most often; e.g., Chatagny et al., 2013). Longitudinal studies, though conducted in relation to infant motor development, are relatively rare and therefore the present study is original thanks to the long time period of observation during the learning phase (over weeks to months). Short daily sessions, during such a long time scale, may explain the very progressive and regular improvement of performance with practice observed in the majority of monkeys. In the present learning data on macaque monkeys, the learning phase may appear rather long for a relatively natural motor task, such as the precision grip performed in the modified Brinkman board task, at least in some individuals (Table 1). This underlies the fact that precision grip is an exquisite motor function subjected to very fine and progressive adjustments with practice. For instance, it was reported that the even more sophisticated skill in rolling cigars may still improve after many years (up to seven) of practice (Crossman, 1959).

Comparison with Previous Studies

Comparing the present behavioral data with the literature is limited to some extent, as the manual dexterity performance and variability strongly depends on the animal/primate species, on practice schedule (Stelmach, 1968), on expertise level (Schorer, Baker, Fath, & Jaitner, 2007), as well as on the type of task. Individual differences are indeed strongly task specific, corresponding to the theory of specificity (see e.g., Marteniuk, 1974). Even close species such as *Macaca fascicularis* and *Macaca mulatta* have different hand size (e.g., finger length), larger for the latter, corresponding consequently to different manual dexterity abilities (see e.g., Darling et al., 2013 for more details). A direct comparison of the present macaque data with rodent data (mainly rats) remains questionable, due to the strong difference between the pincer grasp (or precision grip) in primates and the arpeggio/power grasp in rodents (Klein et al., 2012). In the context of motor specificity, a strong influence is exerted by the size and shape of the object to be manipulated, as well as by the size of the well containing the object, when applicable. In a human study focused on precision grasps (Wong & Whishaw, 2004), it was shown that there was a high degree of variability of grasping pattern within and between subjects, like in our group of monkeys. Wong and Whishaw (2004) reported up to seven grasp types in human subjects, involving the thumb and various combinations of other digits, depending on the size of the bead being held. The proper precision grip (opposition of thumb and index finger only) was highly predominant when grasping the smallest beads, whereas the involvement of other fingers increased when progressively larger beads were grasped. In the present study on monkeys, only the proper precision grip was observed (opposition of thumb and index finger) because the food pellet was small compared to the finger size. Wong and Whishaw (2004) reported also in human subjects a large variability of first contact strategy with an object, depending on which and how the first finger contacted the object. This observation is in line with the large inter-individual variability observed here for the monkeys in the first digit used to contact the pellet in the horizontal slots (see results paragraph Variable Patterns of Food Pellet Grasping). The large inter- and intra-individual variability of grasping patterns observed in our monkeys and in humans (Wong & Whishaw, 2004) is consistent with the exquisitely complex somatotopic organization in mosaics of the primary motor cortex in primates (e.g., Schieber, 2001) as well as with complex movements synergies elicited in primates by microstimulation of the primary motor cortex (Graziano, Taylor, & Moore, 2002).

In two studies conducted on *Macaca fascicularis* (Brinkman, 1984) and *Macaca mulatta* (Brinkman & Kyupers, 1973), using a very comparable task (the original Brinkman board task), the data were mostly reported in a qualitative manner (movement pattern), preventing a direct comparison with the present quantitative data. The same limitation applies to other macaque studies using different manual tasks (e.g., Glees & Cole, 1950; Ogden & Franz, 1917; Passingham et al., 1983). In several studies on non-human primates (as listed in the introduction) involving a lesion of the motor system followed by functional recovery, the pre-lesion behavioral data were often limited to very few baseline data points, if not a single one, thus strongly limiting the comparison with the present progressive training phase over weeks, followed then by a long period of performance stabilization at plateau.

An exception is the study by Pizzimenti et al. (2007) conducted on *Macaca mulatta* and using a somewhat different behavioral apparatus, modified from the often used dexterity *Klüver* board. Although different from our modified Brinkman board, the wells A and B in the dexterity board used by Pizzimenti et al. (2007) had a size comparable to our slots. The manual dexterity was assessed quantitatively in three monkeys, using the so-called performance ratio, defined as the average score divided by the *SD* of the score, derived from five pre-lesion sessions (plateau). For the preferred hand, the performance ratios ranged from 2.5 to 3.0 in well A and from 3.5 to 8 in well B, the latter being the least difficult. Taking our data from the modified Brinkman board at plateau (Table 1) and computing similarly the performance ratio, values ranging from 4.4 to 14.0 (average = 9.3) among the 20 monkeys were obtained, thus corresponding to a generally better manual dexterity performance in our monkeys. However, such direct comparison may be biased due to important differences, such as species, manual task, duration of the considered plateau phase, scoring, as well as the time interval between the sessions (1-2 weeks in Pizzimenti et al., 2007 versus 1-3 days in our study). Furthermore, the monkeys of Pizzimenti et al. (2007) worked from their home cage (in a primate chair here).

As far as the reach and grasp drawer task is concerned, slightly different versions of the original set-up (Kazennikov et al., 1994) were used along the years (Kazennikov et al., 1998; Kazennikov et al., 1999; Kermadi, Liu, Tempini, & Rouiller, 1997; Kermadi, Liu, Tempini, Calciati, & Rouiller, 1998; Kermadi, Liu, & Rouiller, 2000), with special emphasis put on the issue of inter-limb coordination. In the current report, the reach and grasp drawer task was used in its unimanual version only, with focus on the assessment of the grip and load forces, a situation more closely related to studies on human subjects performing the reach and grasp drawer task (e.g., Grichting, Hediger, Kaluzny, & Wiesendanger, 2000; Serrien & Wiesendanger, 1999; Serrien, Kaluzny, Wicki & Wiesendanger, 1999). Interestingly, as compared to intact human subjects, cerebellar patients overestimated the proactive grip force requested to pull the drawer (Serrien & Wiesendanger, 1999). It can thus be expected that the reach and grasp drawer task will also be pertinent in macaque monkeys to evaluate deficits related to various motor dysfunctions (e.g., Parkinson disease, cortical lesion, spinal cord lesion) and to follow the time course and extent of functional recovery. In particular, it will be interesting to compare the properties of the initial learning phase of a motor task with those of the re-learning phase of the same task in the same animals following a lesion, in absence (spontaneous recovery) or presence of a specific treatment (induced recovery).

Acknowledgements

The authors wish to thank the technical assistance of Françoise Tinguely, Josef Corpataux, Laurent Bossy, Jacques Maillard (animal care taking), André Gaillard (mechanics), Bernard Aebischer (electronics), Laurent Monney (informatics). Over the years, previous members of the laboratory were involved in some of the experiments: Dr. Alexander Wyss, Dr. Shahid Bashir, Dr. Yu Liu and Dr. Abderraouf Belhaj-Saif.

References

Adi-Japha, E., Karni, A., Parnes, A., Loewenschuss, I., & Vakil, E. (2008). A shift in task routines during the learning of a motor skill: group-averaged data may mask critical phases in the individuals' acquisition of skilled performance. *Journal of Experimental Psychology: Learning, Memory, and Cognition, 34,* 1544-1551.

Alstermark, B., & Isa, T. (2002). Premotoneuronal and direct corticomotoneuronal control in the cat and macaque monkey. *Advances in experimental medicine and biology, 508,* 281-297.

Alstermark, B., Pettersson, L. G., Nishimura, Y., Yoshino-Saito, K., Tsuboi, F., Takahashi, M., & Isa, T. (2011). Motor command for precision grip in the macaque monkey can be mediated by spinal interneurons. *Journal of Neurophysiology, 106,* 122-126.

Alstermark, B., & Isa, T. (2012). Circuits for skilled reaching and grasping. *Annual Review of Neuroscience, 35,* 559-578.

Armand, J., Edgley, S. A., Lemon, R. N., & Olivier, E. (1994). Protracted postnatal development of corticospinal projections from the primary motor cortex to hand motoneurones in the macaque monkey. *Experimental Brain Research, 101,* 178-182.

Armand, J., Olivier, E., Edgley, S. A., & Lemon, R. N. (1997). Postnatal development of corticospinal projections from motor cortex to the cervical enlargement in the macaque monkey. *Journal of Neuroscience, 17,* 251-266.

Bashir, S., Kaeser, M., Wyss, A., Hamadjida, A., Liu, Y., Bloch, J., . . . Rouiller, E. M. (2012). Short-term effects of unilateral lesion of the primary motor cortex (M1) on ipsilesional hand dexterity in adult macaque monkeys. *Brain Structure and Function, 217,* 63-79.

Beaud, M. L., Schmidlin, E., Wannier, T., Freund, P., Bloch, J., Mir, A., . . . Rouiller, E. M. (2008). Anti-Nogo-A antibody treatment does not prevent cell body shrinkage in the motor cortex in adult monkeys subjected to unilateral cervical cord lesion. *BMC Neuroscience, 9,* 5.

Beaud, M. L., Rouiller, E. M., Bloch, J., Mir, A., Schwab, M. E., Wannier, T., & Schmidlin, E. (2012). Invasion of lesion territory by regenerating fibers after spinal cord injury in adult macaque monkeys. *Neuroscience, 227,* 271-282.

Bihel, E., Pro-Sistiaga, P., Letourneur, A., Toutain, J., Saulnier, R., Insausti, R., . . . Touzani, O. (2010). Permanent or transient chronic ischemic stroke in the non-human primate: behavioral, neuroimaging, histological, and immunohistochemical investigations. *Journal of Cerebral Blood Flow and Metabolism, 30,* 273-285.

Borra, E., Belmalih, A., Gerbella, M., Rozzi, S., & Luppino, G. (2010). Projections of the hand field of the macaque ventral premotor area F5 to the brainstem and spinal cord. *Journal of Comparative Neurology, 518,* 2570-2591.

Bortoff, G. A., & Strick, P. L. (1993). Corticospinal terminations in two new-world primates: further evidence that corticomotoneuronal connections provide part of the neural substrate for manual dexterity. *Journal of Neuroscience, 13,* 5105-5118.

Brinkman, C. (1984). Supplementary motor area of the monkey's cerebral cortex: short- and long-term deficits after unilateral ablation and the effects of subsequent callosal section. *Journal of Neuroscience, 4,* 918-929.

Brinkman, J., & Kuypers, H. G. J. M. (1973). Cerebral control of contralateral and ipsilateral arm, hand and finger movements in the split-brain rhesus monkey. *Brain, 96,* 653-674.

Carron, A. V., & Leavitt, J. L. (1968). Individual differences in two motor learning tasks under massed practice. *Perceptual and Motor Skills, 27,* 499-504.

Chalmeau, R., Visalberghi, E., & Gallo, A. (1997). Capuchin monkeys, *Cebus apella* fail to understand a cooperative task. *Animal Behaviour, 54,* 1215-1225.

Chatagny, P., Badoud, S., Kaeser, M., Gindrat, A. D., Savidan, J., Fregosi, M., . . . Rouiller, E. M. (2013). Distinction between hand dominance and hand preference in primates: a behavioral investigation of manual dexterity in nonhuman primates (macaques) and human subjects. *Brain and Behavior, 3,* 575-595.

Christel, M. I., & Billard, A. (2002). Comparison between macaques' and humans' kinematics of prehension: the role of morphological differences and control mechanisms. *Behavioural Brain Research, 131,* 169-184.

Costello, M. B., & Fragaszy, D. M. (1988). Prehension in *Cebus* and *Saimiri*: I. Grip type and hand preference. *American Journal of Primatology, 15,* 235-245.

Courtine, G., Bunge, M. B., Fawcett, J. W., Grossman, R. G., Kaas, J. H., Lemon, R., . . . Edgerton, V. R. (2007). Can experiments in nonhuman primates expedite the translation of treatments for spinal cord injury in humans? *Nature Medicine, 13,* 561-566.

Crossman, E. R. F. W. (1959) A theory of the acquisition of speed-skill. *Ergonomics 2*, 153-166.

Dancause, N., Barbay, S., Frost, S. B., Plautz, E. J., Chen, D. F., Zoubina, E. V., . . .Nudo, R. J. (2005). Extensive cortical rewiring after brain injury. *Journal of Neuroscience, 25,* 10167-10179.

Dancause, N., Barbay, S., Frost, S. B., Zoubina, E. V., Plautz, E. J., Mahnken, J. D., & Nudo, R. J. (2006). Effects of small ischemic lesions in the primary motor cortex on neurophysiological organization in ventral premotor cortex. *Journal of Neurophysiology, 96,* 3506-3511.

Dancause, N., & Nudo, R. J. (2011). Shaping plasticity to enhance recovery after injury. *Progress in Brain Research, 192,* 273-295.

Darian-Smith, I., Galea, M. P., & Darian-Smith, C. (1996). Manual dexterity: how does the cerebral cortex contribute? *Clinical and Experimental Pharmacology and Physiology, 23,* 948-956.

Darian-Smith, I., Galea, M. P., Darian-Smith, C., Sugitani, M., Tan, A., & Burman, K. (1996). The anatomy of manual dexterity. The new connectivity of the primate sensorimotor thalamus and cerebral cortex. *Advances in Anatomy, Embryology and Cell Biology, 133,* 1-140.

Darian-Smith, I., Burman, K., & Darian-Smith, C. (1999). Parallel pathways mediating manual dexterity in the macaque. *Experimental Brain Research, 128,* 101-108.

Darling, W. G., Pizzimenti, M. A., Rotella, D. L., Peterson, C. R., Hynes, S. M., Ge, J., . . . Morecraft, R. J. (2009). Volumetric effects of motor cortex injury on recovery of dexterous movements. *Experimental Neurology, 220,* 90-108.

Darling, W. G., Pizzimenti, M. A., Rotella, D. L., Hynes, S. M., Ge, J., Stilwell-Morecraft, K. S., . . . Morecraft, R. J. (2010). Minimal forced use without constraint stimulates spontaneous use of the impaired upper extremity following motor cortex injury. *Experimental Brain Research, 202,* 529-542.

Darling, W. G., Pizzimenti, M. A., Hynes, S. M., Rotella, D. L., Headley, G., Ge, J., . . . Morecraft, R. J. (2011). Volumetric effects of motor cortex injury on recovery of ipsilesional dexterous movements. *Experimental Neurology, 231,* 56-71.

Darling, W. G., Helle, N., Pizzimenti, M. A., Rotella, D. L., Hynes, S. M., Ge, J., . . . Morecraft, R. J. (2013). Laterality affects spontaneous recovery of contralateral hand motor function following motor cortex injury in rhesus monkeys. *Experimental Brain Research, 228,* 9-24.

Eisner-Janowicz, I., Barbay, S., Hoover, E., Stowe, A. M., Frost, S. B., Plautz, E. J., & Nudo, R. J. (2008). Early and late changes in the distal forelimb representation of the supplementary motor area after injury to frontal motor areas in the squirrel monkey. *Journal of Neurophysiology, 100,* 1498-1512.

Falk, D., Pyne, L., Helmkamp, R. C., & DeRousseau, C. J. (1988). Directional asymmetry in the forelimb of Macaca mulatta. *American Journal of Physical Anthropology, 77,* 1-6.

Flament, D., Hall, E. J., & Lemon, R. N. (1992). The development of cortico-motoneuronal projections investigated using magnetic brain stimulation in the infant macaque. *Journal of Physiology, 447,* 755-768.

Fragaszy, D. M., & Adams-Curtis, L. E. (1997). Developmental changes in manipulation in tufted capuchins (*Cebus apella*) from birth through 2 years and their relation to foraging and weaning. *Journal of Comparative Psychology, 111,* 201-211.

Fragaszy, D. M. (1998). How non-human primates use their hands. In K. J. Connolly (Ed.), *The psychobiology of the hand* (pp. 77-96). London, UK: Mac Keith Press.

Freund, P., Schmidlin, E., Wannier, T., Bloch, J., Mir, A., Schwab, M. E., & Rouiller, E. M. (2006). Nogo-A-specific antibody treatment enhances sprouting and functional recovery after cervical lesion in adult primates. *Nature Medicine, 12,* 790-792.

Freund, P., Wannier, T., Schmidlin, E., Bloch, J., Mir, A., Schwab, M. E., & Rouiller, E. M. (2007). Anti-Nogo-A antibody treatment enhances sprouting of corticospinal axons rostral to a unilateral cervical spinal cord lesion in adult macaque monkey. *Journal of Comparative Neurology, 502,* 644-659.

Freund, P., Schmidlin, E., Wannier, T., Bloch, J., Mir, A., Schwab, M. E., & Rouiller, E. M. (2009). Anti-Nogo-A antibody treatment promotes recovery of manual dexterity after unilateral cervical lesion in adult primates--re-examination and extension of behavioral data. *European Journal of Neuroscience, 29,* 983-996.

Friel, K. M., & Nudo, R. J. (1998). Recovery of motor function after focal cortical injury in primates: compensatory movement patterns used during rehabilitative training. *Somatosensory and Motor Research, 15,* 173-189.

Friel, K. M., Heddings, A. A., & Nudo, R. J. (2000). Effects of postlesion experience on behavioral recovery and neurophysiologic reorganization after cortical injury in primates. *Neurorehabilitation and Neural Repair, 14,* 187-198.

Frost, S. B., Barbay, S., Friel, K. M., Plautz, E. J., & Nudo, R. J. (2003). Reorganization of remote cortical regions after ischemic brain injury: A potential substrate for stroke recovery. *Journal of Neurophysiology, 89,* 3205-3214.

Galea, M. P., & Darian-Smith, I. (1994). Multiple corticospinal neuron populations in the macaque monkey are specified by their unique cortical origins, spinal terminations, and connections. *Cerebral Cortex, 4,* 166-194.

Galea, M. P., & Darian-Smith, I. (1995). Postnatal maturation of the direct corticospinal projections in the macaque monkey. *Cerebral Cortex, 5,* 518-540.

Galea, M. P. & Darian-Smith, I. (1997). Corticospinal projection patterns following unilateral section of the cervical spinal cord in the newborn and juvenile macaque monkey. *Journal of Comparative Neurology, 381,* 282-306.

Gash, D. M., Zhang, Z. M., Umberger, G., Mahood, K., Smith, M., Smith, C., & Gerhardt, G. A. (1999). An automated movement assessment panel for upper limb motor functions in rhesus monkeys and humans. *Journal of Neuroscience Methods, 89,* 111-117.

Glees, P., & Cole, J. (1950). Recovery of skilled motor function after small repeated lesions of motor cortex in macaque. *Journal of Neurophysiology, 13,* 137-148.

Graziano, M. S., Taylor, C. S., & Moore, T. (2002). Complex movements evoked by microstimulation of precentral cortex. *Neuron, 34,* 841-851.

Grichting, B., Hediger, V., Kaluzny, P., & Wiesendanger, M. (2000). Impaired proactive and reactive grip force control in chronic hemiparetic patients. *Clinical Neurophysiology, 111,* 1661-1671.

Hamadjida, A., Wyss, A. F., Mir, A., Schwab, M. E., Belhaj-Saif, A., & Rouiller, E. M. (2012). Influence of anti-Nogo-A antibody treatment on the reorganization of callosal connectivity of the premotor cortical areas following unilateral lesion of primary motor cortex (M1) in adult macaque monkeys. *Experimental Brain Research, 223,* 321-340.

Hoffman, D. S., & Strick, P. L. (1986). Step-tracking movements of the wrist in humans. I. Kinematic analysis. *Journal of Neuroscience, 6,* 3309-3318.

Hoogewoud, F., Hamadjida, A., Wyss, A. F., Mir, A., Schwab, M. E., Belhaj-Saif, A., & Rouiller, E. M. (2013). Comparison of functional recovery of manual dexterity after unilateral spinal cord lesion or motor cortex lesion in adult macaque monkeys. *Frontiers in Neurology,* (in press).

Iwaniuk, A. N., Pellis, S. M., & Whishaw, I. Q. (1999). Is digital dexterity really related to corticospinal projections?: a re-analysis of the Heffner and Masterton data set using modern comparative statistics. *Behavioural Brain Research, 101,* 173-187.

Iwaniuk, A. N., & Whishaw, I. Q. (1999). How skilled are the skilled limb movements of the raccoon (*Procyon lotor*)? *Behavioural Brain Research, 99,* 35-44.

Iwaniuk, A. N., & Whishaw, I. Q. (2000). On the origin of skilled forelimb movements. *Trends in Neuroscience, 23,* 372-376.

Kaeser, M., Wyss, A. F., Bashir, S., Hamadjida, A., Liu, Y., Bloch, J., . . . Rouiller, E. M. (2010). Effects of unilateral motor cortex lesion on ipsilesional hand's reach and grasp performance in monkeys: Relationship with recovery in the contralesional hand. *Journal of Neurophysiology, 103,* 1630-1645.

Kaeser, M., Brunet, J. F., Wyss, A., Belhaj-Saif, A., Liu, Y., Hamadjida, A., . . . & Bloch, J. (2011). Autologous adult cortical cell transplantation enhances functional recovery following unilateral lesion of motor cortex in primates: a pilot study. *Neurosurgery, 68,* 1405-1416.

Kaeser, M., Wannier, T., Brunet, J. F., Wyss, A., Bloch, J., & Rouiller, E. M. (2013). Representation of motor habit in a sequence of repetitive reach and grasp movements performed by macaque monkeys: Evidence for a contribution of the dorsolateral prefrontal cortex. *Cortex, 49,* 1404-1419.

Kakebeeke, T. H., Caflisch, J., Chaouch, A., Rousson, V., Largo, R. H., & Jenni, O. G. (2013). Neuromotor development in children. Part 3: motor performance in 3- to 5-year olds. *Developmental Medicine and Child Neurology, 55,* 248-256.

Kazennikov, O., Wicki, U., Corboz, M., Hyland, B., Palmeri, A., Rouiller, E. M., & Wiesendanger, M. (1994). Temporal structure of a bimanual goal-directed movement sequence in monkeys. *European Journal of Neuroscience, 6,* 203-210.

Kazennikov, O., Hyland, B., Wicki, U., Perrig, S., Rouiller, E. M., & Wiesendanger, M. (1998). Effects of lesions in the mesial frontal cortex on bimanual co-ordination in monkeys. *Neuroscience, 85,* 703-716.

Kazennikov, O., Hyland, B., Corboz, M., Babalian, A., Rouiller, E. M., & Wiesendanger, M. (1999). Neural activity of supplementary and primary motor areas in monkeys and its relation to bimanual and unimanual movement sequences. *Neuroscience, 89,* 661-674.

Kermadi, I., Liu, Y., Tempini, A., & Rouiller, E. M. (1997). Effects of reversible inactivation of the supplementary motor area (SMA) on unimanual grasp and bimanual pull and grasp performance in monkeys. *Somatosensory and Motor Research, 14,* 268-280.

Kermadi, I., Liu, Y., Tempini, A., Calciati, E., & Rouiller, E. M. (1998). Neuronal activity in the primate supplementary motor area and the primary motor cortex in relation to spatio-temporal bimanual coordination. *Somatosensory and Motor Research, 15,* 287-308.

Kermadi, I., Liu, Y., & Rouiller, E. M. (2000). Do bimanual motor actions involve the dorsal premotor (PMd), cingulate (CMA) and posterior parietal (PPC) cortices? Comparison with primary and supplementary motor cortical areas. *Somatosensory and Motor Research, 17,* 255-271.

King, B. J. (1986). Extractive foraging and the evolution of primate intelligence. *Journal of Human Evolution, 1,* 361-372.

King, J., & Landau, V. (1993). Manual preference in varieties of reaching in squirrel monkeys. In J. Ward & W. Hopkins (Eds.), *Primate laterality* (pp. 107-124). New York, NY: Springer.

Kinoshita, M., Matsui, R., Kato, S., Hasegawa, T., Kasahara, H., Isa, K., . . . Isa, T. (2012). Genetic dissection of the circuit for hand dexterity in primates. *Nature, 487,* 235-238.

Klein, A., Sacrey, L. A., Whishaw, I. Q., & Dunnett, S. B. (2012). The use of rodent skilled reaching as a translational model for investigating brain damage and disease. *Neuroscience and Biobehavioral Reviews, 36,* 1030-1042.

Lacreuse, A., & Fragaszy, D. M. (1999). Left hand preferences in capuchins (Cebus apella): role of spatial demands in manual activity. *Laterality, 4,* 65-78.

Lacroix, S., Havton, L. A., McKay, H., Yang, H., Brant, A., Roberts, J., & Tuszynski, M. H. (2004). Bilateral corticospinal projections arise from each motor cortex in the macaque monkey: A quantitative study. *Journal of Comparative Neurology, 473,* 147-161.

Lashley, K. S. (1930) Basic neural mechanisms in behavior. *Psychological Review, 37*, 1-24.

Lawrence, D. G., & Hopkins, D. A. (1976). The development of motor control in the rhesus monkey: evidence concerning the role of corticomotoneuronal connections. *Brain, 99,* 235-254.

Lawrence, D. G., Porter, R., & Redman, S. J. (1985). Corticomotoneuronal synapses in the monkey: light microscopic localization upon motoneurons of intrinsic muscles of the hand. *Journal of Comparative Neurology, 232,* 499-510.

Leca, J. B., Gunst, N., & Huffman, M. (2011). Complexity in object manipulation by Japanese macaques (*Macaca fuscata*): A cross-sectional analysis of manual coordination in stone handling patterns. *Journal of Comparative Psychology, 125,* 61-71.

Lemon, R. N., Johansson, R. S., & Westling, G. (1996). Modulation of corticospinal influence over hand muscles during gripping tasks in man and monkey. *Canadian Journal of Physiology and Pharmacology, 74,* 547-558.

Lemon, R. N. (1999). Neural control of dexterity: what has been achieved? *Experimental Brain Research, 128,* 6-12.

Lemon, R. N., & Griffiths, J. (2005). Comparing the function of the corticospinal system in different species: organizational differences for motor specialization? *Muscle Nerve, 32,* 261-279.

Lemon, R. N. (2008). Descending pathways in motor control. *Annual Review of Neuroscience, 31,* 195-218.

Lindshield, S. M., & Rodrigues, M. A. (2009). Tool use in wild spider monkeys (*Ateles geoffroyi*). *Primates, 50,* 269-272.

Liu, Y., & Rouiller, E. M. (1999). Mechanisms of recovery of dexterity following unilateral lesion of the sensorimotor cortex in adult monkeys. *Experimental Brain Research, 128,* 149-159.

Maier, M. A., Armand, J., Kirkwood, P. A., Yang, H. W., Davis, J. N., & Lemon, R. N. (2002). Differences in the corticospinal projection from primary motor cortex and supplementary motor area to macaque upper limb motoneurons: an anatomical and electrophysiological study. *Cerebral Cortex, 12,* 281-296.

Manoel, E. J., & Connolly, K. J. (1995). Variability and the development of skilled actions. *International Journal of Psychophysiology, 19,* 129-147.

Marshall, J. W., Ridley, R. M., Baker, H. F., Hall, L. D., Carpenter, T. A., & Wood, N. I. (2003). Serial MRI, functional recovery, and long-term infarct maturation in a non-human primate model of stroke. *Brain Research Bulletin, 61,* 577-585.

Marteniuk, R. G. (1974). Individual differences in motor performances and learning. *Exercise and Sport Sciences Reviews, 2,* 103-130.

McNeal, D. W., Darling, W. G., Ge, J., Stilwell-Morecraft, K. S., Solon, K. M., Hynes, S. M., . . . Morecraft, R. J. (2010). Selective long-term reorganization of the corticospinal projection from the supplementary motor cortex following recovery from lateral motor cortex injury. *Journal of Comparative Neurology, 518,* 586-621.

Murata, Y., Higo, N., Oishi, T., Yamashita, A., Matsuda, K., Hayashi, M., & Yamane, S. (2008). Effects of motor training on the recovery of manual dexterity after primary motor cortex lesion in macaque monkeys. *Journal of Neurophysiology, 99,* 773-786.

Nahallage, C. A. D., & Huffman, M. A. (2007). Acquisition and development of stone handling behavior in infant Japanese macaques. *Behaviour, 144,* 1193-1215.

Newell, K. M., Liu, Y. T., & Mayer-Kress, G. (2001). Time scales in motor learning and development. *Psychological Review, 108,* 57-82.

Nishimura, Y., Onoe, H., Morichika, Y., Perfiliev, S., Tsukada, H., & Isa, T. (2007). Time-dependent central compensatory mechanisms of finger dexterity after spinal cord injury. *Science, 318,* 1150-1155.

Nudo, R. J., Wise, B. M., SiFuentes, F., & Milliken, G. W. (1996). Neural substrates for the effects of rehabilitative training on motor recovery after ischemic infarct. *Science, 272,* 1791-1794.

Nudo, R. J., & Milliken, G. W. (1996). Reorganization of movement representations in primary motor cortex following focal ischemic infarcts in adult squirrel monkeys. *Journal of Neurophysiology, 75,* 2144-2149.

Ogden, R., & Franz, S. I. (1917). On cerebral motor control: the recovery from experimentally produced hemiplegia. *Psychobiology, 1,* 33-49.

Ogihara, N., & Oishi, M. (2012). Muscle dimensions in the Japanese macaque hand. *Primates., 53,* 391-396.

Olivier, E., Edgley, S. A., Armand, J., & Lemon, R. N. (1997). An electrophysiological study of the postnatal development of the corticospinal system in the macaque monkey. *Journal of Neuroscience, 17,* 267-276.

Padberg, J., Franca, J. G., Cooke, D. F., Soares, J. G., Rosa, M. G., Fiorani, M. Jr., . . . Krubitzer, L. (2007). Parallel evolution of cortical areas involved in skilled hand use. *Journal of Neuroscience, 27,* 10106-10115.

Passingham, R. E., Perry, V. H., & Wilkinson, F. (1983). The long-term effects of removal of sensorimotor cortex in infant and adult rhesus monkeys. *Brain, 106 (Pt 3),* 675-705.

Pizzimenti, M. A., Darling, W. G., Rotella, D. L., McNeal, D. W., Herrick, J. L., Ge, J., . . . Morecraft, R. J. (2007). Measurement of reaching kinematics and prehensile dexterity in nonhuman primates. *Journal of Neurophysiology, 98,* 1015-1029.

Plautz, E. J., Barbay, S., Frost, S. B., Friel, K. M., Dancause, N., Zoubina, E. V., . . . Nudo, R. J. (2003). Post-infarct cortical plasticity and behavioral recovery using concurrent cortical stimulation and rehabilitative training: a feasibility study in primates. *Neurological Research, 25,* 801-810.

Pouydebat, E., Laurin, M., Gorce, P., & Bels, V. (2008). Evolution of grasping among anthropoids. *Journal of Evolutionary Biology, 21,* 1732-1743.

Pouydebat, E., Gorce, P., Coppens, Y., & Bels, V. (2009). Biomechanical study of grasping according to the volume of the object: human versus non-human primates. *Journal of Biomechanisms, 42,* 266-272.

Pouydebat, E., Reghem, E., Borel, A., & Gorce, P. (2011). Diversity of grip in adults and young humans and chimpanzees (*Pan troglodytes*). *Behavioural Brain Research, 218,* 21-28.

Rathelot, J. A., & Strick, P. L. (2009). Subdivisions of primary motor cortex based on cortico-motoneuronal cells. *Proceedings of the National Academy of Sciences of the United States of America, 106,* 918-923.

Roitberg, B., Khan, N., Tuccar, E., Kompoliti, K., Chu, Y., Alperin, N., . . . Emborg, M. E. (2003). Chronic ischemic stroke model in cynomolgus monkeys: behavioral, neuroimaging and anatomical study. *Neurological Research, 25,* 68-78.

Rosenblatt, N. J., Hurt, C. P., Latash, M. L., & Grabiner, M. D. (2014) An apparent contradiction: increasing variability to achieve greater precision? *Experimental Brain Research, 232,* 403-413.

Rouiller, E. M., Moret, V., Tanné, J., & Boussaoud, D. (1996). Evidence for direct connections between the hand region of the supplementary motor area and cervical motoneurons in the macaque monkey. *European Journal of Neuroscience, 8,* 1055-1059.

Rouiller, E. M., Yu, X. H., Moret, V., Tempini, A., Wiesendanger, M., & Liang, F. (1998). Dexterity in adult monkeys following early lesion of the motor cortical hand area: the role of cortex adjacent to the lesion. *European Journal of Neuroscience, 10,* 729-740.

Sacrey, L. A., Alaverdashvili, M., & Whishaw, I. Q. (2009). Similar hand shaping in reaching-for-food (skilled reaching) in rats and humans provides evidence of homology in release, collection, and manipulation movements. *Behavioural Brain Research, 204,* 153-161.

Sasaki, K., & Gemba, H. (1984). Compensatory motor function of the somatosensory cortex for dysfunction of the motor cortex following cerebellar hemispherectomy in the monkey. *Experimental Brain Research, 56,* 532-538.

Sasaki, S., Isa, T., Pettersson, L. G., Alstermark, B., Naito, K., Yoshimura, K., . . . Ohki, Y. (2004). Dexterous finger movements in primate without monosynaptic corticomotoneuronal excitation. *Journal of Neurophysiology, 92,* 3142-3147.

Schieber, M. H. (2001). Constraints on somatotopic organization in the primary motor cortex. *Journal of Neurophysiology, 86,* 2125-2143.

Schmidlin, E., Wannier, T., Bloch, J., & Rouiller, E. M. (2004). Progressive plastic changes in the hand representation of the primary motor cortex parallel incomplete recovery from a unilateral section of the corticospinal tract at cervical level in monkeys. *Brain Research, 1017,* 172-183.

Schmidlin, E., Wannier, T., Bloch, J., Belhaj-Saïf, A., Wyss, A., & Rouiller, E. M. (2005). Reduction of the hand representation in the ipsilateral primary motor cortex following unilateral section of the corticospinal tract at cervical level in monkeys. *BMC Neuroscience, 6:56.*

Schmidlin, E., Kaeser, M., Gindrat, A. D., Savidan, J., Chatagny, P., Badoud, S., . . . Rouiller, E. M. (2011). Behavioral assessment of manual dexterity in non-human primates. *Journal of Visualized Experiments, 57:* 3258.

Schmidt, R. A., & Lee, T. D. (2011). Individual differences and capabilities. In *Motor control and learning: a behavioral emphasis* (5th ed., pp. 297-324). Champaign, IL: Human Kinetics.

Schmidt, R. A., & Lee, T. D. (2011). Motor learning concepts and research methods. In *Motor control and learning: a behavioral emphasis* (5th ed., pp. 327-346). Champaign, IL: Human Kinetics.

Schorer, J., Baker, J., Fath, F., & Jaitner, T. (2007). Identification of interindividual and intraindividual movement patterns in handball players of varying expertise levels. *Journal of Motor Behavior, 39,* 409-421.

Serrien, D. J., & Wiesendanger, M. (1999). Grip-load force coordination in cerebellar patients. *Experimental Brain Research, 128,* 76-80.

Serrien, D. J., Kaluzny, P., Wicki, U., & Wiesendanger, M. (1999). Grip force adjustments induced by predictable load perturbations during a manipulative task. *Experimental Brain Research, 124,* 100-106.

Spinozzi, G., Castorina, M. G., & Truppa, V. (1998). Hand preferences in unimanual and coordinated-bimanual tasks by tufted capuchin monkeys (*Cebus apella*). *Journal of Comparative Psychology, 112,* 183-191.

Spinozzi, G., Truppa, V., & Lagana, T. (2004). Grasping behavior in tufted capuchin monkeys (*Cebus apella*): grip types and manual laterality for picking up a small food item. *American Journal of Physical Anthropology, 125,* 30-41.

Spinozzi, G., Lagana, T., & Truppa, V. (2007). Hand use by tufted capuchins (*Cebus apella*) to extract a small food item from a tube: digit movements, hand preference, and performance. *American Journal of Primatology, 69,* 336-352.

Stelmach, G. E. (1968). Distribution of practice in individual differences and intra-variability. *Perceptual and Motor Skills, 26,* 727-730.

Sugiyama, Y., Higo, N., Yoshino-Saito, K., Murata, Y., Nishimura, Y., Oishi, T., & Isa, T. (2013). Effects of early versus late rehabilitative training on manual dexterity after corticospinal tract lesion in macaque monkeys. *Journal of Neurophysiology, 109,* 2853-2865.

Tomassini, V., Jbabdi, S., Kincses, Z. T., Bosnell, R., Douaud, G., Pozzilli, C., . . . Johansen-Berg, H. (2011). Structural and functional bases for individual differences in motor learning. *Human Brain Mapping, 32,* 494-508.

Travis, A. M. (1955). Neurological deficiencies after ablation of the precentral motor area in *Macaca mulatta*. *Brain, 78,* 155-173.

Van Schaik, C. P., Deaner, R. O., & Merrill, M. Y. (1999). The conditions for tool use in primates: implications for the evolution of material culture. *Journal of Human Evolution, 36,* 719-741.

Wannier, T., Schmidlin, E., Bloch, J., & Rouiller, E. M. (2005). A unilateral section of the corticospinal tract at cervical level in primate does not lead to measurable cell loss in motor cortex. *Journal of Neurotrauma, 22,* 703-717.

Whishaw, I. Q., Whishaw, P., & Gorny, B. (2008). The structure of skilled forelimb reaching in the rat: a movement rating scale. *Journal of Visualized Experiments, 18*: 816.

Whishaw, I. Q., Travis, S. G., Koppe, S. W., Sacrey, L. A., Gholamrezaei, G., & Gorny, B. (2010). Hand shaping in the rat: conserved release and collection vs. flexible manipulation in overground walking, ladder rung walking, cylinder exploration, and skilled reaching. *Behavioural Brain Research, 206,* 21-31.

Wiesendanger, M. (1999). Manual dexterity and the making of tools - an introduction from an evolutionary perspective. *Experimental Brain Research, 128,* 1-5.

Wong, Y. J., & Whishaw, I. Q. (2004). Precision grasps of children and young and old adults: individual differences in digit contact strategy, purchase pattern, and digit posture. *Behavioural Brain Research, 154,* 113-123.

Wu, H. G., Miyamoto, Y. R., Gonzalez Castro, L. N., Ölveczky, B. P., & Smith, M. A. (2014) Temporal structure of motor variability is dynamically regulated and predicts motor learning ability. *Nature Neuroscience, 17,* 312-321.

Wyss, A. F., Hamadjida, A., Savidan, J., Liu, Y., Bashir, S., Mir, A., . . . Belhaj-Saif, A. (2013). Long-term motor cortical map changes following unilateral lesion of the hand representation in the motor cortex in macaque monkeys showing functional recovery of hand functions. *Restorative Neurology and Neuroscience, 31,* 733-760.

Zhao, D., Hopkins, W. D., & Li, B. (2012). Handedness in nature: first evidence on manual laterality on bimanual coordinated tube task in wild primates. *American Journal of Physical Anthropology, 148,* 36-44.

12

Thinking Pigs: A Comparative Review of Cognition, Emotion, and Personality in *Sus domesticus*

Lori Marino[1,2] & Christina M. Colvin[3]
The Kimmela Center for Animal Advocacy[1], The Someone Project[2]
Emory University, USA[3]

While relatively little is known about the psychology of domestic pigs, what is known suggests that pigs are cognitively complex and share many traits with animals whom we consider intelligent. This paper reviews the scientific evidence for cognitive complexity in domestic pigs and, when appropriate, compares this literature with similar findings in other animals, focusing on some of the more compelling and cutting-edge research results. The goals of this paper are to: 1) frame pig cognition and psychology in a basic comparative context independent of the livestock production and management setting; and 2) identify areas of research with pigs that are particularly compelling and in need of further investigation. We summarize and discuss several areas of comparative psychology, including nonsocial and social cognition, self-awareness, emotion, and personality. We conclude that there are several areas of research in which the findings are suggestive of complex psychology in pigs. We conclude by calling for more noninvasive cognitive and behavioral research with domestic pigs in non-laboratory settings that allow them to express their natural abilities.

The animal cognition literature is rich in information about certain types of animals, including primates, rodents, birds, and, increasingly, dogs. From the standpoint of our basic understanding of the range of cognition in the animal kingdom, pigs, as even-toed ungulates, are a taxonomic group that is not as well represented in the comparative psychology literature as these other groups. In fact, no ungulate groups are well-studied compared with the aforementioned animals who are, in contrast, frequently considered. Because of their status as an under-represented ungulate group, there exists a very basic need to bring together what we do know about pigs in order to build on our current understanding and gain further insights into the distribution of various cognitive and behavioral levels of sophistication in mammals and other taxa.

The scientific literature on pig psychology and behavior has been dominated by applied themes and settings relating to welfare in intensive farming. These kinds of applied frameworks likely impact and shape our understanding of pigs from both a scientific and public perspective. While some studies have been done that do not frame pigs within an applied setting, these are far less numerous than those with direct reference to behavioral management in an agricultural or laboratory setting.

This paper examines both categories of research – applied and basic – in an effort to begin to fill out and reframe our understanding of pig intelligence, cognition, and overall psychology on a basic comparative-

Please send correspondence to Dr. Lori Marino, The Kimmela Center for Animal Advocacy. USA. (Email:lorimarino@kimmela.org)

evolutionary level. We also identify research findings that are particularly promising and interesting from the point of view of revealing complex abilities of pigs. We do not purport to offer an exhaustive review of all studies of cognition and emotion in pigs. Instead, we have chosen to focus on the more complex capacities in pigs that are arguably at the leading edge of intelligence and sentience and to identify compelling and promising areas of cognition, emotion, and sociality which, we contend, should be investigated in future studies.

Species-specific Factors to Consider When Assessing Findings on Pig Behavior and Cognition

Evolution and History of Domestication

As with any group, species-specific factors need to be considered when interpreting cognitive, emotional, and social capacities in pigs, as well as when comparing their capacities to other species. It is especially important to keep in mind that not all domesticated animals are bred for the same characteristics. For instance, while dogs were selected for traits promoting human companionship and work, pigs were selected for the ability to produce meat.

Domestic pigs descended from wild boars (*Sus scrofa*), a gregarious species that underwent the first phase of domestication in the Near East about 9,000 years ago (Giuffra,, Kijas, Amarger, Carlborg, Jeon & Andersson, 2000). Multiple smaller domestication events occurred over time, with much crossbreeding between Asian and European groups (Giuffra et al., 2000; Larson, Dobney, Albarella, Fang, Matisoo-Smith, Robins, & Cooper, 2005). Importantly, although during domestication there was some artificial selection for an easy temperament, most of the selective breeding of pigs has been for production traits, especially growth and reproduction. As a result, modern domesticated pigs are not too dissimilar, cognitively and behaviorally, from ancestral and modern wild boars (Held, Cooper, & Mendl, 2009).

This is especially true of their social behavior; for both domesticated pigs and wild boars, the basic social unit is several females and their offspring, with strong parallels in reproductive behavior, parenting, and development (Graves, 1984; Jensen, 1986). Preliminary comparisons of cognition and learning in wild boars and domestic pigs indicate that often ontogeny and early experience have more of an impact on these processes than selection during domestication (Albiach-Serrano, Brauer, Cacchione, Zickert, & Amici, 2012). Therefore, the capacities and behaviors of domesticated pigs appear to have been developed through adaptations based in the physical and social environment of their wild ancestors and relatives.

Sensory Abilities

Assessments of cognitive capacity in any species are dependent upon using stimuli and settings appropriate to the sensory capabilities of that species, i.e., those that resemble the mass of sensory information the animal is adapted to perceiving and processing (Geiling, Nordquist, & van der Staay, 2011). Therefore, it is critical to recognize that domestication has not substantially altered the type of environmental information domesticated pigs are capable of detecting (Held et al., 2009; Jensen, 1986). They use a wide range of stimuli both in their physical and social environments.

It should not come as a surprise, considering the gregarious nature of their wild counterparts, that pigs are highly social animals and that tactile information plays an important role in their behavior. The highest density of tactile receptors is found in the pig's snout (Kruska, 1988), as they use their snouts to engage in highly manipulative behaviors such as rooting, carrying and pushing, and social interactions (Stolba & Wood-Gush, 1989). Olfaction is the pig's keenest sense. Thus, they learn olfactory discriminations more easily than discriminations in other modalities (Croney, 1999). As opportunistic omnivores, they rely heavily on odors and flavors to find appropriate food items when foraging (Croney, Adams, Washington, & Stricklin, 2003). Furthermore, their sensitivity in the olfactory domain is not limited to foraging for food, but is used heavily in the social domain in a wide range of contexts, including discriminating social identity (Mendl, Randle, & Pope, 2002, sexual state (Signoret, Baldwin, Fraser, & Hafez, 1975) and the emotional state of other pigs in aggressive encounters (McGlone, 1990), as well as in creating dominance hierarchies (Mendl, Randle, & Pope, 2002).

Audition is used by pigs in many social contexts, including communication. Identity and arousal state can be conveyed through vocalizations (Manteuffel, Puppe, & Schon, 2004), and these are used extensively in mother-offspring interactions (Weary, Lawson, & Thompson, 1996; Weary, Ross, & Fraser, 1997). The hearing range of pigs spans from 42-40,500 Hz (Heffner & Heffner, 1992), making them sensitive in the ultrasound range.

Pigs typically use vision along with other senses, particularly olfaction and touch, to discriminate objects in the natural environment (Arave, 1996; Lomas, Piggins, & Phillips, 1998). Nevertheless, they are capable of discriminating objects by vision alone in the absence of other cues (Koba & Tanida, 2001). Moreover, both vision and audition are used more than olfaction when discriminating between humans (Tanida & Nagano, 1998).

The Scientific Literature

Research Methods

Here we present a summary of cognitive, emotional, personality and social characteristics of pigs from a comprehensive review of the scientific literature. We conducted online Google-based direct searches through all of the major peer-reviewed journals in these areas (Table 1). We used familiar and broad terms relevant to intelligence, cognition, and behavior and key terms from existing papers (e.g., intelligence, cognition, behavior, learning, memory, sociality, self-awareness, self-recognition, etc.). We also used more specific search terms, e.g., spatial memory, navigation, deception, etc., within these broader categories when necessary. Additionally, we used these terms to search on ScienceDaily for relevant news items and the peer-reviewed papers they described. We also conducted a complete search of the websites of the major authors in these fields for all of their relevant projects. Finally, we searched the reference section of each paper to find additional papers in additional miscellaneous journals (not listed in Table 1) and ensured that our search was comprehensive. We included books, book chapters, and dissertation theses as well as both empirical and review papers (which provided further description and interpretation of the empirical data) and included both the basic comparative psychology literature and the applied literature. We did not place time restrictions on articles, but we did give priority to more recent papers when appropriate. The reference section shows the full breadth of the sources we consulted.

We divide our findings into five broad categories: Nonsocial Cognition, Social Cognition, Self-awareness, Emotion, and Personality, with sub-categories within some.

Findings from the Literature

Nonsocial Cognition

Nonsocial cognition refers to how animals perceive, mentally represent, and process physical components of their environment. It includes problem solving in the physical realm, object discrimination, spatial cognition, and other elements of learning and memory in the physical/object domain, including time perception. In this paper we distinguish nonsocial from social cognition for the sake of presentation but do not presume that all aspects of social and nonsocial cognition are mutually exclusive.

Table 1. *List of major peer-reviewed journals searched*

Journals	
Animal Behavior	*Domestic Animal Endocrinology*
Animal Cognition	*Hormones and Behavior*
Animal Welfare	*International Journal of Comparative Psychology*
Applied Animal Behavior Science	*Journal of Animal Science*
Applied Animal Behavior Ethology	*Journal of Comparative Psychology*
Behaviour	*Journal of Mammalogy*
Behavioural Brain Research	*Nature*
Behavioural Processes	*Physiology and Behavior*
Brain, Behavior and Evolution	*Public Library of Science (PLoS) Biology and PLoS One*
Current Biology	*Science*

Object discrimination learning. Object discrimination learning involves the ability to learn to discriminate stimuli or objects on the basis of various attributes of those stimuli through differential reinforcement contingencies (Kehoe, 2008). Clearly, object discrimination is a necessary foundation for other forms of cognition. Object discrimination makes categorization and concept formation possible; these capacities, in turn, can provide cognitive scaffolding for other complex capacities. All animals possess some ability to learn to discriminate objects, and these capacities range from discriminations of simple concrete stimuli to complex and even abstract concepts.

Pigeons and other bird species are capable of categorizing and differentiating various stimuli, e.g., distinguishing between photos with and without humans (Huber, Apfalter, Steurer, & Prossinger, 2005). Many mammals, including rodents and primates, are capable of rather complex discriminations (Fagot, 2000; Matsuzawa, 2001; Zentall & Wasserman, 2006). And dogs are able to classify color photographs of natural stimuli such as other dogs and landscapes (Range, Aust, Steurer, & Huber, 2008).

When it comes to robust object discrimination capacities, pigs are no exception. Complex object discrimination has been demonstrated in pigs in a range of situations requiring a robust memory (Croney et al, 2003; Hemsworth, Verge, & Coleman, 1996; Tanida & Nagano, 1998. In one study in which the spontaneous response of pigs to novel and familiar objects was assessed, after exposure to a sample object for two days, pigs remembered the object for at least five days and showed a preference for novel objects over familiar ones (Gifford, Sylvie Cloutier, & Newberry, 2007), demonstrating their capacity for long-term memory.

Moreover, pigs can prioritize *important* memories, such as the requirements of a food-searching task. When given the opportunity to access only one of two food sources, they regularly preferred the one with more food and remembered that site (Held, Baumgartner, Kilbride, Byrne, & Mendl, 2005). Pigs can also use either or both visual and olfactory cues while foraging. Rather than rely on the spatial placement of a location that previously contained food, pigs can follow both certain colors and food extract odors to find a food source, showing that they can make discriminations in both modalities, that is, between colors and odors (Croney et al. 2003).

Some of the most compelling studies on object discrimination with pigs were designed to parallel the *symbolic language comprehension* research with dolphins (*Tursiops truncatus*, Herman, 1980, 1987; Herman, Hovanick, Gory, & Bradshaw, 1989) and sea lions (*Zalophus californianus*, Schusterman, 1993). These marine mammals can utilize visual (gestural) and auditory stimuli to successfully process semantic (meaning) and syntactic (sequential) components of an artificial language. When given a similar task, two Vietnamese potbellied pigs (*Sus scrofa domesticus*) demonstrated comprehension of gestural and verbal symbols representing objects (frisbee, ball, dumbbell) and actions (sit, fetch, jump). They were also able to distinguish these items from one another (Cerbulis, 1994). Moreover, they learned to comprehend a combination of symbols for actions and objects (e.g., *fetch the frisbee*), discriminating among three objects, and, like dolphins and sea lions, performed the action-object task presented to them. Although there has been controversy over whether these kinds of responses to symbols represent more than stimulus response-learning, the pigs, like the dolphins, exhibited complex three-choice object discrimination and three-object, one action combination discrimination as well. These capacities lend support to the view that their performance on the task may require a more complex explanation. The basic ability to appropriately respond to symbols representing objects and actions in pigs suggests that further studies of this kind would be worth pursuing in order to explore the differences and similarities in levels of cognitive complexity in this situation between pigs and marine mammals.

Time perception. One area of longstanding interest in comparative cognition is time perception, i.e., the ability to detect the passage of time and anticipate the future. Basic time perception is not entirely synonymous with, but is arguably a basis for, more sophisticated mental time travel, the conscious ability to mentally represent the past and the future. That is, when coupled with an episodic memory system, time perception may become part of an autobiographical sense of self in the past, present and future.

There is substantial evidence that other animals have internal timing mechanisms that help them know the time of day and predict when events will occur (Gallistel, 1994). Western scrub jays (*Aphelocoma californica*) are able to anticipate future events and act accordingly during food-caching episodes (Raby, Alexis, Dickinson, & Clayton, 2007). Chimpanzees (*Pan troglodytes*) and other great apes clearly possess an autobiographical self, as they are able to prepare themselves for future actions (e.g., tool use), even as much as a day in advance (Beran, Pate, Washburn, & Rumbaugh 2004, 2012; Mulcahy & Call, 2006; Osvath & Osvath, 2008) and demonstrate a capacity for episodic memory. They can remember highly specific contextual elements, that is, the *what, where and when* of events when hours, weeks and even years have passed (Martin-Ordas, Berntsen, & Call, 2013; Martin-Ordas, Haun, Colmenares, & Call, 2010).

Although there has been no conclusive work on time perception in pigs, the research that has been done is intriguing and points toward the value of further work in this area. In one study female pigs were given a choice between two crates that differed mainly with respect to the duration of confinement they imposed, which was either 30 min (short) or 240 min (long). The pigs showed an overall preference for confinement in crates associated with short durations instead of those associated with longer durations, demonstrating that they were sensitive to differences in elapsed time in the two crates. Furthermore, the pigs used a variety of sensory cues (visual patterns and direction) to make that decision (Spinka, Duncan, & Widowski, 1998). However, the pigs in this study did not show all the behaviors expected from the time perception hypothesis. That is, there was no measurable hesitancy to enter crates where they would be confined for long duration. One would hypothesize that if the pigs strongly preferred short-duration to long-duration crates that they would hesitate to enter the long-duration crates. The authors concluded, however, that although there was a preference the long duration period was not very aversive for the pigs. Also, the apparatus used was not symmetrical and the pigs initially showed some bias towards one side versus the other. This bias had to be overcome by modifications in the apparatus. Therefore, there were a number of components of the study that need to be explored more closely before it can be taken as definitive evidence of time perception.

Another study used an operant set-up requiring a foot lever press by six female, pre-adolescent mini-pigs who performed tasks thought to measure some aspect of timing behavior through temporal response differentiation requiring the pigs to hold down a lever for a specific number of seconds. The authors concluded that the cognitive aspects of the task were likely to be within the capacity of the pigs but that the required physical response was too difficult, i.e., their hooves slipped off the lever and many of the pigs tried to respond with their snouts instead of feet, showing that they likely understood the cognitive requirements of the task, despite the physical limitations (Ferguson, Gopee, Paule, & Howard, 2009).

In another study, pigs were able to anticipate positive and negative situations (Imfeld-Mueller, van Wezemaela, Stauffachera, Gygax, & Hillmann, 2011). Pigs were kept in a waiting box and cued with tones signaling whether they would be able to go into a room with a bowl of popcorn (positive) or cross a ramp provoking a visual cliff response (negative). When anticipating the negative situation, the proportion of pigs uttering high-frequency vocalizations was significantly higher, pigs turned around more often, and the latency to move was longer after door opening, than when waiting for the positive situation. However, heart rate, heart rate variability and locomotive activity were not influenced by the valence of the situation but differed depending on the phase (waiting, tone, anticipation and end) of the trial. Although the authors considered the high-pitched vocalization to be the most sensitive parameter of the pigs' emotional responses, the results demonstrate various behaviors indicative of an emotional response in anticipation of two different events.

Although there is insufficient data to draw definitive conclusions regarding the complexity of time perception in pigs, the research described above suggests that further research on time perception, anticipation, and, if these abilities turn out to be robust in pigs, perhaps even planning (which is based upon these capacities), in pigs would be promising.

Spatial learning and memory. Spatial cognition (learning and memory) refers to the ability to acquire knowledge of, remember, organize and utilize information about spatial aspects of one's environment, including navigation and learning to discriminate and prioritize the locations of objects. Spatial learning is highly dependent upon mental representations in both short and long-term memory and often forms the basis of complex cognitive maps of the environment, providing the foundation for many other social and non-social strategic behaviors during such tasks as foraging and traveling.

The complex spatial abilities of food-caching birds are well known (Balda & Kamil, 2002; Shettleworth, 2002) and many other species display sophisticated navigational and spatial foraging capacities as well, including rodents (Bird, Roberts, Abrams, Kit, & Crupi, 2013) and fish (Brown, 2015). Dogs, too, show complex spatial navigational and search capacities indicating use of cognitive maps. For instance, while navigating toward desired locations and searching for hidden objects, dogs appear to develop novel spatial shortcuts based on their knowledge of previously used paths (Bensky, Gosling, & Sinn, 2013, for a review). Chimpanzees and other nonhuman primates also possess sophisticated spatial-navigational memory and learning capacities in some cases, on a par with four-year old humans (Garber & Dolins, 2014).

Pigs, as foraging animals, are especially good at using spatial information; they are highly competent at learning to navigate mazes and other spatial arrangements (e.g., de Jon et al., 2000; Siegford, Rucker, & Zarella, 2008), although many of these tests are done in highly artificial settings, such as water mazes. Arguably more relevant and revealing are studies of spatial abilities in a foraging context. One of the most ethologically valid and productive methods used to study spatial learning and memory and other cognitive capacities in pigs is the *holeboard* procedure (van der Staay, Gieling, Pinzon, Nordquist, & Ohl, 2012). The holeboard is an open-field arena with numerous holes (or wells) in it that can be baited. This apparatus and procedure allow pigs to *forage* using their snouts as they do in the natural setting. The holeboard protocol has been used to study spatial behavior in a wide variety of species and has been used extensively to study a range of dimensions of spatial behavior, including working memory and foraging strategies. Pigs perform quite well in this spatial discrimination setting, and their performance is robust as it is not affected by an acute social stress, e.g., the presence of a strange pig (Arts, van der Staay, & Ekkel, 2009). For instance, pigs rapidly learn spatial discriminations that depend upon working and reference memory (Bolhuis et al., 2013; Gieling, Arts, Nordquist, & van der Staay, 2012; Gieling et al., 2013; Nawroth & von Borell, 2014).

Pigs also remember the location, content, and relative value of previously discovered sites that contained stimuli of interest. Across 10-minute and 2-hour retention intervals, pigs successfully used spatial memory to search areas for food and to avoid areas previously found to be empty (Mendl, Laughlin, & Hitchcock, 1997). Another experiment showed that pigs were able to learn a win-shift (searching elsewhere after finding food) foraging task faster and with a higher degree of accuracy than a win-stay (returning to the location of previously-discovered food) foraging task, suggesting that pigs have a predisposition to forage in previously unexplored areas (Laughlin & Mendl, 2000). These studies show that pigs can use spatial memory flexibly; they can be trained to either return to a location where they previously found food or to use the memory of a previously discovered food site to forage elsewhere.

In another particularly interesting experiment, pigs were presented with two different food sites that were baited with unequal amounts of food. When made to choose between one of the two locations in a foraging context, pigs showed a preference for visiting the site containing the larger amount of food (Held et al., 2005). These findings suggest that pigs are able to discriminate between and remember the locations of food sites of different relative value. Although it is possible that the pigs were subitizing, a form of pattern recognition that is used to rapidly assess small quantities of items (Cutini & Bonato, 2012), these findings do suggest some level of numerosity in pigs. Of course, more research could be focused on determining the exact cognitive mechanism underlying this ability.

Novelty Seeking, Inquisitiveness and Play. Play is related to creativity and innovation and, therefore, forms the basis for complex object-related and social abilities (Bateson, 2015) in humans and other animals.

Exposure to novelty enhances learning experiences, and responses to novelty can have an impact on performance in other cognitive tasks as well (Kaulfuss & Mills, 2008). Social play, which involves creating new interactions and situations, has an important role in the development of canids and other social mammals (Bekoff, 1974, 2014). Therefore, curiosity and the preference for novelty are, arguably, related to cognitive complexity and certain personality traits (see below).

Play is found most predominantly in the most cognitively complex and adaptable nonhuman species, such as primates (Bencke, 2015), dogs (Bekoff, 2015), dolphins (Janik, 2015) and birds (Emery & Clayton, 2015). However, play behavior also exists in fish and reptiles (Burghardt, 2015), and the most cognitively complex invertebrates, such as the octopus (Zylinski, 2015). Therefore, play appears to be a marker of cognitive complexity.

Pigs, too, are playful animals (Donaldson, Newberry, Spinka, & Cloutier, 2002; Olsen, Simonsen, & Dybkjaer, 2002; Newberry, et al. 1988; Wood-Gush and Vestergaard, 1991, 1993), exhibiting a wide range of behaviors in this domain. A recent study of play behavior in pigs shows that they engage in quite complex types of play that include social play and object play (Horback, 2014). Common object play behaviors in pigs include shaking or carrying an object such as a ball or stick or tossing straw (Bolhuis, Schouten, Schrama, & Wiegant, 2005; Dudink, Simonse, Marks, de Jonge, & Spruijt, 2006; Newberry et al., 1988). Locomotor play includes waving/tossing of the head, scampering, jumping, hopping, pawing, pivoting, and gamboling (energetic running), flopping on the ground, and hopping around (Martin, Ison, & Baxter, 2015). Social play in pigs includes play fighting, pushing and running after each other (Horback, 2014). Many of these categories of play are combined and the behaviors are similar to play behavior in dogs and other mammals.

Play in pigs not only satisfies a need for exploration and discovery, it also is critical for healthy development. Play is best stimulated by diverse, complex, *hands on*, and renewable objects and materials (Martin, et al., 2015; Studnitz, Jensen, & Pederson, 2007; Telkanranta, Bracke, & Valros, 2014). So important is this need that insufficient opportunity to explore leads to behavioral abnormalities (Pedersen et al., 2014; Studnitz et al., 2007; Telkanranta et al., 2014). Young pigs reared in a cognitively challenging and complex environment affording greater interactions with objects and other pigs are more socio-cognitively developed than their counterparts raised in standard farrowing crates (Martin et al., 2014). Olsen et al. (2002) found that when given access to materials allowing for exploration, pigs engaged in more behaviors associated with positive affect, such as play, and especially locomotor play. Also, consistent with these findings is the fact that pigs make more optimistic choices (have a positive bias) when in enriched environments than in others, indicating that they find stimulation rewarding and pleasurable (Douglas, Bateson, Walsh, Bedue, & Edwards, 2012). Therefore, opportunities for play and exploration impact emotional development in pigs as well.

Social Cognition and Complexity

Social cognition is the use of cognitive skills within the social domain and forms the basis for cognitive complexity and intelligence, including culture, across a wide range of species. There is an abundance of empirical evidence showing a positive correlation between various high-level cognitive capacities and measures of social complexity in groups as wide-ranging as primates (e.g., Dunbar, 1998), birds (Burish, Kueh, & Wang, 2004), and cetaceans, e.g.., dolphins and whales (Whitehead & Rendell, 2015). Whereas domestic and wild pigs are social animals, relatively little is known about how these capacities manifest in their natural lives and what cognitive and emotional abilities underwrite their sociality. What is known points to the possibility that pigs are as socially complex as many other highly intelligent animals, possibly sharing a number of cognitive capacities related to social complexity.

Discriminating conspecifics and others. The ability to discriminate among individuals forms the basis for social relationships, hierarchies, and reactions to familiar versus unfamiliar individuals. Individual discrimination is not the same as but is a prerequisite to the more complex capacity for true individual recognition, defined as a mental representation of an individual's identifying characteristics. Thus, individual discrimination is a logical beginning for investigating a species' general social recognition abilities.

A number of animals can discriminate individuals. Dogs can discriminate between barks of other dogs recorded in different contexts from the same individual, as well as from different individuals in the same context (Molnar, Pongracz, Farago, Doka, & Miklosi, 2009). As another example, elephants are well known for their sophisticated recognition of individual conspecifics even over long distances (McComb, Moss, Sayialel, & Baker, 2000). These kinds of capacities not only underlie the ability to recognize kin from non-kin, and stranger from familiar individual, but also allow for finer discriminations of individual identity within one's social network.

Like these other socially complex animals, pigs discriminate among conspecifics and show a preference for familiar individuals over strangers (de Souza, Jansen, Tempelman, Mendl, & Zanella, 2006; Kristensen, Jones, Schofield, White, & Wathes, 2001; McLeman, Mendl, Jones, White, & Wathes, 2005). McLeman et al. (2005), investigated the ability of 6-week-old female pigs to discriminate between pairs of female conspecifics in a Y-maze using a variety of sensory cues. They found that juvenile pigs base discriminations on learning and can differentiate between two familiar conspecifics when allowed to use all normal social cues. They can even discriminate between closely-related individuals.

Young pigs can also discriminate between both familiar and unfamiliar individuals based on urinary samples alone (Mendl et al, 2002). In one study, pigs were able to use olfactory cues to make social discriminations even after chronic exposure to 36 ppm of ammonia, which degraded their sense of smell (Kristensen et al., 2001). Moreover, this ability to make distinctions lasted at least over a 15-minute period, over which the pigs showed habituation to the same odors. In addition to olfactory discrimination, pigs use auditory cues to distinguish among conspecifics, as do dogs (Molnar, Pongracz, Farago, Doka, & Miklosi, 2009). Consistent with this finding is the evidence for the individuality of vocalizations in pigs (Blackshaw, Jones, & Thomas, 1996; Scho¨n, Puppe, Gromko, & Manteufel, 1999). When listening to a playback of piglet vocalizations, sows responded more strongly when the calls of their own piglets were played than when listening to the calls of unfamiliar piglets, showing that they are able to discriminate their offspring from other litters by voice (Illmann, Schrader, Pinka, & Ustr, 2002). Thus, not unlike canids, pigs appear to have strong abilities to flexibly discriminate among conspecifics using various cues and under a variety of circumstances.

It may be argued that it requires even further cognitive flexibility and learning to differentiate members of another species. Dogs can not only discriminate among humans but they can tell the difference between a smiling human face and a neutral expression (Nagasawa, Murai, Mogi, & Kikusui, 2011). These kinds of capacities are not surprising in a species with a history of domestication that involved sensitivity to human cues. Yet pigs, too, can discriminate familiar and unfamiliar humans (Koba & Tanida, 1999; Tanida & Nagano, 1998), though perhaps not with the same degree of subtlety. In a study by Tanida and Nagano (1998), young miniature pigs were handled gently and fed treats for five weeks and then allowed to choose between the handler and a stranger in a Y-maze. The results showed that these pigs were able to discriminate between the handler and a stranger and there were a range of individual differences in the kinds of cues (e.g., olfactory, visual and auditory) each pig used. Surprisingly, olfaction appeared to be the least useful for the pigs in differentiating stranger from familiar handler. In general, this study showed that the pigs were able to use prior experience to discriminate between two humans.

Interestingly, there is some evidence that pigs in commercial settings handled in a negative manner do not discriminate between handlers as they are handled roughly by all handlers in this setting (Hemsworth, Coleman, Cox, & Barnett, 1994), a result that shows that pigs respond adaptively to different kinds of previous treatment. In another set of choice studies similar to those above, Koba and Tanida (1999) found that pigs can discriminate between humans by differences in body size and some aspects of the face when repeatedly exposed to people wearing the same clothes. The pigs' abilities were more attuned to differences in body size than facial characteristics, but these results suggest that pigs may be sensitive, at some level, to facial characteristics in humans. More research is clearly needed to clarify and refine our understanding of these capacities.

Perspective-taking. The ability to take the perspective of another individual is considered a complex mental capacity that may form the basis of a specific kind of social cognition known as Machiavellian Intelligence (Byrne & Whiten, 1988; Humphrey, 1976; Whiten & Byrne, 1997). Machiavellian intelligence is defined by political maneuvering, e.g., deceit and manipulation, and is hypothesized to be a major driver of intelligence in primates and some other species, such as dogs (Humphrey, 1976; Whiten & Byrne, 1997, 1988).

Throughout the general comparative literature and across a variety of species, perspective-taking has been associated with a number of other cognitive capacities, including self-awareness, theory of mind, intentional deception and empathy (Bulloch, Boysen, & Furlong, 2008; de Waal, 2005, 2008a; Gallup, 1998; Towner, 2010, for a comprehensive review of these issues). Even the most basic forms, attention to visual cues and visual perspective-taking, require taking a stance other than one's own and usually using that information to one's advantage. Although responsiveness to cues, such as pointing, is not equivalent to perspective-taking, it can be categorized in a very general way as sensitivity toward some indicating act on the part of another. In this section, we will explore the continuum of cue use and perspective-taking in pigs.

A number of species have demonstrated well-developed capacities in the realm of conspecific perspective-taking, including chimpanzees (Krachun & Call, 2009), and dogs (Bräuer, Bös, Call, & Tomasello, 2013), and Western scrub jays (Clayton, Dally, & Emery, 2007). Pigs exhibit behaviors and patterns of interaction with one another that may be comparable to what has been observed in primates and some birds.

For example, pigs exhibit complex abilities to utilize and manipulate conspecifics to their advantage in social foraging situations. In a protocol requiring pigs to forage in pairs for hidden food, when one pig was informed as to the location of the food and the other was naïve (a scrounger), the latter was able to exploit the knowledge of the informed pig by following him to the food source and displacing him, thus reducing the time it took for the naïve pig to find food on his own (Held, Mendl, Devereux, & Byrne, 2000). Moreover, exploited pigs altered their behavior in response to this exploitation in competitive foraging trials; foraging behavior of individuals who were previously exploited changed to match the circumstances and to decrease the chances of being exploited. For instance, subordinates were more likely to show food-directed behavior when the chances of arriving at the food ahead of their exploiters was high (Held, Mendl, Devereux, & Byrne, 2002; Held, Mendl, Laughlin, & Byrne, 2002). In a similar study, subordinates increased their foraging speed to stay ahead of exploiters (Held et al., 2010).

These kinds of strategic behaviors and counter-behaviors are described as tactical deception when observed in great apes (Bräuer, Call, & Tomasello, 2007; Byrne & Whiten, 1988, 1992), and these observations in pigs suggest that pigs may have a complex level of perspective-taking. As one of the authors stated: "Our results suggest that pigs can develop quite sophisticated social competitive behavior, similar to that seen in some primate species." (Mendl, 2002, British Association for the Advancement of Science conference). Like primates, the ability to take the perspective of another is most apparent in competitive situations in pigs.

Some other species, such as apes (Hostetter, Russell, Freeman, & Hopkins, 2007), dogs (Gacsi, Miklosi, Varga, Topalo, & Csanyi, 2004; Kaminski, Brauer, Call, & Tomasello, 2009) and horses (Proops & McComb, 2010) are sensitive to the attentional state of humans. This capacity is not surprising in dogs and horses, as these species were selected for purposes of interacting with humans, and these factors enhanced their skills in reading human communicative cues. Apes and other primates quite naturally use visual cues in their social interactions with conspecifics.

But pigs, domesticated mainly for meat production, are also sensitive to the attention state of humans. In a paradigm requiring active choice between two humans, Nawroth, Ebersbach, and von Borell (2013a, b) found that young pigs are quite skillful at utilizing human head cues to discriminate between different attention states in humans (Nawroth et al., 2013a). They prefer humans who are being attentive to those who are not. Additionally, pigs can use pointing by humans (under certain circumstances) to lead them to a food reward (Nawroth et al., 2013b). There are some differences in these capacities between dogs and pigs. For instance, pigs had more trouble with distant rather than proximal pointing, but it is notable that pigs can be meaningfully engaged in these kinds of perspective-taking tasks and do relatively well under some circumstances. These findings suggests that sensitivity to human visual perspective and indicators in pigs may be extensions of the complexity of their natural social interactions with conspecifics to humans (Nawroth et al., 2013b).

Self-awareness

Self-awareness is a component of cognition that has to do with sense of self in both the physical and mental domains. In the physical domain, ethologists have traditionally tested self-awareness by determining if an animal recognizes himself in a mirror (i.e., mirror self-recognition, MSR); however, some authors suggest that this method might not be a suitable test of self-recognition for all species (Coren, 2004).

In the mental realm, self-awareness takes the form of metacognition, the ability to think about one's own thoughts and feelings. Both involve having an autobiographical self—a sense of "I" - on some level (Marino, 2010). Although the mirror test tends to create the impression that self-awareness is unitary, it is probably more accurately understood as a continuum of subtle and complex abilities (Bekoff & Sherman, 2004).

MSR is usually tested by determining whether an animal uses a mirror to investigate a part of his own body and is usually demonstrated in a controlled setting by placing a mark on a part of the body not visible without a mirror and determining whether a mirror-experienced subject exhibits mark-directed behaviors at the mirror. To date, mirror self-recognition has been convincingly demonstrated in all great apes (Anderson & Gallup, 2011 for a review of this literature), Asian elephants (*Elephas maximus*) (Plotnik, de Waal & Reiss, 2006) bottlenose dolphins (*Tursiops truncatus*) (Reiss & Marino, 2001), and magpies (*Pica pica*) (Prior, Schwarz, & Gunturkun, 2008). In chimpanzees, for instance, MSR is tested by providing mirror-naïve individuals with a mirror to determine if they show indications that they understand the mirror image is not another chimpanzee and begin to use the mirror to investigate their body. The definitive test is to apply a non-tactile mark to their forehead or ear while they are unaware and determine whether they later use the mirror to investigate the new mark on their own body. European magpies show MSR by pecking at the mark with their beaks, elephants by investigating the mark with their trunks, and dolphins by maneuvering in front of the mirror to expose the newly marked part of their body.

On the other hand, some animals, such as monkeys, do not show definitive evidence of MSR but are able to use mirrors as a tool to find hidden items. For instance, Japanese monkeys (*Macaca fuscata fuscata*) found hidden apples that were only visible in a mirror (Itakura, 1987).

When confronted with a mirror, pigs, like many other animals, do not display clear indicators of mirror self-recognition. However, there is evidence that they are able to use mirrors as a tool to find hidden items. Broom, Sena, and Moynihan (2009) exposed young pigs to a mirror and found that seven out of eight mirror-experienced pigs were able to use the mirror to find hidden food (i.e., mirror-mediated spatial localization); the eighth pig looked behind the mirror for the food.

> After 5 h spent with a mirror, the pigs were shown a familiar food bowl, visible in the mirror but hidden behind a solid barrier. Seven out of eight pigs found the food bowl in a mean of 23s by going away from the mirror and around the barrier. Naïve pigs shown the same, looked behind the mirror. (Broom, 2010, p. 5)

Moreover, upon encountering a mirror for the first time, some of the pigs in this study made repetitive movements while apparently watching themselves in the mirror.

> After initially encountering the mirror the pigs moved back from the mirror surface, oriented nose and eyes towards it apparently looking at it and made movements looking again from different angles. Three pigs showed some weaving movements. (Broom, 2009, p. 1039)

These behaviors are interesting because they are similar to the contingency-checking behaviors displayed by other animals e.g., elephants, dolphins and chimpanzees (Plotnik et al., 2006; Reiss & Marino, 2001), who pass the definitive mark test, suggesting the pigs could have been monitoring their own movements in the mirror.

As compelling as these findings are, another study showed that these results are not as robust as they may seem. That is, in a similar situation with similar research subjects, only two pigs out of eleven in the first study and one pig out of eleven in a second study used the mirror to find food (Geiling et al., 2014). The authors suggest that mirror use may not be robust in pigs and/or that differences in the findings between the two studies might be due to the use of different genetic lines of pigs. Clearly, more research is needed to determine the robustness of mirror-mediated spatial capacities in pigs and to determine if they engage in any behaviors suggesting they are testing the relationship between their own body and the mirror image.

From a comparative perspective, similar unclear results are found in dogs. Howell and Bennett (2011) found that when placed in front of a mirror with their human guardian standing behind them, only two out of 40 dogs were able to understand the actual location of the human. Howell, Toukhsati, Conduit, and Bennett (2013) adapted a similar paradigm to that used by Broom et al. (2009) to dogs and found that more dogs could find the location of hidden food reflected in an angled mirror than those in a control group without a mirror. These responses to mirrors and the ability to use the mirror as a tool to locate hidden items is very similar to the level of understanding of mirrors found in monkeys. Like rhesus macaques (Rajala, Reininger, Lancaster, & Populin, 2010), pigs and dogs can use mirrors to solve problems and may understand something about how they are spatially oriented in relationship to other objects. But the cognitive foundation and robustness of these interesting capacities require much more elucidation.

Pigs have also demonstrated another compelling behavior that may be related to self-awareness. Croney (1999) found that pigs were able to manipulate a modified joystick in order to move an on-screen cursor. In a study designed to assess how well pigs would acquire this kind of task to obtain an on-screen target, Croney (1999) found that all pigs in the study were able to acquire the task, despite dexterity and visual-capacity constraints of the joystick task. Dogs, however, did not do as well on the same tasks (Croney, 2014). Manipulating a joystick to attain a target arguably requires a complex capacity known as self-agency: the ability to recognize actions caused by oneself. Self-agency is a fundamental component of autonomy and purposeful behavior. Pigs may share this capacity with chimpanzees, who are able to distinguish a computer cursor controlled by themselves from motion caused by someone else (Kaneko & Tomonaga, 2011). Again, much more research is needed to determine the exact nature of the pigs' responses to this task and whether it overlaps in any way with self-awareness and self-agency.

Emotion

Emotions are comprised of behavioral, neurophysiological, cognitive and conscious subjective processes (Mendl & Paul, 2004; Paul, Harding, & Mendl, 2005) and can interact with other processes by shaping attention, decision-making, and memory. Emotions, themselves, are influenced by such cognitive abilities as situational awareness and sensitivities to the experience of others. Emotions and cognition, therefore, are often intimately tied together in a complex interplay e.g., recollection of memories can generate strong emotions and, in turn, modulate one's response to various stimuli (Mendl, Burman, Parker, & Paul, 2009; Ohl, Arndt, & van der Staay, 2008; Paul et al., 2005).

It may be that an exact definition of emotion is impossible, based on the complexity and *fuzzy boundaries* of the concept. If so, then description, rather than categorization and labeling, will be more illustrative of animal capacities. Regardless, emotional experience is a felt blend of mood, current responses, cognitive biases, and memory, as becomes clear when looking at the literature of emotion, regardless of species. Murphy, Nordquist, and van der Staay (2014) reviewed behavioral methods used to study pig cognition and emotion and suggested a list of eight criteria by which these studies can be assessed. The authors came to the conclusion that, among other important factors, such as replicability, a major dimension that is often overlooked in studies of pig emotion is ethological validity, which, in many ways, sets the context for other important criteria, such as the ability of the animal to express natural and spontaneous behaviors. For instance, findings in many classical comparative psychology tests of emotion, especially anxiety and fear, are often inconsistent and difficult to interpret and may not be ethologically valid for pigs, as many have been developed for testing laboratory-reared rats.

Emotions tend to influence more than one individual in a group. For instance, they can be shared through a process known as emotional contagion, the arousal of emotion in one individual upon witnessing the same emotion in another individual (Hatfield, Cacciopo, & Rapson, 1993). Emotional contagion is considered, by some investigators, to be a simple form of empathy, the ability to feel the emotional state of another from the other's perspective (de Waal, 2008b). Emotional contagion may be the phylogenetically oldest level of empathy and a building block of more complex forms of empathy; it is difficult to imagine the capacity for empathy without the ability to share or match emotional experience at some level. de Waal (2008b) suggests that emotional contagion forms the basis of sympathetic concern (which involves some perspective-taking) and these lead to empathy-based altruism. Therefore, it is important to follow this line of reasoning and determine, first, if a species is capable of emotional contagion.

Emotional contagion has been demonstrated in many socially complex groups such as dogs (Joly-Mascheroni, Senju, & Shepherd, 2008), wolves (*Canis lupus*) (Romero, Ito, Saito, & Hasegawa, 2014), great apes (Anderson, Myowa-Yamakoshi, & Matsuzawa, 2004; Palagi, Norscia & Demuru, 2014) and only a few other nonhuman species, including pigs. Emotional contagion, like other proximate psychological mechanisms, serve the ultimate purpose of providing a way for social animals, including pigs, to take in social cues about important circumstances and respond accordingly.

Some of the more interesting studies demonstrating emotional contagion in pigs involve responses to other pigs' anticipation of positive or negative events, revealing the importance of social factors in emotion. In one study, naïve test pigs were exposed to pen mates who had been trained to anticipate upcoming rewarding events (receiving straw and chocolate raisins) or aversive events (social isolation). When the naïve pigs were placed in the company of the trained pigs they adopted the same emotional anticipatory behaviors (e.g., ear and tail postures, increased cortisol release) as the trained pigs with the direct experience. These findings show that not only can pigs connect with the emotions of other pigs, but they can also do so with pigs who are responding emotionally in anticipation of future events (Reimert, Bolhuis, Kemp, & Rodenburg, 2013).

In a recent extension of this study, Reimert, Bolhuis, Kemp, and Rodenburg (2014) housed pigs in groups of six and trained two of the pigs from each group to anticipate something positive (food) or something negative (social isolation and handling). They did this by training the pigs to associate a piece of music with one of the two outcomes – for half of the training pigs Bach was played for the positive event and a military march for the negative event and for the other half the opposite was the case. All the naïve pigs were then played the music that held meaning to the trained pigs. A few of the trained pigs showed that they learned what the music predicted for them, showing either *happy* behaviors (play behavior, wagging their tail and barking) or stress (standing *alert*, putting their ears back, urinating and defecating). The authors wanted to determine if the naïve pigs would react to the behavior of the trained pig when they heard the music predicting a positive or negative outcome. They found that when a naïve pig was near a trained pig that was acting stressed, the naïve pig also became more alert and also put her ears back. This happened to a much greater degree than when naïve pigs were paired with pigs that acted *happy*. The researchers could be sure that the naïve pigs were reacting to the behavior of the other pigs and not just the sound of the music because when they just played music, this had no effect on their behavior at all. This study indicates that pigs are sensitive to the emotions of other pigs even when the other pigs are responding to a learned cue about a positive or negative outcome. This and the study above provide promising evidence for emotional contagion in pigs. Further work could help to better explicate the parameters of this response and help to clarify the degree to which it is related to empathy.

Finally, Murphy et al. (2014) suggest that play could be useful for the study of emotion in pigs. As mentioned above, pigs engage in a range of play behaviors and Murphy et al. (2014) suggest that object play, and most (but not all) forms of social play, are motivated by positive affect and are indirect indicators of emotion. Indeed, naïve pigs in the studies above showed increases in play behavior when anticipating a positive event, even when the event was only happening to the trained pigs. The study of both positive, especially play, behavior and negative responses, in naturalistic settings will likely prove to elucidate more dimensions of emotional responses in pigs.

Personality

Personality is a complex phenomenon with ambiguous boundaries. Even in the human domain there is no consensus on a single definition of personality. However, one definition that captures the phenomenon for purposes of comparison is: "Those characteristics of individuals that describe and account for temporally stable patterns of affect, cognition, and behavior" (Gosling, 2008, p. 986). However, personality adds a dimension of complexity to assessments of comparative psychology and is critically important for understanding that other animals, as humans, are individuals with their own combination of psychological and behavioral characteristics.

The study of personality in other animals is not only important because it is necessary for understanding and dealing with inter-individual variability in research subjects, but, from a more theoretical point of view, personality in other animals demonstrates a basic psychological continuity across species and with humans. Acknowledgement of personality in other animals becomes a path by which individuality can be recognized and other animals can be viewed not as one-dimensional interchangeable members of a species, but rather as more complex individuals. Personality interacts with cognition and emotion and is, therefore, an important dimension in understanding behavior and intelligence in any animal.

Studies of personality in nonhuman animals have shown that personality traits are ubiquitous in the animal kingdom; a wide range of fish, birds, and mammals show persistent individual differences that can be organized along core personality dimensions, many of which overlap with those found in humans (Gosling, 2008; Gosling & John, 1999). Although some authors prefer to refer to *behavioral syndromes* or *temperament* in other animals, there is little distinction between these phenomena and personalities as observed and documented (Gosling, 2008). The different labels refer, with only slight variation of meaning, to the same category of phenomena.

Given the wide range of species that possess personality traits, an analysis of comparative traits profits most from a discussion of how these traits are structured. Debate exists over the number and types of dimensions needed to characterize personality variation in most species of animals (Gosling, 2008). In humans, there is broad agreement on a five-factor model of personality that includes the dimensions of openness, conscientiousness, extraversion, agreeableness, and neuroticism (McCrae & Costa, 2008). Some studies of personality in other animals indicate fewer or more personality traits than have been identified in humans. However, much of this issue has to do with how much one combines or separates behavioral traits. Personality studies of pigs are important for understanding what traits pigs share with other species, including humans, as well as for better understanding individual variability in cognitive performance (Carere & Locurto, 2011; Sih & Bell, 2008).

Pigs display consistent behavioral and emotional characteristics that have been described variously as personality. e.g., coping styles, response types, temperament, and behavioral tendencies (Brown et al., 2009; D'Eath, 2002; D'Eath & Burn, 2002; Hessing et al., 1993; Ijichi, Collins, & Elwood, 2013; Janczak, Peddersen, & Bakken, 2003; Lawrence, Terlouw, & Illius, 1991; Melotti, Oostindger, Bolhuis, Held, & Mendl, 2011; Ruis et al., 2000 van Erp-van der Kooij et al, 2002). Individual differences tend to be consistent over time. A number of studies have found personality profiles, dimensions, and structure in pigs comparable to other species (Forkman, Furuhaug, & Jensen, 1995; Gosling & John, 1999).

Ruis et al. (2000) found that when put in a group-feeding competition setting, individual aggression emerged as a stable personality feature of female pigs. In another illustrative example, Forkman et al. (1995) examined how piglets respond to different situations (being held down for several seconds, social isolation, contact with an unfamiliar piglet, and the introduction of novel objects) and measured various behaviors, including vocalization, aggression, approaches, and others. Using principal component analysis to determine which factors were closely correlated with others, the authors derived at least three personality factors in pigs: aggression, sociability, and exploration. Forkman, Furuhaug, and Jensen noted that these personality factors are very similar to those identified in many other species. Moreover, Gosling and John (1999) suggested that the factors revealed by Forkman et al. (1995) map onto the human dimensions of agreeableness, extraversion, and openness. All of these studies point to the presence of stable individual behavioral traits that reveal a complex personality in pigs that overlaps with that of other animals, including humans. As with any comparative scientific issue, the study of personality in pigs and how it interacts with their other characteristics is critical for a full understanding of who they are.

Conclusion

In this paper we have identified a number of findings from studies of pig cognition, emotion, and behavior which suggest that pigs possess complex ethological traits similar, but not identical, to dogs and chimpanzees. The main conclusion from this review is that essentially every domain of research with pigs would profit from further explanation as many of the current findings are promising but only suggestive. In general, the study of pig psychology lags behind comparative research with some other species (e.g., dogs, chimpanzees, elephants, cetaceans). Therefore, in order to investigate the leading edges of cognition in pigs, in a comparative framework, we recommend the following for further research areas:

1) Discrimination and comprehension of symbolism and the meaning of various combinations and sequences of symbolic cues.
2) The ability to not only anticipate an event but to prepare or plan for an event behaviorally.
3) The capacity for numerical understanding, particular in a foraging situation.
4) Play and exploration and how different forms are combined and are related to social relationships.
5) Level of sophistication in social discriminations of conspecifics and humans, including the nature and subtlety of cues used in these circumstances.
6) Whether discrimination of individuals is also accompanied by true recognition of conspecifics and/or humans.

7) Taking the perspective of a conspecific or human, including understanding eye and head orientation as it relates to attention.
8) Understanding and using pointing and other indicating actions by humans.
9) The question of contingency-checking behaviors at a mirror and, especially, the robustness and parameters of mirror-mediated behaviors.
10) Parameters of emotional contagion and the presence of cognitive empathy
11) Personality structure as it compares with other species, including humans.

Acknowledgments

We wish to thank Donald Broom, Bruce Friedrich, Mark Bekoff, Joyce D'Silva and Hope Ferdowsian, and two anonymous reviewers for their guidance and suggestions for improving this manuscript.

References

Albiach-Sewrrano, A., Brauer, J., Cacchione, T., Zickert, N., & Amici, F. (2012). The effect of domestication and ontogeny in swine cognition (*Sus scrofa scrofa* and *S. s. domestica). Applied Animal Behavior Science, 141*, 25-35.

Anderson, J. R. & Gallup, Jr., G. G. (2011). Which primates recognize themselves in mirrors? *PLoS Biology, 9*, e1001024. doi:10.1371/journal.pbio.1001024.

Anderson, J. R., Myowa-Yamakoshi, M., & Matsuzawa, T. (2004). Contagious yawning in chimpanzees. *Proceedings of the Royal Society, B 271*(Suppl. 6), S468-S470.

Arave, C. W. (1996). Assessing sensory capacity of animals using operant technology. *Journal of Animal Science 74*, 1996-2009.

Arts, J. W. M., van der Staay, F. J., & Ekkel, E. D. (2009). Working and reference memory of pigs in the spatial holeboard discrimination task. *Behavioural Brain Research, 205*, 303–306.

Balda, R. P. & Kamil, A. C. (2002). Spatial and social cognition in corvids: An evolutionary approach. In M. Bekoff, C. Allen, & G. M. Burghardt (Eds.), *The cognitive animal* (pp.129-134). Cambridge, MA: MIT Press.

Bekoff, M. (2015). Playful fun in dogs. *Current Biology, 25*(1), R4-R7.

Bekoff, M. (2014). The significance of ethological studies: Playing and peeing. In A. Horowitz (Ed.), *Dog Behavior and Cognition* (pp. 59-78). New York, NY: Springer.

Bekoff, M. (1974). Social play and play-soliciting by infant canids. *American Zoology, 14*, 323-340.

Bekoff, M., & Sherman, P. W. (2004). Reflections on animal selves. *Trends in Ecology and Evolution, 19*, 176-180.

Bencke, I. (2015). Play in the Peter Pan ape. *Current Biology, 25*(1), R24-R27.

Bensky, M. K., Gosling, S. D., & Sinn, D. L. (2013). The world from a dog's point of view: A review and synthesis of dog cognition research. *Advances in the Study of Behavior, 45*, 209-406.

Beran, M., Pate, J., Washburn, D., & Rumbaugh, D. (2004). Sequential responding and planning in chimpanzees (*Pan troglodytes*) and rhesus macaques (*Macaca mulatta*). *Journal of Experimental Psychology: Animal Behavior Processes, 30*, 203-212.

Blackshaw, J. K., Jones, D. N., & Thomas, F. J. (1996). Vocal individuality during suckling in the intensively housed domestic pig. *Applied Animal Behaviour Science, 50*, 33–41.

Bird, L. R., Roberts, W. A., Abroms, B., Kit, K. A., & Crupi, C. (2003). Spatial memory for food hidden by rats (*Rattus norvegicus*) on the radial maze: studies of memory for where, what, and when. *Journal of Comparative Psychology 117*, 176–187.

Bolhuis, J. E., Oostindjer, M., Hoeks, C. W. F., de Haas, E. N., Bartels, A. C., Ooms, M., & Kemp, B. (2013). Working and reference memory of pigs (*Sus scrofa domesticus*) in a holeboard spatial discrimination task: The influence of environmental enrichment. *Animal Cognition, 16*, 845-850.

Bolhuis, J. E., Schouten, W. G. P., Schrama, J. W., & Wiegant, V. M. (2005). Behavioural development of pigs with different coping characteristics in barren and substrate-enriched housing conditions. *Applied Animal Behavior Science, 93*, 213–228.

Bräuer, J., Bös, M., Call, J., & Tomasello, M. (2013). Domestic dogs (*Canis familiaris*) coordinate their actions in a problem-solving task. *Animal Cognition, 16*, 273–285.

Bräuer, J., Call, J., & Tomasello, M. (2007). Chimpanzees really know what others can see in a competitive situation. *Animal Cognition, 10*, 439-448.

Broom, D. (2010). Cognitive ability and awareness in domestic animals and decisions about obligations to animals. *Applied Animal Behavior Science, 126*, 1-11.

Broom, D., Sena, H., & Moynihan, K. L. (2009). Pigs learn what a mirror image represents and use it to obtain information. *Animal Behaviour, 78*, 1037-1041.

Brown, C. (2015). Fish intelligence, sentience, and ethics. *Animal Cognition, 18,* 1-17.

Brown, J. A., Dewey, C., Delange, C. F. M., Mandell, I. B., Purslow, P. P., Widowski, T. M. (2009). Reliability of temperament tests on finishing pigs in group-housing and comparison to social tests. *Applied Animal Behaviour Science, 118*, 28-35.

Bulloch, M. J., Boysen, S. T., & Furlong, E. E. (2008). Visual attention and its relation to knowledge states in chimpanzees, *Pan troglodytes. Animal Behaviour, 76*, 1147- 1155.

Burghardt, G. (2015). Play in fishes, frogs and reptiles. *Current Biology, 25*(1), R9-R10.

Burish, M. J., Kueh, H. Y., & Wang, S. H. (2004). Brain architecture and social complexity in modern and ancient birds. *Brain, Behavior and Evolution, 63*, 107-124.

Byrne, R. W. & Whiten, A. (1988) *Machiavellian intelligence: Social expertise and the evolution of intellect in monkeys, apes and humans*. Oxford , England: Oxford University Press.

Byrne, R. W. & Whiten, A. (1992). Cognitive evolution in primates: evidence from tactical deception. *Man, 27*, 609-627.

Carere, C., & Locurto, C. (2011). Interaction between animal personality and animal cognition. *Current Zoology, 57*, 491–498.

Cerbulis, I. G. (1994). Cognitive abilities of the domestic pig (*Sus scrofa*), Thesis in Department of Psychology, Ohio State University, 1-108.

Clayton, N. S., Dally, J. M., & Emery, N. J. (2007). Social cognition by food-caching corvids. The western scrub-jay as a natural psychologist. *Philosophical Transactions of the Royal Society B: Biological Sciences, 362*, 507-522.

Coren, S. (2004). *How dogs think: Understanding the canine mind.* New York, NY: Free Press.

Croney, C. C. (1999). *Cognitive abilities of domestic pigs*. Thesis in Animal Science, The Pennsylvania State University, College of Agricultural Sciences, 1-105.

Croney, C. C., Adams, K. M., Washington, C. G., & Stricklin, W. R. (2003). A note on visual, olfactory and spatial cue use in foraging behaviour of pigs: indirectly assessing cognitive abilities. *Applied Animal Behaviour Science, 83,* 303–308.

Cutini, S., & Bonato, M. (2012). Subitizing and visual short-term memory in human and nonhuman species: A common shared system? *Frontiers in Psychology, 3*, 469. doi:10.3389/fpsyg.2012.00469

D'Eath, R. B. (2002). Individual aggressiveness measured in a resident intruder test predicts the persistence of aggressive behaviour and weight gain of young pigs after mixing. *Applied Animal Behaviour Science, 77*, 267–283.

D'Eath, R. B. & Burn, C. C. (2002). Individual differences in behaviour: a test of 'coping style' does not predict resident-intruder aggressiveness in pigs. *Behaviour, 139*, 1175–1194.

De Souza, A. S., Jansen, J., Tempelman, R. J., Mendl, M., & Zanella, A. J. (2006). A novel method for testing social recognition in young pigs and the modulating effects of relocation. *Applied Animal Behavior Science, 99*, 77-87.

de Waal, F. B. M. (2005). Intentional deception in primates. *Evolutionary Anthropology, 1*, 86-92.

de Waal, F. B. M. (2008a). The thief in the mirror. *PLoS Biology 6*(8), e201.

de Waal, F. B. M. (2008b). Putting the altruism back into altruism: the evolution of empathy. *Annual Review of Psychology, 59*, 279-300.

Donaldson, T. M., Newberry, R. C., Spinka, M., & Cloutier, S. (2002). Effects of early play experience on play behavior of piglets after weaning. *Applied Animal Behaviour Science, 79*, 221-231.

Douglas, C., Bateson, M., Walsh, C., Bedue, A. & Edwards, S.A. (2012). Environmental enrichments induces optimistic cognitive biases in pigs. *Applied Animal Behaviour Science, 139*, 65-73.

Dudink, S., Simonse, H., Marks, I., de Jonge, F. H., & Spruijt, B. M. (2006). Announcing the arrival of enrichment increases play behavior and reduces weaning-stress-induced behaviours of piglets directly after weaning. *Applied Animal Behaviour Science, 101*, 86–101.

Dunbar, R. I. (1998). The social brain hypothesis. *Brain, 9*(10), 178-190.

Emery, N. J., & Clayton, N. S. (2015). Do birds have the capacity for fun? *Current Biology 25*(1), R16-R20.

Fagot, J. (2000). *Picture Perception in Animals*. East Sussex, England: Psychology Press Ltd.

Ferguson, S. A., Gopee, N. V., Paule, M. G., & Howard, P. C. (2009). Female mini-pig performance of temporal response differentiation, incremental repeated acquisition, and progressive ration operant tasks. *Behavioural Processes, 80*, 28-34.

Forkman, B., Furuhaug, I. L., & Jensen, P. (1995). Personality, coping patterns, and aggression in piglets. *Applied Animal Behaviour Science, 45*, 31-42.

Gácsi, M., Miklosi, A., Varga, O., Topal, J., & Csanyi, V. (2004). Are readers of our face readers of our minds? Dogs (*Canis familiaris*) show situation-dependent recognition of human's attention. *Animal Cognition, 7*, 144–153.

Gallistel, C. R. (1994). Space and time. In N. J. Mackintosh (Ed.), *Animal learning and cognition* (pp. 221-253). San Diego, CA: Academic Press.

Gallup, Jr. G. G. (1998). Self-awareness and the evolution of social intelligence. *Behavioural Processes, 42*, 239-247.

Garber, P. A. & Dolins, F. L. (2014). Primate spatial strategies and cognition: Introduction to this special issue. *American Journal of Primatology, 76,* 393-398.

Gieling, E. T., Arts, J. Nordquist, R. E., & van der Staay, F. J. (2012). Measuring spatial discrimination performance in (mini) pigs using the cognitive holeboard task. *Ellegaard Newsletter, 38*, 4-7.

Gieling, E. T., Mijdam, E., van der Staay, F. J., & Nordquist, R. E. (2014). Lack of mirror use by pigs to locate food. *Applied Animal Behavior Science, 154*, 22-29.

Gieling, E. T., Nordquist, R. E., & van der Staay, F. J. (2011). Assessing learning and memory in pigs. *Animal Cognition, 14*, 151-173.

Gieling, E. T., Wehkamp, W., Willigenburg, R., Nordquist, R. E., Ganderup, N. C., & van der Staay, F. J. (2013). Performance of conventional pigs and Gottingen miniature pigs in a spatial holeboard task: Effects of the putative muscarinic cognition impairer Biperidon. *Behavioural and Brain Functions, 9*, 4- 10.

Gifford, A., Sylvie Cloutier, K., & Newberry, R. C. (2007). Objects as enrichment: Effects of object exposure time and delay interval on object recognition memory of the domestic pig. *Applied Animal Behaviour Science, 107*, 206-217.

Giuffra, E., Kijas, J. M. H., Amarger, V., Carlborg, O, Jeon, J. T., & Andersson, L. (2000). The origin of the domestic pig: Independent domestication and subsequent introgression. *Genetics, 154*, 1785-1791.

Gosling, S., & John, O. P. (1999). Personality dimensions in nonhuman animals. *Current Directions in Psychological Science, 8*, 69-75.

Gosling, S. (2008). Personality in nonhuman animals. *Social and Personality Psychology Compass 2*, 985 – 1001.

Graves, H. B. (1984). Behavior and ecology of wild and feral swine (*Sus scrofa*). *Journal of Animal Science, 58*, 482-492.

Hatfield, E., Cacioppo, J. T. & Rapson, R. L. (1993). Emotional contagion. *Current Directions in Psychological Science 2*, 96-9.

Heffner, H. E. & Heffner, R. S. (1992). Auditory perception. In C.J.C. Phillips & D. Piggins (Eds.), *Farm Animals and the Environment* (pp. 159-184). Wallingford, UK: CABI.

Held, S., Baumgartner, J., Kilbride, A., Byrne, R.W., & Mendl, M. (2005). Foraging behaviour in domestic pigs (*Sus scrofa*): Remembering and prioritizing food sites of different value. *Animal Cognition, 8,* 114-121.

Held, S., Byrne, R. W., Jones, S., Murphy, E., Friel, M., & Mendl, M. T. (2010). Domestic pigs, *Sus scrofa*, adjust their foraging behavior to whom they are foraging with. *Animal Behaviour, 79*, 857-862.

Held, S., Cooper, J. J., & Mendl, M. T. (2009). Advances in the study of cognition, behavioural priorities and emotions. In J. N. Marchant-Forde (Ed.), *The welfare of pigs* (pp. 47-94), Springer Science Business Media B.V.

Held, S., Mendl, M., Devereux, C., & Byrne, R. W. (2000). Social tactics of pigs in a competitive foraging task: the 'informed forager' paradigm. *Animal Behaviour, 59*, 579-576.

Held, S., Mendl, M. Devereaux, C., & Byrne, R. W. (2002). Foraging pigs alter their behavior in response to exploitation. *Animal Behaviour, 64*, 157-166.

Held, S., Mendl, M., Laughlin, K., & Byrne, R. W. (2002). Cognition studies with pigs: Livestock cognition and its implication for production. *Journal of Animal Science, 80* (E Suppl. 1), E10-E17.

Hemsworth, P. H., Coleman, G. J., Cox, M. L., & Barnett, J. L. (1994). Stimulus generalization: The inability of pigs to discriminate between humans on the basis of their previous handling experience. *Applied Animal Behavior Science, 40*, 129–142.

Hemsworth, P. H., Verge, J, & Coleman, G. J. (1996). Conditioned approach avoidance responses to humans: the ability of pigs to associate feeding and aversive social experiences in the presence of humans with humans. *Applied Animal Behaviour Science, 50*, 71–82.

Herman, L. M. (1980). Cognitive characteristics of dolphins. In L. Herman (Ed.), *Cetacean behavior: Mechanisms and functions* (pp. 363-429). New York, NY: John Wiley & Sons.

Herman, L.M. (1987). Receptive competencies of language-trained animals. In J. S. Rosenblatt, C. Beer, M. Busnel, and J. Slater (Eds.), *Advances in the Study of Behavior, 17*, 1-60.

Herman, L., Hovanick, J. Gory, J., & Bradshaw, G. (1989). Generalization of visual matching by a bottlenose dolphin (*Tursiops truncatus*): Evidence for invariance of cognitive performance with visual and auditory materials. *Journal of Experimental Psychology: Animal Behavior Processes, 15*, 124-136.

Hessing, M. J. C., Hagelso, A. M., van Beek, J. A. M., Wiepkema, P. R. Schouten, W. G. P., & Krukow, R. (1993). Individual behavioural characteristics in pigs. *Applied Animal Behaviour Science, 37*, 285-295.

Hostetter, A. B., Russell, J. L., Freeman, H., & Hopkins, W. D. (2007). Now you see me, now you don't: evidence that chimpanzees understand the role of eyes in attention. *Animal Cognition, 10*, 55-62.

Horback, K. (2014). Nosing around: Play in pigs. *Animal Behavior and Cognition, 1*(2), 186-196.

Howell, T. J., & Bennett, P. C. (2011). Can dogs (*Canis familiaris*) use a mirror to solve a problem? *Journal of Veterinary Behavior: Clinical Applications and Research, 6,* 306-312.

Howell, T. J., Toukhsati, S., Conduit, R., & Bennett, P. (2013). Do dogs use a mirror to find hidden food? *Journal of Veterinary Behavior, 8*, 425-430.

Huber, L., Apfalter, W., Steurer, M., & Prossinger, H. (2005). A new learning paradigm elicits fast visual discrimination in pigeons. *Journal of Experimental Psychology: Animal Behavior Processes, 31*, 237–246.

Humphrey, N. K. (1976). The social function of intellect. *Growing Points in Ethology*, 303-317.

Illmann, G., Schrader, L., Pinka, M., & Ustr, P. (2002). Acoustical mother-offspring recognition in pigs (*Sus scrofa domesticus*). *Behaviour, 139*, 487-505.

Ijichi, C. L., Collins, L. M., & Elwood, R.W. (2013). Evidence for the role of personality in stereotypy predisposition. *Animal Behaviour, 85*, 1145-1151. Need first initial.

Imfeld-Mueller, S., Van Wezemaela, L., Stauffachera, M., Gygax, L., & Hillmann, E. (2011). Do pigs distinguish between situations of different emotional valences during anticipation? *Applied Animal Behavior Science, 131,* 86-93.

Itakura, S. (1987). Mirror-guided behavior in Japanese macaques (*Macaca fuscata fuscata*). *Primates, 28*, 149-161.

Janczak, A. M., Pedersen, L. J., & Bakken, M. (2003). Aggression, fearfulness and coping styles in female pigs. *Applied Animal Behaviour Science, 81*, 13-28.

Janik, V. (2015). Play in dolphins. *Current Biology, 25*(1), R7-R8.

Jensen, P. (1986). Observations on the maternal behavior of free-ranging domestic pigs. *Applied Animal Behavior Science, 16*, 131-142.

Joly-Mascheroni, R. M., Senju, A., & Shepherd, A. (2008). Dogs catch human yawns. *Biology Letters, 4*, 446–448.

Kaminski, J., Bräuer, J., Call, J., & Tomasello, M. (2009). Domestic dogs are sensitive to a human's perspective. *Behaviour, 146,* 979–998.

Kaneko, T., & Tomonaga, M. (2011). The perception of self-agency in chimpanzees (*Pan troglodytes*). *Proceedings of the Royal Society B., 278,* 3694-3702.

Kaulfuss, P., & Mills, D.S. (2008). Neophilia in domestic dogs (*Canis familiaris*) and its implication for studies of dog cognition. *Animal Cognition, 11*, 553-556.

Kehoe, E. J. (2008). Discrimination and generalization. In R. Menzel (Vol. Ed.), *Learning Theory and Behavior. Vol. 1.* of J. Byrne (Ed.), *Learning and memory: A comprehensive reference*, (pp. 123–150). Oxford, United Kingdom: Elsevier.

Koba, Y., & Tanida, H. (2001). How do miniature pigs discriminate between people? Discrimination between people wearing coveralls of the same colour. *Applied Animal Behaviour Science, 73*, 45-58.

Krachun, C., & Call, J. (2009). Chimpanzees (*Pan troglodytes*) know what can be seen from where. *Animal Cognition, 12*, 317-331.

Kristensen, H. H., Jones, R. B., Schofield, C. P., White, R. P., & Wathes, C. M. (2001). The use of olfactory and other cues for social recognition by juvenile pigs. *Applied Animal Behaviour Science, 72*, 321-333.

Kruska, D. (1988). Mammalian domestication and its effect on brain structure and behavior. In H.J. Jerison & Jerison, I. (Eds.) *Intelligence and evolutionary biology* (pp. 211-250). Berlin, Germany: Springer-Verlag.

Larson, G., Dobney, K., Albarella, U., Fang, M., Matisoo-Smith, E., Robins, J., & Cooper, A. (2005). Worldwide phylogeography of wild boar reveals multiple centers of pig domestication. *Science, 307*, 1618-1621.

Laughlin, K., & Mendl. M. (2000). Pigs shift too: foraging strategies and spatial memory in the domestic pig. *Animal Behavior, 60*, 403-410.

Lawrence, A. B., Terlouw, E. M. C., & Illius, A. W. (1991). Individual differences in behavioural responses of pigs exposed to non-social and social challenges. *Applied Animal Behaviour Science, 30*, 73-86.

Lomas, C. A., Piggins, D., & Phillips, C. J. C. (1988). Visual awareness. *Applied Animal Behaviour Science, 57,* 247-257.

Manteuffel, G., Puppe, B., & Schon, P. C. (2004). Vocalization of farm animals as a measure of welfare. *Applied Animal Behavior Science, 88*, 163-182.

Marino, L. (2010). Sentience. *Encyclopedia of animal behavior*, Vol. 3, M. Breed & J. Moore (Eds.) (pp. 132-138). Oxford: UK: Academic Press.

Martin, J. E., Ison, S. H., & Baxter, E. M. (2015). The influence of neonatal environment on piglet play behaviour and post-weaning social and cognitive development. *Applied Animal Behaviour Science, 163*, 69-79.

Martin–Ordas, G., Berntsen, D., & Call, J. (2013). Memory for distant past events in chimpanzees and orangutans. *Current Biology, 23*, 1-4.

Martin-Ordas, G., Haun, D., Colmenares, F., & Call, J. (2010). Keeping track of time: Evidence for episodic-like memory in great apes. *Animal Cognition, 13,* 331-340.

Matsuzawa, T. (2001). *Primate Origins of Human Cognition and Behavior*. Tokyo, Japan: Springer

McComb, K., Moss, C., Sayialel, S., & Baker, L. (2000). Unusually extensive networks of vocal recognition in African elephants. *Animal Behavior, 59*, 1103-1109.

McCrae, R. R., & Costa, P. T. (2008).The five-factor theory of personality. In O. P. John, R. W. Robins, & L. A. Pervin (Eds.), *Handbook of personality* (pp. 159-181). New York, NY: Guildford Press.

McGlone, J. J. (1990). Olfactory signals that modulate pig aggressive and submissive behavior. In R. Zayan & R. Dantzer (Eds.), *Social stress in domestic animals*, 86-109. Dordrecht: Kluwer Academic Press.

McLeman, N. A., Mendl, M., Jones, R. B., White, R., & Wathes, C. M. (2005). Discrimination of conspecifics by juvenile domestic pigs, *Sus scrofa. Animal Behavior, 70*, 451-461.

Melotti, L., Oostindjer, M., Bolhuis, J. E., Held, S., & Mendl, M. (2011). Coping personality type and environmental enrichment affect aggression at weaning in pigs. *Applied Animal Behaviour Science, 133*, 144-153.

Mendl, M. (2002). British Association for the Advancement of Science Conference.

Mendl, M., Burman, O., Parker, R. M. A., & Paul, E. S. (2009). Cognitive bias as an indicator of animal emotion and welfare: emerging evidence and underlying mechanisms. *Applied Animal Behavior Science, 118*, 161–181

Mendl, M., Laughlin, K., & Hitchcock, D. (1997). Pigs in space: spatial memory and its susceptibility to interference. *Animal Behaviour, 54,* 1491–1508.

Mendl, M., & Paul, E. S. (2004). Consciousness, emotion and animal welfare: insights from cognitive science. *Animal Welfare, 13*, S17-25.

Mendl, M., Randle, K., & Pope, S. (2002). Young female pigs can discriminate individual differences in odours from conspecific urine. *Animal Behaviour, 64*, 97-101.

Molnar, C., Pongracz, P., Farago, T., Doka, A., & Miklosi, A. (2009). Dogs discriminate between barks: The effects of context and identity of the caller. *Behavioural Processes, 82*, 198–201

Mulcahy, N. J. & Call, J. (2006). Apes save tools for future use. *Science, 312*, 1038-1040.

Murphy, E., Nordquist, R., & van der Staay, F. J. (2014). A review of behavioural methods to study emotion and mood in pigs, *Sus scrofa. Applied Animal Behaviour Science*, 159, 9-28.

Nagasawa, M., Murai, K., Mogi, K., & Kikusui, K. (2011). Dogs can discriminate human smiling faces from blank expressions. *Animal Cognition, 14*, 525-533.

Nawroth, C., Ebersbach, M., von Borell, E. (2013a). Are juvenile domestic pigs (*Sus scrofa domesticus*) sensitive to the attentive states of humans? – The impact of impulsivity on choice behavior. *Behavioral Processes, 96*, 53-58.

Nawroth, C., Ebersbach, M., & von Borell, E. (2013b). Juvenile domestic pigs (*Sus scrofa domesticus*) use human-given cues in an object choice task. *Animal Cognition, 17*, 701-713.

Nawroth, C., & von Borell, E. (2014). Do young domestic pigs (*Sus scrofa domestica*) rely on object-specific cues in a simultaneous discrimination task?. *PeerJ2*: e281v1.

Newberry, R. C., Wood-Gush, D. G. M., & Hall, J. W. (1988). Playful behavior in piglets. *Behavioural Processes, 17*, 205-216.

Ohl, F., Arndt, S., & van der Staay, F. J. (2008). Pathological anxiety in animals. *Veterinary Journal, 175*, 18–26.

Olsen, A. W., Simonsen, H. B., & Dybkjaer, L. (2002). Effect of access to roughage and shelter on selected behavioural indicators of welfare in pigs housed in a complex environment. *Animal Welfare, 11*, 75–87.

Osvath, M., & Osvath, H. (2008). Chimpanzee (*Pan troglodytes*) and orangutan (*Pongo abelii*) forethought: self-control and pre-experience in the face of future tool use. *Animal Cognition, 11*, 661-674.

Palagi, E., Norscia, I., & Demuru, E. (2014) Yawn contagion in humans and bonobos: emotional affinity matters more than species. *PeerJ2*:e519 http://dx.doi.org/10.7717/peerj.519

Paul, E. S., Harding E. J., & Mendl, M. (2005). Measuring emotional processes in animals: The utility of a cognitive approach. *Neuroscience and Bio-Behavioral Reviews, 29,* 469–491.

Pedersen, L. J., Herskin, M. S.,Forkman, B., Halekoh, U., Kristensen, K. M., & Jensen, M. B. (2014). How much is enough? The amount of straw necessary to satisfy pigs' need to perform exploratory behavior. *Applied Animal Behavior Science, 160*, 46-55.

Plotnik, J. M., de Waal, F. B. M., & Reiss, D. (2006). Self-recognition in an Asian elephant. *Proceedings of the National Academy of Sciences, 103*, 17052-17057.

Prior, H., Schwarz, A., & Gunturkun, O. (2008). Mirror-induced behavior in the magpie (*Pica pica*): Evidence of self-recognition. *PLoS Biology 6: 1642-1650*, doi:10.1371/journal.pbio.0060202.

Proops, L., & McComb, K. (2010). Attributing attention: The use of human-given cues by domestic horses (*Equus caballus*). *Animal Cognition, 13*, 197-205.

Raby, C. R., Alexis, D. M., Dickinson, A., Clayton, N. S. (2007). Planning for the future by western scrub-jays. *Nature, 445*, 919–921.

Rajala, A. Z., Reininger, K. R, Lancaster, K. M., & Populin, L. C. (2010). Rhesus monkeys (*Macaca mulatta*) do recognize themselves in the mirror: Implications for the evolution of self-recognition. *PLoS ONE 5*, e12865.

Range, F., Aust, U., Steurer, M., & Huber, L. (2008). Visual categorization of domestic stimuli by domestic dogs. *Animal Cognition, 11,* 338-347.

Reimert, I., Bolhuis, J. E., Kemp, B., & Rodenburg, T. B. (2014). Emotions on the loose: emotional contagion and the role of oxytocin in pigs. *Animal Cognition,18:* 517- 532.

Reimert, I., Bolhuis, J. E., Kemp, B., & Rodenberg, T. (2013). Indicators of positive and negative emotions and emotional contagion in pigs. *Physiology and Behavior, 109*, 42-50.

Reiss, D., & Marino, L. (2001). Self-recognition in the bottlenose dolphin: A case of cognitive convergence. *Proceedings of the National Academy of Sciences USA 98*, 5937-5942.

Romero, T., Ito, M., Saito, A., & Hasegawa, T. (2014), Social modulation of contagious yawning in wolves. *PLoS One*, e105963. doi: 10.1371/journal.pone.0105963

Ruis, M. A. W., Brake, J. H., VandeBurgwal, J. A., deJong, I. C., Blokhuis, H. J., & Koolhaas, J. M. (2000). Personalities in female domesticated pigs: Behavioural and physiological indications. *Applied Animal Behavior Science, 66*, 31-47.

Scho¨n, P., Puppe, B., Gromyko, T., & Manteuffel, G. (1999). Common features and individual differences in nurse grunting of domestic pigs (*Sus scrofa*): a multi-parametric analysis. *Behaviour, 136*, 49–66.

Schusterman, R.J. (1993). Artificial language comprehension in dolphins and sea lions: The essential cognitive skills. *The Psychological Record, 38*, 311-348.

Shettleworth, S. J. (2002). Spatial behavior, food storing, and the modular mind. In The Cognitive Animal. In M. Bekoff, C. Allen, & G.M. Burghardt (Eds.), *The cognitive animal* (pp.123 - 128). Cambridge, MA: MIT Press.

Siegford, J. M., Rucker, G., & Zanella, A. J. (2008). Effects of pre-weaning exposure to a maze on stress responses in pigs at weaning and on subsequent performance in spatial and fear-related tests. *Applied Animal Behavior Science, 110*, 189–202.

Signoret, J. P., Baldwin, B. A., Fraser, S., & Hafez, E. S. E. (1975). In E. S. E. Hafez (Ed.), *The behaviour of domestic animals* (pp. 295-329). London, UK: Bailliere, Tindall and Cox.

Sih, A., & Bell, A. M. (2008). Insights for behavioral ecology from behavioral syndromes. *Advances in the Study of Behavior, 38*, 227–281.

Spinka, M., Duncan, I. J. H., & Widowski, T. M. (1998). Do domestic pigs prefer short-term to medium-term confinement? *Applied Animal Behaviour Science, 58*, 221-232.

Stolba, A., & Wood-Gush, D. G. M. (1989). The behavior of pigs in a semi-natural environment. *Animal Production 48*, 419-425.

Studnitz, M., Jensen, M. B., & Pedersen, L. J. (2007). Why do pigs root and in what will they root? A review on the exploratory behavior of pigs in relation to environmental enrichment. *Applied Animal Behavior Science, 107*, 183-197.

Tanida, H., & Nagano, Y. (1998). The ability of miniature pigs to discriminate between a stranger and their familiar handler. *Applied Animal Behaviour Science 56*, 149–159

Tanida, H., Senda, K., Suzuki, S., Tanaka, T., Yoshimoto, T. (1991). Color discrimination in weaning pigs. *Animal Science and Technology (Jpn.), 62*, 1029–1034.

Telkanranta, H., Bracke, M. B. M., & Valros, A. (2014). Fresh wood reduced tail and ear biting and increases exploratory behavior in finishing pigs. *Applied Animal Behavior Science*, *161*, 51-59.

Towner, S. (2010). Concept of mind in non-human primates. *Bioscience Horizons, 3*, 96-104.

Van der Staay, F. J., Gieling, E. T., Pinzon, N. E., Nordquist, R. E., & Ohl, F. (2012). The appetitively motivated "cognitive" holeboard: A family of complex spatial discrimination tasks for assessing learning and memory. *Neuroscience and Biobehavioral Reviews*, *36*, 379-403.

Van Erp-van der Kooij, E., Kuijpers, A. H., Schrama, J. W., van Eerdenburg, F. J. C. M., Schouten, W. G. P., & Tielen, M. J. M. (2002). Can we predict behaviour in pigs? Searching for consistency in behaviour over time and across situations. *Applied Animal Behaviour Science, 75*, 293–305.

Weary, D. M., Lawson, G. L., & Thompson, B. K. (1996). Sows show stronger responses to isolation calls of piglets associated with greater levels of piglet need. *Animal Behaviour, 52*, 1247-1253.

Weary, D. M., Ross, S., & Fraser, D. (1997). Vocalisations by isolated piglets: A reliable indicator of piglet need directed towards the sow. *Applied Animal Behaviour Science, 53*, 249-257.

Whitehead, H., & Rendell, L. (2015). *The cultural lives of whales and dolphins*. Chicago,IL: University of Chicago Press.

Whiten, A., & Byrne, R.W. (1997). Machiavellian intelligence. II. Cambridge, UK: Cambridge University Press.

Whiten, A., & Byrne, R.W. (1988). Tactical deception in primates. *Behavioural and Brain Sciences, 11*, 233-273.

Wood-Gush, D. G. M., & Vestergaard, K. (1993). Inquisitive exploration in pigs. *Animal Behaviour, 45*, 185-187.

Wood-Gush, D. G. M., & Vestergaard, K. (1991). The seeking of novelty and its relation to play. *Animal Behaviour*, *42*, 599–606.

Zentall, T., & Wasserman, E. (2006). *Comparative cognition: Experimental explorations of animal intelligence.* New York, NY: Oxford University Press.

Zylinski, S. (2015). Fun and play in invertebrates. *Current Biology, 25*(1), R10-R12.

13

Diversity of Adjustments to Reward Downshifts in Vertebrates

Mauricio R. Papini
Texas Christian University

This review focuses on reward-schedule effects, a family of learning phenomena involving surprising devaluations in reward quality or quantity (as in incentive contrast), and reward omissions (as in appetitive extinction), as studied in three taxonomic groups of vertebrates: mammals, birds, and amphibians. The largest database of dependable data comes from research with mammals in general, and with rats in particular. These experiments show a variety of behavioral adjustments to situations involving reward downshifts. For example, rats show disruption of instrumental and consummatory behavior directed at a small reward after receiving a substantially larger reward (called successive negative contrast, SNC)—a *reward-schedule effect*. However, instrumental SNC does not seem to occur when animals work for sucrose solutions—a *reversed* reward-schedule effect. Similar modes of adjustment have been reported in analogous experiments with avian and amphibian species. A review of the evidence suggests that carry-over signals across successive trials can acquire control over behavior under massed practice, but emotional memory is required to account for reward-schedule effects observed under widely spaced practice. There is evidence for an emotional component to reward-schedule effects in mammals, but similar evidence for other vertebrates is scanty and inconsistent. Progress in the comparative analysis of reward-schedule effects will require the intense study of a set of selected species, in selected reward-downshift situations, and aiming at identifying underlying neural mechanisms.

Bitterman (1975) reviewed evidence suggesting discontinuities among vertebrates in the mechanisms underlying several sets of learning phenomena, including probability learning, discrimination reversal, and *reward-schedule effects* (*RSEs*). This article concentrates on the latter—a family of phenomena characterized by the adjustment to the unexpected devaluation or omission of rewards. These involve effects such as successive negative contrast (SNC), the magnitude of reinforcement extinction effect (MREE), and the partial reinforcement extinction effect (PREE), among others, most extensively studied in mammals (for a brief characterization, see Table 1 and references therein). These three effects illustrate the two basic *reward downshift* manipulations; in *reward devaluation* (e.g., SNC), the downshift is to a nonzero reward value, whereas in *reward omission* (e.g., MREE, PREE), the downshift is to a zero reward value. Bitterman (1975) summarized evidence from several nonmammalian species suggesting that these RSEs were not always found in analogous experiments. For example, goldfish (*Carassius auratus*) trained under either instrumental (Lowes & Bitterman, 1967) or consummatory (Couvillon & Bitterman, 1985) conditions showed a gradual adjustment or no adjustment whatsoever to reward devaluation, although they clearly differentiated reward types and magnitudes. A reward devaluation paradigm that yields evidence of quality or magnitude differentiation, but no evidence of SNC, will be qualified as *reversed*; for example, the behavioral outcome of the goldfish

Please send correspondence to Dr. Papini, Department of Psychology, Texas Christian University, Fort Worth, TX 76129, USA (Email: m.papini@tcu.edu).

experiments just described is referred to as a *reversed SNC effect*. Mammals such as rats, however, exhibited an exaggerated response to the devaluation, with extensive (albeit transient) deterioration of either instrumental or consummatory behavior (see Flaherty, 1996). Bitterman (1975) emphasized the co-variation of RSEs in any given species, that is, they either occurred or did not occur, and derived two major hypotheses. First, that such co-variation suggested common underlying mechanisms among RSEs, and second, that reversed RSEs in fish suggested an evolutionary transition in learning processes which, in turn, implied that different theories of learning were required for different vertebrate taxa.

This review concentrates on research with representatives of three vertebrate classes: mammals, birds, and amphibians (RSEs are virtually unexplored in cartilaginous and jawless fish; for research with bony fish and reptiles, see Macphail, 1982; Papini, 2006). An analysis of RSEs requires many experimental manipulations performed under analogous conditions varying training factors that affect behavior. Isolated experiments in a single species may be informative, but, as in other research areas (e.g., fruit flies and mice in genetics), what is required are systematic variations in a relatively small number of selected species and situations. Based on this type of evidence, this review will show that there are several modes of adjustment to situations involving reward downshifts that resist a unitary theoretical treatment. Two possible mechanisms, *carry-over signals* and *emotional memory*, are described and considered in some detail in the final section. Moreover, some traditional categories provide little guidance to organize the literature. This is the case with the classic distinction between general-process and ecological views of the evolution of learning (Papini, 2002, 2008; Shettleworth, 2010; Thorndike, 1911). The general-process view maintains that learning processes are basically common to a wide variety of species otherwise divergent in their morphology and physiology. Indeed, there is remarkable constancy in basic learning phenomena across species, from simple acquisition and extinction, to compound conditioning effects and even seemingly cognitive processes. By contrast, the ecological view suggests that learning is closely tied to ecological pressures. It seems obvious that the relevance of perceptual, motivational, and motor capacities of any given species (i.e., contextual variables; Bitterman, 1960) for understanding their behavior in learning situations cannot be ignored—and is not actually ignored when designing apparatus and testing procedures (Timberlake & Lucas, 1989). But it turns out that it is rather difficult to demonstrate that ecological pressures affect behavior by shaping learning mechanisms, rather than by shaping these other contextual variables. Evidence consistent with this view comes from artificial selection studies based on learned behaviors (Brush, 1985; Torres & Sabariego, 2014). For example, rat strains originally selected for good vs. poor avoidance learning apparently diverged on the basis of differences in what might be loosely called *emotionality*, rather than in terms of evolving different associative processes. Conservation in the evolution of learning mechanisms is likely more the rule than the exception, as suggested by wide phylogenetic homologies in cell-molecular cascades involved in synaptic plasticity in mollusks, arthropods, and vertebrates (Lonze & Ginty, 2002; Sakamoto, Karelina, & Obrietan, 2011; Silva, Kogan, Frankland, & Kida, 1998).

One aspect of the terminology used in this review needs clarification. A description of experimental outcomes in terms of the presence or absence of a given RSE is insufficient because *absence* is ambiguous. There are two potential outcomes that might be described as the absence of a RSE: either because some other effect is present or because there are no differences between the experimental conditions throughout the experiment. Figure 1 shows the regular RSE and these two additional outcomes using idealized data in the PREE and SNC situations: the RSE (1A and 1D), the reversed RSE (1B and 1E), and a null result (1C and 1F). The phrase *reversed RSE*, as used above to describe the effect of reward devaluation in experiments with goldfish (Couvillon & Bitterman, 1985; Lowes & Bitterman, 1967), refers to reward conditions that can be shown to differentially control behavior, but that produce a gradual adjustment, rather that the abrupt changes in behavior typical of RSEs. In some experiments (e.g., the goldfish experiments just cited), different reward values generate differential preshift performance (i.e., they are discriminable), but following reward

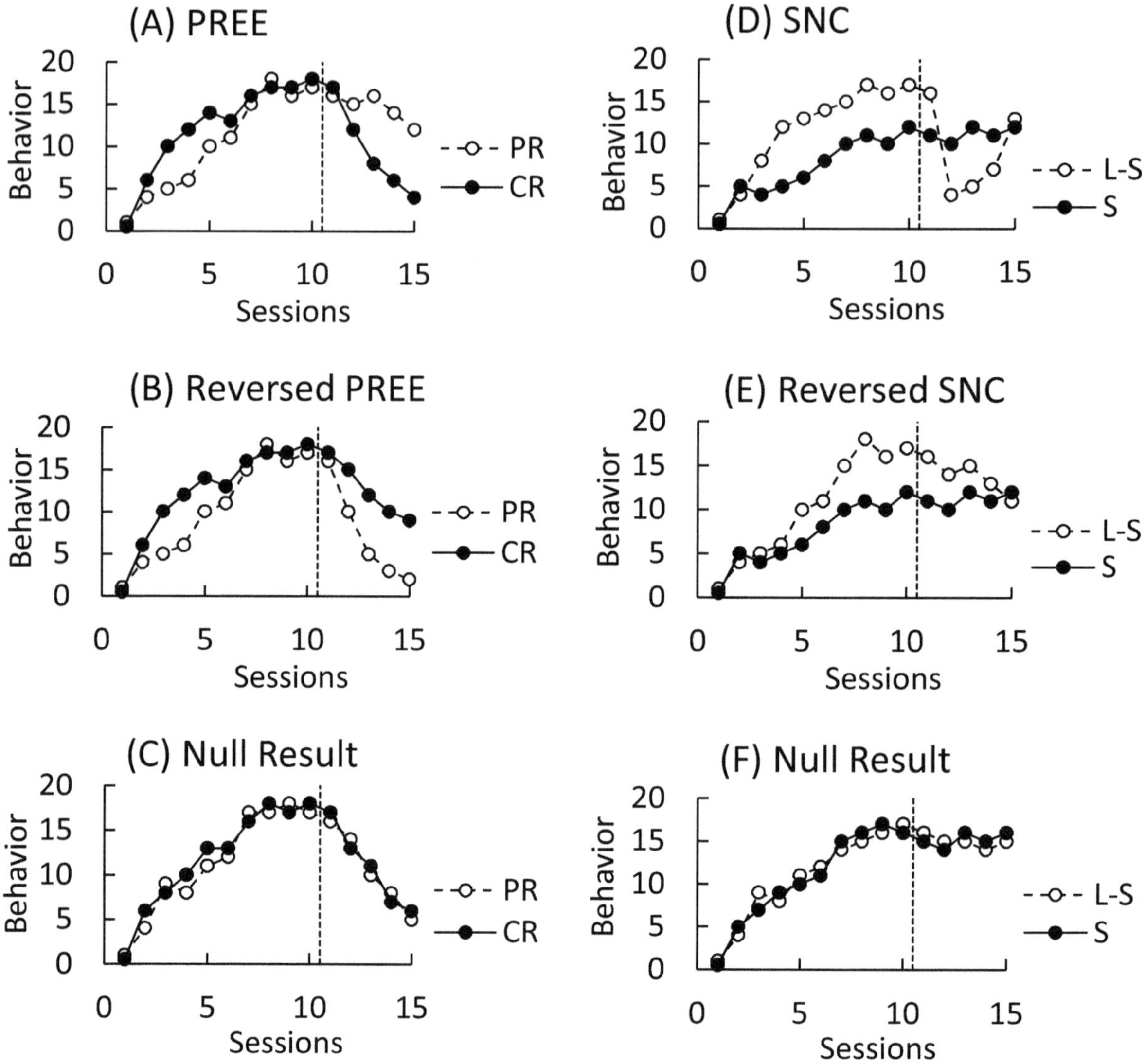

Figure 1. Idealized representation of three possible outcomes of RSEs illustrated in terms of the partial reinforcement extinction effect (PREE) and successive negative contrast (SNC). (A) The *PREE* varies across experiments in terms of the acquisition profile. Here partial reinforcement (PR) animals are slower to acquire than continuous reinforcement (CR) animals, but reach the same asymptote. In other cases, PR animals end at a lower or higher asymptote compared to CR animals. In extinction, however, the PREE involves higher responding or slower extinction rate in PR animals relative to CR animals. (B) The *reversed PREE* involves higher responding or slower extinction rate in CR animals, relative to PR animals, just the opposite. The effect is *reversed* because the difference between groups in extinction is statistically significant (either in terms of a main schedule effect or as a schedule by session interaction). (C) A *null PREE* occurs when neither the acquisition nor the extinction effects of schedule or of schedule by session interaction are significant. In this case, it is parsimonious to attribute the absence of the PREE to a failure of the animals to discriminate the schedules. (D) The regular *SNC effect* involves an exaggerated response of the downshifted animals (large to small reward: L-S) during postshift sessions, relative to animals always given access to the small reward (S). There may be or not behavioral differences in preshift sessions. (E) The *reversed SNC effect* occurs when groups differ during the postshift sessions, but without the exaggerated response by the downshifted animals. There may be an adjustment to the new reward, as shown in here, or downshifted animals may remain at their preshift behavioral level. In the latter case, it is assumed that given a sufficient number of sessions, downshifted animals would drop their behavior to the level of unshifted controls. There must be evidence of control by reward magnitude or quality before the shift. (F) A *null SNC effect* occurs when there are no differences between groups before and after the reward downshift. Again, the most parsimonious hypothesis is that the two chosen rewards did not control behavior differentially, so the reward downshift was not detected by the animals.

devaluation the behavior of downshifted animals exhibits no change. For simplicity it will be assumed that given a sufficient number of trials, a gradual adjustment would have been observed, so that this outcome is also characterized here as a reversed RSE. A null effect, however, can be dismissed on a purely procedural basis; the absence of group differences suggests the parsimonious (and uninteresting) alternative that the RSE failed to occur because the conditions of reinforcement were not discriminable to the animal.

This review aims at describing the diversity of behavioral adjustments to situations involving reward downshifts in vertebrates. It illustrates major trends, suggests areas requiring additional experimental attention, identifies brain processes engaged in these situations, and recognizes some factors that account for the spectrum of outcomes observed in vertebrates. I focus first on the mammalian model *par excellence*: the rat.

RSEs in Rats and Other Mammals

Several results inconsistent with Bitterman's (1975) co-variation of RSEs have emerged in experiments with rats. Whatever their comparative implications, these apparently inconsistent results demonstrate that even within a single species, several modes of adjustment are observed in situations involving the unexpected devaluations or omissions of rewards. This makes it difficult for a single set of mechanisms to account for the available evidence. Let's begin by asking what factors lead to apparent inconsistencies in the outcomes of reward-schedule experiments. Three factors are identified here: behavior, reward, and training procedure. Importantly, experiments differ in terms of the distribution of practice. *Massed practice* refers to the administration of sessions with multiple trials separated by intertrial intervals in the order of seconds to a few minutes, whereas *spaced practice* refers to sessions with trials separated by intervals ranging from one hour to days (e.g., one trial per day). A *trial* involves the presentation of one signal-outcome pairing (Pavlovian) or one response-outcome pairing (instrumental), in which the outcome could be reward (R) or nonreward (N).

Anticipatory vs. Consummatory Behavior

To be sure, rats do not always produce evidence of RSEs. Consider the two most typical behaviors engaged in animal learning experiments. In *anticipatory* behavior, the target response occurs before the animal reaches the reward, whereas in *consummatory* behavior, the response involves a direct interaction with the reward. Examples of anticipatory behavior include running in runways and lever pressing in Skinner boxes, whereas fluid consumption is typically used in experiments involving consummatory behavior.

A striking dissociation of RSEs has been demonstrated in the runway situation, using sucrose solutions as the reward. Flaherty and Caprio (1976) have shown, *in the same animals*, that reinforcing rats with sucrose in the goal box yields a reversed iSNC effect in running behavior (anticipatory), but a strong cSNC in licking behavior (consummatory). Thus, there are conditions that promote consummatory contrast, but fail to influence anticipatory behavior in the same direction. This dissociation between anticipatory and consummatory behavior is also present in terms of the effect of some neurobiological manipulations. Several experiments involving brain lesions show that whether an effect on behavior is observed depends critically on the type of behavior. For example (Leszczuk & Flaherty, 2000), electrolytic lesions of the nucleus accumbens had no detectable effect on cSNC or cANC (Table 1), whether at the level of overall consummatory behavior or in terms of lick microstructure (e.g., burst duration, number of licks per burst). However, the same lesions eliminated the iSNC effect in the section of the runway closest to the goal. A similar dissociation was reported after Ibotenic acid lesions of the hippocampus (Flaherty, Coppotelli, Hsu, & Otto, 1998). However, the

Table 1. *A brief characterization of some reward-schedule effects (RSEs) induced by unexpected reward devaluation or omission cited in the article*

Acronym	Behavior	Dependent Variable	Description
cANC	Consummatory	Lick frequency	Reduced consummatory behavior of a low-value incentive when followed by a high-value incentive (low→high), relative to one followed by a low-value incentive (low→low), in daily training trials.
iMREE **cMREE**	Anticipatory Consummatory	Latency, response rate Goal-tracking time	Faster extinction of anticipatory or consummatory behavior after acquisition with a large, rather than with a small incentive.
OEE	Anticipatory	Latency	Faster extinction after a greater amount of acquisition training than after a relatively shorter number of acquisition sessions.
ORE	Anticipatory	Latency	Faster reversal learning after greater amount of discrimination training than after a relatively small amount of discrimination training.
PPEE	Anticipatory	Latency	Faster extinction after continuous food reinforcement, than after partial punishment superimposed on a continuous food reinforcement schedule.
PRAE	Anticipatory	Latency	Higher acquisition performance in a group receiving partial reinforcement training than in one receiving continuous reinforcement training.
iPREE **cPREE**	Anticipatory Consummatory	Latency, response rate Goal-tracking time	Faster extinction of anticipatory or consummatory behavior after acquisition with continuous, rather than with partial incentive training.
iSNC **cSNC**	Anticipatory Consummatory	Latency, response rate Fluid intake, lick frequency, goal-tracking time	Greater deterioration of anticipatory (induced via instrumental or Pavlovian procedures) or consummatory behavior in animals downshifted from a large to a small incentive, relative to unshifted controls exposed to the small incentive.
SPC	Anticipatory	Latency	Increased responding for a large reward after training with a small reward, relative to an unshifted control always trained with the large reward.
VMREE	Anticipatory	Latency	Faster extinction after acquisition with small reward than with an unpredictable mixture of large and small rewards.

Note. Lower case prefixes stand for instrumental (i) and consummatory (c) procedures. ANC: anticipatory negative contrast. MREE: magnitude of reinforcement extinction effect. OEE: overtraining extinction effect. ORE: overtraining reversal effect. PPEE: partial punishment extinction effect. PRAE: partial reinforcement acquisition effect. PREE: partial reinforcement extinction effect. SNC: successive negative contrast. SPC: successive positive contrast. VMREE: variable magnitude of reinforcement extinction effect. The procedures to induce instrumental effects are in some cases Pavlovian (i.e., response-independent reward presentations). The word *anticipatory* is intended to encompass both instrumental and Pavlovian procedures since in both cases the target behavior is measured before the animal reaches the goal. In *consummatory* situations, the target behavior is the animal's interaction with (i.e., consumption of) the reward. The prefix *i* (*instrumental*, e.g., iSNC) is left in place, even when the procedure was Pavlovian, because it has become established in the literature, although perhaps *a* (*anticipatory*) would be more precise. Some key references (see text for additional references): Amsel (1992), Amsel and Stanton (1980), Bitterman (2000), Flaherty (1996), and Papini (2006).

opposite pattern of results was reported for excitotoxic lesions of the gustatory thalamus—impairment of cSNC, but not of iSNC (Sastre & Reilly, 2006).

There are also discrepancies between different RSEs when the task requires different types of behavior. For example, although rats readily yield the iPREE and iMREE in autoshaping after being reinforced with food pellets in acquisition (Boughner & Papini, 2006; Papini, Ludvigson, Honeycutt, & Boughner, 2001), they show reversed cPREE and cMREE during consummatory extinction, after being offered sucrose solutions for consumption (Mustaca, Freidin, & Papini, 2002). These reversed effects in consummatory extinction, cPREE and cMREE, also point to an inconsistency with cSNC, which is routinely observed in analogous experiments (e.g., Flaherty, 1996). In fact, consummatory extinction and cSNC sometimes yield opposite results for the same manipulation. For example, ethanol reduces cSNC (Kamenetzky, Mustaca, & Papini, 2008) and thus one would expect that it would also reduce consummatory extinction; in fact, ethanol enhances extinction after consummatory training (Kamenetzky, Mustaca, Pedron, Cuenya, & Papini, 2009). To the extent that these effects are based on the same mechanisms, they should obey Bitterman's (1975) co-variation prediction. In these cases, as in those reviewed above (i.e., iSNC vs. cSNC), requiring different responses also usually implies the administration of different rewards, which itself may be responsible for the inconsistency (see below).

Psychological-level concepts, such as expectancy, incentive comparisons, and frustration, may apply equally to situations involving similar procedures (e.g., reward downshift), but the actual implementation of the procedure can engage different brain mechanisms. Thus, when the reward downshift is implemented using anticipatory behaviors, the nucleus accumbens and the hippocampus are more critical than when the operation is implemented in a consummatory situation. One corollary of these results for comparative analyses of learning processes reminds us of the distinction between homology (similarity of characters by inheritance from a common ancestor) and homoplasy (similarity of characters by common selective pressures, but evolved from different ancestors) in evolutionary theory (Papini, 2002). Two different species may show very similar behavioral adjustments based on independently evolved mechanisms, just as two behaviorally similar tasks engage different mechanisms even in the same animal. Behavioral similarities do not demonstrate homology of mechanism; it is analysis at lower mechanistic levels (i.e., brain circuitry, neurochemical systems, and synaptic plasticity) that has the potential to distinguish between these possibilities (Papini, 2002, 2003).

Food Pellets vs. Sucrose Solutions as the Reward

As mentioned previously, rats trained to run down a runway or lever press for sucrose reinforcement usually yield evidence of a reversed iSNC (Barnes & Tombaugh, 1973; Flaherty & Caprio, 1976; Flaherty, Riley, & Spear, 1973; Goodrich & Zaretsky, 1962; Pellegrini & Papini, 2007; Rosen, 1966; Rosen & Ison, 1965; Sastre, Lin, & Reilly, 2005; Shanab, Domino, & Ralf, 1978; Spear & Hill, 1965). This is perhaps one of the most puzzling results in the entire field of incentive contrast, one that, to my knowledge, has not been clarified despite having been identified in the 1960s. Trained under these conditions, rats adjust their performance after the downshift but exhibit no contrast effect, much like nonmammalian vertebrates do in analogous experiments with solid or liquid reinforcers (e.g., Papini, 1997). There is some indication that iSNC also fails to occur when sucrose pellets are downshifted in terms of the sucrose concentration or in terms of the number of pellets (Burns, McCrary, McRae, & Lorig, 1984; Shanab et al., 1978). An apparent demonstration of iSNC with a downshift in sucrose concentration can be explained in terms of cSNC (Weinstein, 1970). In Weinstein's experiment, rats deprived of food and water received lever-pressing, free-operant training for access to either 16% or 4% sucrose. However, the lever and dipper were sufficiently close spatially for rats to operate the lever and drink the solution at the same time. After a downshift from 16% to 4% sucrose, rats exhibited a significant decrease in response rate below the level of the unshifted 4% controls. Although technically a case of iSNC the close spatial proximity between lever and sucrose, the use of a free-operant procedure, and the continuous reinforcement schedule suggest that the reduction in lever pressing resulted from withdrawal from the reward area, a behavior observed in the cSNC situation (Pellegrini & Mustaca, 2000). This artifact is prevented in the runway situation, where the anticipatory response and the goal response are spatially segregated (Flaherty & Caprio, 1976).

As a reinforcer, however, sucrose exhibits standard properties. For example, both sucrose and food pellets support single alternation patterning (Burns, 1984), suggesting that their stimulus traces can acquire control over instrumental behavior. Rats can also anticipate the presentation of a 30% sucrose solution when R and N trials alternate regularly within a session (Burns & Wiley, 1984). In one experiment, rats trained with an R–N–N sequence exhibited lower performance on the second trial than rats trained with an R–N–R sequence, suggesting anticipation of the 30% sucrose reward in the latter group. In turn, this suggests that a representation of sucrose reward can be accessed in a cued-recall situation, something that would be required for animals to show evidence of the iSNC effect (Papini & Pellegrini, 2006). Notice, however, that unlike the single alternation of R and N trials, the iSNC effect requires a comparison between two different sucrose concentrations. Would rats show behavioral patterning when exposed to two different concentrations of sucrose solutions? A negative result would suggest that rats fail to produce the iSNC effect with sucrose solutions as rewards because they have a limited ability to anticipate the sweetness of a sucrose solution.

Successive vs. Anticipatory Contrast

One set of inconsistent results comes from different types of reward downshift situations. Consider cSNC and cANC (see Table 1). These two situations may be designed such that they involve the same rewards, but presented in different arrangements. For example, whereas in cSNC a rat may receive 32% sucrose for 10 daily trials followed by 4% sucrose for five additional trials (with a 4-to-4% sucrose unshifted control), in cANC rats may receive two trials per day, separated by a brief interval, in which the first provides access to 4% sucrose and the second to 32% sucrose (vs. a 4-to-4% sucrose each day). In cANC, consummatory behavior in the first trial is lower in the 4-to-32% sucrose condition than in the first trial of the 4-to-4% sucrose control (Flaherty, 1996).

Although a priori one could apply the same psychological mechanisms to both situations (e.g., an explanation based on Amsel's, 1992, frustration theory), psychopharmacological evidence suggests that these two situations engage different neurochemical mechanisms (Flaherty, 1996). For example, whereas cSNC is attenuated by benzodiazepine anxiolytics such as diazepam and chlordiazepoxide (e.g., Flaherty, Grigson, & Rowan, 1986; Mustaca, Bentosela, & Papini, 2000; Ortega, Glueck, et al., 2014), there is no evidence that cANC is influenced by these drugs (Flaherty & Rowan, 1988). Similarly, whereas corticosterone administration immediately after the first downshift experience impairs subsequent consummatory behavior in the cSNC situation, the same treatment has no measurable effect on cANC (Ruetti, Justel, Mustaca, & Papini, 2009).

Thus, even under generally similar conditions of training, with the same rewards (albeit presented in different arrangements), dissimilar brain mechanisms are engaged in the same species.

Generality of RSEs Among Mammals

Although the largest amount of systematic data comes from experiments with rats, there have been a handful of additional experiments on RSEs and related situations with other mammalian species. SNC is the situation that has attracted most attention using mammals other than rats, but, occasionally, the effects of unexpected reward omissions in other situations have also been reported. For example, appetitive extinction has been shown to be accompanied by increased pituitary and adrenal hormonal activity in pigs, Alpine goats, squirrel monkeys, and rats (Carbonaro, Friend, Dellmeier, & Nuti, 1992; Coe, Stanton, & Levine, 1983; Davis, Memmott, MacFadden, & Levine, 1976; Lyons, Fong, Schrieken, & Levine, 2000), and increased aggressive behavior in pigs and rats (Dantzer, Arnone, & Mormede, 1980; Thompson & Bloom, 1966; for the opposite result, see Mustaca, Martinez, & Papini, 2000). Preventing access to food has also been shown to induce goal-avoidance behavior and reduce activity in the prefrontal cortex measured by functional near-infrared spectroscopy in dwarf goats (Gygax, Reefmann, Wolf, & Langbein, 2013). This evidence is consistent with the view that reward loss can have emotional significance for mammalian species, as is further shown by experiments on SNC reviewed below.

One drawback of isolated experiments is that they can tell us relatively little about the conditions that enhance and reduce the size of RSEs. Additionally, until reversed RSEs were recognized as providing positive information, the absence of a regular RSE was often taken as a null result (e.g., compare Figure 1E vs. 1F); such conclusions probably resulted in the editorial rejection of the submission. A null result unworthy of publication is one in which the behavior of animals in groups treated with different reward magnitudes or schedules does not differ before and after the critical downshift (see Figure 1C and 1F; e.g., Bergvall, Rautio, Luotola, & Leimar, 2007). In a case like this, the most parsimonious explanation for the absence of a RSE after the downshift is that the two reward conditions failed to differentially control behavior. However, if there is evidence of control by reward magnitude or schedule before the downshift, then the absence of a RSE in postshift behavior is informative (i.e., a reversed RSE; see Figure 1B and 1E). Thus, for example, the lack of iSNC with sucrose rewards (see above) represents a reversed iSNC effect, rather than a null result (Sastre et al., 2005). Therefore, we cannot be sure that we have a reasonably full list of conditions that promote reversed RSEs in mammals. With this caveat in mind, what do analogous SNC experiments with mammalian species other than rats show?

Papini, Mustaca, and Bitterman (1988) reported significant cSNC effects in experiments with two species of didelphid marsupials (*Lutreolina crassicaudata, Didelphis albiventris).* These animals were exposed to conditions similar to those used with rats: 32% and 4% sucrose solutions, one 5-min trial per day, and consummatory behavior as the dependent variable. In addition, they received four successive 32-to-4% sucrose downshifts. In rats, repeated downshifts cause no measurable changes in the size of the cSNC effect (Flaherty, Clarke, & Coppotelli, 1996), but in didelphid marsupials, the cSNC effect actually increased in size across the four downshift events. The reasons for this discrepancy and its significance are not known. Red opossums (*L. crassicaudata*) also showed an increase in running speed during appetitive extinction (Papini & Ramallo, 1990); this effect is reminiscent of the extinction burst or spike also observed in rats under a variety of situations (e.g., Dudley & Papini, 1995; Stout, Boughner, & Papini, 2003; Thomas & Papini, 2001).

Similar SNC effects have been reported in a variety of mammalian species. In one of the first demonstrations, Tinklepaugh (1928; Watanabe, 1996) trained rhesus monkeys (*Macacca* sp.) to choose one of two cups for rewards that could be either highly preferred (a piece of banana) or not very appealing, but acceptable (a leaf of lettuce). The monkeys first saw the experimenter depositing the reward under one of the cups and then, after a short retention interval with a screen preventing the monkey from accessing the cups, the monkeys could choose a cup and consume the reward. On some probe trials, the monkey saw the experimenter depositing a piece of banana under the cup, but it did not see the experimenter replacing the banana for lettuce during the retention interval. When the screen was raised and the monkey could choose, the banana-to-lettuce downshift often resulted in the animal refusing to consume the food and behaving aggressively toward the experimenter. This can be understood as a special case of cSNC with repeated qualitative downshifts and relatively massed conditions of training. Similar cSNC effects have been reported in human babies (Kobre & Lipsitt, 1972) and mice (*Mus musculus*; Mustaca, Bentosela, & Papini, 2000) using more conventional procedures with sucrose solutions. Human babies also demonstrate a variety of behavioral changes in instrumental situations (Lewis, Alessandri, & Sullivan, 1990; Mast, Fagen, Rovee-Collier, & Sullivan, 1980). For example, 82-112-day old infants who could move a mobile attached to their legs by kicking exhibited increased kicking and negative vocalizations (e.g., crying, fuzzing) when the number of pieces in the mobile was reduced from 10 to 2. The increased kicking may seem puzzling, but rats also increase the rate of anticipatory behavior after reward devaluations or omissions (e.g., Dudley & Papini, 1995; Stout et al., 2003). These instrumental effects with human babies were observed under relatively massed conditions of training. Similar results were observed under massed-training conditions with dogs (*Canis familiaris*) in reward devaluation (Bentosela, Jakovcevic, Elgier, Mustaca, & Papini, 2009) and reward omission paradigms (Bentosela, Barrera, Jakovcevic, Elgier, & Mustaca, 2008). In one experiment (Bentosela et al., 2009), dogs exposed to a qualitative downshift in food availability (from dry liver to dog pellets) rejected the reward more than unshifted controls, and also withdrew from the experimenter and exhibited a reduction in gaze duration.

Thus, it seems that mammalian species trained under conditions of reward devaluation tend to exhibit changes in behavior that are congruent with SNC effects. The conditions of training vary across species and the actual behaviors measured are also adjusted to the peculiar repertoire of the animal. The phenomenon is there in these mammalian species, but what is lacking in these cases is a detailed analysis of the underlying mechanisms, something that has only been done with some degree of depth for rats.

RSEs in Mammals: Conclusions

Several conclusions can be reached from the research reviewed in this section. Despite being well-represented in published articles, there are still several outstanding issues that remain to be resolved. First, RSEs can be dissociated in rats behaviorally (e.g., cSNC and reversed iSNC, cSNC and reversed cPREE), in terms of brain lesions (e.g., hippocampal damage affects iSNC, but not cSNC), and pharmacologically (e.g., ethanol affects cE and iE in opposite directions). What brain processes are responsible for these behavioral dissociations? Second, why do rats show a reversed iSNC in the runway with a downshift in sucrose concentration? Third, there are entire mammalian orders that have not been studied in terms of the RSEs. Especially intriguing is the status of RSEs in evolutionarily conservative species: Would these effects be observed in experiments with monotremes (egg-laying mammals), marsupials, edentates (e.g., armadillos), and insectivores (e.g., hedgehogs)? Do RSEs reflect the operation of a brain circuit common to all mammals?

RSEs in Birds

As with rats and other mammals, the research on RSEs using birds also yields outcomes that are inconsistent with Bitterman's (1975) co-variation hypothesis. The picture is most complete for pigeons (*Columba livia*), which are used extensively in animal learning experiments based on instrumental conditioning procedures. Papini (1997) reported evidence of a reversed iSNC using a key-pecking procedure with pigeon-formula food pellets as the reward. A single trial per day was used and 10 responses were required to receive the reward, either 1 pellet or 15 pellets. Although pigeons acquired the pecking response faster when reinforced with 15 pellets than with 1 pellet, thus showing control of behavior by reward magnitude, a 15-to-1 pellet reward downshift only yielded evidence of adjustment, without contrast—a reversed iSNC. Further experiments based on the same procedure showed that extinction of key-pecking was faster after acquisition with a small reward than with a large reward—a reversed iMREE (Papini, 1997; Papini & Thomas, 1997).

A similar reversed iMREE effect was obtained with male quail (*Coturnix japonica*) using copulation with females as the reinforcer (Baquero, Puerta, & Gutierrez, 2009). Males were trained to run to the goal box of a runway for access to either 8 females or just 1 female (i.e., a magnitude of sexual reinforcement manipulation). Although running latencies were very similar during acquisition, the large-reward group continued to run for a larger number of trials in extinction (when no females were available in the goal box) than the small-reward group. A second experiment showed that males preferred access to 8 females rather than one, suggesting that they differentiated the two magnitudes. This is where the agreement with Bitterman's (1975) co-variation hypothesis stops. There are two exceptions to the co-variation hypothesis, one involving a demonstration of cSNC with starlings (*Sturnus vulgaris*) and the other involving demonstrations of the iPREE in pigeons and quail.

Freidin, Cuello, and Kacelnik (2009) reported evidence of cSNC in starlings, using solid food and a qualitative downshift in reward from mealworms to turkey crumbs. Starlings in the downshift condition received access to mealworms in one of three cups for 15 trials, at a rate of 3 trials per daily session separated by a fixed 90-min intertrial interval; these were followed by 9 trials with the same temporal spacing (3 trials/session) in which they had access to turkey crumbs in all three cups. The amount of food consumed was measured. Downshifted starlings consume more food than unshifted controls (receiving turkey crumbs throughout training) during preshift trials, but they consumed less food during postshift trials, thus exhibiting a cSNC effect. In addition, downshifted animals switched between feeders more than unshifted controls during postshift trials, when all three cups contained turkey crumbs for all the animals. Because these measures (food consumption and feeder switching) occurred after contact with the reward, they can be both considered consummatory measures. A third measure, probing the target feeder cup (i.e., the one containing mealworms on preshift trials), possibly an instrumental response, did not yield group differences. Experiments with rats in which both cSNC and iSNC are studied simultaneously generally show that conditions that fail to promote contrast in anticipatory behavior, can produce evidence of contrast in consummatory behavior (e.g., with sucrose solutions as the reward; Flaherty & Caprio, 1976). Because demonstrations of reverse SNC effects in birds are instrumental (e.g., Papini, 1997), it is possible that the cSNC procedure would be more sensitive to the behavioral effects of reward devaluation with avian species, as shown by this experiment with starlings. This remains to be seen.

The second source of variance with respect to Bitterman's (1975) co-variation hypothesis comes from experiments involving spaced-trial outcome uncertainty. Pigeons reinforced with solid food either to peck a localized light (Papini, Thomas, & McVicar, 2002) or to run down a runway (Roberts, Bullock, & Bitterman, 1963; Thomas & Papini, 2003) demonstrated stronger resistance to extinction after 50% partial reinforcement training than after continuous reinforcement. Extinction was also retarded after training with variable magnitudes of reinforcement (the VMREE; see Table 1), using the same reward amounts that yield evidence of a reversed iMREE (Thomas & Papini, 2003). A similar iPREE was obtained in a spaced-trial runway experiment with solid food using quail as subjects (Butiricá, Ortega, Papini, & Gutierrez, 2013). Thus, there seems to be no co-variation of RSEs in pigeons, which show reverse iSNC and iMREE, but regular iPREE and VMREE under spaced practice.

To avoid the potentially unreliable comparison across experiments, Thomas and Papini (2003) trained pigeons in a four-group experiment designed to test the iMREE and iPREE within the same conditions of training. The performance of a 50% partial reinforcement group receiving 5 g of mixed grain on R trials and nothing on N trials (for a total of 48 daily trials) was compared to the performance of three groups receiving continuous reinforcement. The iPREE was assessed against continuous groups also reinforced with 5 g of mixed grain and matched either in terms of total trials (48; but then receiving twice as many rewards) or R trials (24; but then receiving half as many trials). Importantly, the continuous group matched for rewards was trained on days in which partial animals were scheduled to receive an R trial; thus, these groups were matched in the number and temporal distribution of R trials. The iMREE was assessed by adding a fourth group receiving 1 g of mixed grain in a continuous reinforcement schedule for 48 daily trials. All animals received one trial per day. Across twenty extinction trials, the performance of these groups showed the following effects: (1) iPREE: there was hardly any change in runway behavior for pigeons trained under partial reinforcement, which extinguished more slowly in comparison to continuous reinforcement groups matched in terms of trials or rewards. (2) Reversed iMREE: continuous reinforcement with 5 g of mixed grain extinguished more slowly than with 1 g of mixed grain. (3) Reversed overtraining extinction effect (OEE; see Table 1): pigeons receiving 24 acquisition trials extinguished faster than pigeons receiving 48 acquisition trials, all under continuous reinforcement. In the OEE, greater amount of acquisition training leads to faster extinction. This RSE has been shown in rats (e.g., Ison, 1962) and in turtles (*Geoclemys reevesii*; Ishida & Papini, 1997), but the reversed version was observed with pigeons and amphibians (see below). Using a similar design, Gonzalez and Bitterman (1969) reported both iPREE and iMREE under spaced practice (1-h intertrial interval) in rats. To complicate matters further, Papini et al. (2002) showed that pigeons did show co-variation of reversed iPREE and reversed iMREE in a spaced-trial (24-h intertrial interval), key-pecking experiment based on a within-subject design. Thus, pigeons extinguished fastest to a key light paired with continuous/small reward, intermediate to another key light paired with partial/large reward, and slowest to yet another key light paired with continuous/large reward.

How is this dissociation of iPREE and iMREE in pigeons to be understood? One possibility is that there is something inadequate about the training parameters leading to dissociated outcomes. This seems unlikely because the adjustment to reward magnitude and schedule in pigeons before the shift to extinction shows nothing unusual. Moreover, as noted above, the same reward magnitudes that produce a reversed iMREE also yield a regular VMREE. A second possibility is that the similarities among the spaced-practice iPREEs observed in birds (pigeons and quail) and mammals (rats) are the result of different underlying mechanisms. Direct comparisons between pigeons and rats suggest different underlying mechanisms. For example, in reward devaluation tasks, the behavior of rats in downshifted trials in consummatory and instrumental tasks, and whether SNC is induced or not, is controlled by the ratio of the reward magnitudes obtained in postshift and those expected from preshift sessions, rather than by their absolute magnitude (Papini & Pellegrini, 2006; Pellegrini & Papini, 2007; Pellegrini, Lopez-Seal, & Papini, 2008). In pigeons, however, postshift key-pecking performance is controlled by the absolute magnitude of the preshift reward (Pellegrini et al., 2008). Using a spatial discrimination reversal task in which successive reversals occurred in the middle of the session, Rayburn-Reeves, Stagner, Kirk, and Zentall (2013) reported that pigeons adjusted to the reversal by making anticipatory errors (before the reversal) and then perseverative errors (after the reversal). Unlike pigeons, the discriminative behavior of rats was more closely controlled by the response-outcome contingencies of previous trials. Tight control of behavior by the long-term memory of a preshift reward magnitude connects seemingly disparate findings from reward devaluation (Papini, 1997; Pellegrini et al., 2008), reward omission (Papini & Thomas 1997; Thomas & Papini, 2003), and perseverative errors in successive reversals (Rayburn-Reeves et al., 2013). There is a component of flexibility in the behavior of rats under shifting reward conditions that seems to be attenuated or missing in pigeons. Negative emotions such as anticipatory frustration induced by prior experience with surprising nonreward may accelerate the detachment from a signal or location previously paired with reward. This process, termed *incentive disengagement* (Papini, 2003), may induce escape behavior and facilitate a switch to a searching mode or to an alternative previously paired with reward.

There is surprisingly little evidence involving manipulations of brain processes during appetitive extinction in birds that produce known effects in mammals. For example, Lengersdorf, Stüttgen, Uengoer, and Güntürkün (2014) infused the sodium channel blocker tetrodotoxin into the pigeon hippocampus during contextual appetitive extinction to produce a temporary inactivation of neural activity. They reported that, as in rats, hippocampal inactivation impaired the retrieval of the extinction memory in pigeons, thus leading to higher levels of spontaneous recovery. Although suggestive, the effects of hippocampal inactivation in pigeons were not tested in relation to reward schedule or magnitude, thus bearing less relevance to the issue under discussion. Using a pharmacological approach, Thomas and Papini (2003) tested three different drugs in the iPREE runway situation with pigeons. The drugs were chosen according to known effects on the iPREE in rats: chlordiazepoxide (a benzodiazepine anxiolytic that eliminates the rat iPREE), nicotine (a cholinergic drug that increases the rat iPREE), and haloperidol (a dopamine antagonist that has no detectable effect on the rat iPREE). In pigeons, however, the effects of these drugs were different. Chlordiazepoxide retarded the pigeon iPREE, but did not eliminate it, whereas nicotine and haloperidol did eliminate the pigeon iPREE. The possibility that the iPREE is based on GABAergic transmission in mammals, but on dopaminergic transmission in birds needs careful examination. These experiments illustrate the type of approach needed to resolve the issue of the behavioral similarity in the spaced-trial iPREE among pigeons and rats.

RSEs in Birds: Conclusions

As shown in this review, birds have provided the best evidence against Bitterman's (1975) co-variation hypothesis. Pigeons readily show reversed iSNC and reversed iMREE, while simultaneously exhibiting the iPREE. This dissociation could provide insights into the differences in brain processes underlying RSEs and reversed RSEs in the same animals. The intriguing results with starlings in the cSNC situation merit further evaluation of consummatory procedures with avian species.

RSEs in Amphibians

There is a slowly emerging literature on learning in toads in situations involving reward devaluation and omission that takes advantage of the adaptive significance of water balance for these animals. The toad *Rhinella arenarum* (formerly *Bufo arenarum*) is a terrestrial anuran that, like most amphibians, returns to water ponds daily for rehydration (Wells, 2007). In the lab, these animals can be maintained for months in good conditions and show excellent motivation to work for an opportunity to sit on a bowl containing distilled water (toads *drink* by absorption through a patch of ventral skin). Reward magnitude can be manipulated by allowing animals to sit on different amounts of water or for different amounts of time in a water container. The consequences of consumption can be assessed by measuring the change in weight before and after a given trial, to ascertain whether indeed different amounts of water were absorbed. Using these procedures, toads were shown to acquire and extinguish an approach response in a runway, and to acquire a spatial discrimination in a Y-maze followed by a discrimination reversal, all under massed practice (Schmajuk, Segura, & Reboreda, 1980). These learning effects were supported by a 2-min of access to water in each of five trials per session (1-min intertrial intervals). In a subsequent experiment, different groups were given five trials per session (30-s intertrial intervals) ending with access to the goal box of a runway for 3.5 min where they found different amount of water. These amounts resulted in 0.5 or 5 g of weight gain per session on average. These two reward magnitudes produced different acquisition functions, but a downshift from the large to the small magnitude led to an adjustment without contrast—a reversed iSNC effect (Schmajuk, Segura, & Ruidiaz, 1981). Similar reversed iSNC effects were observed under spaced practice (one trial per day) in animals given access to water for either 1,280 s or 80 s (Papini, Muzio, & Segura, 1995). In this case, water uptake was measured for each trial thus yielding data on the effects of the reward devaluation in a consummatory measure. There was no evidence of cSNC; rather, the amount of water uptake was essentially dependent on the absolute value of the current reward magnitude. This experiment had two unshifted controls which were then trained in extinction, after 24 daily acquisition trials. The performance of both groups converged during extinction without yielding any evidence of the iMREE. In another spaced-practice experiment (Muzio, Segura, & Papini, 1992), independent groups of toads received reward magnitudes of 20, 80, 320, or 1280 s of access to water, yielding differential gains in body weight, except for the two lowest magnitudes, and differential terminal performance in acquisition for each of the four magnitudes. In extinction, however, there was again a convergence of performance among all groups with no evidence of an iMREE.

The toad's skin can also detect the salinity of the water and react accordingly depending on whether they are hydrating or dehydrating. Thus, by varying the concentration of sodium in the water offered to the toads, one can manipulate the hedonic value of the solution. For example, a 300 mM (slightly hypertonic) sodium solution is a neutral solution that leads neither to gain nor loss of water, whereas an 800 mM strongly hypertonic solution results in dehydration. Toads exposed to an inescapable immersion (Pavlovian) in an 800 mM solution or to an immersion that can be avoided (instrumental) respond, respectively, with an anticipatory increase in heart rate and avoidance of the goal compartment in a one-way active avoidance task (Daneri, Papini, & Muzio, 2007). Response latency in a runway also varies with the degree of hydration: Toads learn to approach the goal for distilled water, show a mild tendency to approach for a 300 mM solution, and one trial of immersion in an 800 mM solution is enough for them to stay away from the goal (i.e., passive or inhibitory avoidance) during 17 subsequent daily trials (Muzio et al, 2011). Using this runway procedure with the neutral, 300 mM solution, Muzio et al. (2011) also found reversed MREE, SNC, and SPC effects (i.e., an upshift from 300 mM to distilled water; see Table 1) in several dependent variables, including running latency, consummatory behavior, changes in coloration of the ventral skin where water uptake occurs, contact time with the reward, and rubbing behavior during water uptake (Muzio et al., 2011). Moreover, a downshift from distilled water to three molarities slightly more appetitive than the neutral (225, 212, and 200 mM solutions) all yielded reversed iSNC and cSNC, with one caveat. Albeit nonsignificant, the mean consummatory behavior of these downshifted groups fell below that of unshifted controls, providing a hint of a cSNC effect (Muzio et al., 2011). Given that cSNC seems more sensitive than iSNC in rats and possibly in birds (see above), this hint deserves further exploration.

Additional studies have dealt with appetitive extinction in amphibians in relation to partial reinforcement and amount of acquisition training. Comparisons between partial vs. continuous reinforcement have produced reversed iPREEs in two species of toads, *R. arenarum* and *Bombina orientalis*. Experiments with *R. arenarum* using the water-reinforced runway procedure described above, spaced practice (24-h intertrial intervals), and runway response have uniformly shown slower extinction after continuous than 50% partial reinforcement with trials equated and, thus, with a different number and temporal distribution of reinforcements (Muzio et al., 1992, 1994). Similarly, an experiment involving solid food (crickets), spaced practice (48-h intertrial intervals), and tongue-snapping responses with *B. orientalis* produced evidence of a reversed iPREE after either 6 or 12 acquisition trials, with a single-alternation schedule of partial reinforcement and conditions matched by trials (Ramsay, Ikura, & Laberge, 2013). In this experiment there was also a continuously reinforced group that received twice the amount of food for six trials; a comparison with the small reward condition yielded evidence of a reversed iMREE. Muzio et al. (2011) reported an additional experiment that combined access to distilled water (positive reinforcer) with access to a hypertonic 800 mM solution (negative reinforcer) in randomly presented daily trials. This design was intended to mimic the partial punishment procedure used by Brown and Wagner (1964), in which rats were reinforced with food in every trial, but with the addition of electric shock in the goal box in a random half of the trials. Rats developed persistence in extinction compared to animals given only food reward—a PPEE (see Table 1). Toads, however, showed no acquisition of runway performance when half the trials involved access to the hypertonic solution. Additionally, a group receiving the neutral 300 mM solution (mimicking a nonreinforced trial) showed a reversed iPREE (Muzio et al., 2011).

What exactly determines resistance to extinction in amphibians? Because experiments involving partial reinforcement usually match the number of trials and the intertrial interval, 50% partial reinforcement groups received half the number of reinforcements with twice the length of the interreinforcement interval compared to continuously reinforced groups. Experiments varying the number of reinforced trials provide evidence of a direct relationship between the number of acquisition trials and the strength of the response during extinction. Such reversed OEEs were reported in toads (Muzio, Ruetti, & Papini, 2006; Ramsay et al., 2013) and newts (*Cynops pyrrhogaster*; Shibasaki & Ishida, 2012). Interestingly, a continuously reinforced group receiving R trials only on days when the partial reinforcement group also received R trials, thus matching the number of reinforcements and their temporal distribution, yielded an extinction performance analogous to that of a regular 50% partial reinforcement group (Muzio et al., 2006; for a similar result in pigeons, see Thomas & Papini, 2003). This last result suggests that reversed iPREEs in toads may result not so much from the schedule of partial reinforcement as from the distribution of R trials in time, as if the reward memory were to weaken in time. To test this memory-decay hypothesis, Puddington, Papini, and Muzio (2013) interpolated retention intervals of 1, 4, 8, 16, 32, or 64 days between the last acquisition and first extinction trials using the runway procedure and found that extinction performance weakened as the retention interval increased. An additional experiment showed that a large reward (600 s of access to distilled water) led to increased responding in extinction compared to a small reward (30 s) with an 8-day retention interval, a result also consistent with the memory-decay hypothesis. Thus, although toads, like most (if not all) animals tested in conditioning experiments, exhibit a reduction in the strength of an acquired response during extinction, thus implying control of instrumental behavior by nonreinforcement, memory decay and limited amounts of acquisition training also weaken extinction performance.

A few experiments have explored the effects of medial pallium lesions on reward devaluation and omission in toads. Based on afferent/efferent connections, the amphibian medial pallium has been hypothesized to be the homolog of the subiculum and CA fields of the mammalian hippocampal formation (Northcutt & Ronan, 1992). Hippocampal lesions in rats eliminate the iSNC even when relatively short intertrial intervals are used (e.g., 5-8 min; Flaherty et al., 1998; Franchina & Brown, 1971). However, hippocampal lesions eliminate the iPREE with spaced practice (Rawlins, Feldon, & Gray, 1980), but not with very short (1-2 s) intertrial intervals (Rawlins, Feldon, Ursin, & Gray, 1985). These effects are eliminated because lesions of the hippocampus *increase* resistance to change, whether in extinction after continuous reinforcement or in contrast after reward downshift; however, these lesions *reduce* persistence in extinction after partial reinforcement. *Increased* resistance to extinction after continuous reinforcement or reward downshift was also observed in toads with medial pallium lesions (Muzio et al., 1993, 1994; Papini et al., 1995), thus showing results consistent with analogous experiments with rats. However, unlike in hippocampectomized rats, medial pallium lesions also *increase* persistence in extinction after partial reinforcement in toads (Muzio et al., 1994). Thus, hippocampal lesions produce opposite effects on extinction after continuous vs. partial reinforcement in rats, suggesting that these situations engage different neural processes; however, hippocampal lesions produce the same effects on extinction after continuous vs. partial reinforcement in toads, suggesting that learning in these two situations engages the same mechanisms.

Like pigeons, amphibians tested in situations involving reward devaluations and omissions show a type of behavioral adjustment that one might label as lacking in flexibility when compared to mammalian behavior. Is this true in other situations? Toads can learn a discrimination reversal based on appetitive reinforcement (Jenkin & Laberge, 2010), but it is unclear what type of adjustment they would exhibit in midsession reversal procedures of the type explored with rats and pigeons (Rayburn-Reeves et al., 2013). Reversals are also observed in toads trained to solve spatial problems in a T-maze, where they tend to show a response strategy in probe trials in which the spatial and response strategies are pit against each other (Daneri, Casanave, & Muzio, 2011). The decay of the reward memory, N trials, reward magnitude, and amount of training are some of the acquisition parameters that determine the reverse RSEs observed in amphibians.

RSEs in Amphibians: Conclusions

Unlike birds, research with amphibians provides support for Bitterman's (1975) co-variation hypothesis. However, additional processes have been identified. There are indications that memory decay for R episodes plays an important role in amphibians, something that is also apparent in analogous experiments with pigeons, as shown above. The relevance of this potential mechanism needs careful attention. Moreover, consummatory situations may prove valuable in uncovering the capacity to show RSEs in amphibians, just as it is suggested above for birds.

Further Comments

This review of RSEs in vertebrates brings to the foreground the diversity of behavioral adjustments that have been discovered in analogous experiments sharing reward devaluation and reward omission as their common procedural denominator. RSEs and reversed RSEs have been described in the three taxonomic groups covered in this review. In mammals, for example, reward devaluations lead to iSNC with solid rewards, but reversed iSNC with sucrose solutions (see references above). Because sucrose solutions yield cSNC effects, it seems likely that the reversed iSNC is the result of a peculiar interaction of the instrumental procedure and sucrose solutions as stimuli, rather than resulting from the engagement of different learning mechanisms. One possibility that needs examination suggests that rats find it difficult to anticipate specific sucrose concentrations. This could be tested by exposing rats to specific sequences of reinforcements in the runway, with short intertrial intervals, and with solutions of different sucrose concentrations. For example, a group trained with 32%-4%-32% exhibiting a shorter latency in the second trial than a group trained with 32%-4%-4% would provide evidence inconsistent with this hypothesis.

In birds, RSEs and reversed RSEs have been observed within the same experiment (Thomas & Papini, 2003). For example, in a runway situation, pigeons exhibit both the iPREE and a reversed iMREE. Moreover, using the same reward magnitudes that yield a reversed iMREE, pigeons showed the VMREE also in the runway. Across-species discrepancies were also noted: a reversed iSNC in pigeons (Papini, 1997), but a cSNC effect in starlings (Freidin et al., 2009). A similar situation has also been observed in experiments with amphibians. I mentioned above a hint of a cSNC effect with downshifts in the sodium concentration of drinking water (Muzio et al., 2011). There was also direct evidence within a single experiment of a dissociation of RSEs: Toads produce an iPREE with 15-s intertrial intervals, but a reversed iPREE with 300-s intertrial intervals (Muzio et al., 1992). Toads also exhibited a performance resembling that of a partially-reinforced group when given training with continuous reinforcement, but with the spacing of rewards equal to that of a partially reinforced condition (Muzio et al., 2006).

As far as I know, there is currently no single learning theory that could accommodate these inconsistencies across species. They challenge two seminal ideas suggested by Bitterman (1975), namely, that RSEs such as the PREE, MREE, and SNC are produced by a common set of underlying mechanisms (e.g., Amsel, 1992), and that their co-variation across species, with RSEs in mammalian and reversed RSEs in nonmammalian vertebrates, suggests the evolution of novel learning mechanisms in mammalian ancestors not present in other vertebrates (e.g., Papini, 2002, 2003, 2006). The first hypothesis, that RSEs are the result of a common set of learning mechanisms, has been challenged independently of the comparative research reviewed here. For example, rats produced an iPREE when trained under either spaced (24-h intertrial intervals) or massed practice (intervals of a few seconds), but the same brain lesion (e.g., hippocampal ablation) disrupts the spaced-practice iPREE (Jarrard, Isaacson, & Wickelgren, 1964; Rawlins et al., 1980), but not the massed-practice PREE (Rawlins et al., 1985).

Practice spacing has, in fact, been used to account for the dissociation of RSEs observed in comparative research, including the toad's iPREE/reversed-iPREE results mentioned above (Muzio et al., 1992). Massed-practice iPREEs have been reported in bony fish (*Carassius auratus*, *Tilapia macrocephala*) and turtles (*G. reevesii*, *Pseudemys scripta*, *Chrysemys picta*) trained in runway situations (Gonzalez & Bitterman, 1967; Gonzalez, Eskin, & Bitterman, 1963; Ishida & Kitamura, 1988; Murillo, Diercks, & Capaldi, 1961; Wise & Gallagher, 1964), although spaced-practice analogues result in reversed iPREEs in bony fish and turtles (Ishida & Papini, 1993; Pert & Bitterman, 1970). It is conceivable that a short intertrial interval may allow the aftereffects (e.g., sensory or short-term memory aftereffects) of one trial to control behavior in the subsequent trial, a mechanism known as *signal carry over* first suggested by Sheffield (1949). Such signal carry-over mechanism was specifically tested in goldfish under training conditions that yield the massed-practice iPREE (Gonzalez & Bitterman, 1967). Couvillon (1984) showed that massed practice produced a reversed iPREE when nontarget trials were interpolated between trials with a target stimulus trained either under partial or continuous reinforcement. This result suggests that goldfish relay on carry-over signals to produce the massed-practice iPREE, a result also consistent with reversed iPREE under spaced-practice conditions (Schutz & Bitterman, 1969). The rationale behind such procedure was to interfere with carry-over signals by interpolating nontarget trials. Using the same procedure, but with pigeons, interpolated trials did not eliminate the iPREE (Couvillon, Brandon, Woodard, & Bitterman, 1980), suggesting that pigeons do not relay on carry-over signals to develop this effect, a result consistent with the spaced-trial iPREE reported in these animals (Roberts et al., 1963; Thomas & Papini, 2003). Thus, there is support for the hypothesis that carry-over signals across trials can produce RSEs under relatively massed-practice conditions (with intertrial intervals from seconds to a few minutes) in all vertebrates studied thus far. However, such a mechanism cannot account for RSEs produced under spaced practice (with intervals in the order of hours to days) because carry-over signals would decay in time during the interval, thus not being available to control behavior in the following trial.

There is substantial evidence of an *emotional memory* component contributing to the spaced-practice RSEs in rats (Papini, Fuchs, & Torres, submitted; Papini, Wood, Daniel, & Norris, 2006). First, behavioral manipulations thought to reduce the impact of negative emotions on behavior, such as counterconditioning resulting from partial reinforcement training (pseudo random alternation of 32% sucrose and water trials), ameliorate the impact of reward devaluation in the cSNC situation (Cuenya et al., 2012; Pellegrini, Muzio, Mustaca, & Papini, 2004). Furthermore, administration of the benzodiazepine anxiolytic chlordiazepoxide before each N trial (i.e., water only) during the preshift period eliminates the effects of partial reinforcement during the 32-to-4% downshift period (Pellegrini et al., 2004). There are also several behavioral tests yielding results consistent with an emotional component to reward downshift. For example, aggressive behavior (Mustaca, Martinez, & Papini, 2000) and male sexual behavior (Freidin & Mustaca, 2004) are impaired, and pain sensitivity heightened (Mustaca & Papini, 2005) immediately after a downshift in the consummatory situation. Furthermore, presession induction of peripheral pain by a subcutaneous injection of formalin in a hind foot (Ortega, Daniel, Davis, Fuchs, & Papini, 2011) or by restraint stress (Ortega, Prado-Rivera et al., 2013) enhance the cSNC effect.

Second, pharmacological manipulations with drugs that affect emotion and mood modulate RSEs. Presession administration of benzodiazepine anxiolytics (Flaherty et al., 1986; Iwahara, Nagamura, & Iwasaki, 1967; Mustaca et al., 2000; Rosen & Tessel, 1970), ethanol (Becker & Flaherty, 1982; Kamenetzky et al., 2008), opioid agonists (Le Moal, Koob, & Bloom, 1979; Rowan & Flaherty, 1987; Wood, Daniel, & Papini, 2005; Wood, Norris, Daniel, & Papini, 2008), and cannabinoid agonists (Genn, Tucci, Parikh, & File, 2004) reduce RSEs in rats. The effects of benzodiazepine anxiolytics on cSNC are mediated by the amygdala, since infusions of diazepam there, but not in the hippocampus, also reduce the cSNC effect (Liao & Chuang, 2003). In the case of opioid receptors, there is evidence that antagonists like naloxone and naltrindole produce the opposite effect, enhancing the cSNC, instrumental extinction, and consummatory extinction (Norris, Daniel, & Papini, 2008; Norris, Perez-Acosta, Ortega, & Papini, 2009; Pellegrini, Wood, Daniel, & Papini, 2005). Antidepressants such as imipramine and citalopram also modulate instrumental appetitive extinction (Huston, van den Brink, Komorowski, Huq, & Topic, 2012) and testosterone has an anxiolytic-like effect ameliorating cSNC (Justel, Ruetti, Mustaca, & Papini, 2012; Justel, Ruetti, Bentosela, Mustaca, & Papini, 2012).

Third, reward devaluation and omission lead to hypothalamic-pituitary-adrenal axis activation. In the cSNC situation, reward devaluation is accompanied by release of stress hormones like the adrenocorticotropic hormone and corticosterone (Flaherty, Becker, & Pohorecky, 1985; Mitchell & Flaherty, 1998; Pecoraro, de Jong, & Dallman, 2009). Reward omission also induces the release of stress hormones in both Skinner box and runway situations (Coe et al., 1983; Coover, Goldman, & Levine, 1971; Romero, Levine, & Sapolsky, 1995). Corticosterone release in appetitive extinction was also higher after acquisition with a large reward than with a small reward (Kawasaki & Iwasaki, 1997). Corticosterone administered immediately after the first devaluation session also enhances cSNC (Bentosela, Ruetti, Muzio, Mustaca, & Papini, 2006; Ruetti et al., 2009), a memory effect that might be mediated by N-methyl-D-aspartate receptors (Norris, Ortega, & Papini, 2011).

Fourth, several areas in the prefrontal cortex known to be implicated in emotion regulation have also been shown to modulate cSNC in rats. For example, lesions of the anterior cingulate cortex retard recovery from reward downshift (Ortega, Uhelski, Fuchs, & Papini, 2011), whereas lesions of the insular cortex eliminate the cSNC effect (Lin, Roman, & Reilly, 2009). Moreover, the ventrolateral orbital cortex seems to control the level of drive during reward devaluation (Ortega, Glueck, Uhelski, Fuchs, & Papini, 2013). These results are potentially relevant to an understanding of RSEs from a comparative perspective. Although precursor cells from all brain areas, including the neocortex, are present in most, if not all, vertebrates, the layered architecture of the mammalian neocortex is unique among the vertebrates (Butler, & Hodos, 2005). It is possible that the functional properties of cortical circuits are necessary for the RSEs observed in mammals, a possibility that has not yet received appropriate attention.

Finally, there is extensive data from selective breeding studies. Roman rat strains selected for high vs. low performance in a two-way active avoidance task exhibit correlated changes in RSE situations. The high-avoidance strain, which shows resilience in a variety of anxiety-inducing situations (Torres & Sabariego, 2014), also demonstrates reduced cSNC (Gomez, Escarabajal et al., 2009), impaired appetitive and aversive iSNC (Rosas et al., 2007; Torres et al., 2005), increased resistance to appetitive extinction (Gomez, de la Torre et al., 2009), and no evidence of iPREE (Gómez et al., 2008) relative to the low-avoidance strain. In another study, Long-Evans rats selected for fast vs. slow recovery from reward devaluation responded differentially to selective breeding (Ortega, Norris, Lopez-Seal, Ramos, & Papini, 2014). Whereas slow-recovery rats were no different form randomly selected controls, fast-recovery rats evolved reduced cSNC effects across seven generations. Interestingly, fast-recovery rats also showed no evidence of PRAE (see Table1) and iPREE, both of which were present in slow-recovery and random rats.

Compelling evidence for an emotional component in reward devaluation and omission comes from studies in which rats are allowed access to anxiolytics after the training session. In one study (Manzo et al., 2014), low-avoidance Roman rats (but not high-avoidance Roman rats) increased their voluntary oral consumption of ethanol immediately after consummatory and instrumental extinction sessions. These rats did not consume more ethanol after acquisition sessions. Moreover, control groups with postsession access to water did not show elevated levels of consumption, thus showing that this effect was driven by ethanol intake, rather than just drinking behavior. Increased oral consumption of the benzodiazepine anxiolytic chlordiazepoxide, as well as ethanol, was also observed after reward devaluation in the cSNC runway situation in Wistar rats (Manzo, Sabariego, Donaire, Papini, & Torres, submitted). These effects were interpreted as anti-anxiety self-medication since these particular drugs have been shown to have anxiolytic properties in reward devaluation and omission situations (see references above).

The evidence for an emotional memory component in RSE experiments with mammals is persuasive, but, one could ask, is there similar evidence in experiments with nonmammalian vertebrates? In this case, the data are scanty and inconsistent. In agreement with an emotional component in RSEs, pigeons exhibit aggressive behavior toward signals of reward omission (Terrace, 1972) and toward another pigeon present during appetitive extinction (Azrin, Hutchinson, & Hake, 1966; Rilling, Askew, Ahlskog, & Kramer, 1969; Rilling & Caplan, 1973). Fowls (*Gallus gallus*) also exhibit aggressive responses when exposed to inaccessible food (Duncan & Wood-Gusch, 1971) and during appetitive extinction (Kuhne, Sauerbrey, & Adler, 2013). Pigeons also learn to turn off a visual stimulus signaling nonreinforcement (Terrace, 1971). These aggressive and escape behaviors are similar to what has been described in several mammalian species exposed to analogous conditions (see Papini & Dudley, 1997). However, an emotional component is inconsistent with some results that show qualitative differences in behavior between mammals and birds. For example, procedures that increase responding after surprising nonreward in rats (Stout et al., 2003) do not invigorate key pecking in pigeons (Papini & Hollingsworth, 1998; Stout, Muzio, Boughner, & Papini, 2002). As already mentioned, chlordiazepoxide eliminates the iPREE in rats (Rosen & Tessel, 1970), but it delays its emergence without eliminating it in pigeons (Thomas & Papini, 2003). There are no comparable data from other nonmammalian vertebrates. Still, what is needed is a systematic study of the mechanisms underlying extinction-induced aggression, escape from signals and contexts associated to nonreinforcement, and behavioral invigoration following surprising nonreward in mammals and birds to determine whether these behavioral similarities are homologous or homoplasic.

Although there seems to be no theoretical framework that can account for the diversity of adjustments to situations involving reward devaluations and omissions in vertebrates, two mechanisms stand out as relatively well tested: carry-over signals and emotional memory. The former mechanism is especially well suited to deal with the results of experiments based on massed practice and is possibly common to all vertebrates, whereas the latter mechanism deals best with spaced-practice experiments and could be unique to mammals. None of these mechanisms can account for RSEs in species that otherwise show reversed RSEs, such as the iPREE in pigeons (Thomas & Papini, 2003) and the OEE and ORE (see Table 1) in turtles (Ishida & Papini, 1997) because they should lead to co-variation of RSEs. But they offer a good starting point for an analysis of neural processes underlying the behavioral adjustments of a few selected vertebrates in a few selected testing conditions aimed at identifying common and divergent mechanisms engaged by surprising changes in reward conditions. As Bitterman (1975) put it:

> The learning processes that we now are able to infer from performance in learning situations are far removed, of course, from learning mechanisms. [...] At the present stage of the inquiry, the question whether the processes of learning are the same in all animals reduces to the question whether the performance of all animals can be deduced from a common set of principles or whether different principles are necessary. It should be evident that the answer to this question must come not from casual work with a large assortment of animals but from intensive work with a small number of widely divergent forms. (pp. 706-707)

References

Amsel, A. (1992). *Frustration theory*. Cambridge, UK: Cambridge University Press.

Amsel, A., & Stanton, M. (1980). Ontogeny and phylogeny of paradoxical reward effects. In J. S. Rosenblatt, R. A. Hinde, C. Beer, & M. Busnel (Eds.), *Advances in the study of behavior* (pp. 227-274). New York, NY: Academic Press.

Azrin, N. H., Hutchinson, R. R., & Hake, D. F. (1966). Extinction-induced aggression. *Journal of the Experimental Analysis of Behavior, 9*, 191-204.

Baquero, A., Puerta, A., & Gutiérrez, G. (2009). Magnitude effects of sexual reinforcement in Japanese quail (*Coturnix japonica). International Journal of Comparative Psychology, 22*, 113-126.

Barnes, W., & Tombaugh, T. N. (1973). Another failure to obtain negative incentive contrast following reductions in sucrose reward. *Psychological Reports, 33*, 801–802.

Becker, H. C., & Flaherty, C. F. (1982). Influence of ethanol on contrast in consummatory behavior. *Psychopharmacology*, *77*, 253-258.

Bentosela, M., Barrera, G., Jakovcevic, A., Elgier, A. M., & Mustaca, A. E. (2008). Effect of reinforcement, reinforcer omission and extinction on a communicative response in domestic dogs (*Canis familiaris*). *Behavioural Processes, 78,* 464–469.

Bentosela, M., Jakovcevic, A., Elgier, A. M., Mustaca, A. E., & Papini, M. R. (2009). Incentive contrast in domestic dogs (*Canis familiaris*). *Journal of Comparative Psychology, 123*, 125-130.

Bentosela, M., Ruetti, E., Muzio, R. N., Mustaca, A. E., & Papini, M. R. (2006). Administration of corticosterone after the first downshift trial enhances consummatory successive negative contrast. *Behavioral Neuroscience, 120,* 371–376.

Bergvall, U. A., Rautio, P., Luotola, T., & Leimar, O. (2007). A test of simultaneous and successive negative contrast in fallow deer foraging behaviour. *Animal Behaviour, 74*, 395-402.

Bitterman, M. E. (1960). Toward a comparative psychology of learning. *American Psychologist, 15*, 704-712.

Bitterman, M. E. (1975). The comparative analysis of learning. *Science, 188*, 699-709.

Bitterman, M. E. (2000). Cognitive evolution: A psychological perspective. In C. Heyes & L. Huber (Eds), *The evolution of cognition* (pp. 61-79). Cambridge, MA: Bradford Press.

Boughner, R. L., & Papini, M. R. (2006). Survival of the partial reinforcement extinction effect after contextual shifts. *Learning and Motivation*, *37*, 304-323.

Brown, R. T., & Wagner, A. R. (1964). Resistance to punishment and extinction following training with shock or nonreinforcement. *Journal of Experimental Psychology, 68*, 503–507.

Brush, F. R. (1985). Genetic determinants of avoidance learning: Mediation by emotionality? In F. R. Brush & J. B. Overmier (Eds.), A*ffect, conditioning, and cognition: Essays on the determinants of behavior* (pp. 27–42). Hillsdale, NJ: Erlbaum.

Burns, R. A. (1984). The goal units dimension in negative contrast failures with sucrose. *Journal of General Psychology, 111*, 9–23.

Burns, R. A., McCrary, M. D., McRae, H. L., & Lorig, T. S. (1984). Sucrose pellet reduction and runway performance. *Journal of General Psychology, 111*, 25–30.

Burns, R. A., & Wiley, L. P. (1984). Interevent anticipation of liquid and solid sucrose rewards. *Bulletin of the Psychonomic Society, 22*, 571–573.

Buriticá, J., Ortega, L. A., Papini, M. R., & Gutiérrez, G. (2013). Extinction of food-reinforced instrumental behavior in Japanese quail (*Coturnix japonica*). *Journal of Comparative Psychology, 127*, 33-39.

Butler, A. B., & Hodos, W. (2005). Co*mparative vertebrate neuroanatomy: Evolution and adaptation.* 2nd Edition. New York, NY: Wiley.

Carbonaro, D. A., Friend, T. H., Dellmeier, G. R., & Nuti, L. C. (1992). Behavioral and physiological responses of dairy goats to food thwarting. *Physiology & Behavior, 51*, 303–308.

Coe, C. L., Stanton, M. E., & Levine, S. (1983). Adrenal responses to reinforcement and extinction: Role of expectancy versus instrumental responding. *Behavioral Neuroscience, 97*, 654-657.

Couvillon, P. A. (1984). Performance of goldfish (*Carassius auratus*) in patterned sequences of rewarded and nonrewarded trials. *Journal of Comparative Psychology, 98*, 333-344.

Couvillon, P. A., & Bitterman, M. E. (1985). Effect of experience with a preferred food on consummatory responding for a less preferred food in goldfish. *Animal Learning & Behavior, 13*, 433-438.

Couvillon, P. A., Brandon, S E., Woodard, W. T., & Bitterman, M. E (1980). Performance of pigeons in patterned sequences of rewarded and nonrewarded trials. *Journal of Experimental Psychology: Animal Behavior Processes, 6,* 137-154.

Cuenya, L., Sabariego, M., Donaire, R., Fernández-Teruel, A., Tobeña, A., Gómez, M. J., Mustaca, A. E., & Torres, C. (2012). The effect of partial reinforcement on instrumental successive negative contrast in inbred Roman High- (RHA-I) and Low- (RLA-I) Avoidance rats. *Physiology & Behavior, 105*, 1112-1116.

Coover, G. D., Goldman, L., & Levine, S. (1971). Plasma corticosterone increases produced by extinction of operant behavior in rats. *Physiology & Behavior, 6*, 261-263.

Daneri, M. R., Casanave, E., & Muzio, R. N. (2011). Control of spatial orientation in terrestrial toads (*Rhinella arenarum*). *Journal of Comparative Psychology, 125*, 296–307.

Daneri, M. F., Papini, M. R., & Muzio, R. N. (2007). Common toads (*Bufo arenarum*) learn to anticipate and avoid hypertonic saline solutions. *Journal of Comparative Psychology, 121*, 419-427.

Dantzer, R., Arnone, M., & Mormede, P. (1980). Effects of frustration on behaviour and plasma corticosteroid levels in pigs. *Physiology & Behavior, 24*, 1-4.

Davis, H., Memmott, J., MacFadden, L., & Levine, S. (1976). Pituitary-adrenal activity under different appetitive extinction procedures. *Physiology & Behavior, 17*, 687–690.

Dudley, R. T., & Papini, M. R. (1995). Pavlovian performance of rats following unexpected reward omissions. *Learning & Motivation, 26*, 63–82.

Duncan, I. J. H., & Wood-Gush, D. G. M. (1971). Frustration and aggression in the domestic fowl. *Animal Behaviour, 19*, 500-504.

Flaherty, C. F. (1996). *Incentive relativity.* Cambridge, UK: Cambridge University Press.

Flaherty, C. F., Becker, H. C., & Pohorecky, L. (1985). Correlation of corticosterone elevation and negative contrast varies as a function of postshift day. *Animal Learning & Behavior, 13*, 309-314.

Flaherty, C. F., & Caprio, M. (1976). Dissociation between instrumental and consummatory measures of incentive contrast. *American Journal of Psychology, 89*, 485-498.

Flaherty, C. F., Clarke, S., & Coppotelli, C. (1996). Lack of tolerance to contrast-reducing actions of chlordiazepoxide with repeated reward reductions. *Physiology & Behavior, 60*, 645-652.

Flaherty, C. F., Coppotelli, C., Hsu, D., & Otto, T. (1998). Excitotoxic lesions of the hippocampus disrupt runway but not consummatory contrast. *Behavioural Brain Research, 93*, 1-9.

Flaherty, C. F., Grigson, P. S., & Rowan, G. A. (1986). Chlordiazepoxide and the determinants of contrast. *Animal Learning & Behavior, 14*, 315-321.

Flaherty, C. F., Riley, E. P., & Spear, N. E. (1973). Effect of sucrose concentration and goal units on runway behavior in the rat. *Learning & Motivation, 4*, 163-175.

Flaherty, C. F., & Rowan, G. A. (1988). Effect of intersolution interval, chlordiazepoxide, and amphetamine on anticipatory contrast. *Animal Learning & Behavior, 16*, 47-52.

Franchina, J. J., & Brown, T. S. (1971). Reward magnitude shift effects in rats with hippocampal lesions. *Journal of Comparative & Physiological Psychology, 76*, 365–370.

Freidin, E., Cuello, M. I., & Kacelnik, A. (2009). Successive negative contrast in a bird: Starlings' behaviour after unpredictable negative changes in food quality. *Animal Behaviour, 77*, 857-865.

Freidin, E., & Mustaca, A. E. (2004). Frustration and sexual behavior in male rats. *Learning & Behavior, 32*, 311-320.

Genn, R. F., Tucci, S., Parikh, S., & File, S. E. (2004). Effects of nicotine and a cannabinoid receptor agonist on negative contrast: Distinction between anxiety and disappointment? *Psychopharmacology, 177*, 93-99.

Gómez, M. J., de la Torre, L., Callejas-Aguilera, J. E., Lerma-Cabrera, J. M., Rosas, J. M., Escarabajal, M. D., Agüero, A., Tobena, A., Fernandez-Teruel, A., & Torres, C. (2008). The partial reinforcement extinction effect (PREE) in female Roman high- (RHA-I) and low-avoidance (RLA-I) rats. *Behavioural Brain Research, 194*, 187-192.

Gómez, M. J., de la Torre, L., Callejas-Aguilera, J. E., Rosas, J. M., Escarabajal, M. D., Agüero, Á., Tobena, A., Fernandez-Teruel, A., & Torres, C. (2009). Differences in extinction of an appetitive instrumental response in female inbred Roman high- (RHA-I) and low- (RLA-I) avoidance rats. *Psicológica, 30*, 181-188.

Gómez, M. J., Escarabajal, M. D., de la Torre, L., Tobeña, A., Fernández-Teruel, A., & Torres, C. (2009). Consummatory successive negative and anticipatory contrast effects in inbred Roman rats. *Physiology & Behavior, 97*, 374-380.

Gonzalez, R. C., & Bitterman, M. E. (1967). Partial reinforcement effect in the goldfish as a function of amount of reward. *Journal of Comparative & Physiological Psychology*, *64*, 163-167.

Gonzalez, R. C., & Bitterman, M. E. (1969). Spaced-trials partial reinforcement effect as a function of contrast. *Journal of Comparative & Physiological Psychology*, *69*, 94-103.

Gonzalez, R. C., Eskin, R. M., & Bitterman, M. E. (1963). Further experiments on partial reinforcement in the fish. *American Journal of Psychology*, *76*, 366-375.

Goodrich, K. P., & Zaretsky, H. (1962). Running speed as a function of concentration of sucrose during pretraining. *Psychological Reports, 11*, 463–468.

Gygax, L., Reefmann, N., Wolf, M., & Langbein, J. (2013). Pefrontal cortex activity, sympatho-vagal reaction and behaviour distinguish between situations of feed reward and frustration in dwarf goats. *Behavioural Brain Research*, *239*, 104-114.

Huston, J. P., van den Brink, J., Komorowski, M., Huq, Y., & Topic, B. (2012). Antidepressants reduce extinction-induced withdrawal and biting behaviors: A model for depressive-like behavior. *Neuroscience, 210*, 249-257.

Ishida, M., & Kitamura, G. (1988). Partial reinforcement and its extinction in the turtle, *Geoclemys reevesii. Memoirs of Osaka Kyoiku University*, *37*, 29-34.

Ishida, M., & Papini, M. R. (1993). Spaced training and instrumental performance in the turtle (*Geoclemys reevesii*). *Memoirs of Osaka Kyoiku University*, *41*, 153-161.

Ishida, M., & Papini, M. R. (1997). Massed-trial overtraining effects on extinction and reversal performance in turtles (*Geoclemys reevesii*). *Quarterly Journal of Experimental Psychology*, *50B*, 1-16.

Ison, J. R. (1962). Experimental extinction as a function of number of reinforcements. *Journal of Experimental Psychology, 64*, 314-317.

Iwahara, S., Nagamura, N., & Iwasaki, T. (1967). Effect of chlordiazepoxide upon experimental extinction in the straight runway as a function of partial reinforcement in the rat. *Japanese Psychological Research, 9*, 128-134.

Jarrard, L. E., Isaacson, R. L., & Wickelgren, W. O. (1964). Effects of hippocampal ablation and intertrial interval on runway acquisition and extinction. *Journal of Comparative & Physiological Psychology, 57*, 442-444.

Jenkin, S. E. M., & Laberge, F. (2010). Visual discrimination learning in the fire-bellied toad *Bombina orientalis. Learning & Behavior, 38*, 418-425.

Justel, N., Ruetti, E., Mustaca, A. E., & Papini, M. R. (2012). Effects of pretraining treatment with testosterone on successive and anticipatory negative contrast. *Physiology & Behavior, 105*, 933-937.

Justel, N., Ruetti, E., Bentosela, M., Mustaca, A. E., & Papini, M. R. (2012). Effects of testosterone administration and gonadectomy on incentive downshift and open field activity in rats. *Physiology & Behavior, 106*, 657-663.

Kamenetzky, G. V., Mustaca, A. E., & Papini, M. R. (2008). An analysis of the anxiolytic effects of ethanol on consummatory successive negative contrast. *Advances in Latin American Psychology, 26*, 135-144.

Kamenetzky, G. V., Mustaca, A. E., Pedron, V. T., Cuenya, L., & Papini, M. R. (2009). Ethanol facilitates consummatory extinction. *Behavioural Processes 82*, 352-354.

Kawasaki, K., & Iwasaki, T. (1997). Corticosterone levels during extinction of runway response in rats. *Life Sciences, 61*, 1721-1728.

Kobre, K. R., & Lipsitt, L. P. (1972). A negative contrast effect in newborns. *Journal of Experimental Child Psychology, 14*, 81–91.

Kuhne, F., Sauerbrey, A. F. C., & Adler, S. (2013). The discrimination-learning task determines the kind of frustration-related behaviours in laying hens (*Gallus gallus domesticus*). *Applied Animal Behaviour Science*, 148, 192-200.

Le Moal, M., Koob, G. F., & Bloom, F. E. (1979). Endorphins and extinction: Differential actions on appetitive and aversive tasks. *Life Sciences, 24*, 1631-1636.

Lengersdorf, D., Stüttgen, M. C., Uengoer, M., & Güntürkün, O. (2014). Transient inactivation of the pigeon hippocampus or the nidopallium caudolaterale during extinction learning impairs extinction retrieval in an appetitive conditioning paradigm. *Behavioural Brain Research, 265*, 93-100.

Leszczuk, M. H., & Flaherty, C. F. (2000). Lesions of nucleus accumbens reduce instrumental but not consummatory negative contrast in rats. *Behavioural Brain Research, 116*, 61-79.

Lewis, M., Alessandri, S. M., & Sullivan, M. W. (1990). Violation of expectancy, loss of control, and anger expressions in young infants. *Developmental Psychology, 26*, 745–751.

Liao, R. M., & Chuang, F. J. (2003). Differential effects of diazepam infused into the amygdala and hippocampus on negative contrast. *Pharmacology, Biochemistry & Behavior, 74*, 953-960.

Lin, J., Roman, C., & Reilly, S. (2009). Insular cortex and consummatory successive negative contrast in the rat. *Behavioral Neuroscience, 123,* 810–814.

Lonze, B. E., & Ginty, D. D. (2002). Function and regulation of CREB family transcription factors in the nervous system. *Neuron, 35*, 605-623.

Lowes, G., & Bitterman, M. E. (1967) Reward and learning in the goldfish. *Science, 157*, 455-457.

Lyons, D. M., Fong, K. D., Schrieken, N., & Levine, S. (2000). Frustrative nonreward and pituitary-adrenal activity in squirrel monkeys. *Physiology & Behavior, 71*, 559-563.

Macphail, E. M. (1982). *Brain and intelligence in vertebrates*. Oxford, UK: Clarendon Press.

Manzo, L., Gómez, M. J., Callejas-Aguilera, J. E., Fernández-Teruel, A., Papini, M. R., & Torres, C. (2014). Anti-anxiety self-medication induced by incentive loss in rats. *Physiology & Behavior, 123*, 86-92.

Mast, V. K., Fagen, J. W., Rovee-Collier, C. K., & Sullivan, M. W. (1980). Immediate and long-term memory for reinforcement context: The development of learned expectancies in early infancy. *Child Development, 51*, 700-707.

Mitchell, C., & Flaherty, C. F. (1998). Temporal dynamics of corticosterone elevation in successive negative contrast. *Physiology & Behavior, 64*, 287-292.

Murillo, N. R., Diercks, J. K., & Capaldi, E. J. (1961). Performance of the turtle, *Pseudemys scripta troostii*, in a partial-reinforcement situation. *Journal of Comparative & Physiological Psychology, 54*, 204-206.

Mustaca, A. E., Bentosela, M., & Papini, M. R. (2000). Consummatory successive negative contrast in mice. *Learning & Motivation, 31*, 272-282.

Mustaca, A. E., Freidin, E., & Papini, M. R. (2002). Extinction of consummatory behavior in rats. *International Journal of Comparative Psychology, 15*, 1-10.

Mustaca, A. E., Martínez, C., & Papini, M. R. (2000). Surprising nonreward reduces aggressive behavior in rats. *International Journal of Comparative Psychology, 13*, 91-100.

Mustaca, A. E., & Papini, M. R. (2005). Consummatory successive negative contrast induces hypoalgesia. *International Journal of Comparative Psychology, 18*, 255-262.

Muzio, R. N., Pistone-Creydt, V., Iurman, M., Rinaldi, M. A., Sirani, B., & Papini, M. R. (2011). Incentive or habit learning in amphibians? *PLoS ONE, 6*, 1-12.

Muzio, R. N., Ruetti, E., & Papini, M. R. (2006). Determinants of instrumental extinction in terrestrial toads (*Bufo arenarum*). *Learning & Motivation, 37*, 346-356.

Muzio, R. N., Segura, E. T., & Papini, M. R. (1992). Effect of schedule and magnitude of reinforcement on instrumental learning in the toad (*Bufo arenarum*). *Learning & Motivation, 23*, 406-429.

Muzio, R. N., Segura, E. T., & Papini, M. R. (1993). Effects of lesions in the medial pallium on instrumental learning in the toad (*Bufo arenarum*). *Physiology & Behavior, 54*, 185-188.

Muzio, R. N., Segura, E. T., & Papini, M. R. (1994). Learning under partial reinforcement in the toad (*Bufo arenarum*): Effects of lesions in the medial pallium. *Behavioral & Neural Biology, 61*, 36–46.

Norris, J. N., Daniel, A. M., & Papini, M. R. (2008). Spontaneous recovery of consummatory behavior, but not of consummatory successive negative contrast. *Learning & Motivation, 39*, 296-312.

Norris, J. N., Ortega, L. A., & Papini, M. R. (2011). Posttrial D-cycloserine enhances the emotional memory of an incentive downshift event. *Behavioural Brain Research, 223*, 348-355.

Norris, J. N., Pérez-Acosta, A. M., Ortega, L. A., & Papini, M. R. (2009). Naloxone facilitates appetitive extinction and eliminates escape from frustration. *Pharmacology, Biochemistry & Behavior, 94*, 81-87.

Northcutt, R. G., & Ronan, M. (1992). Afferent and efferent connections of the bullfrog medial pallium. *Brain, Behavior & Evolution, 40*, 1-16.

Ortega, L. A., Daniel, A. M., Davis, J. B., Fuchs, P. N., & Papini, M. R. (2011). Peripheral pain enhances the effects of incentive downshifts. *Learning & Motivation, 42*, 203-209.

Ortega, L. A., Glueck, A. C., Daniel, A. M., Prado-Rivera, M. A., White, M. M., & Papini, M. R. (2014). Memory interfering effects of chlordiazepoxide on consummatory successive negative contrast. *Pharmacology Biochemistry & Behavior, 116*, 96-106.

Ortega, L. A., Glueck, A. C., Uhelski, M., Fuchs, P. N., & Papini, M. R. (2013). Role of the ventrolateral orbital cortex and medial prefrontal cortex in incentive downshift situations. *Behavioural Brain Research, 244*, 120-129.

Ortega, L. A., Norris, J. N., Lopez-Seal, M. F., Ramos, T., & Papini, M. R. (2014). Correlates of recovery from incentive downshift: A preliminary selective breeding study. *International Journal of Comparative Psychology, 27*, 18-44.

Ortega, L. A., Prado-Rivera, M. A., Cárdenas-Poveda, D. C., McLinden, K. A., Glueck, A. C., Gutiérrez, G., Lamprea, M. R., & Papini, M. R. (2013). Tests of the aversive summation hypothesis in rats: Effects of restraint stress on consummatory successive negative contrast and extinction in the Barnes maze. *Learning & Motivation, 44*, 159-173.

Ortega, L. A., Uhelski, M., Fuchs, P. N., & Papini, M. R. (2011). Impairment of recovery from incentive downshift after lesions of the anterior cingulate cortex: Emotional or cognitive deficits? *Behavioral Neuroscience, 125*, 988-995.

Papini, M. R. (1997). Role of reinforcement in spaced-trial operant learning in pigeons (*Columba livia*). *Journal of Comparative Psychology, 111*, 275–285.

Papini, M. R. (2002). Pattern and process in the evolution of learning. *Psychological Review, 109*, 186-201.

Papini, M. R. (2003). Comparative psychology of surprising nonreward. *Brain, Behavior & Evolution, 62*, 83-95.

Papini, M. R. (2006). Role of surprising nonreward in associative learning. *Japanese Journal of Animal Psychology, 56*, 35-54.

Papini, M. R. (2008). *Comparative psychology: Evolution and development of behavior. 2nd Edition.* New York: Psychology Press.

Papini, M. R., & Dudley, R. T. (1997). Consequences of surprising reward omissions. *Review of General Psychology, 1*, 175-197.

Papini, M. R., & Hollingsworth, P. R. (1998). Role of nonreinforcement in the fixed-interval performance of pigeons. *Psychonomic Bulletin & Review, 5*, 84-90.

Papini, M. R., Ludvigson, H. W., Huneycutt, D., & Boughner, R. L. (2001). Apparent contrast effects in autoshaping with rats. *Learning & Motivation, 32*, 434-456.

Papini, M. R., Mustaca, A. E., & Bitterman, M. B. (1988). Successive negative contrast in the consummatory responding of didelphid marsupials. *Animal Learning & Behavior, 16*, 53-57.

Papini, M. R., Muzio, R. N., & Segura, E. T. (1995). Instrumental learning in toads (*Bufo arenarum*): reinforcer magnitude and the medial pallium. *Brain, Behavior, & Evolution, 46*, 61–71.

Papini, M. R., & Pellegrini, S. (2006). Scaling relative incentive value in consummatory behavior. *Learning & Motivation, 37*, 357-378.

Papini, M. R., & Ramallo, P. (1990). Primary frustration in the red opossum, *Lutreolina crassicaudata. International Journal of Comparative Psychology, 3*, 235–242.

Papini, M. R., & Thomas, B. (1997). Spaced-trial learning with purely instrumental contingencies in pigeons (*Columba livia*). *International Journal of Comparative Psychology, 10*, 128–136.

Papini, M. R., Thomas, B., & McVicar, D. G. (2002). Between-subject PREE and within-subject reversed PREE spaced-trial extinction with pigeons. *Learning & Motivation, 33*, 485-509.

Papini, M. R., Wood, M., Daniel, A. M., & Norris, J. N. (2006). Reward loss as psychological pain. *International Journal of Psychology & Psychological Therapy*, *6*, 189-213.

Pecoraro, N., de Jong, H., & Dallman, M. R. (2009). An unexpected reduction in sucrose concentration activates the HPA axis on successive post shift days without attenuation by discriminative contextual stimuli. *Physiology & Behavior, 96*, 651-661.

Pellegrini, S., Lopez-Seal, M. F., & Papini, M. R. (2008). Scaling relative incentive value: Different adjustments to incentive downshift in pigeons and rats. *Behavioural Processes*, *79*, 182-188.

Pellegrini, S., & Mustaca, A. E. (2000). Consummatory successive negative contrast with solid food. *Learning & Motivation*, *31*, 200-209.

Pellegrini, S., Muzio, R. N., Mustaca, A. E., & Papini, M. R. (2004). Successive negative contrast after partial reinforcement in the consummatory behavior of rats. *Learning and Motivation*, *35*, 303-321.

Pellegrini, S., & Papini, M. R. (2007). Scaling relative incentive value in anticipatory behavior. *Learning & Motivation, 38*, 128-154.

Pellegrini, S., Wood, M., Daniel, A. M., & Papini, M. R. (2005). Opioid receptors modulate recovery from consummatory successive negative contrast. *Behavioural Brain Research, 164*, 239-249.

Pert, A., & Bitterman, M. E. (1970). Reward and learning in the turtle. *Learning & Motivation, 1*, 121-128.

Puddington, M. M., Papini, M. R., & Muzio, R. N. (2013). Vulnerability of long-term memory to temporal delays in amphibians. *Behavioural Processes, 99*, 7-11.

Ramsay, Z. J., Ikura, J., & Laberge, F. (2013). Modification of a prey catching response and the development of behavioral persistence in the fire-bellied toad (*Bombina orientalis*). *Journal of Comparative Psychology, 127*, 399-411.

Rayburn–Reeves, R. M., Stagner, J. P., Kirk, C. R., & Zentall, T. R. (2013). Reversal learning in rats (*Rattus norvegicus*) and pigeons (*Columba livia*): Qualitative differences in behavioral flexibility. *Journal of Comparative Psychology, 127*, 202-211.

Rawlins, J. N. P., Feldon, J, & Gray J. A. (1980). The effects of hippocampectomy and of fimbria section upon the partial reinforcement extinction effect in rats. *Experimental Brain Research, 38*, 273-283.

Rawlins, J. N. P., Feldon, J., Ursin, H., & Gray, J. A. (1985). Resistance to extinction after schedules of partial delay or partial reinforcement in rats with hippocampal lesions. *Experimental Brain Research, 59*, 273-281.

Rilling, M., Askew, H. R., Ahlskog, J. E., & Kramer, T. J. (1969). Aversive properties of the negative stimulus in a successive discrimination. *Journal of the Experimental Analysis of Behavior, 12*, 917–932.

Rilling, M., & Caplan, H. J. (1973). Extinction-induced aggression during errorless discrimination learning. *Journal of the Experimental Analysis of Behavior, 20*, 85-92.

Roberts, W. A., Bullock, D. H., & Bitterman, M. E. (1963). Resistance to extinction in the pigeon after partially reinforced instrumental training under discrete-trials conditions. *American Journal of Psychology, 76*, 353-365.

Romero, L. M., Levine, S., & Sapolsky, R. M. (1995). Adrenocorticotropin secretagog release: stimulation by frustration and paradoxically by reward presentation. *Brain Research, 676*, 151-156.

Rosas, J. M., Callejas-Aguilera, J. E., Escarabajal, M. D., Gómez, M. J., de la Torre, L., Agüero, Á., Tobena, A., Fernandez-Teruel, A., & Torres, C. (2007). Successive negative contrast effect in instrumental runway behaviour: A study with Roman high- (RHA) and Roman low- (RLA) avoidance rats. *Behavioural Brain Research, 185,* 1-8.

Rosen, A. J. (1966). Incentive-shift performance as a function of magnitude and number of sucrose rewards. *Journal of Comparative and Physiological Psychology, 62*, 487–490.

Rosen, A. J., & Ison, J. R. (1965). Runway performance following changes in sucrose rewards. *Psychonomic Science, 2*, 335–336.

Rosen, A. J., & Tessel, R. E. (1970). Chlorpromazine, chlordiazepoxide and incentive shift performance in the rat. *Journal of Comparative & Physiological Psychology, 72*, 257-262.

Rowan, G. A., & Flaherty, C. F. (1987). The effects of morphine in the consummatory contrast paradigm. *Psychopharmacology, 93*, 51-58.

Ruetti, E., Justel, N., Mustaca, A. E., & Papini, M. R. (2009). Posttrial corticosterone administration enhances the effects of incentive downshift: Exploring the boundaries of this effect. *Behavioral Neuroscience, 123*, 137-144.

Sakamoto, K., Karelina, K., & Obrietan, K. (2011). CREB: A multifaceted regulator of neuronal plasticity and protection. *Journal of Neurochemistry, 116*, 1-9.

Sastre, A., & Reilly, S. (2006). Excitotoxic lesions of the gustatory thalamus eliminate consummatory but not instrumental successive negative contrast in rats. *Behavioural Brain Research, 170*, 34-40.

Sastre, A., Lin, J.-Y., & Reilly, S. (2005). Failure to obtain instrumental successive negative contrast in tasks that support consummatory successive negative contrast. *International Journal of Comparative Psychology, 18*, 307-319.

Schmajuk, N. A., Segura, E. T., & Reboreda, J. C. (1980). Appetitive conditioning and discriminatory learning in toads. *Behavioral & Neural Biology, 28*, 392-397.

Schmajuk, N. A., Segura, E. T., & Ruidiaz, A. C. (1981). Reward downshift in the toad. *Behavioral & Neural Biology, 33*, 519-523.

Schutz, S. L., & Bitterman, M. E. (1969). Spaced trials partial reinforcement and resistance to extinction in the goldfish. *Journal of Comparative & Physiological Psychology, 68,*126-128.

Shanab, M. E., Domino, J., & Ralf, L. (1978). The effects of repeated shifts in magnitude of food reward upon the barpress rate in the rat. *Bulletin of the Psychonomic Society, 12*, 29–31.

Sheffield, V. F. (1949). Extinction as a function of partial reinforcement and distribution of practice. *Journal of Experimental Psychology, 39*, 511-526.

Shettleworth, S. J. (2010). *Cognition, evolution, and behavior.* (2nd ed.). New York, NY: Oxford University Press.

Shibasaki, M., & Ishida, M. (2012). Effects of overtraining on extinction in newts (*Cynops pyrrhogaster*). *Journal of Comparative Psychology, 126*, 368-371.

Silva, A. J., Kogan, J. H., Frankland, P. W., & Kida, S. (1998). CREB and memory. *Annual Review of Neuroscience, 21*, 127-148.

Spear, N. E., & Hill, W. F. (1965). Adjustment to new reward: Simultaneous- and successive-contrast effects. *Journal of Experimental Psychology, 70*, 510–519.

Stout, S. C., Boughner, R. L., & Papini, M. R. (2003). Reexamining the frustration effect in rats: Aftereffects of surprising reinforcement and nonreinforcement. *Learning & Motivation, 34*, 437-456.

Stout, S. C., Muzio, R. N., Boughner, R. L., & Papini, M. R. (2002). Aftereffects of the surprising presentation and omission of appetitive reinforcers on key pecking performance in pigeons. *Journal of Experimental Psychology: Animal Behavior Processes*, *28*, 242-256.

Terrace, H. S. (1971). Escape from S-. *Learning & Motivation, 2*, 148-163.

Terrace, H. S. (1972). By-products of discrimination learning. *Psychology of Learning & Motivation, 5*, 195-265.

Thomas, B., & Papini, M. R. (2001). Adrenalectomy eliminates the extinction spike in autoshaping with rats. *Physiology & Behavior*, *62*, 543-547.

Thomas, B., & Papini, M. R. (2003). Mechanism of spaced-trial runway extinction in pigeons. *Learning & Motivation*, *34*, 104-126.

Thompson, T., & Bloom, W. (1966). Aggressive behavior and extinction-induced response-rate increase. *Psychonomic Science, 5*, 335-336.

Thorndike, E. L. (1911). *Animal intelligence: Experimental studies*. New York, NY: Macmillan.

Timberlake, W., & Lucas, G. A. (1989). Behavior systems and learning: From misbehavior to general principles. In S. B. Klein & R. R. Mowrer (Eds.), *Contemporary learning theories. Instrumental conditioning and the impact of biological contraints on learning* (pp. 237-275). Hillsdale, NJ: Erlbaum.

Tinklepaugh, O. L. (1928). An experimental study of representative factors in monkeys. *Journal of Comparative Psychology, 8*, 197-236.

Torres, C., Cándido, A., Escarabajal, M. D., de la Torre, L., Maldonado, A., Tobeña, A., & Fernández-Teruel, A. (2005). Successive negative contrast in one-way avoidance learning in female Roman rats. *Physiology & Behavior, 85*, 377-382.

Torres, C., & Sabariego, M. (2014). Incentive relativity: Gene-environment interactions. *International Journal of Comparative Psychology*, *27*, 446-458.

Watanabe, M. (1996). Reward expectancy in primate prefrontal neurons. *Nature, 382*, 629-632.

Weinstein, L. U. (1970). Negative incentive contrast effects with saccharin vs. sucrose and partial reinforcement. *Psychonomic Science, 21*, 276–278.

Wells, K. D. (2007). *The ecology and behavior of amphibians*. Chicago, IL: University of Chicago Press.

Wood, M. D., Daniel, A. M., & Papini, M. R. (2005). Selective effects of the delta opioid receptor agonist DPDPE on consummatory successive negative contrast. *Behavioral Neuroscience*, *119*, 446-454.

Wood, M. D., Norris, J. N., Daniel, A. M., & Papini, M. R. (2008). Trial-selective effects of U50,488H, a kappa-opioid receptor agonist, on consummatory successive negative contrast. *Behavioural Brain Sciences, 193*, 28-36.

Wise, L. M., & Gallagher, D. P. (1964). Partial reinforcement of a discriminative response in the turtle. *Journal of Comparative & Physiological Psychology*, *57*, 311-313.

14

Ordinal Pattern Analysis in Comparative Psychology: A Flexible Alternative to Null Hypothesis Significance Testing Using an Observation Oriented Modeling Paradigm

David Philip Arthur Craig and Charles I. Abramson

Oklahoma State University, U.S.A.

The data of comparative psychology generally differ from the majority of data collected within mainstream psychology in several key respects – most notably in the diversity of forms of measurement and fewer number of subjects. We believe null hypothesis significance testing may not be the most appropriate method of analysis for comparative psychology for these reasons. Comparative psychology has a rich history of performing several analyses on a few subjects due to a philosophical interest in individual subject behavior, along with group assessments. Since first being published in 2011, Observation Oriented Modeling has successfully been used to analyze individual subjects' responses from honey bees, horses, humans, and rattlesnakes. Observation Oriented Modeling is highly flexible and has allowed comparative researchers to perform a variety of assessments comparable to null hypothesis significance testing's *T*-Tests, One-way ANOVA, and Repeated-Measures ANOVA while producing easily-interpretable and, most importantly, relevant results. This paper describes the diverse manners in which comparative psychologists can assess individual and group performances without concerns of statistical assumptions and limitations that complicate assessments when employing Null Hypothesis Significance Testing.

Comparative psychology is insulated from the majority of psychology sub-fields due to inherent differences in data collection between human and animal models. In practice, measuring animal behavior is based in a fundamentally different methodology compared to measuring human behavior. Comparative data are generally collected in-line with the traditional (Michell, 2014) definition of measurement (i.e., $a=r*b$ where r is a unit and b is a magnitude). In contrast, modern human behavioral data are generally collected following Stevens' (1946) redefinition of measurement (i.e., the assignment of numbers to properties following a rule). These different definitions of measurement solidified a major difference between psychometric and physics-based science (Humphry, 2013), and comparative psychology began using both forms of measurement due to strong influences from both biology and psychology. While psychology's influence from biology and the physics-based sciences initially impressed a use of both continuous and discrete measurement, throughout the later part of the 20th century, influences from psychometric and cognitive research introduced more qualitative measures into comparative psychology (Whissell, Abramson, & Barber, 2013). The common use of these different forms of measurement across the sub-fields requires comparative psychologists use both psychometric and physics-based methods.

Please send correspondence to David Philip Arthur Craig, Oklahoma State University, U.S.A. (Email: dpac007@gmail.com)
Support for this research was provided by grants NSF-REU (2016-1560389), and NSF-OISE (2015-1545803).
* Dr. H. M. Hill acted as action editor on this paper for the special issue.

Measurement Redefined

After Stevens' (1946) redefinition of measurement, psychometricians' data required clarification to contend with diminishing effect sizes. After all, imprecise measurement without clear units led to relatively unclear data (John, Loewenstein, & Prelec, 2012), and these data required enhanced new data analyses methods to observe significant differences. The emphasis on operationalism and representationalism of Stevens' (1946) measurement created an artificial focus on instrumentation, application, and permissibility that drew attention away from the equivocation concerns around the actual term of measurement. Before Stevens (1946) redefined measurement in psychology, Ferguson et al. (1940) specifically referenced the measurement reported in Stevens and Davis (1938) as an example of why true quantitative measurement was impossible for psychometricians. The invention and adoption of Stevens' measurement validated and encouraged estimates of sensory events, and the focus on the four scales of measurement raised more questions about scale transformations and permissibility rather than if the proxy scale, and actual attribute being estimated, was actually a quantitative measure (Michell, 2008). The quantitative imperative (viz., knowledge and science require quantitative measurement) was left unaddressed, and the relevancy of the quantitative hypothesis (viz., measured mental attributes are actually quantitative) was largely untested. Instead, psychologists successfully emulated other sciences in competition for grant money by using quantitative methods for measures on interval and ratio scales (Solovey, 2004).

By using quantitative methods, psychometricians appeared to be performing quantitative science, and successfully avoided criticism for not adhering to the quantitative imperative (Michell, 2008). Of these quantitative methods, parametric Null Hypothesis Significance Testing, or the process of predicting there is no mean difference in populations, became the most popular analysis tool for psychometric science. Parametric Null Hypothesis Significance Testing further strengthened the psychometricians' confidence in satisfying the requirements of the quantitative imperative, and thus helped perpetuate the claims that psychology was a quantitative science. While psychometric data were treated as if they are quantitative, neither the observed measure, nor the operationalized construct, had been demonstrated to actually be quantitative. While not actually measuring quantitative data, the use of parametric Null Hypothesis Significance Testing treated the data (and most importantly, the construct) as if they were quantitative, but this quantitative hypothesis has largely been untested within psychology (Michell, 2008). Rather than address this fundamental quantitative assumption, psychometricians increasingly relied on larger sample sizes, group designs, and corrective transformations to assess their data and obtain significant, publishable results using parametric Null Hypothesis Significance Testing. Significance replaced meaningfulness, and psychologists began estimating population parameters under a hypothesis no mean differences exist in the population (Gigerenzer, 2004).

Despite this shift in measurement and the accompanying analyses, comparative psychologists and radical behaviorists largely continued measuring and collecting data in the traditional sense and conformed to Hölder's axioms of quantity (Michell & Ernst, 1997). Common comparative measures like inter-response time clearly fit Hölder's axioms (viz., communitive, associative, and transitive properties, and a sums of magnitudes are greater than individual magnitudes). Comparative psychological data also largely conformed to Hölder's additional requirements of density to be able to consider a quantitative measure as continuous (i.e., consistency of magnitudes and upper/lower bounds). Measures such as response time contained clear units, were continuous, and thus suitable for undergoing the additive multiplicative operations required when calculating a mean. These comparative data were tangible and real, and the effects of manipulations could easily be deciphered by, for example, visually displaying a cumulative number of responses across time. Comparative data were already quantitative and satisfied the quantitative imperative, so unlike the psychometricians, comparative researchers did not need to use parametric Null Hypothesis Significance Testing to validate reliance on qualitative measurement.

Null Hypothesis Significance Testing in Comparative Psychology

However, most comparative psychologists are now trained as general psychologists; given the diminishing number of course and curriculum options for students interested in comparative psychology, few other data analysis options are afforded to comparative psychology students (Abramson, 2015). Perhaps because of these shared curriculums, Null Hypothesis Significance Testing has slowly been adopted by the comparative sub-field rather than being leveraged for methodological or metaphysical reasons. In practice, the use of Null Hypothesis Significance Testing may also have been stimulated by comparative psychology's tendency to publish in a wide variety of journals, and the differences in these other sub-fields' journal standards. As comparative psychology differs in fundamental ways compared to the rest of psychology's sub-fields, and data analyses methods should be selected based on the type of data to be analyzed, the use of Null Hypothesis Significance Testing (NHST) may not be the most appropriate of available options for the comparative psychologist. Comparative researchers should not feel obliged to use NHST simply because their colleagues do so with their human models. In light of the differences between human and animal data, we pose the use of NHST may not have been the most suitable analysis method for comparative psychology. Three key aspects of comparative research encourage critically evaluating the continued use of NHST in comparative psychology:

1) Behavioral or physiological data are the only available dependent variables for comparative psychologists; after all, communication barriers between species make self-report assessments useless. Comparative psychologists have continued to explore and refine measures that are more likely to be based and occur in reality. The measurement of dependent variables based in space-time (e.g., length, duration, responses per minute, inter-response time, temperature) requires the use of units (i.e., common standards), ratios of magnitudes (i.e., consistent standards), and continuity (i.e., additive and density mathematical properties), and thus continues the traditional form of measurement. Indeed, Herman von Helmholtz (1887) was among the first to question how to know if an attribute was additive; even though Helmholtz was measuring reaction time (a continuous quantitative measure), this form of critical inquiry and assessment-checking had a firm tradition in comparative work prior to the sub-field's genesis.

In contrast, modern human psychological investigators favor both Stevens' (1946) redefinition of measurement and invented four forms of measurement: nominal, ordinal, interval, and ratio measures. Despite his clear arguments as to why ordinal data could not undergo multiplicative operations (e.g., to calculate a mean) due to a lack of continuity, Stevens' (1946) sent modern psychology toward a discussion of statistical permissibility (Velleman, & Wilkinson, 1993). Despite the rigorous methods and discussion (Schorske, 1997), it seems the majority of modern human psychological researchers incorrectly classify their data. For example, Likert data, data which can only be considered ordinal, are treated as interval data that may then be averaged. Hölder's axioms are still the benchmark to allow additive and multiplicative mathematical properties for certain types of numbers and data; psychometric data are no exception. However, the influence of psychometrics on comparative psychology is undeniable (Whissell, et al., 2013), so because of its history of measurement, comparative psychology will likely continue to collect both continuous and discrete quantitative data (along with qualitative data as psychometrics is further adopted into animal research). A method of data analysis that contends with all three forms of data (continuous quantitative, discrete quantitative, qualitative) would best serve a sub-field that collects a diverse form of data due to a mix of influence of traditional measurement, and the psychometrican's form of measurement.

2) Comparative psychological research seldom relies on introductory psychology students to serve as subjects to quickly build large Ns; animal husbandry requirements, barriers to field data collection, and other

logistical difficulties of animal data collection result in a sub-field that publishes with a relatively lower *N* compared to the standards of other psychological sub-fields. Throughout its history, comparative psychology has demonstrated a keen focus on individual subject behaviors (Mace & Kratochwill, 1986). For example, Skinner Boxes originally showed cumulative responding for individual subjects, and Skinner's qualitative cumulative curves forced the use of response rate as a dependent variable. Experiments with individual assessments of thousands of trials for a single subject clearly exhibits an interest in the individual subject (e.g., Ferster & Skinner, 1957). After all, learning occurs in an individual subject, not in a group average. Within-subjects designs were popular in radical behaviorism, and along with group analyses, single-subject and other designs with lower *N*s are still popular within comparative psychology. For example, recent subject sizes in three of the most popular comparative and social psychology journals highlight this stark contrast (Table 1).

Table 1

Comparison of Ns in Popular Animal and Human Psychology Journals

Journal	Date of Publication	Median N per Experiment	Median N per Publication
Journal of Comparative Psychology	Nov/2017	8	12
Behavioural Processes	Dec/2017	16	16
Journal of Experimental Analysis of Behavior	Nov/2017	9	8
Social Behavior and Personality	Oct/2017	298	305
Journal of Experimental Social Psychology	Nov/2017	154	810
The Journal of Social Psychology	Nov/2017	187	277

Ultimately, these lower *N*s impact the comparative psychologist's ability to generalize findings and make convincing conclusions about a population based on a relatively small sample. For example, how could comparative researchers with a sample size of four turtle doves (Lejeune & Richelle, 1982) or eight Aldabra giant tortoises (Spiezio, Leonardi, & Regaiolli, 2017) meaningfully generalize findings to a population that is not critically endangered? The use of Null Hypothesis Significance Testing (NHST) may not be the most ideal form of analysis for comparative psychology because truly representative samples are rarely assessed in the field. Data analysis methods that do not abstract to assessments of a population parameter and can perform individual subject analyses may better serve a researcher with fewer subjects. However, this inability to generalize to a population is not an inherent issue with data collection or analysis, just in the ability to draw generalizable conclusions.

3) Due to the difference in subject size and the established interest in individual subject performance, we believe comparative psychology's data analysis methods should be focused more on individual subjects and observations rather than abstracting observed data to a population parameter based on aggregate assessments. Group assessments and aggregate analyses are certainly helpful for initial analyses, but individual analyses allow researchers to further investigate the observed data, and may reveal artifacts associated with aggregate based analyses. Indeed, comparative psychology's literature is rich with well-articulated points

(Branch & Gollub, 1974; Bakan, 1967; Meehl, 1978; Skinner, 1956; Dews, 1978; Schneider, 1969; Zeiler & Powell, 1994) against dependence on aggregate, and especially mean and variance based, analyses. These cautionings should continue to encourage comparative psychologists to consider other data analysis methods that assess individual subject performances. With lower *N*s, comparative psychologists can dedicate more attention to individual subjects and rely more on within-subjects and single-subjects designs. Data analyses that favor individual observations within and between subjects, do not need data transformations, and offer standardized and clear output could be expected to especially appeal to comparative psychologists.

Alternatives to Null Hypothesis Significance Testing

Statisticians such as Russell, Campbell, Nagel, and Stevens invented a series of regression analyses that are easy to misunderstand (e.g., the focus on the p-value above an effect size, the definition of a p-value, the implications of statistical significance, meaningfulness) and misinterpret (Cohen, 1994; Gigerenzer, 2004). The statistical misuse outside of comparative psychology is likely to blame for the unprecedented replication failures experienced within the more popular sub-fields like cognitive or social psychology (Doyen, Klein, Pichon, & Cleeremans, 2012; Nosek et al., 2015). However, by remaining based in traditional measurement and demonstrating a historical interest in individual subjects, comparative psychology does not need to depend on NHST like the psychometric or cognitivist sub-fields.

More recently, NHST advocates are being challenged in many scientific fields (Woolston, 2015; Beghetto, 2014; Gigerenzer, 2004), but NHST has been criticized throughout comparative psychology's history (Skinner, 1972) likely because behavioral data frequently do not meet the assumptions required to perform NHST (Laurent & Lejeune, 1985). A field using real idemnotic measurement, with a focus on individual subjects that utilizes small sample sizes with non-normal and non-homogeneous data could benefit from exploring alternatives to NHST. Comparative psychology's continued use of NHST should be questioned, not just because of NHST's own limitations, but because there was never a need for NHST in a sub-field that was focused on individual subjects and performed real measurement.

As comparative psychology becomes a rarer course in collegiate catalog offerings (Abramson, 2015), a bridge between physics-based science and mainstream psychology diminishes, and animal researchers will continue to use the only option that is seemingly available for psychological data analysts: NHST. Bayesian methods could be classified as the top alternative option to NHST, but Bayesian methods may be hard to adopt in sub-fields that collect and report data as frequencies rather than probabilities (Gigerenzer & Marewski, 2015). Frequency-based assessments may better serve the comparative psychologist, so a different alternative to Bayesian methods may be more appropriate for animal researchers. We believe implementing frequency-based data analysis methods that focus on individual subjects may be integral to the continued growth of comparative psychology. Moreover, Bayesian methods also abstract to population parameters and thus may be less useful for a sub-field with lower sample sizes and an interest in explanatory inferences. The established focus on individuals in comparative psychology stems from a desire to describe the causal mechanisms (viz., contingencies) impacting the individual's behavior, so this established and careful use of abductive inferences may further decrease the likelihood of adoption of an 'inference machine' like Bayesian methods. Like Bayesian methods, we also do not consider Latent Class Modeling an ideal approach for comparative psychologists. While Latent Class Modeling has relatively fewer assumptions than parametric NHST, Latent Class Modeling is still designed to estimate population parameters of unobservable mental constructs. Like all Structural Equation Modeling, Latent Class Modeling is generally less helpful for comparative researchers that perform behavioral and physiological measurement and adopt a behaviorist tendency to avoid abstraction to unobservable attributes.

Observational Oriented Modeling

Observation Oriented Modeling (Grice, 2011) is an established method of data analysis that is capable of assessing the types of data that are collected by comparative researchers, and doing so without taking an aggregate to summarize the individual observations. Fundamentally, Observation Oriented Modeling (OOM) focuses scientific descriptions on the actual observed data: individual subjects making individual responses. Philosophically, OOM empowers comparative psychology to align all of its methods with its metaphysics. The use of NHST stands in contrast with the rich tradition of quantitative measurement of individual subject behavior within comparative psychology. Practically, OOM empowers comparative psychology to actually ask questions that matter to the sub-field. NHST cannot answer the simple question: *were more responses observed in A versus B?*. NHST only allows researchers to reject a null hypothesis that the population parameters of the observed data differ when compared to a supposedly normal distribution. Prior to ever being used to analyze comparative psychological data, Grice (2011) specifically identified behaviorists (and by extension, comparative researchers) would most likely be the first psychologists to understand the benefits of OOM. Below, we explain why the flexibility of OOM's Ordinal Pattern Analysis should appeal to comparative psychologists that are interested in performing traditional measurement and assessing individual subject behavior.

Ordinal Pattern Analysis

Within the philosophy of OOM, the Ordinal Pattern Analysis (Grice, Craig, & Abramson, 2015), seems especially useful for comparative psychologists. Ordinal Pattern Analysis (OPA) is a highly-flexible assessment that allows analysts to make any number of *a priori* ordinal predictions (e.g., an FR 2 schedule of reinforcement would produce lower responding than an FR 4). The observed data are then compared to the ordinal prediction to calculate a Percent Correct Classification Value (PCC Value) before the observed data are randomized a set number of times. Each of these randomizations is then compared to the ordinal prediction to create a distribution of PCC values that are then compared to the observed data's PCC Value. The comparison of the randomizations' PCC values versus the observed data's PCC value produces a probability statistic, a chance value (*c*-value). The PCC value is an effect size and displays the number of observed data that match the ordinal prediction compared to the total number of performed ordinal comparisons. The assessment is simple at its core and thus easy to understand and leverage to draw clear conclusions. Additionally, researchers may also include the presentation of the lowest and highest PCC values obtained from the randomization comparisons along with the PCC value and *c*-value. In doing so, OPA can more easily be understood by those based in an NHST paradigm; the PCC value is an effect size, the c-value is a probability statistic, and the randomization range is analogous to a confidence interval.

When performing pair-wise assessments, OPA calculates a PCC value and accompanying c-value. However, ordinal predictions with more than two orders can also be made and assessed in OOM. When performing omnibus assessments, OOM performs both pair-wise and omnibus assessments and calculates a PCC value for all of the pair-wise assessments, and a Complete Percent Correct Classification Value (CPCC Value) for the omnibus assessment. The CPCC value compares all of the observations to the entire ordinal prediction whereas the pair-wise assessments compare all observations against segments of the ordinal prediction. If a single subject had three observations of movement (15 cm, 12 cm, 18 cm) compared to a monotonically increasing ordinal prediction, the CPCC value would be 0 because a perfect match was not observed, but the PCC value would be 66.66%. With this CPCC value, OPA can be extended to compare any number of groups or conditions.

Moreover, OPA can perform both dependent and independent analyses. Dependent Ordinal Analyses simply compare each observation as relevant without involving other observations. For example, a two-subject pre-test versus post-test assessment would perform two ordinal comparisons (i.e., A1 vs B1; A2 vs B2). Independent Ordinal Analyses can be performed by comparing combinations of observations. For example, a two subject assessment would perform four ordinal comparisons (i.e., A vs C; A vs D; B vs C; B vs D). If comparing more than two conditions, repeated measures assessments can be performed for dependent data. For example, a two-subject pre-test versus post-test versus follow-up assessment would perform eight assessments (i.e., 1A vs 1B; 1A vs 1C; 1B vs 1C; 1A vs 1B vs 1C; 2A vs 2B; 2A vs 2C; 2B vs 2C; 2A vs 2B vs 2C). If comparing more than two groups, multiple combination assessments can be performed as a natural extension of a two group comparison. For example, a three group comparison with two-subjects each would perform 16 pair-wise assessments and 8 omnibus assessments.

Inherent Flexibility of OPA

The diversity of OPA is of particular importance for a sub-field that must contend with instrumental (viz., procedural) differences when making indirect comparisons between species. Being able to leverage similar analyses for individual subjects addresses analytical and procedural differences to better facilitate making inter-species comparisons. Rather than using different types of tests across different forms of data, OPA is just one type of test. This robustness of OPA is inherent in its methods of analysis: the ordinal comparisons, the calculated PCC value, and the randomizations.

1. A major contributor to this flexibility are the ordinal comparisons themselves; the observed data are treated in a non-parametric manner. While seemingly conservative, treating observations as discrete quantities, or as the observations are actually collected, eschews the difference between parametric and non-parametric data assessments (allowing for an even greater number of comparisons), and thus aligns the analysis with the observation. In the process, an ordinal analysis side-steps theoretical implications of violations of continuity in measurement. For example, should a clearly discrete binomial observation, such as a response (Michell 1994; 1997), be treated as a continuous observation if divided by an interval of time? Does the division of time and transformation to a response rate suddenly justify the use of parametric assessments for data that are otherwise clearly discrete? If a numerator does not adhere to the density property, division by a continuous variable may not be appropriate. OPA's treatment of the observations in an ordinal manner eschews deviating definitions of measurement (and assumptions of continuity) to allow a wide variety of forms of data to be assessable via the same analysis method. OPA may be valuable for comparative psychologists that otherwise may face difficult decisions about the composition and constitution of an observation, and thus the most appropriate NHST assessment to perform. Theoretically, OPA maintains how the observations and data are treated by the researcher; discrete and continuous data can be analyzed in the same manner. Practically, OPA bypasses assumptions requiring considerations of statistical permissibility along with qualifying and inconsistent corrections processes.

2. PCC values are an ideal effect size because the value occurs on a 0-100 scale (percent), so indirect comparisons via outcomes from a data analysis tool is not methodologically offensive when using OOM (as long as procedural considerations are made). Because OPA's PCC value is calculated purely on comparisons

of the individual observations and without the use of aggregates from a particular set of observations, the PCC values are easy to compare across datasets. As the PCC value is not calculated with an aggregate such as a standard deviation, the PCC value is not vulnerable to aggregate artifacts. Moreover, conventions of interpretation, such as for Pearson's *r*, Cohen's *d*, and η^2 are not required because a PCC is displayed as a standard percent. In contrast, many common effect sizes in NHST such as Cohen's *d* and η^2, do not have clear and absolute limits, meaning, or methods of interpretation without arbitrary guidelines. Several common effect sizes in NHST make indirect comparisons via data analysis impossible because these values are relative to the observed data set. The PCC value's absolute standard facilitates making indirect comparisons and may be a more effective effect size for comparative psychologists using common effect sizes with NHST. The PCC value is highly transparent, simple to compute, easy to understand, and thus an ideal effect size to interpret. For example, if a comparative researcher were to predict subject lever-press responding decreases across 5 trials in an extinction contingency, and the PCC value for dolphin responding was 75.00, but the PCC value for shark responding was 50.00, the PCC value alone could be used to indirectly compare extinction across species and allow the researcher to conclude dolphin responding was more sensitive to the extinction contingency than shark responding. The same type of indirect comparison of η^2 in a repeated measures ANOVA would not be as easy to interpret.

3. Randomization-generated probability statistics are more robust than assessments with requirements that the data (and assumed population) occur on a specific type of distribution (Manly, 2006). By generating a randomized distribution, observations are catered to what was actually observed, not what is assumed could potentially occur for some population. Concerns around kurtosis, skew, and assumptions of normalcy are irrelevant with randomization. Unlike the *p*-value, the *c*-value is transparent and easy to interpret and use to perform abduction because it simply shows the number of randomized assessments that better fit the ordinal prediction compared to the observed data.

Extended Flexibilities of OPA

While OPA compares individual observations, the assessment is not limited to assessing individual subjects' responding. Group assessments can be performed by pooling individual subjects' data and comparing every groups' individuals' responses. Pooling simply combines observations, but unlike an aggregate, no attempts to describe the individual data are attempted when pooling observations. Instead, OOM compares the observed data, not descriptions (such as measures of central tendency) of the data. As statistical power is irrelevant with OOM, performing both group and individual subject analyzes is permissible and encouraged. Moreover, by using pooling to perform dependent analyses, OOM allows researchers to perform assessments with unequal response observations. This adaptability is greatly beneficial to comparative psychologists that perform measurement in the field and cannot perfectly control variables such as trial/session duration. This flexibility may also appeal to researchers attempting to make indirect comparisons across species. Statistical limitations of data analyses that make no real theoretical violations, such as unequal numbers of observations or insufficient degrees of freedom, introduce artificial barriers that are not based in the organic reality of the observations, or the context in which the data are collected. Fields wherein data collection cannot occur in rigid circumstances may be especially stifled by the adoption of assumption-laden data analysis methods.

Indeed, OPA is extremely flexible in part because it eschews many of the assumptions traditionally expected in data analysis due to the monopolistic omnipresence of NHST. Dinges et al. (2013) outline four clear differences in assumptions between OOM vs NHST.

1. OPA does not make assumptions regarding *continuity*. While parametric NHST's assumption of continuity is more frequently violated by psychometric measurement, comparative psychology does use dependent variables with discrete quantities (e.g., response counts) that should not undergo multiplicative properties like means (or medians with equal *N*s). The frequent violation of the continuity assumption is troubling because there is no corrective action to perform when Hölder's axioms are not met. When parametric NHST is used to assess qualitative data, the actual transformations of the data violate the mathematical properties of the observations (e.g., additive and multiplicative). Calculating a mean for a Likert scale, or any qualitative data, is not mathematically permissible as fundamental properties about the observations have not been met, and many of these aggregates (e.g., standard deviation, mean) that are critical to calculate a probability statistic are functionally meaningless because these aggregates cannot possibly exist in reality. The eschewing of the continuity assumption makes the Ordinal Analysis versatile and capable of analyzing all forms of quantitative data. Measures of both time (continuous) and responses (discrete) can be observed with the same test, using the same calcuations, and providing the same values (PCC and *c*-value). Treating data as discrete quantities aligns with how observations are generally recorded (viz., counting); continuous data are rarely recorded continuously. By treating observations in an ordinal manner, frequencies can be compared in the same manner as numerical relations. OPA does not assume the collected data have been measured, in the strictest sense, and thus allows for qualitative and quantitative data analyses.

2. OPA does not make assumptions regarding *homogeneity* (or sphericity). While parametric NHST is dependent on calculating aggregates such as means, variances, standard deviations, and sums of squares, OOM never uses an aggregate for data analysis purposes. Comparative psychologists will likely encounter homogeneity concerns when making comparisons between species; variability in discrimination capabilities in honey bees compared to rats or pigeons shouldn't prevent direct species comparisons. It is reasonable to expect species' responding will differ in different ways, and comparative psychologists need a data analysis tool that allows direct comparisons of these types of data.

3. OPA does not compare observations to a hypothetical distribution, so topics associated with *normality* are all eschewed. OPA does not use alpha-levels, and thus does not have concerns around power or degrees of freedom. By using randomizations to generate distributions, OPA empowers researchers to perform data analyses on smaller subject sizes. Given comparative psychology generally assesses smaller sample sizes compared other sub-fields within psychology, this feature of OPA is especially relevant for animal researchers. However, the gains of side-stepping assumptions around normality allows researchers to analyze the same data in numerous ways without artificial limitations surrounding the number of allotted assessments that can be performed on a series of data. For this reason, OPA allows comparing the observed data to any number of ordinal predictions to determine which ordinal prediction best characterizes the data. OPA removes concerns related to retesting previously assessed data, such as when a new species' data can be compared to historical information in the literature. Additionally, assessing different aspects of the observed data (e.g., a post-reinforcement pause versus general inter-response times) doesn't lead to conceptual issues related to power or degrees of freedom.

4. OOM does not make assumptions regarding *dependency*. OOM uses the same mathematical process to assess dependent observations as it does to assess independent observations. This means longitudinal data could be analyzed alongside cross-sectional data. Independent and dependent *T*-Tests do not use the same exact methods of analyzing independent vs dependent data. The only difference between dependent data versus independent data assessments in OPA would be to perform combination assessments for independent assessments. Unlike a dependent *t*-test, no subtraction is performed in OPA.

OOM's adaptability allows for analyses of data collected from a wide variety of procedures, and OOM has successfully been used to analyze established and common assessments performed by comparative psychologists and radical behaviorists. OOM has been utilized to assess data collected from discrimination (Dinges et al., 2013), fixed interval (Craig et al., 2014, Craig & Abramson, 2015), reversal (Abramson, Craig, Varnon, & Wells, 2015), and fixed ratio (Place, Varnon, Craig, & Abramson, 2017) procedures. Within the comparative literature, OOM has been used to assess responding in honey bees (Dinges et al., 2013, Craig et al., 2014), horses (Craig, Varnon, Pollock, & Abramson, 2015), and rattlesnakes (Place et al., 2017). Observation Oriented Modeling was not designed with animal researchers specifically in mind, but its flexibility naturally appeals towards comparative psychology.

Examples of Ordinal Pattern Analysis in Comparative Psychology

Prior to the development of OPA within the context of OOM, ordinal analyses had been recommended as a solution to effectively analyze individual data within the comparative literature (Gentry, Weiss, & Laties, 1983). Additionally, Thorngate and Carroll (1986) specifically recommended the use of an Ordinal Pattern Analysis, and have successfully published an alternative Ordinal Pattern Analysis (Thorngate & Edmonds, 2013) than the OPA within OOM that is described here. Thorngate's OPA and OOM's OPA are similar in their pairwise ordinal comparisons; Thorngate's Index of Fit is analogous to OOM's PCC value. However, there are two main differences between Thorngate's OPA and OOM's OPA. First, Thorngate and Ma (2016) indicate their OPA only performs pair-wise assessments to calculate their Index of Fit (like OOM's PCC value). However, OOM can also calculate a CPCC value to perform omnibus comparisons (e.g., $A < B < C$), so OOM is not limited to only performing pair-wise assessments. Second, Thorngate and Ma (2016) indicate a general disinterest in calculating a probability statistic, so their OPA does not have a process similar to OOM's randomizations and subsequent comparisons of the randomized data to the ordinal prediction. At their core, these different OPA methods are very similar. While the use of Ordinal Analyses is not a novel idea within comparative psychology and psychology in general, OOM's OPA was originally published as a method of analysis for comparative research to assess individual honey bee data. The following four honey bee investigations demonstrate OOM's OPA's flexibility across a variety of common comparative and behaviorist protocols.

OOM's OPA was first developed, described, and published to circumvent a repeated measure ANOVA's inability to properly assess the inter-session-interval (inter-visit-interval) between honey bees visiting an artificial flower and returning to the hive (Craig et al., 2012). In the experiment, Craig et al. (2012) prevented honey bees from returning to the hive for zero, five, or ten minutes by trapping the subject in the artificial flower (post-reinforcement delay). The honey bee data contained extreme outlier observations (intervals frequently ranged between five to ten minutes, but hour-long intervals were observed and terminated a subject's session), insufficient degrees of freedom (due to subject size and number of observations despite $N = 10$ per group), and 'missing' data (subjects were free-flying and could cease returning to the artificial flower). Based on the four conditions, five groups, and the goal of collecting twenty trials' worth of data for each subject, a twenty order prediction was generated under the hypothesis that subjects would fly back to the flower at increasingly shorter intervals if never trapped, but would fly back to the flower at increasingly longer intervals if trapped. Craig et al. (2012) observed groups and individuals with more extreme post-reinforcement intervals better fit the twenty order prediction, so trapping subjects for a longer duration resulted in longer inter-visit-intervals. While many individuals fit this pattern, a handful of individual subjects deviated from these general trends. Further descriptions and analyses of these data (along with a comparison between OPA and NHST) appears in Grice, et al. (2015).

Dinges et al. (2013) investigated aversive discrimination learning sex-differences in honey bees and was the first to generalize the comparative capabilities of OPA. Dinges et al. (2013) assessed aversive learning in a shuttle-box that could deliver shock on either half of the apparatus. In three separate experiments, OPA was utilized to assess behavior within trials (to assess individual learning), and between groups (to compare: master vs yoke, worker vs drone, and color discrimination of yellow versus blue). Indirect comparisons of PCC values from different ordinal assessments revealed stark individual differences within conditions and sexes. Overall, masters better matched the ordinal predictions than yokes, worker subjects tended to better match the ordinal predictions than drones, and both workers and drones tended to more accurately discriminate when shock was paired with the color blue rather than yellow. While Dinges et al. (2013) measured continuous temporal variables (e.g., response frequency, and latency to respond), several of the observations were partitioned into bins in order to perform comparisons within a single trial. The method of separating a single trial into bins is common within comparative psychology, but the practice loses the granularity of continuous responding and arguably requires discrete analysis and may not meet the assumptions of continuity. Moreover, responses are discrete observations that were then binned to create an arbitrary response rate; this transformation is frequently performed in comparative analyses, but this practice is questionable. For these reasons, the use of NHST to assess the data reported in Dinges et al. (2013) via a repeated measures ANOVA would require violations of critical assumptions. Practically, the most disruptive consideration was if the response frequency would be considered discrete or continuous. In order to demonstrate the impact of a potentially incorrect decision to treat discrete data as continuous in NHST, Dinges et al. (2013) also inappropriately analyzed the data with both Freedmen's assessments and repeated measures ANOVAs and treated the data as if they were continuous. Indeed, treating the data as being continuous resulted in significant *p*-values whereas the same data were not significantly different when considered discrete. Given the division of responses into equal bins creates constant denominators, the data are not fundamentally different, so the fact that separate NHST assessments of the same data can be used to draw different conclusions is worrisome. Moreover, due to violated sphericity assumptions, both a Greenhouse–Geisser correction and Huynh–Feldt correction were performed as a demonstration of the differences in correction processes, and Dinges et al. (2013) reported some cases wherein the latter was significant when the former was not. This inconsistency is also troubling. If a researcher were to select the wrong correction method, incorrect conclusions may be drawn, and clear guidance on the proper usage of a Greenhouse–Geisser correction versus Huynh–Feldt correction is not established. These types of complications that are more common in behavioral data can be by-passed with OPA.

Craig, Varnon, Sokolowski, Abramson, and Wells (2014) further established the generalizability of OPA by extending the number of independent group comparisons from two orders (analogous to an independent *t*-test) to three orders (analogous to a one-way ANOVA). This generalization was needed in order to compare the response rates of three different groups of honey bees' response levels during an extinction contingency. Similar to Craig et al. (2012), use of NHST by Craig et al. (2014) would have provided highly qualified results because of unequal numbers of observations associated with voluntary attrition (honey bees were free-flying). Additionally, homogeneity assumption violations, normalcy assumption violations, and an insufficient degrees of freedom would have prevented sufficient analyses of the data. Craig et al. (2014) exposed honey bee responding to fixed interval schedules of reinforcement using an artificial flower, and analyzed three of the more popular measures of temporal control (i.e., binned response rates, post-reinforcement pauses, cumulative curves). The three-order extinction ordinal prediction was: FI 0-sec < FI 15-sec < FI 30-sec. The pair-wise analyses indicated the data matched this ordinal prediction fairly well (PCC = 0.67, *c*-value = .001), but the three-way ordinal prediction was far less impressive despite the failure of all 1,000 randomizations to be better characterized by the ordinal prediction than the observed data (CPCC = 0.34, *c*-value = .001). While insightful, additional pair-wise analyses were required to explain the distinction between the pair-wise ordinal comparisons versus the complete three-order comparison; a direct pair-wise comparison between the two experimental groups (FI 15-sec < FI 30-sec) revealed no clear difference in responding in an extinction contingency between these groups of subjects. Craig and Abramson (2015) performed a more detailed level of analysis of several measures of temporal control in honey bees (i.e., cumulative curves, response bin levels, quarter lives, IRTs, response duration, and trial duration). None of these measures displayed clear evidence of individual subject responding coming under temporal control, but pooling groups' individuals' responses did manifest evidence of temporal control. OPA empowers researchers to add these types of clarifying statements to group analyses; if individual subjects do not fit a researchers' model (e.g., an ordinal prediction), conclusions based solely on group analyses may be an analytical artifact.

Abramson et al. (2015) measured binomial response data (proboscis extension, or no proboscis extension) in honey bees across multiple sessions in a reversal protocol, and assessed honey bee reversal behavior under varying doses of ethanol. Given the observed data were binomial, dependent, and had multicollinearity and quasi-complete complications when comparing CS+, CS-, and US dependent variable, a logistical regression assessment was not ideal for the collected data. With a reversal design, OPA compared responding before and after the reversal and produced two orders of observations; with two orders of observations, a total of three ordinal predictions can be made (A > B, A < B, A = B). To thoroughly investigate the effect of ethanol on reversal learning, 510 ordinal comparisons were performed across three experiments using these three ordinal predictions. Given the reversal's design, many of the ordinal predictions comparing the CS+ responding or the CS- responding aligned with, or countered, the experimental hypothesis for some assessments. CS+ and CS- between- and within-group analyses were both performed, individuals were assessed on their own and were pooled into appropriate groups, and the comparisons combined to reveal a clear trend in CS+, CS-, and US responding. Three main-effects were assessed: reversal (control or experimental), ethanol dose (0%, 2.5%, 5%, 10%, and 20%), and ethanol administration (administered prior to training, or after training). Unsurprisingly, OPA revealed CS+ responding decreased and CS- responding increased after a reversal, and US responding did not differ between control subjects versus subjects undergoing a reversal. OPA also revealed higher doses of ethanol decreased CS+ and US responding, but did not seem to impact CS- responding. After observing these main-effects, Abramson et al. (2015) further solidified the generalizability of OPA by performing two notable interaction assessments. Using OPA, a reversal-dose interaction was observed; at higher doses, CS+ and CS- responding were more resistant to the reversal contingency change whereas the responding for subjects in the lower dosage groups displayed stronger evidence of reversal learning. Beyond this two-variable interaction, a reversal-dose-administration interaction was observed for CS- responding; administering higher doses of ethanol just prior to the reversal contingency produced higher CS- responding while administering the same doses of ethanol prior to the original discrimination training produced lower CS- responding. In this sense, Abramson et al. (2015) refined the PCC comparison process to approximate a factorial ANOVA analysis.

OPA's flexibility and ability to analyze a wide-variety of data was pioneered using honey bee data. Since establishing OPA analysis methods in honey bees, OPA has since been used to assess data from horses (Craig, Varnon, Pollock, & Abramson, 2015), humans (Jaeger, Cox, Craig, & Grice, 2016; Jordan & Thomas, 2017), and rattlesnakes, (Place et al., 2017). However, these investigations not only generalized the types of species data to have been assessed with OPA, but further extended the types of procedures to have been assessed with OPA. Further examples of OPA's generalizability exemplify its potential utility for comparative researchers.

Craig et al. (2015) employed OPA to describe horse responding under fixed interval and peak procedure contingencies, and observed clear trends in horse responding coming under temporal control. Craig et al. (2015) administered three baseline sessions for all subjects before switching to either an FI 60-sec, FI 90-sec, or FI 180-sec contingency, and as the final contingency, subjects were exposed to the peak procedure. Similar to the previous honey bee fixed interval assessments, Craig et al. (2015) assessed multiple measures of temporal control including response levels via bins, quarter life, latency to first response (post-reinforcement pause), break point (when responding shifts from low levels to higher levels), and inter-response time. These analyses in OPA revealed horse responding under fixed interval contingencies was better categorized as 'break-and-run' rather than 'scalloped', and longer fixed intervals produced clearer evidence of temporally controlled responding. To analyze the peak procedure data, each trial was divided in half, and an ordinal prediction was made for each half of the trial: responding was expected to monotonically increase for the first half of the trial, and monotonically decrease for the second half of the trial. All eleven subjects' responding monotonically increased throughout the first half of the trial, and seven of the eleven subjects' responding monotonically decreased throughout the second half of the trial. In addition to dividing the peak procedure trial in half, Craig et al. (2015) also assessed the entire peak procedure trials under the prediction responding would increase until the trial was half-way complete, and then decrease for the remainder of the trial. Four of the eleven subjects' responding fit the full prediction, so this indicates responding did 'peak' approximately half-way through the peak procedure trial for these subjects.

In a truly comparative analysis, Craig (2015) performed extensive indirect comparisons between honey bee and horse responding on FI scheduled of reinforcement via the usage of CPCC values and found horse responding came under stronger temporal control than honey bee responding via this method. Four bin response frequency ordinal assessments revealed horse responding produced higher CPCC values than honey bee responding on break-and-run ordinal predictions (e.g., $1 = 2 < 3 < 4$). Additionally, between-schedule comparisons of quarter life, index of curvature, and latency to first response reveled increasing the duration of a fixed interval schedule increased these measures of temporal control, and that horses produced higher PCC values of these assessments than honey bees. Moreover, individual subject analyses displayed higher diversity in performance in honey bees while horse responding was comparatively more uniform. Additionally, horses generally produced monotonically decreasing inter-response times within an interval while honey bee responding produced higher PCC values when comparing the data to a monotonically increase prediction (i.e., honey bees took longer to respond as the fixed interval continued while horses responded increasingly rapidly as the interval continued). OPA allows comparative researchers to indirectly compare species' performances across a variety of measures due to the simplicity of the PCC and CPCC values. These types of assessments in NHST would not be possible.

Place et al. (2017) collected response rate data for rattlesnake responding in varying fixed ratio schedule of reinforcement contingencies, and compared responding across conditions via the use of combinations. Rather than simply performing a three-way comparison like Craig et al. (2014), Place et al. (2017) compared data in shaping, CRF, FR1, FR2, FR3, and extinction conditions. Because of the number of conditions, Place et al. (2017) assessed all six of these combinations in a single ordinal assessment, but also performed more narrow comparisons (e.g. FR1 < FR2 < FR3, Shaping < FR1 < FR2). Place et al. (2017) also performed within-condition assessments and expected response rates would monotonically increase across shaping sessions, but monotonically decrease across extinction conditions. For the first time since OOM's inception, Place et al. (2017) deviated from the analysis of individual data, and instead assessed trial aggregates for individual subjects (i.e., rather than assessing responses via bins, the total number of responses in a session were pooled into appropriate conditions, and conditions were then compared). Additionally, the IRT analyses detailed in Place et al. (2017) assessed trial aggregates, and compared the usage of means or medians in OPA;

clear differences in OPA's results were observed when comparing median versus mean ordinal predictions during the extinction condition. This difference in aggregate-based comparisons serves as a reminder of the potential pitfalls associated with aggregate-based data analysis methods; which measure of central tendency is most appropriate when not relying on individual data analyses? While these types of questions encourage the use of individual analyses tools, Place et al. (2017) effectively used an individual data analysis tool to assess measures of central tendency in a given trial. With OPA, researchers are able to assess aggregates (e.g., trial average IRTs) as well as the observed individual data (individual IRTs with a trial), so researchers are certainly not limited to only performing individual analyses of raw data. So long as the measure is quantitative, appropriate aggregates are calculated, and the interpreter of the data analysis recognizes that artifacts and abstractions may remove the analyst from the real observations, there is nothing inherently preventing a researcher from using OPA to assess data summaries. Of course, this aggregate usage is not how the tool was intended to be used, but OPA certainly does not prevent a researcher from performing this type of assessment. Individual observations, as well as summaries of these observations, can be analyzed with OPA.

Ultimately, comparative researchers need to be able to draw comparisons between animal and human behavior. While comparative psychologists may be more cautious about the usage of self-reports, Jaeger et al. (2016) used OPA to assess muscle-twitch differences between self-reported extraverts, introverts, and ambiverts at varying decibel levels (50 dB, 60 dB, 70 dB, 80 dB, 90 dB, and 100 dB). In doing so, Jaeger et al. (2016) generalized the types of data to have been analyzed by OPA; for the first time, physiological data (rather than only behavioral) data were assessed. Response frequency, response amplitude, and muscle tension were assessed under the prediction introverts would produce higher metrics compared to extraverts, and ambiverts would produce middling metrics (i.e., introverts > ambiverts, introverts > extraverts, ambiverts > extraverts). From the pair-wise predictions, ambiverts did not produce response frequency data that differed from extravert or introvert data, but only comparing introverts against extraverts produced a far better match to the ordinal predictions. Via indirect comparisons of PCC values, Jaeger et al. (2016) also observed louder stimuli revealed starker differences between self-reported personality types, and introverts were more likely to respond at higher frequencies and amplitudes than extraverts.

Comparative psychology is frequently type-cast as animal research, but this caricature of comparative psychologists is narrow and dismisses the common interests and methods comparative psychology shares with other psychological sub-fields. For example, infant developmental psychologists must also contend with a language barrier, and thus are more inclined towards physiological data and behavioral scoring rather than self-reports. Andrew (1963) hypothesized facial expressions evolved in primates because these behaviors could increase social communication, and later research (Izard, 1994) into innate infant facial behaviors help support these comparative and evolutionary hypotheses. In a similar vein, Jordan and Thomas (2017) used OPA to analyze the duration and intensity of contagious human infant facial affect as recorded on an *AFFEX* scale (see Izard, Dougherty, & Hembree, 1983) and extended the generality of OPA to include analyses of qualitative, categorical data. The *AFFEX* scale involves observing three regions of a participant's face and then rating intensity and duration of movement on a 5-point Likert scale. Rather than employ Kruskal–Wallis and Mann–Whitney U non-parametric assessments, OPA was used to perform pairwise and omnibus ordinal comparisons between three stimulus conditions (audio, audio-visual, control) and two age groups (5 months and 10 months). Jordan and Thomas (2017) assessed changes in affect across these conditions and within subjects and found the audio and audio-visual stimulus conditions produced higher positive affect compared to the control condition, but did not observe a clear difference between the audio and audio-visual conditions; in contrast, negative affect differences were not clearly observed between conditions. Jordan and Thomas (2017) also compared responding in infants aged 5 months compared to 10 months with the expectation older infants would have higher affect responding, but did not observe a clear age difference in negative and positive affective responding for these pair-wise ordinal assessments when pooling appropriate conditions or ages. In addition to behavioral and physiological data, OPA is a clear alternative for researchers collecting (or assigning) Likert scales as a form of qualitative data collection.

In perhaps its widest deviation from comparative psychological methods, OPA has been used to analyze historical data from the 15th and 16th centuries to understand how slave population frequencies in the Crimean Khanate varied across years based on the Ottoman Empire's economic fluctuations (Broyes, 2014). For these data, Broyes (2014) collected archival records of slave raids, and thus estimations of the number of slaves from the Crimean Khanate for a given year. To test the hypothesis that increases in economic prosperity were associated with increases of slave frequencies, Broyes (2014) used bureaucratically recorded economic data from the Ottoman Empire to create ordinal predictions in OPA. The Ottomon Empire saw general increases in economic prosperity up until approximately 1575 when Anatolia suffered great economic downturn, but saw general economic improvement thereafter and until the end of the 17th century. Broyes (2014) assessed the difference in slave frequencies before and after 1575 and found approximately 65% of the reported slave frequencies after 1575 were greater than frequencies prior to 1575, and a thousand randomizations of the collected data could not produce a single occurrence that better matched the ordinal prediction than the observed data. While these data and hypothesis may not be of specific interest to comparative researchers, this type of investigation could be helpful for population ecologists and evolutionary psychologists and serves as a stark example of the flexibility of OPA. Moreover, Broyes (2014) is an excellent example of how researchers can generate ordinal predictions based on hypotheses and established theories from a variety of fields and interests.

Discussion

The above use of OPA has allowed for comparative, human, and historical researchers to perform statistical analyses without the use of the following different NHST assessments:

- Dependent/Independent *T*-Tests / Chi-squares (Dinges et al., 2013)
- One-Way ANOVA (Place et al., 2017)
- Repeated Measures ANOVA / Freedman's (Craig et al., 2012)
- Factorial ANOVA / Logistical Regression (Abramson et al., 2015)
- Kruskal–Wallis / Mann–Whitney U (Jordan & Thomas, 2017)

The above comparison between NHST and OPA is intended for analogical purposes; in actuality, OPA offers far more to comparative researchers than simply being a mere substitute for NHST because of three major differences between the methods.

1. Individual vs Aggregate Analyses

OPA, and OOM in general, does not depend on aggregate analyses like NHST. Instead, OOM assesses the actual observations as they occurred in reality without performing any transformations, or relying on summaries of the observations. If only the aggregate behaviors are compared, researchers fail to ask a critical follow-up question: how well do the individuals compare? Moreover, analyzing the observed data as they were collected (in an individual, discrete manner) reduces the requirements and assumptions of the data to be analyzed. Functionally, this allows OPA to analyze all forms of measurement, including both traditional and the psychometrican's measurement. Nominal data frequencies, ordinal/discrete observations, as well as discrete and continuous measures can all be analyzed in the same manner. In this sense, OPA makes no assumptions that attributes are quantitative; instead, OPA treats no attributes as being quantitative (i.e., aligns with the quantity objection). If trained under the popular measurability thesis (i.e., some attributes are measureable), siding with the quantity objection may be uncomfortable, but Michell (1999) articulates the measurability thesis is largely based in the embedded quantitative imperative and presumption that quantitative data are better than qualitative data.

OPA is conservative in that the method treats measured quantitative data (either discrete, or continuous) as ordinal data. In doing so, the assessment eschews many assumptions of parametric testing and increases its generalizability, but does render a researcher's analyses as qualitative. If entrenched in the positivism of the quantitative imperative, qualitative analyses may seem to have less merit. However, the quantitative imperative has likely contributed to much of the statistical misuse in psychology. Critically evaluating the relevancy of the perhaps antiquated quantitative imperative (Michell, 2003), especially when quantitate observations may not be continuous at a quantum and micro level (Craig, 2016), may serve comparative psychology well. OPA is more robust, makes fewer assumptions, and provides clearer output to better allow a researcher to perform abduction. Perhaps OPA's gains of flexibility outweigh the loss of fidelity in treating continuous quantitative measures as ordinal frequencies. Ultimately, OPA's focus on the individual observations rather than transformations of these observations may be more appropriate for a sub-field with a historical sensitivity towards extrapolating towards unobservable constructs, like an aggregate.

2. Sample Observations vs Population Parameters

The most critical difference between OOM and NHST is that OOM does not attempt to estimate a population parameter. This means OOM and NHST ask fundamentally different questions and provide different output. NHST asks a basic question: does a difference exist? Indeed, Fisher (1955, 1956) indicated NHST should be used for initial testing when little is known about the phenomena; NHST does not get an analyst very far because of the tendency to treat null as nil. The method of posting an alternative to the null hypothesis frequently introduces concerns about the direction of an implied difference when the null is rejected, and the alternative is never directly tested. Because one alternative is all that is frequently offered (rather than divide an alpha level), a researcher may incorrectly make an assumption about the direction of this difference when simply observing a significant *p*-value (i.e., make a type III error). OPA asks a different question: how well do the data conform to an ordinal prediction? Rather than only asking if a difference exists like NHST, OPA asks the specific direction, or directions, of observed differences.

The next logical question would then be: what is the magnitude of the difference for the actual observations as they were collected? NHST cannot answer this question without abstracting to a population parameter and without calculating an aggregate, nor can OPA if used strictly within the framework of OOM due to the need to calculate an aggregate (e.g., sum of differences). After performing analyses in OPA to identify the direction of a difference, traditional quantitative measures could then undergo subtraction to reveal the magnitude of the difference, but this would require aggregate comparisons (via additive transformations) and would counter the metaphysics of OOM by losing focus on the actual observations themselves.

Additionally, by not extrapolating to estimating a population and not assessing a null hypothesis of nil population differences, Type I and Type II errors are not relevant with OPA. There is no possibility of incorrectly rejecting, or failing to reject, a null hypothesis of nil differences in a population parameter. Hence, the only relevant error would be left to a researcher drawing a conclusion not supported by the PCC value, but this would be a failure of abduction, not of OPA. Ultimately, OPA's focus on individual subjects rather than estimating a population parameter may be more appropriate for a sub-field with relatively small sample sizes.

3. Simplicity vs Complexity

Of greatest practical importance: OPA offers simple and transparent output that can be clearly interpreted on a standard (0-100 for the PCC value, and 0-1 for the *c*-value). Analysis tools must provide researchers with the ability to draw clear conclusions and make abductive comparisons without requiring qualifying statements due to violated assumptions, the appropriateness of a particular assessment, and a complete dependence on the aggregate rather than the object of interest – the individual. The simplicity of OOM creates its transparency and its flexibility. Rather than needing a decision tree to determine the appropriate form of assessment to use, OPA assesses a wide variety of data in the same manner.

In our experience, newer students of statistics struggle with understanding the definition of *p*-values, and the rampant implementation of NHST. This struggle is not a deficit at these newer students' learning abilities, or the learning-curve of introductory statistics courses, but speaks to the inherent confusion imbedded into NHST. NHST requires years of training because its methods are so counter-intuitive and seemingly complex. Simplicity and transparency in methods should be celebrated, but psychology leveraged overly-complex methods, appeared as a quantitative science, and has largely ignored criticism of its quantitative analyses (Michell, 2008). Ultimately, OPA's flexibility may be more appropriate for a field that assesses continuous and discrete quantities along with qualitative observations.

Conclusion

While the above examples of OPA's wide utility serve as clear evidence of why OPA is a viable alternative to NHST, the prevailing weakness of OPA, and OOM in general, is psychology's hesitancy to consider alternative data analyses compared to NHST. This criticism is an appeal to popularity, and is not a substantive weakness of the data analysis method itself. However, OPA does have a handful of identified minor weaknesses. The most obvious is the treatment of truly quantitative data as ordinal data. Because only ordinal comparisons are made, OPA can be extremely sensitive. For example, OPA does not adjust for practically identical data differences (e.g., a comparison of 598.21 versus 598.209). OPA has a threshold adjustment feature (Classification Imprecision value) to contend with this high-degree of sensitivity. Using this feature, researchers can 'pad' the observed values' analyses to be less sensitive by a fixed value (e.g., an analyst could set this threshold value to '1.00' to require an observed ordinal difference be at least '1.00' for the data to be considered to substantially different). This threshold adjustment feature has not yet been utilized in OPA due to requirements of an arbitrary threshold value being selected by the analyst, but this threshold adjustment feature can be used to reduce the sensitivity of OPA's analyses.

Computational space can be a practical limitation of the Ordinal Analysis, like all individual data analyses. However, OPA's use of combinations can result in hundreds of millions of ordinal comparisons if enough observations are collected. This is not especially impressive, but once the data are randomized thousands of times, billions of comparisons may actually be made via OPA to generate the *c*-value. In this sense, OPA may discourage the comparison of very large sample-sizes or observations in a single ordinal pattern assessment, or may just require usage of the PCC value rather than a *c*-value in these types of circumstances. Perhaps the limits of computational memory serve as a practical limitation to indicate the researcher may be more interested in aggregate or populations than assessing individuals; for these types of researchers, OPA's *c*-value may not be the most appropriate alternative at a fundamental level (though the PCC value may still be a preferable effect size). Outside of its conservative treatment of continuous observations as orders and modern computer memory limitations, OPA's flexibility is limited to its users' creativity. As long as the user can articulate ordinal hypotheses to describe a phenomenon (or construct), OOM's Ordinal Pattern Analysis can analyze the provided available data.

Comparative psychology is positioned to be able to appreciate the need to shift use away from NHST to an option that may more suitable. Comparative psychology's established interests in individual observations, individual subjects, and the use of diverse forms of measurement does not align with other psychology sub-fields – why then, should comparative psychology's data analysis methods? The continued adoption of NHST within comparative psychology simply because these forms of assessments are used in other more mainstream sub-fields may stifle the growth of comparative psychology. Comparative psychology needs a more flexible data analysis option that allows for a wide variety of direct and indirect comparisons and produces standard and easily interpretable results. OOM's Ordinal Pattern Analysis is a viable contender as a preferred analysis tool for a sub-field with an established sensitivity to continuity and quantitative concerns, a history of observing individual subjects, a need for flexible assessments, and a suspended willingness to extrapolate to unobservable constructs such as a population parameter, or aggregate.

References

Abramson, C. I. (2015). A crisis in comparative psychology: Where have all the undergraduates gone? Additional comments. *Innovative Teaching*, *4*, 7.

Abramson, C. I., Craig, D. P. A., Varnon, C. A., & Wells, H. (2015). The effect of ethanol on reversal learning in honey bees (*Apis mellifera anatolica*): Response inhibition in a social insect model. *Alcohol*, *49*, 245–258.

Andrew, R. J. (1963). The origin and evolution of the calls and facial expressions of the primates. *Behavior*, *20*, 1–109.

Bakan, D. (1967). *On method: Toward a reconstruction of psychological investigation*. San Francisco, CA: Jossey-Bass.

Branch, M. N., & Gollub, L. R. (1974). A detailed analysis of the effects of d-amphetamine on behavior under fixed-interval schedules. *Journal of the Experimental Analysis of Behavior*, *21*, 519–539.

Broyes, S. C. (2014). *Slavery and the Ottoman-Crimean khanate connection* (Master's Thesis). Retrieved from: https://hdl.handle.net/11244/14742

Beghetto, R.A. (2014). Toward avoiding an empirical march to nowhere. *Psychology of Aesthetics, Creativity, and the Arts*, *8*, 18–20.

Cohen, J. (1994). The earth is round ($p < .05$). *American Psychologist*, *49*, 997–1003.

Craig, D. P. A (2015). *An assessment of multiple measures of honey bee (Apis mellifera ligustica) and horse (Equus ferus caballus) responding on fixed interval schedules: An individual versus aggregate analysis* (Doctoral dissertation). Retrieved from: https://hdl.handle.net/11244/33403

Craig, D. P. A. (2016). Shedding the quantitative imperative. *Social Behavior Research and Practice*, *1*, 10–12.

Craig, D. P. A., & Abramson C. I. (2015). A need for individual data analyses for assessments of temporal control: Invertebrate fixed interval performance. *International Journal of Comparative Psychology - Special Issue on Timing and Time Perception*, *28*, 1–39.

Craig, D. P. A., Grice, J. W., Varnon, C. A., Gibson, B., Sokolowski, M. B. C., & Abramson, C. I. (2012). Social reinforcement delays in free-flying honey bees (*Apis mellifera L.*). *PLoS One, 7*, e46729.

Craig, D. P. A., Varnon, C. A., Pollock, K. L., & Abramson, C. I. (2015). An assessment of horse (*Equus ferus caballus*) responding on fixed interval schedules of reinforcement: An individual analysis. *Behavioural Processes, 120*, 1–13.

Craig, D. P. A., Varnon, C. A., Sokolowski, M. B. C., Abramson, C. I., & Wells, H. (2014). An assessment of fixed interval timing in free-flying honey bees (*Apis mellifera ligustica*): An analysis of individual performance. *PLoS One, 9*, e101262.

Dews, P. B. (1978). Studies on responding under fixed-interval schedules of reinforcement: II. The scalloped pattern of the cumulative record. *Journal of the Experimental Analysis of Behavior*, *29*, 67–75.

Dinges, C. W., Avalos, A., Abramson, C. I., Craig, D. P. A., Austin, Z. M., Varnon, C. A., ... Wells, H. (2013). Aversive conditioning in honey bees (*Apis mellifera anatolica*): A comparison of drones and workers. *The Journal of Experimental Biology, 216*, 4124–4134.

Doyen, S., Klein, O., Pichon, C.-L., Cleeremans, A. (2012). Behavioral priming: It's all in the mind, but whose mind? *PLoS ONE*, *7,* e29081.

Ferguson, A., Myers, C. S., Bartlett, R. J., Banister, H., Bartlett, F. C., Brown W., ... Tucker, W.S. (1940). Quantitative estimates of sensory events: Final report of the committee appointed to consider and report upon the possibility of quantitative estimates of sensory events. *Advancement of Science*, *1*, 331–349.

Ferster, C. B., & Skinner, B. F. (1957). *Schedules of reinforcement.* New York, NY: Appleton-Century-Crofts.

Fisher, R.A. (1955). Statistical methods and scientific induction. *Journal of the Royal Statistical Society (B)*, *17*, 69–77.

Fisher, R.A. (1956). *Statistical Methods and Scientific Inference*. Edinburgh, Scotland: Oliver & Boyd.

Gentry, G. D., Weiss, B., & Laties, V. G. (1983). The microanalysis of fixed-interval responding. *Journal of the Experimental Analysis of Behavior*, 39, 327–343.

Gigerenzer, G., (2004). Mindless statistics. *The Journal of Socio-Economics*, *33*, 587–606.

Gigerenzer, G., & Marewski, J. N., (2015). Surrogate Science: the idol of a universal method for scientific inference. *Journal of Management*, *41*, 421–440.

Grice, J. W. (2011). *Observation oriented modeling: Analysis of cause in the behavioral sciences*. San Diego, CA: Elsevier.

Grice, J. W., Craig, D. P. A., & Abramson, C. I. (2015). A simple and transparent alternative to Repeated Measures ANOVA. *SAGE Open*, *5*, 1–13.

Helmholtz, H. Von (1887). Numbering and measuring from an epistemological viewpoint. In P. Hertz, & M. Schlick (Eds.), *Hermann von Helmhotlz: Epistemological writings* (pp. 72–114). Dordrecht, Holland: Reidel.

Humphry, S. (2013). Understanding measurement in light of its origins. *Frontiers in Psychology*, *4*, 113.

Izard, C. E. (1994). Innate and universal facial expressions: Evidence from developmental and cross-cultural research. *Psychological Bulletin*, *115*, 288–299.

Izard, C., Dougherty, L., & Hembree, E. (1983). *A system for identifying affect expressions by holistic judgments (Affex)*. Newark, DE: Instructional Resources Center, University of Delaware.

Jaeger, K. M., Cox, A. H., Craig, D. P. A., & Grice, J. W. (2016). Auditory startle response predicts introversion: An individual analysis. *Modern Psychological Journal, 23*, 67–78.

John, L. K., Loewenstein, G., & Prelec, D. (2012). Measuring the prevalence of questionable research practices with incentives for truth telling. *Psychological Science*, *23*, 524–532,

Jordan, E. M., & Thomas, D. G. (2017). Contagious positive affective responses to laughter in infancy. *Archives of Psychology*, *1*, 1–21.

Laurent, E., & Lejeune, H. (1985). Temporal regulation of behavior in a fresh water turtle, Pseudemys scripta elegans (Wied). *Behavioural Processes*, *10*, 159–160.

Lejeune, H., & Richelle, M. (1982). Fixed-interval performance in turtle doves: A comparison with pigeons and rats. *Behaviour Analysis Letters*, *2*, 87–95.

Mace, C., & Kratochwill, T. (1986). The individual subject in behavioral analysis research. In J. Valsiner (Ed.), *The individual subject and scientific psychology* (pp. 153–180). New York, NY: Plenum.

Manly, B. F. (2006). *Randomization, bootstrap and Monte Carlo methods in biology* (3rd ed.). New York, NY: Chapman and Hall/CRC.

Meehl, P. E. (1978). Theoretical risks and tabular asterisks: Sir Karl, Sir Ronald, and the slow progress of soft psychology. *Journal of Consulting and Clinical Psychology*, *46*, 806–834

Michell, J. (1994). Measuring dimensions of belief by unidimensional unfolding. *Journal of Mathematical Psychology*, *38*, 244–273.

Michell, J. (1997). Quantitative science and the definition of measurement in psychology. *British Journal of Psychology*, *88*, 355–383.

Michell, J. (1999). *Measurement in psychology: Critical history of a methodological concept*. Cambridge, England: Cambridge University Press.

Michell, J. (2003). The quantitative imperative, positivism, naïve realism and the place of qualitative methods in psychology. *Theory & Psychology*, *13*, 5–31.
Michell, J. (2008). Is psychometrics pathological science? *Measurement*, *6*, 7–24.
Michell, J. (2014). Numbers as quantitative relations and the traditional theory of measurement. *The British Journal for the Philosophy of Science*, *45*, 389–406.
Michell, J., & Ernst C. (1997). The axioms of quantity and the theory of measurement: Translated from Part I of Otto Hölder's German Text "Die Axiome der Quantität und die Lehre vom Mass". *Journal of Mathematical Psychology*, *40*, 235–252.
Nosek, B., et al. (2015). Estimating the reproducibility of psychological science. *Science*, *349*, aac4716.
Place, A. J., Varnon, C. V., Craig, D. P. A., & Abramson C. I. (2017). Exploratory investigations in operant thermoregulation in rattlesnakes (*Crotalus atrox*). In M. J. Dreslik, W. K. Hayes, S. J. Beaupre, & S. P. Mackessy (Eds.), *The biology of rattlesnakes II* (pp. 213–227). Rodeo, NM: ECO Herpetological Publishing and Distribution.
Schorske, C. E. (1997). The new rigorism in the human sciences 1940-1960. In T. Bender & C. E. Schorske (Eds.), *American academic culture in transformation: Fifty years, four disciplines* (pp. 309–329). Princeton, New Jersey: Princeton University Press.
Schneider, B. A. (1969). A two-state analysis of fixed-interval responding in the pigeon. *Journal of the Experimental Analysis of Behavior*, *12*, 677–687.
Skinner, B. F. (1956). A case history in scientific method. *American Psychologist*, *11*, 221–233.
Skinner, B. F. (1972). *Cumulative record*. New York, NY: Appleton-Century- Crofts.
Solovey, M. (2004). Riding natural scientists' coattails onto the endless frontier: The SSRC and the quest for scientific legitimacy. *Journal of the History of the Behavioral Sciences*, *40*, 393–422.
Spiezio, C., Leonardi, C., & Regaiolli, B. (2017). Assessing colour preference in Aldabra giant tortoises (*Geochelone gigantea*). *Behavioural Processes*, *145*, 60–64.
Stevens, S. S. (1946). On the theory of scales of measurement. *Science*, *103*, 677–680.
Stevens, S. S., & Davis, H. (1938). *Hearing: Its psychology and physiology*. New York,NY: Wiley.
Thorngate, W., & Carroll, B. (1986). Ordinal Pattern Analysis: A strategy for assessing hypotheses about individuals. In J. Valsiner (Ed.), *The individual subject and scientific psychology* (pp. 201–232). New York, NY: Plenum Press.
Thorngate, W., & Edmonds, B. (2013). Measuring simulation observation fit: An introduction to Ordinal Pattern Analysis. *Journal of Artificial Societies and Social Simulation*, *16*. Retrieved from http://jasss.soc.surrey.ac.uk/16/2/4.html.
Thorngate, W., & Ma, C. (2016). Wiggles and curves: The analysis of ordinal patterns. *Problemy Zarządzania*, *14*, 160–172.
Velleman, P. F., & Wilkinson, L. (1993). Nominal, ordinal, interval, and ratio typologies are misleading. *The American Statistician*, *47*, 65–72.
Whissell, C., Abramson, C. I., & Barber, K. R. (2013). The search for cognitive terminology: An analysis of comparative psychology journal titles. *Behavioural Sciences*, *3*, 133–142.
Woolston, C. (2015). Psychology journal bans P values. *Nature*, *519*, 9.
Zeiler, M. D., & Powell, D. G. (1994). Temporal control in fixed-interval schedules. *Journal of the Experimental Analysis of Behavior*, *61*, 1–9.

15

The Importance of Comparative Psychology in Equine-Assisted Activities and Therapies

Emily Kieson

Oklahoma State University, U.S.A.

Practitioners of Equine Assisted Activities and Therapies (EAAT) use these therapies to help individuals suffering from a wide range of physical and psychological disorders as an alternative practice in physical and psychotherapy. Although there is plenty of research to support the benefits of these therapies, there is little research in equine behavior in this context, specifically how equine behaviors can best be utilized to improve the health of the human component. Although much of EAAT uses horses in physical therapy, newer practices in EAAT focus on assisting individuals in building and improving interpersonal skills through practicing those skills with horses. To fully understand and develop this area of EAAT, researchers need to look at the behavioral patterns of horses, how they learn and adapt to changes in human emotions and behaviors, and how these behaviors correspond to bonding within equine-human interactions. To do this, scientists need to rely upon the principles of learning theory and behavioral sciences associated with comparative psychology. The scientific methods used in comparative psychology provide a strong foundation from which to research these areas of EAAT.

There is plenty of research to support the physical and psychological benefits of Equine Assisted Activities and Therapies (EAAT), but little research into equine behavioral psychology or how different types of interactions can benefit both horse and human. A number of EAAT methods and models have been designed to provide physical and psychological therapies to individuals with physical and developmental disabilities as well as those with varying degrees of psychological disorders (Kendall, Maujean, Pepping, & Wright, 2014). These models, however, are focused primarily on the outcome of therapeutic practices for humans and fail to explore the elements of equine-human interactions that facilitate this outcome (Kieson & Abramson, 2016). Furthermore, the historic use of negative reinforcement as the primary means of training horses for transportation and work ignores the possible consequences on the subsequent human-horse relationship (Bierke, Meinen, Wilkens, Leponiemi, & Hiney, 2013; Cooper, 2007; McLean & Christensen, 2017; Murphy & Arkins, 2007b). Despite efforts to incorporate more positive reinforcement techniques during horse training (Craig, Varnon, Pollock, & Abramson, 2015; Ninomiya, Mitsumasu, Aoyama, & Kusunose, 2007), limited knowledge exists about how the horses perceive these hypothetically more socially-rewarding contexts. As a result, EAAT models rely on knowledge and practices based on historical training methods which depend on negative reinforcement with limited knowledge as to how to interact with horses in ways that mimic social bonding for both species.

As horses transition from the role of work and transportation into therapy and companion animals, researchers need to develop new ways humans can interact with these animals that facilitate the EAAT goals of interspecies social bonding. Most developed countries no longer rely on horses as a primary means of transportation or as work animals which corresponds to an increasing trend for people to view their horses as companions (Keaveney, 2008). This new role in society facilitated the transition to using equines in therapy and created the need to develop the new methods of interaction. Despite this transition, however, individuals still rely on traditional horse training techniques based on negative reinforcement (McLean & Christensen, 2017). This dependence on old techniques is due to a lack of research in interspecies social bonding within the

Please send correspondence to Emily Kieson, Oklahoma State University, 116 N. Murray, OSU, Stillwater, OK 74078-3064, U.S.A. (Email: ekieson@okstate.edu)

horse-human dyad. For EAAT to achieve its goals of promoting trust, companionship, and interpersonal bonding through horsemanship, researchers need to study equine behavioral psychology in this context through the methods and concepts originating in comparative psychology.

Current State of EAAT

EAAT uses equine interactions as part of physical or psychological therapies for individuals suffering from a variety of disorders. Although riding is not always a component of EAAT, hippotherapy (the use of riding horses to produce bilateral rhythmic stimulation of the pelvis and back) can improve the health of various populations by reducing symptoms associated with muscular and skeletal disorders (Debuse, Gibb, & Chandler, 2009; Lechner, Kakebeeke, Hegemann, & Baumberger, 2007; Shurtleff, Standeven, & Engsberg, 2009). Similarly, mechanical versions of horses are associated with improved physical strength for elderly patients (De Araújo et al., 2013). Some popular models in EAAT include non-riding elements designed to provide psychological benefit to the client by focusing on behavioral interactions between human and horse (Kieson & Abramson, 2016; Latella & Abrams, 2015). These types of interactions have been shown to improve the mental health of individuals with autism, whether clients worked with the horse on the ground (Hameury et al., 2010) or while riding (Gabriels et al., 2012; Jenkins & Digennaro Reed, 2013). Additionally, EAAT has been shown to lower basal cortisol levels in young adults (Pendry, Smith, & Roeter, 2014). The physical benefits of EAAT and hippotherapy are well researched as are the psychological benefits to the participants. The actual behavioral interactions of the horse and the resulting welfare, however, are less understood.

In the context of EAAT, equine behavior is often used to convey meaning to the client or allow them to practice behavior, but very little attention is paid to the psychology of the horse. For example, horses in EAAT are used as a means to practice empathy, initiate conversation with the therapist, or develop compassion in the client (Kieson & Abramson, 2016). Since little little attention is paid to equine behavioral psychology, it is not uncommon for practitioners of EAAT to report wide variations in their interpretations of equine behavior. This misunderstanding of equine behavior and the appropriate learning theory application may be part of the reason why researchers have found that riding horses in therapeutic programs can often result in increased stress for the horse (Fazio, Medica, Cravana, & Ferlazzo, 2013). Furthermore, although most quantitative studies find similar results regarding benefits to clients, qualitative studies that focus on equine-human interactions often contradict one another with regards to interpreting equine behavior in the horse-human interaction (Pauw, 2000). For example, a unique three-year study in Kansas using 26 adolescents with moderate to severe behavioral disorders found little change in empathetic capabilities, self-esteem, or emotional control (Ewing, MacDonald, Taylor, & Bowers, 2007). Variations in individual interviews and differences in interpretations of equine behavior, however, suggests more research needs to be conducted into equine-human interactions and why EAAT works (Ewing et al., 2007). Both researchers and practitioners need to develop a better understanding of equine behavior in the horse-human interaction through promoting research in equine learning theory and its application in EAAT.

Research of Equine Behavior in EAAT

Despite a lack in research directly affecting the role of horses in EAAT, there is evidence to suggest that equine behavior and equine psychology are affected by human interaction. Most of the existing research in horse behavior in this context, however, is focused on stress responses and confusion behaviors. To study equine stress, researchers commonly use salivary cortisol, heart rate variability, behavioral indicators, and eye temperatures to determine short-term stress responses of horses during human interaction (Borstel, Visser, & Hall, 2017). Horses, like other animals, exhibit stress behaviors as a response to both physical and psychological stresses which means it can be difficult for researchers and equitation (EAAT) practitioners to determine the cause of stress (Borstel et al., 2017). With regards to pleasurable response, there is some research to indicate that horses show positive voluntary responses to familiar humans with whom they have shared positive experiences (Sankey, Richard-Yris, Leroy, Henry, & Hausberger, 2010), but there is little evidence to suggest what, if any, behaviors indicate a social bonding between horse and human.

Considering that horses used in EAAT are used to practice empathy, compassion, and interpersonal bonding, this lack of knowledge is of primary concern within the industry. Research indicates that healthy interpersonal relationships are based on trust, dependability (consistency), feelings of safety and security, and positive interactions (Gambetta, 1990; Rempel, Holmes, & Zanna, 1985) with punishment negatively impacting close relationships between people (Vollan, 2011). Historically, horse-human interactions are primarily based on negative reinforcement and positive punishment (Bierke et al., 2013; Cooper, 2007; McGreevy, 2011; McLean & Christensen, 2017; Murphy & Arkins, 2007b). Consequently, EAAT practitioners and researchers need to find new ways to interact with horses that more closely resemble the positive reinforcement associated with healthy human relationships. Although there are positive reinforcement techniques available to train horses with food (Craig et al., 2015; Ninomiya et al., 2007), researchers have not explored how these techniques affect the horse-human bond.

In EAAT, humans rely upon the accurate interpretation of equine behavior to provide clients with a context in which to engage with the animal and explore how their actions affect others. Existing methods in EAAT utilize a variety of interactions with horses to achieve results for human benefit. Some of these methods involve leading or riding the horse, grooming, or using negative reinforcement to force the horse to move around a pen or over obstacles (Kieson & Abramson, 2016). In most of these models, the goal is to use the horse as a tool for therapy and, while EAAT practitioners claim to use the horse as a "therapeutic partner", the different models often focus primarily on the use of negative reinforcement and contradict one another as to their interpretations of equine behavior (Kieson & Abramson, 2016). For example, in Natural Lifemanship, the client is often asked to move a horse around a round pen by using negative reinforcement as a means of practicing control over the environment (or people). According to the model, the horse "bonds" with the human when it finally stops resisting the pressure (Kieson & Abramson, 2016). In contrast, the Professional Association of Therapeutic Horsemanship (PATH) emphasizes less pressure and more physical touch (such as grooming) to create a "bond" between horse and human, relying primarily on the relaxation of muscles and submissive behaviors to indicate horse "bonding" (Kieson & Abramson, 2016).

Although there are no standardized interpretations of equine behavior in EAAT, there is plenty of scientific and anecdotal evidence to suggest that changes in human behavior result in changes in equine behavior. For example, human vocalizations gets a horses' attention if a human is present and the horses show changes in behavior based on variations of vocal tone (Merkies, MacGregor, Ouimette, Bogart, & Miraglia, 2013). Furthermore, horses in pasture vary their reactions based on differences in human approach speed and behaviors (Birke et al., 2011). These studies support the idea that horses respond to observed changes in human behaviors, but there is also some evidence to suggest that horses may respond to human moods as well (Keeling, Jonare, & Lanneborn, 2009; Merkies et al., 2014). Considering the emotional and behavioral variations in individuals participating in EAAT, more research is needed to look at correlations between equine behaviors and different emotional or behavioral changes in humans.

The Horse-Human Bond and Practicing Interpersonal Relationships

To support the use of horses in EAAT for developing interpersonal and relationship skills, researchers need to look at how humans behaviorally bond and connect with other humans, how horses bond with other conspecifics, and how humans might use this knowledge to understand and study if or how horses might bond socially with humans. Researchers understand the behaviors humans and other primates use in social bonding, but there is no evidence to suggest these same behaviors can be used to bond with horses. Humans and primates, for example, use food as a social bonding tool (de Waal, 1989; Jaeggi, De Groot, Stevens, & Van Schaik, 2013; Koster & Leckie, 2014; Stirrat, Gumert, & Perrett, 2011) even correlating with oxytocin levels (Carter & Wilkinson, 2015). With regards to horses, however, researchers have so far focused on stress behaviors and cortisol response of horses resulting from human interactions (Dai et al., 2015; Mullard, Berger, Ellis, & Dyson, 2017; Wathan, Burrows, Waller, & McComb, 2015) with no known studies on how horses socially bond with humans.

Unlike traditional animals bred for companionship, previous studies in comparative psychology of cows and sheep demonstrates that, even with social interactions, herbivores do not display behavioral or neurological indicators indicative of interspecies bonding with humans. Although dogs demonstrate both behavioral and physiological indictors of social bonding with their owners (Berns, Brooks, & Spivak, 2015; Cook, Prichard, Spivak, & Berns, 2016; Konok, Nagy, & Miklósi, 2015), studies with lambs and cows show no obvious emotional bonds or connections with familiar humans, especially under stress conditions or potential opportunities for bonding (Coulon et al., 2013; Rushen, Munksgaard, Marnet, & DePassillé, 2001). There is evidence, however, to suggest conspecifics bond within herds of cows (Marino & Allen, 2017) and horses (Hartmann, Søndergaard, & Keeling, 2012) and additional support of interspecies social bonding in groups of mixed herbivores (Proops, Burden, & Osthaus, 2012). These studies suggest that domestic herbivores are capable of social bonding within and between species. Since EAAT focuses on using horses to practice interpersonal relationships, more research is needed to determine if horses socially bond with humans. Experiments conducted through comparative psychology and applied learning theory would help researchers and EAAT practitioners develop a better understanding of equine behavior in interspecies interactions and its applicability to EAAT.

Comparative Psychology and EAAT Research

By researching equine behavior and learning theory through the comparative method, researchers can help practitioners develop models of EAAT that mimic actual interspecies bonding that would facilitate their goals of paralleling interpersonal relationships in EAAT. This understanding would maintain and improve welfare of the horse, help individuals understand their own actions in the context of what is considered punishment versus negative reinforcement for establishing boundaries, and create an environment to practice trust, consistency, and positive reinforcement that are conducive to healthy human relationships (Gambetta, 1990; Rempel et al., 1985).

EAAT is based on behavioral interactions, not training, so researching positive interactions and interspecies bonding between horse and human is critical for the future of EAAT. Scientists already know that horses can be trained to perform tasks through the use of negative and positive reinforcement (Bierke et al., 2013; Briefer Freymond et al., 2014; Heidenreich, 2007; Hockenhull & Creighton, 2013; Innes & McBride, 2008; McGreevy, 2007; Slater & Dymond, 2011) and through the use of positive punishment (Hockenhull & Creighton, 2013). Only recently have researchers looked closely at the relationship between learning theory and equitation and the overwhelming use of negative reinforcement and positive punishment with regards to how humans communicate with horses (Hockenhull & Creighton, 2013; McGreevy, 2007; McLean & Christensen, 2017; Murphy & Arkins, 2007a). These results suggest that researchers have accurately captured the nature of communication between humans and horses and the manipulation of horses for training purposes. It also suggests that scientists understand how horses learn with regards to human interactions in the context of reinforcement and punishment and the need to develop more ways to interact with horses through the use of positive reinforcement for use in EAAT.

Due to increased interest in animal-human interactions and animal-assisted therapies, researchers have begun to explore new perspectives into how animals perceive their human counterparts and the use of positive reinforcement. Much of this research, however, has been performed with dog-human interactions. Dogs have historically been linked to humans as both companions and work animals (Hoummady et al., 2016; McGreevy, Starling, Branson, Cobb, & Calnon, 2012; Pennisi, 2002; Vilà et al., 1997), but, unlike studies on horses, research on the dog-human connection and interspecies communication indicates a very close social relationship between dogs and their human counterparts. For example, canines tested in fMRI machines while awake and subsequently observed for behavior in a choice preference test demonstrated that they preferred human vocal praise over food rewards (Cook et al., 2016), suggesting that the social bond is stronger than food rewards. Another study found that when humans and their dogs made eye contact, there was a positive oxytocin feedback loop in both human and canine, suggesting a neurologically-based bonding association based on previous social connections (Nagasawa et al., 2015).

There are no such studies on horses, however, and, other than anecdotal evidence, there is little to indicate a strong social connection between horses and humans from the equine perspective. If horses are to be used as interpersonal connections, there needs to be significantly more research in this area to determine if they will remain as simple tools in this context, or if researchers can study and manipulate interspecies communication and bonding between horse and human to improve methods of EAAT. There is also some discourse in the scientific community to support an increase in involvement of comparative psychology as well as evolutionary psychology in order to improve the understanding of similarities between species and their interconnectivity (Vonk & Shackelford, 2015). This consideration is especially important due to an increasing interest in animal welfare and exploration into emotional states of domestic animals (Boissy & Erhard, 2014; Broom, 2010; Cory, 2013; Manteuffel, Langbein, & Puppe, 2009), and in this case relating to horse management and handling (Hall, Goodwin, Heleski, Randle, & Waran, 2008; Horseman, Buller, Mullan, & Whay, 2016; Sarrafchi & Blokhuis, 2013).

Researching the horse-human interaction has unique challenges, however, due to the size and cost of maintaining the animals. Although utilizing large sample sizes is common in science to study population parameters and make inferences to assumed populations (Preacher, Rucker, MacCallum, & Nicewander, 2005), such methods are rarely used when studying horse-human interactions since horses are large, expensive animals and necessitate smaller sample size. Creating a better understanding of equine behavior in human interactions is focused primarily on understanding the individual interactions so that more individualized models of EAAT based on client-horse interaction may be utilized.

Given the limitations of sample size and the goal of studying individual client-horse interactions, researchers should utilize scientific methods based in comparative psychology. Comparative psychology traditionally focuses on small sample sizes and behavior of individuals and small groups and utilizes experiments that elucidate behavioral patterns, such as the reinforcement requirements of horses during interactions with humans. Implementing comparative psychology-based designs will provide the basis for better understanding of how horses perceive humans within the environment and if horses might choose to interact with humans in ways that parallel the behavioral conditions associated with human-human interactions.

Further Discussion

Unlike cows and lambs, horses were domesticated for close interaction with humans for use in transportation and work and, unlike dogs, did not and do not have a primary role as companion animals. As a result, there is a lot of research as to how horses have played a role in history and how they have learned from humans through negative reinforcement (Brubaker & Udell, 2016; Linklater, 2007; Sigurjónsdóttir, 2007). In contrast to their historical use, however, transitioning horses from work animals into therapy requires a more thorough understanding of this new horse-human interaction.

Since horses are expensive and each comes with unique breeding and experience, it can be difficult to isolate variables. Rather than approach research questions using parameter-based statistics, alternative methods may be better suited (i.e., Observation Oriented Modeling, which allows data to be analyzed for behavioral pattern analysis, comparison, and examining dyads within the context of the study or previous data). Although some population parameters may be applicable to human-horse interactions, especially those pertaining to species-specific behavioral reactions, the relationship between one human and one horse is especially difficult to study. Much like the experiments with dogs and their owners, each of these dyads is different and learning theories are critical to understanding how interspecies relationships between horse and human are formed and maintained. More research in horse behavior under rewarding conditions and how these behaviors might manifest in human interactions. Furthermore, researchers need to look at when horses voluntarily repeat behaviors on their own, with other conspecifics, and with humans to determine what constitutes a reward within each context. A more thorough evaluation of horse behavioral psychology, human-horse interactions, and the application of comparative psychology in EAAT can help improve not only the welfare of the horse, but the efficacy of the entire field of EAAT.

References

Berns, G. S., Brooks, A. M., & Spivak, M. (2015). Scent of the familiar: An fMRI study of canine brain responses to familiar and unfamiliar human and dog odors. *Behavioural Processes, 110*, 37–46. http://doi.org/10.1016/j.beproc.2014.02.011

Bierke, C. M., Meinen, R. H., Wilkens, E. E., Leponiemi, M. A., & Hiney, K. M. (2013). A comparison of negative and positive reinforcement in naïve horses. *Journal of Equine Veterinary Science*, *33*, 397. http://doi.org/10.1016/j.jevs.2013.03.170

Birke, L., Hockenhull, J., Creighton, E., Pinno, L., Mee, J., & Mills, D. (2011). Horses' responses to variation in human approach. *Applied Animal Behaviour Science*, *134*, 56–63. http://doi.org/10.1016/j.applanim.2011.06.002

Boissy, A., & Erhard, H. W. (2014). How studying interactions between animal emotions, cognition, and personality can contribute to improve farm animal welfare. In T. Grandin & M. Deesing, (Eds.), *Genetics and the behavior of domestic animals* (2nd ed.) (pp. 81–113). Elsevier Inc. http://doi.org/10.1016/B978-0-12-394586-0.00003-2

Borstel, U. K., Visser, E. K., & Hall, C. (2017). Indicators of stress in equitation. *Applied Animal Behaviour Science, 190*, 43–56. http://doi.org/10.1016/j.applanim.2017.02.018

Briefer Freymond, S., Briefer, E. F., Zollinger, A., Gindrat-von Allmen, Y., Wyss, C., & Bachmann, I. (2014). Behaviour of horses in a judgment bias test associated with positive or negative reinforcement. *Applied Animal Behaviour Science*, *158*, 34–45. http://doi.org/10.1016/j.applanim.2014.06.006

Broom, D. M. (2010). Cognitive ability and awareness in domestic animals and decision about obligations to animals. *Applied Animal Behaviour Science*, *126*, 1–11.

Brubaker, L., & Udell, M. A. R. (2016). Cognition and learning in horses (*Equus caballus*): What we know and why we should ask more. *Behavioural Processes*, *126*, 121–131. http://doi.org/10.1016/j.beproc.2016.03.017

Carter, G. G., & Wilkinson, G. S. (2015). Intranasal oxytocin increases social grooming and food sharing in the common vampire bat Desmodus rotundus. *Hormones and Behavior, 75,* 150–153. http://doi.org/10.1016/j.yhbeh.2015.10.006

Cook, P. F., Prichard, A., Spivak, M., & Berns, G. S. (2016). Awake canine fMRI predicts dogs' preference for praise vs food. *Social Cognitive and Affective Neuroscience*, *11,* 1853–1862. http://doi.org/10.1093/scan/nsw102

Cooper, J. J. (2007). Equine learning behaviour: Common knowledge and systematic research. *Behavioural Processes*, *76*, 24–26. http://doi.org/10.1016/j.beproc.2006.12.009

Cory, J. (2013). Identification and management of cognitive decline in companion animals and the comparisons with Alzheimer disease: A review. *Journal of Veterinary Behavior: Clinical Applications and Research*, *8*, 291–301. http://doi.org/10.1016/j.jveb.2012.08.001

Coulon, M., Nowak, R., Andanson, S., Ravel, C., Marnet, P. G., Boissy, A., & Boivin, X. (2013). Human-lamb bonding: Oxytocin, cortisol and behavioural responses of lambs to human contacts and social separation. *Psychoneuroendocrinology*, *38*, 499–508. http://doi.org/10.1016/j.psyneuen.2012.07.008

Craig, D. P. A., Varnon, C. A., Pollock, K. L., & Abramson, C. I. (2015). An assessment of horse (*Equus ferus caballus*) responding on fixed interval schedules of reinforcement: An individual analysis. *Behavioural Processes*, *120*, 1–13. http://doi.org/10.1016/j.beproc.2015.08.006

Dai, F., Cogi, N. H., Heinzl, E. U. L., Dalla Costa, E., Canali, E., & Minero, M. (2015). Validation of a fear test in sport horses using infrared thermography. *Journal of Veterinary Behavior: Clinical Applications and Research*, *10*, 128–136. http://doi.org/10.1016/j.jveb.2014.12.001

De Araújo, T. B., De Oliveira, R. J., Martins, W. R., De Moura Pereira, M., Copetti, F., & Safons, M. P. (2013). Effects of hippotherapy on mobility, strength and balance in elderly. *Archives of Gerontology and Geriatrics*, *56*, 478–481. http://doi.org/10.1016/j.archger.2012.12.007

de Waal, F. B. M. (1989). Food sharing and reciprocal obligations among chimpanzees. *Journal of Human Evolution, 18*, 433–459. http://doi.org/10.1016/0047-2484(89)90074-2

Debuse, D., Gibb, C., & Chandler, C. (2009). Effects of hippotherapy on people with cerebral palsy from the users' perspective: A qualitative study. *Physiotherapy Theory and Practice*, *25*, 174–192. http://doi.org/10.1080/09593980902776662

Ewing, C. A., MacDonald, P. M., Taylor, M., & Bowers, M. J. (2007). Equine-facilitated learning for youths with severe emotional disorders: A quantitative and qualitative study. *Child and Youth Care Forum*, *36*, 59–72. http://doi.org/10.1007/s10566-006-9031-x

Fazio, E., Medica, P., Cravana, C., & Ferlazzo, A. (2013). Hypothalamic-pituitary-adrenal axis responses of horses to therapeutic riding program: Effects of different riders. *Physiology and Behavior*, *118*, 138–143. http://doi.org/10.1016/j.physbeh.2013.05.009

Gabriels, R. L., Agnew, J., Holt, K. D., Shoffner, A., Zhaoxing, P., Ruzzano, S., … Mesibov, G. (2012). Pilot study measuring the effects of therapeutic horseback riding on school-age children and adolescents with autism spectrum disorders. *Research in Autism Spectrum Disorders*, *6*, 578–588. http://doi.org/10.1016/j.rasd.2011.09.007

Gambetta, D. (1990). Can we trust trust? In D. Gambetta (Ed.), *Trust: Making and breaking coopeative relations*, (pp. 213–237) electronic version. Oxford, UK: Blackwell. http://doi.org/10.1.1.24.5695

Hall, C., Goodwin, D., Heleski, C., Randle, H., & Waran, N. (2008). Is there evidence of learned helplessness in horses? *Journal of Applied Animal Welfare Science : JAAWS*, *11*, 249–66. http://doi.org/10.1080/10888700802101130

Hameury, L., Delavous, P., Teste, B., Leroy, C., Gaboriau, J. C., & Berthier, A. (2010). Équithérapie et autisme. *Annales Medico-Psychologiques*, *168*, 655–659. http://doi.org/10.1016/j.amp.2009.12.019

Hartmann, E., Søndergaard, E., & Keeling, L. J. (2012). Keeping horses in groups: A review. *Applied Animal Behaviour Science*, *136*, 77–87. http://doi.org/10.1016/j.applanim.2011.10.004

Heidenreich, B. (2007). An introduction to positive reinforcement training and its benefits. *Journal of Exotic Pet Medicine*, *16*, 19–23. http://doi.org/10.1053/j.jepm.2006.11.005

Hockenhull, J., & Creighton, E. (2013). Training horses: Positive reinforcement, positive punishment, and ridden behavior problems. *Journal of Veterinary Behavior: Clinical Applications and Research*, *8*, 245–252. http://doi.org/10.1016/j.jveb.2012.06.002

Horseman, S. V., Buller, H., Mullan, S., & Whay, H. R. (2016). Current welfare problems facing horses in Great Britain as identified by equine stakeholders. *PLoS ONE*, *11*(8), 1–19. http://doi.org/10.1371/journal.pone.0160269

Hoummady, S., Peron, F., Grandjean, D., Clero, D., Bernard, B., Titeux, E., ... Gilbert, C. (2016). Relationships between personality of human-dog dyads and performances in working tasks. *Applied Animal Behaviour Science*, *177*, 42–51.

Innes, L., & McBride, S. (2008). Negative versus positive reinforcement: An evaluation of training strategies for rehabilitated horses. *Applied Animal Behaviour Science*, *112*, 357–368. http://doi.org/10.1016/j.applanim.2007.08.011

Jaeggi, A. V., De Groot, E., Stevens, J. M. G., & Van Schaik, C. P. (2013). Mechanisms of reciprocity in primates: Testing for short-term contingency of grooming and food sharing in bonobos and chimpanzees. *Evolution and Human Behavior, 34,* 69–77. http://doi.org/10.1016/j.evolhumbehav.2012.09.005

Jenkins, S. R., & Digennaro Reed, F. D. (2013). An experimental analysis of the effects of therapeutic horseback riding on the behavior of children with autism. *Research in Autism Spectrum Disorders*, *7*, 721–740. http://doi.org/10.1016/j.rasd.2013.02.008

Keaveney, S. M. (2008). Equines and their human companions. *Journal of Business Research*, *61*, 444–454. http://doi.org/10.1016/j.jbusres.2007.07.017

Keeling, L. J., Jonare, L., & Lanneborn, L. (2009). Investigating horse-human interactions: The effect of a nervous human. *Veterinary Journal*, *181*, 70–71. http://doi.org/10.1016/j.tvjl.2009.03.013

Kendall, E., Maujean, A., Pepping, C. & Wright, J. J. (2014). Hypotheses about the psychological benefits of horses. *Explore*, *10*, 81–87. http://doi.org/10.1016/j.explore.2013.12.001

Kieson, E., & Abramson, C. I. (2016). Equines as tools vs partners: a critical look at the uses and beliefs surrounding horses in equine therapies and argument for mechanical horses. *Journal of Veterinary Behavior: Clinical Applications and Research*, *15*, 94–95. http://doi.org/10.1016/j.jveb.2016.08.067

Konok, V., Nagy, K., & Miklósi, Á. (2015). How do humans represent the emotions of dogs? The resemblance between the human representation of the canine and the human affective space. *Applied Animal Behaviour Science*, *162*, 37–46. http://doi.org/10.1016/j.applanim.2014.11.003

Koster, J. M., & Leckie, G. (2014). Food sharing networks in lowland Nicaragua: An application of the social relations model to count data. *Social Networks, 38*, 100–110. http://doi.org/10.1016/j.socnet.2014.02.002

Latella, D., & Abrams, B. N. (2015). The role of the equine in animal-assisted interactions. In A. Fine (Ed.), *Handbook on animal-assisted therapy* (4th ed.) (pp. 115–137). London, UK: Elsevier Inc. http://doi.org/10.1016/B978-0-12-801292-5.00010-9

Lechner, H. E., Kakebeeke, T. H., Hegemann, D., & Baumberger, M. (2007). The effect of hippotherapy on spasticity and on mental well-being of persons with spinal cord injury. *Archives of Physical Medicine and Rehabilitation*, *88*, 1241–1248. http://doi.org/10.1016/j.apmr.2007.07.015

Linklater, W. L. (2007). Equine learning in a wider context--opportunities for integrative pluralism. *Behavioural Processes*, *76*, 53–56. http://doi.org/10.1016/j.beproc.2006.10.015

Manteuffel, G., Langbein, J., & Puppe, B. (2009). Increasing farm animal welfare by positively motivated instrumental behaviour. *Applied Animal Behaviour Science*, *118*, 191–198. http://doi.org/10.1016/j.applanim.2009.02.014

Marino, L., & Allen, K. (2017). The psychology of cows. *Animal Behavior and Cognition*, *4*, 474–498. http://doi.org/10.26451/abc.04.04.06.2017

McGreevy, P. D. (2007). The advent of equitation science. *The Veterinary Journal*, *174*, 492–500. http://doi.org/10.1016/j.tvjl.2006.09.008

McGreevy, P. D. (2011). The fine line between pressure and pain: Ask the horse. *Veterinary Journal*, *188*, 250–251. http://doi.org/10.1016/j.tvjl.2010.10.011

McGreevy, P. D., Starling, M., Branson, N. J., Cobb, M. L., & Calnon, D. (2012). An overview of the dog-human dyad and ethograms within it. *Journal of Veterinary Behavior: Clinical Applications and Research*, *7*, 103–117. http://doi.org/10.1016/j.jveb.2011.06.001

McLean, A. N., & Christensen, J. W. (2017). The application of learning theory in horse training. *Applied Animal Behaviour Science*, *190*, 18–27. http://doi.org/10.1016/j.applanim.2017.02.020

Merkies, K., MacGregor, H., Ouimette, M., Bogart, E., & Miraglia, K. (2013). Does the human voice have a calming effect on horses ? *Journal of Equine Veterinary Science*, *33*, 321–399. http://doi.org/10.1016/j.jevs.2013.03.110

Merkies, K., Sievers, A., Zakrajsek, E., MacGregor, H., Bergeron, R., & von Borstel, U. K. (2014). Preliminary results suggest an influence of psychological and physiological stress in humans on horse heart rate and behavior. *Journal of Veterinary Behavior: Clinical Applications and Research*, *9*,242–247. http://doi.org/10.1016/j.jveb.2014.06.003

Mullard, J., Berger, J. M., Ellis, A. D., & Dyson, S. (2017). Development of an ethogram to describe facial expressions in ridden horses (FEReq). *Journal of Veterinary Behavior: Clinical Applications and Research*, *18*, 7–12. http://doi.org/10.1016/j.jveb.2016.11.005

Murphy, J., & Arkins, S. (2007a). Equine learning behaviour. *Behavioural Processes*, *76*(1), 1–13. http://doi.org/10.1016/j.beproc.2006.06.009

Murphy, J., & Arkins, S. (2007b). Synthesizing what we know of equine learning behaviour. *Behavioural Processes*, *76*, 57–60. http://doi.org/10.1016/j.beproc.2007.02.029

Nagasawa, M., Mitsui, S., En, S., Ohtani, N., Ohta, M., Sakuma, Y., … Kikusui, T. (2015). Oxytocin-gaze positive loop and the coevolution of human-dog bonds. *Science*, *348*, 333–336.

Ninomiya, S., Mitsumasu, T., Aoyama, M., & Kusunose, R. (2007). A note on the effect of a palatable food reward on operant conditioning in horses. *Applied Animal Behaviour Science*, *108*, 342–347. http://doi.org/10.1016/j.applanim.2007.02.010

Pauw, J. (2000). Therapeutic horseback riding studies: Problems experienced by researchers. *Physiotherapy*, *86*, 523–527. http://doi.org/10.1016/S0031-9406(05)60986-8

Pendry, P., Smith, A. N., & Roeter, S. M. (2014). Randomized trial examines effects of equine facilitated learning on adolescents basal cortisol levels. *Human-Animal Interaction Bulliten, 2*, 80–95.

Pennisi, E. (2002). A shaggy dog history. *Science*, *298*, 1540.

Preacher, K. J., Rucker, D. D., MacCallum, R. C., & Nicewander, W. A. (2005). Use of the extreme groups approach: A critical reexamination and new recommendations. *Psychological Methods*, *10*, 178–192. http://doi.org/10.1037/1082-989X.10.2.178

Proops, L., Burden, F., & Osthaus, B. (2012). Social relations in a mixed group of mules, ponies and donkeys reflect differences in equid type. *Behavioural Processes*, *90*, 337–342. http://doi.org/10.1016/j.beproc.2012.03.012

Rempel, J. K., Holmes, J. G., & Zanna, M. P. (1985). Trust in close relationships. *Journal of Personality and Social Psychology*, *49*, 95–112. http://doi.org/10.1037/0022-3514.49.1.95

Rushen, J., Munksgaard, L., Marnet, P. G., & DePassillé, A. M. (2001). Human contact and the effects of acute stress on cows at milking. *Applied Animal Behaviour Science*, *73*(1), 1–14. http://doi.org/10.1016/S0168-1591(01)00105-8

Sankey, C., Richard-Yris, M.-A., Leroy, H., Henry, S., & Hausberger, M. (2010). Positive interactions lead to lasting positive memories in horses, Equus caballus. *Animal Behaviour*, *79*, 869–875. http://doi.org/10.1016/j.anbehav.2009.12.037

Sarrafchi, A., & Blokhuis, H. J. (2013). Equine stereotypic behaviors: Causation, occurrence, and prevention. *Journal of Veterinary Behavior: Clinical Applications and Research*, *8*, 386–394. http://doi.org/10.1016/j.jveb.2013.04.068

Shurtleff, T. L., Standeven, J. W., & Engsberg, J. R. (2009). Changes in dynamic trunk/head stability and functional reach after hippotherapy. *Archives of Physical Medicine and Rehabilitation*, *90*, 1185–1195. http://doi.org/10.1016/j.apmr.2009.01.026

Sigurjónsdóttir, H. (2007). Equine learning behaviour: The importance of evolutionary and ecological approach in research. *Behavioural Processes*, *76*, 40–42. http://doi.org/10.1016/j.beproc.2006.09.019

Slater, C., & Dymond, S. (2011). Using differential reinforcement to improve equine welfare: Shaping appropriate truck loading and feet handling. *Behavioural Processes*, *86*, 329–339. http://doi.org/10.1016/j.beproc.2011.02.001

Stirrat, M., Gumert, M., & Perrett, D. (2011). The effect of attractiveness on food sharing preferences in human mating markets. *Evolutionary Psychology, 9*, 79–91.

Vilà, C., Savolainen, P., Maldonado, J. E., Amorim, I. R., Rice, J. E., Honeycutt, R. L., … Wayne, R. K. (1997). Multiple and ancient origins of the domestic dog multiple and ancient origins of the domestic dog carles vila. *Science*, *276*, 1687–1689. http://doi.org/10.1126/science.276.5319.1687

Vollan, B. (2011). The difference between kinship and friendship: (Field-) experimental evidence on trust and punishment. *Journal of Socio-Economics*, *40*, 14–25. http://doi.org/10.1016/j.socec.2010.10.003

Vonk, J., & Shackelford, T. K. (2015). Comparative evolutionary psychology: Current status and a proposal for a more integrated future. In J. D. Wright (Ed.), *International Encyclopedia of the Social & Behavioral Sciences* (2nd ed.). Elsevier B.V. http://doi.org/10.1016/B978-0-08-097086-8.81015-6

Wathan, J., Burrows, A. M., Waller, B. M., & McComb, K. (2015). EquiFACS: The equine facial action coding system. *PLoS ONE, 10,* e0137818. http://doi.org/10.1371/journal.pone.0131738

Permissions

All chapters in this book were first published in IJCP, by eScholarship Publishing, University of California; hereby published with permission under the Creative Commons Attribution License or equivalent. Every chapter published in this book has been scrutinized by our experts. Their significance has been extensively debated. The topics covered herein carry significant findings which will fuel the growth of the discipline. They may even be implemented as practical applications or may be referred to as a beginning point for another development.

The contributors of this book come from diverse backgrounds, making this book a truly international effort. This book will bring forth new frontiers with its revolutionizing research information and detailed analysis of the nascent developments around the world.

We would like to thank all the contributing authors for lending their expertise to make the book truly unique. They have played a crucial role in the development of this book. Without their invaluable contributions this book wouldn't have been possible. They have made vital efforts to compile up to date information on the varied aspects of this subject to make this book a valuable addition to the collection of many professionals and students.

This book was conceptualized with the vision of imparting up-to-date information and advanced data in this field. To ensure the same, a matchless editorial board was set up. Every individual on the board went through rigorous rounds of assessment to prove their worth. After which they invested a large part of their time researching and compiling the most relevant data for our readers.

The editorial board has been involved in producing this book since its inception. They have spent rigorous hours researching and exploring the diverse topics which have resulted in the successful publishing of this book. They have passed on their knowledge of decades through this book. To expedite this challenging task, the publisher supported the team at every step. A small team of assistant editors was also appointed to further simplify the editing procedure and attain best results for the readers.

Apart from the editorial board, the designing team has also invested a significant amount of their time in understanding the subject and creating the most relevant covers. They scrutinized every image to scout for the most suitable representation of the subject and create an appropriate cover for the book.

The publishing team has been an ardent support to the editorial, designing and production team. Their endless efforts to recruit the best for this project, has resulted in the accomplishment of this book. They are a veteran in the field of academics and their pool of knowledge is as vast as their experience in printing. Their expertise and guidance has proved useful at every step. Their uncompromising quality standards have made this book an exceptional effort. Their encouragement from time to time has been an inspiration for everyone.

The publisher and the editorial board hope that this book will prove to be a valuable piece of knowledge for researchers, students, practitioners and scholars across the globe.

List of Contributors

Takamasa Koyama
Japan Women's University, Japan

Yasuhiro Yasutomi and Tadashi Sankai
National Institutes of Biomedical Innovation, Health and Nutrition, Japan

Maiko Yoshida- Kobayashi
Japan Women's University, Japan
National Institutes of Biomedical Innovation, Health and Nutrition, Japan

Lucas Cuenya
Laboratorio de Psicología Experimental y Aplicada, Instituto de Investigaciones Médicas, CONICET - Universidad de Buenos Aires

Giselle Kamenetzky and Alba E. Mustaca
Laboratorio de Psicología Experimental y Aplicada, Instituto de Investigaciones Médicas, CONICET - Universidad de Buenos Aires
Centro de Altos Estudios en Ciencias Humanas y de la Salud, Universidad Abierta Interamericana (UAI)

Kerry E. Gilroy, Ebony M. Everett and Andrew R. Delamater
Brooklyn College - CUNY, USA

J. Bruce Overmier
University of Minnesota, USA

Julia E. Meyers-Manor
Macalester College, USA

Tohru Taniuchi
Kanazawa University, Japan

Walter T. Herbranson, Patricia M. Xi and Yvan T. Trinh
Whitman College, U.S.A

John W. Donahoe
University of Massachusetts, USA

Bonnie M. Perdue
Department of Psychology, Agnes Scott College, USA

Stephanie M. Himmler, Jena M. Lewis and Sergio M. Pellis
Department of Neuroscience, University of Lethbridge, Lethbridge, Alberta, Canada

Barbara A. Church and J. David Smith
Department of Psychology, University at Buffalo, The State University of New York, USA

Michael J. Beran
Language Research Center and Department of Psychology, Georgia State University, USA

Kenneth J. Leising and Chad M. Ruprecht
Texas Christian University, U.S.A

W. David Stahlman
University of Mary Washington, U.S.A

Mélanie Kaeser, Pauline Chatagny, Anne-Dominique Gindrat, Julie Savidan, Simon Badoud, Michela Fregosi, Véronique Moret, Christine Roulin, Eric Schmidlin and Eric M. Rouiller
Domain of Physiology, Department of Medicine and Fribourg Center for Cognition, University of Fribourg, Chemin du Musée 5, CH-1700 Fribourg, Switzerland

Lori Marino
The Kimmela Center for Animal Advocacy
The Someone Project

Christina M. Colvin
Emory University, USA

Mauricio R. Papini
Texas Christian University

David Philip Arthur Craig and Charles I. Abramson
Oklahoma State University, U.S.A

Emily Kieson
Oklahoma State University, U.S.A

Index

CPSIA information can be obtained
at www.ICGtesting.com
Printed in the USA
LVHW062013100122
708212LV00002B/220